The Political Economy of the United Nations Security Council
Money and Influence

Trades of money for political influence persist at every level of government. Not surprisingly, governments themselves trade money for
political support on the international stage. Strange, however, is the
tale of this book: In this study, legitimacy stands as the central political commodity at stake. The book investigates the ways governments
trade money for favors at the United Nations Security Council, the body
endowed with the international legal authority to legitimize the use of
armed force to maintain or restore peace. With a wealth of quantitative
data, the book shows that powerful countries, such as the United States,
Japan, and Germany, extend financial favors to the elected members
of the Security Council through direct foreign aid and through international organizations, such as the International Monetary Fund and
the World Bank. In return, developing countries serving on the Security
Council must deliver their political support – or face the consequences.

James Raymond Vreeland is Professor of International Relations at
Georgetown University's School of Foreign Service and holds a joint
appointment in the Department of Government.

Axel Dreher is Professor of International and Development Politics at
Heidelberg University.

For our godsons

The Political Economy of the United Nations Security Council

Money and Influence

JAMES RAYMOND VREELAND
Georgetown University

AXEL DREHER
Heidelberg University

CAMBRIDGE
UNIVERSITY PRESS

CAMBRIDGE
UNIVERSITY PRESS

32 Avenue of the Americas, New York, NY 10013-2473, USA

Cambridge University Press is part of the University of Cambridge.

It furthers the University's mission by disseminating knowledge in the pursuit of education, learning, and research at the highest international levels of excellence.

www.cambridge.org
Information on this title: www.cambridge.org/9780521740067

© James Raymond Vreeland and Axel Dreher 2014

First published 2014

A catalog record for this publication is available from the British Library.

Library of Congress Cataloging in Publication Data
Vreeland, James Raymond, 1971–
The Political Economy of the United Nations Security Council : Money and Influence /
James Raymond Vreeland, Georgetown University; Axel Dreher, Heidelberg University.
   pages cm
Includes bibliographical references and index.
ISBN 978-0-521-51841-3 (hbk.) – ISBN 978-0-521-74006-7 (pbk.)
1. United Nations. Security Council – Economic aspects.   I. Dreher, Axel.   II. Title.
JZ5006.7.V74   2014
341.23'23–dc23   2013043783

ISBN 978-0-521-51841-3 Hardback
ISBN 978-0-521-74006-7 Paperback

Contents

Figures

Tables

Acknowledgments

The Godfather, a motion picture about families, presents a logic of trading favors that we use in this book. The book itself would never have taken shape if not for favors – countless favors – that we have received. We thus find ourselves in debt to many friends and colleagues around the world. We like to think of these people as part of various extended families to which we have the good fortune to belong. So, for their innumerable contributions to this book, we thank the "five families."

Coauthors

Our coauthors stand as the first family to acknowledge. This book represents the culmination of several studies on the United Nations Security Council that we have undertaken with various colleagues. These collaborations have transformed our thinking and have thoroughly impacted the writing of this book. We owe our coauthors an enormous debt of gratitude.

We thank Jan-Egbert Sturm, the coauthor of our original studies on the effects of Security Council membership on World Bank and IMF loans. He also continued to work with us on our study of IMF conditionality. We also thank the Swiss Federal Institute of Technology (ETH) Zurich, where Jan-Egbert is "the boss" of the KOF family. Through our affiliations with the KOF Swiss Economic Institute, one of the leading economic think tanks in Switzerland, we first met and began our studies on the Security Council.

We thank Stephan Klasen and Eric Werker, who worked with us on a study of the effects of foreign aid contingent on Security Council membership. We are particularly grateful to Stephan for sharing his expert knowledge on World Bank programs and evaluations, while Eric coauthored (with Ilyana Kuziemko) the original study on the Security Council and U.S. foreign aid that inspired this book.

Matthew Gould and Matthew Rablen (whom we have taken to affectionately calling "the Matthews") coauthored a study on the election of Security Council members. We actually met and did all of our work through the Internet, and so this collaboration represents the most modern kind. We thank them for developing a sophisticated statistical model to estimate the determinants of Security Council elections, as well as for their patience in working with us without face-to-face contact.

B. Peter Rosendorff is currently coauthoring with us an ongoing study of Security Council voting. He provided us immense help with the formal model presented in Chapter 2 (remaining errors are our own).

We also thank Peter Nunnenkamp for coauthoring a study on German foreign aid and the Security Council. No one can write a paper faster.

Students

We have also had the privilege of researching and writing with the next generation of our family of coauthors, our students.

For coauthoring the study on the Security Council and the Asian Development Bank, we thank Daniel Lim, who developed the hypothesis himself. We thank Maya Schmaljohann for coauthoring the study on the Security Council and German foreign aid, and Vera Eichenauer and Kai Gehring for coauthoring the study on foreign aid to UNSC members and economic growth.

We have learned a great deal from our students in general. Many of them have studied drafts of our work and provided constructive feedback. The 2014 Krogh Students merit special note. We are particularly grateful to the numerous students who have taken our courses on international organizations over the years. There are hundreds of them, far too many to list, but we want them to know that they have played an important role in shaping our thoughts about this project and about international relations in general. They will always be a part of us. For helping us conduct our courses, we thank teaching assistants Raphael Cohen, Anjali Dayal, Dani Nedal, Fouad Pervez, Alexandra Rudolph, and Alexandra Stark.

Some of our students have taken the time to provide detailed written assistance on the project. We are especially indebted to Kate Anthony, Timothy Dee, Elisabeth Dorfmeister, Thomas Mancinelli, Hesham

Sallam, and Yuko Shimada. For carefully reading every single page of the manuscript and providing page-by-page suggestions, very special thanks go to Alyssa Huberts. And for incredible research assistance – from checking sources to proofreading our discussions of statistical results – we extend our gratitude to Soumyajit "Shom" Mazumder.

Colleagues in the Professions of Economics and Political Science

We next turn to our extended family of colleagues, a large group that has improved our work in countless ways. We thank them for making our work fun as they interact with us at conferences, seminars, and through e-mail. We have received helpful comments from seminar attendees in many places including Bond University, the Browne Center for International Politics at the University of Pennsylvania, the Centre for International Governance Innovation (CIGI), Chicago University, Columbia University, Duke University, Escuela Superior de Administración y Dirección de Empresas (ESADE), the European Central Bank, the Niehaus Center for Globalization and Governance at Princeton University, Essex University, Facultad Latinoamericana de Ciencias Sociales (FLACSO), Free University of Brussels, Fribourg University, Fundación Juan March, George Washington University, Institut Barcelona d'Estudis Internacionals (IBEI), Instituto de Relações Internacionais (Universidade de São Paulo), Korea University, London School of Economics (LSE), Lund University, Manhattan College, Minnesota University, New York University, Nova Southeastern University, Peking University, Penn State, Pittsburg University, RWI Essen, Solvay Brussels School, University of California at Los Angeles (UCLA), University of Dresden, University of Duisburg-Essen, University of Geneva, University of Giessen, University of Illinois at Urbana-Champaign, University of Kassel, University of Kiel, University of Lucerne, University of Marburg, University of Massachusetts Amherst, University of Milan-Bicocca, University of Osnabrück, University of Pittsburgh, University of St. Gallen, University of Texas at Austin, University of Virginia, University of Wisconsin-Madison, Vassar College, Vienna University of Economics and Business, Villanova University, the World Trade Institute, University of Bayreuth, University of Bergen, WIFO Vienna, and Yale University.

In addition to recognizing these institutions, we wish to acknowledge the following libraries around the world where we found a place to work during our travels and completed much of the work for this project: the Georgetown Neighborhood Library (Washington, DC), the

Joong-Ang Library (Korea University), the Kingston Library (Kingston, NY), the Lauinger Library (Georgetown University), the Lázaro Library (University of Puerto Rico, Río Piedras), the New York Public Library Main Branch (New York, NY), the O'Malley Library (Manhattan College), the Sachem Public Library (Holbrook, NY), the Soundview Library (Bronx, NY), the Weston Branch Library (Weston, FL), and the Zurich Central Library (University of Zurich).

We have received constructive feedback from participants at many conferences as well, including the Political Economy of International Organizations meetings in Geneva, Washington, Zurich, Mannheim/Heidelberg, and Philadephia; the Beyond Basic Questions conferences in Göttingen and Lucerne; the Canadian Economic Association Meeting in Halifax; the Christmas Meeting of the German-Speaking Economists Abroad at Mannheim University; the Effectiveness of Aid for Development workshop in Barcelona; the European Economic Association meeting in Barcelona; the European Economic Association meeting in Budapest; the European Public Choice Society meeting in Amsterdam; the European Public Choice Society meeting in Izmir; the German Development Economics Association meeting in Frankfurt; the International Political Economy Society meeting in Philadelphia; the International Society for New Institutional Economics meeting in Reykjavik; the International Studies Association meeting in Chicago; the National Political Science Association meeting in Boston; the Royal Economic Society Annual Conference in Warwick; and the Silvaplana Workshop on Political Economy in Pontresina.

We are humbled by the valuable insights we have received from many of the participants at the aforementioned presentations and cannot possibly list them all. For specific and written comments, we would like to thank Faisal Ahmed, Tim Allen, Manuela Angelucci, David Bearce, Christian Bjørnskov, Thomas Bräuninger, Lawrence Broz, Tim Büthe, Eugenio Cano, Terrence Chapman, Pamela Chasek, Eunbin Chung, Mark Copelovitch, Christina Davis, Michael Doyle, Peter Egger, Chris Elbers, Ofer Eldar, Marcel Fafchamps, Songying Fang, Christina Fattore, John Freeman, Sumit Ganguly, Ingo Geishecker, Adam Glynn, Joanne Gowa, Lloyd Gruber, Jan Gunning, Birger Heldt, Simon Hug, Ian Hurd, Paul Huth, Nathan Jensen, Dídac Queralt Jiménez, Silva Kantareva, Judith Kelley, Gary King, Stephen Knack, Jean Krasno, Quan Li, Dalton Lin, Phillip Lipscy, Andre Lowe, Colum Lynch, Thomas Markussen, Lisa Martin, Covadonga Meseguer,

Bessma Momani, Kevin Morrison, Hannes Müller, Connor Myers, Steve Nelson, Rich Nielsen, Martin Paldam, Jon Pevehouse, Pablo Pinto, Varun Piplani, Stephanie Rickard, Shanker Satyanath, Mark Sawyer, Holger Schmidt, Friedrich Schneider, Robert Schub, Ken Shadlen, Beth Simmons, Alastair Smith, Stefan Sperlich, Randall Stone, Daniel Y. J. Tan, Eva Terberger, Dustin Tingley, Nathaniel Tisa, Shawn Treier, Burcu Uçaray, Jürgen von Hagen, Robert Wade, Yuval Weber, Scott Wolford, and George L. C. Yin. We are particularly indebted to Christopher Kilby; in addition to reading and offering helpful suggestions on numerous working papers related to this project, Christopher helped us develop the book's title and the title of the first chapter. We also thank the editors and anonymous reviewers of our journal articles on this subject matter, as well as the reviewers of this manuscript for Cambridge University Press.

For supplying important information through interviews and correspondence, we are very grateful to Secretary Madeleine Albright, Ambassador John Bolton, Ben Chang, Andrew S. Natsios, and John Pilger. Their rich experience beyond the halls of academia makes them especially valuable colleagues. We stress that their consent to be quoted should not be taken as an endorsement of any of our conclusions. Indeed, in some cases they disagree with us. Their willingness to share their time and thoughts with us is a testament to their commitment to the free exchange of ideas.

We would also like to express thanks to our editorial team at Cambridge University Press, our editor Deborah Gershenowitz and her assistant Dana Bricken, as well as Joshua Penney, our production editor. We further thank our copy editor, Jane Voodikon, and our indexer, Julia Petrakis. For his patience, professionalism, and endless assistance, special thanks go to Shashank Shankar, our project manager at Aptara, the editorial and composition service company for our book.

Colleagues at Home Institutions

Both of us have moved around a bit while working on this project and thus have benefited from several families at home institutions. We thank all of our wonderful colleagues at these amazing universities. Again, we are humbled by the support that we have received from many people – too many to list here. We would like to make a public expression of gratitude to those colleagues who have provided specific and detailed comments.

From Yale University, we thank Keith Darden, Greg Huber, Stathis Kalyvas, David Mayhew, Harris Mylonas, Bruce Russett, and Kenneth Scheve. For administrative support, we thank Sandy Nuhn. We also thank participants in the Leitner Political Economy Seminar.

From Georgetown University, we thank Marc Busch, Donald Daniel, Raj Desai, Michael Green, Shareen Joshi, Rodney Ludema, Anna Maria Mayda, Kathleen McNamara, Abraham Newman, Anders Olofsgård, Dennis Quinn, Jennifer Tobin, Charles Udomsaph, and Erik Voeten. We acknowledge the William V. O'Brien Endowment for funding student research assistants. For administrative support, we thank Halley Lisuk, Moira Todd, and Eva Zamarippa of the Mortara Center for International Studies. We also thank participants in the Political Economy Tuesday Lunch Group and the Georgetown University International Theory and Research Seminar (GUITARS). Hoya Saxa!

From ETH Zurich, the Georg-August University of Göttingen, and Heidelberg University, we thank Christian Conrad, Andreas Fuchs, Martin Gassebner, Stephan Klasen, Michael Lamla, Christoph Moser, Frank Somogyi, and Jan-Egbert Sturm.

Family

We close our acknowledgments by thanking the people nearest and dearest to us, whose support has carried us through this demanding project and, more generally, our careers.

Vreeland thanks friends of ours, Zé Cheibub, Jennifer Gandhi, Fernando Limongi, Sebastian Saiegh, and the boss, Adam Przeworski.

Vreeland especially wishes to express his gratitude and love to his parents, James and Joan, who have shown unwavering support for him throughout his life. He further thanks his sister Kristen, his brother-in-law Aris, and his nephew Brian for all of their love and support. He also thanks his cousin Bill and his family – Maureen, Billy, and Jenn. Whenever he flew off to meet with colleagues to work on this project, they were always ready to put him up for a night and make runs to the old Idlewild Airport.

Dreher thanks Martin Gassebner, who probably most closely followed the ups and downs involved with working on this project over the years. He thanks his PhD supervisor, Roland Vaubel, for raising his interest in the political economy of international organizations. And most especially, he thanks Diana, not least for accepting the work on this project (and others) when he should have spent more time with her.

Finally, we acknowledge the next generation – for their inspiration to continue our work. We dedicate this book to Adam Michael Arcuik, Lukas Dreher, Alex Raymond Frias, Aris Vreeland Frias, Jonas König, and Juan Carlos Serrano – of course – *our godsons.*

1

Money and Politics on the International Stage

1.1 Trading Favors

Trading money for political influence takes place at every level of government. We may tip the mailman in hope of better service. Lobbyists shower government officials with lavish trips in an effort to convince them to support their cause. A presidential administration may deliver cash to legislators for their support.[1] Some cases are innocent, some questionable, and others illegal, but the fact remains that these kinds of exchanges are commonplace. So it should not be surprising to learn that governments themselves trade money for political influence on the international stage.

Strange, however, is the tale we tell. In our study, the central political commodity that is bought and sold is *legitimacy*. We investigate how governments trade money for political influence – a practice commonly considered illegitimate – to obtain a shroud of legitimacy for their foreign policies.

The story begins in New York City, home of the United Nations, where the Security Council regularly meets to pass resolutions concerning the world's most vital security issues. Uniquely powerful, the Security Council serves as the most important organ of the UN. Its highly visible actions often receive considerable press, in no small part because its powers include imposing economic sanctions on sovereign nations and providing legal authority for military action against them. Famous cases include the authorizing of military force in the Korean Peninsula in 1950, the invasion of Iraq in 1990, and the bombing of Libya in 2011.[2]

---

[1] As in the famous case of the Fujimori government in Peru (see Saiegh 2011: 127–132).

[2] Korean War: Resolution 84 (July 7, 1950), Gulf War in Iraq: Resolution 678 (November 29, 1990), Bombing of Libya: Resolution 1973 (March 17, 2011).

By what authority does the United Nations Security Council (UNSC) take these actions? The UNSC has no military of its own, nor does it have any major financial resources with which to punish or reward. But the UNSC has a certain moral force codified in international law, and it also serves as an informational focal point for the citizens of the world. The power of the UNSC is thus to *legitimate* hostile actions that states may take against each other. Scholars have suggested two types of legitimacy with respect to the UNSC: symbolic and informational. The UNSC has the power to persuade some people because of its moral force and also the power to credibly signal information about the severity of global security threats. For the purposes of our study, we thus define legitimacy broadly as a coordinating mechanism, signaling to the world whether a foreign policy should be supported, tolerated, resisted, or opposed. UNSC resolutions may convey both symbolic and informative legitimacy, as global citizens view the policies approved by the UNSC as normatively and strategically appropriate courses of action.[3] Hence, when the U.S. government, for example, enjoys the backing of the UNSC for its foreign policy actions, it can expect more support from other governments around the world and from its own citizens at home. Some may offer support because of the symbolic value of following international legal procedures, whereas others take UNSC resolutions as a credible signal of the value of the foreign policy in question.

From where does the UNSC derive its authority?[4] The answer to this question is grounded in representation. The UN Charter, which came into force in the aftermath of World War II, grants permanent status on the Security Council to that conflict's victors: China, France, the Soviet Union (now Russia), the United Kingdom, and the United States. Each of these permanent members of the Security Council also has veto power to block any resolution that it strongly opposes.[5]

---

[3] On the symbolic role of the UNSC, see Hurd (2007). Also see Franck (1990), Wendt (1992), Ruggie (1992: 564), and Johnston (2001). On the broader role of ideas in international relations, see Risse-Kappen (1994), McNamara (1998, 1999), and Tannenwald (2005). On the informational role of the UNSC, see Chapman (2009, 2011). Also see Garrett and Weingast (1993), Goldstein and Keohane (1993), Milner (1997), and Fearon and Laitin (2004). For research arguing that the UNSC can promote international norms by devoting attention to an issue, see True-Frost (2007), Hudson (2009), and Carpenter (2012). For legalistic perspectives, see Glennon (2001, 2003), Tharoor (2003) and Slaughter (2003).

[4] Hurd (2007) has greatly influenced our views on this question.

[5] This is also called "Great Power unanimity" (see http://www.un.org/sc/members.asp, accessed June 16, 2011). Because they may abstain rather than oppose a resolution,

Endowing these Great Powers with a privileged position in the organization incentivized them to participate. This was important; without the support of the most powerful countries in the world, a council for global security would not have much strength. Still, such a council would also need support from the rest of the world in order to be viewed as legitimate. The world has become, after all, a place where representation matters. Other, less-powerful countries would also need to have a voice. So, beside the permanent members, the membership of the UNSC would also include countries elected to represent specifically designated regions of the world: Africa, Asia, Eastern Europe, Latin America and the Caribbean, and Western Europe along with its descendent countries.[6]

Beyond the symbolic importance of gathering representatives from the various regions of the world, the breadth of representation has helped ensure a diversity of preferences with respect to the use of forceful foreign policies, such as the imposition of economic sanctions and the use of military force. UNSC resolutions can therefore convey credible signals – of the necessity and appropriateness of such policies – to domestic and international publics that do not enjoy the same privileged access to information about security threats as do the members of the UNSC.

Who are these elected members of the Security Council? We delve into the details later, but for now, consider a country that is poor and small. This minor country may never before have entered into the minds of most citizens of rich and powerful countries – like those of the United States, Japan, and Europe. But during the country's two-year term serving on the UNSC, the entire world may hear about its voting behavior on the nightly news. The government of such a country suddenly has a powerful voice on the international stage. Its opinions over issues of international security are subject to unprecedented levels of scrutiny. Does the North Korean attack on South Korea constitute a breach of the peace, calling for military intervention? Should the UN establish a peacekeeping force in Cyprus? Should the world impose sanctions against the policies of apartheid practiced by the government of South Africa? Can the

---

however, affirmative unanimity is not required. The Great Powers need only be unanimous in their non-opposition.

[6] Before 1966, the elected members included two elected seats for Latin America, one for the Middle East, one for Eastern Europe, one for Western Europe, and one British Commonwealth country. The number of elected members expanded from six to ten in the aftermath of decolonization to afford better representation for the expanded UN membership. For more, see Russett (1997), Russett, O'Neill, and Sutterlin (1997), Hurd and Cronin (2008), Voeten (2008), Hovet (1960: 2), Bailey and Daws (1998: 168–173), Daws (1997), and Kahler (2011: 21–22).

world tolerate Iraq's invasion of Kuwait? Should outside forces restore the rule of democracy in Haiti? Should we intervene in the Rwandan genocide? Should the world permit North Korea and Iran to develop nuclear weapons? Should the Libyan and Syrian governments be stopped from killing their own citizens? Not only do citizens of the United States and other rich countries learn about how this small country votes on these and similar issues; research even suggests that they may also judge their own government's performance based on whether its security policies have the approval of the UNSC. During this small country's two-year term on the UNSC, the governments of the United States, Japan, and European countries have a vested political interest in its public declarations and voting behavior.

But what does the government of a small country care if the United States takes action somewhere way off in another region? Take Zimbabwe, for example. Issues at home are far more pressing on its government than are the events unfolding around the globe. Its economy is languishing. Its citizens, suffering from poverty and hunger, might turn violent if the economy takes another turn for the worse. Rather than worry about issues of international security, this government cares more about domestic political issues. It does not value a powerful voice on issues of global security – this government would prefer foreign aid from the global community.

Herein lies the crux of this book: Trades are possible, and they happen. The governments of rich and powerful countries such as the United States and Japan care more about votes and discussions at the UNSC than they do about foreign aid, which amounts to a paltry sum in their overall budgets. Developing countries, by contrast, may care more about foreign aid than about the global security issues considered by the UNSC. Typically, governments of developing countries stay out of foreign policy matters – they may not even have well-developed policy positions. Exceptions arise, of course, and the governments of some developing countries have strong and sincere preferences concerning certain issues of global security. Yet, when weighing the salience of most foreign policy concerns against the prospect of foreign aid, the latter often trumps.

This study thus addresses the political economy of the UNSC. Focusing on the elected members, we consider whether governments trade money for political influence on the international stage of the UNSC. In the pages that follow, we present evidence that when governments serve on the UNSC, they receive more bilateral aid from the United States, Japan, and Germany. During their UNSC service, they also receive better treatment from multilateral organizations where the United States, Japan, and Germany, as well as France and the United Kingdom, have historically exerted political control. The International Monetary Fund (IMF) provides UNSC members more loans and attaches softer conditionality to these loans. UNSC elected members also receive more project loans from the World Bank.[7]

The core evidence that we present is statistical in nature and robust. Our quantitative approach allows us to summarize multiple observations of countries both on and off the UNSC, showing that there are real perks to membership in terms of bilateral and multilateral aid from the global community. The statistical significance of the evidence indicates only a small chance of observing these patterns if there really were no relationship between increased aid and UNSC membership. And the results generally hold, whether we present a simple depiction of the descriptive data or subject the data to complex statistical models that account for a myriad of factors specific to country and year. Beyond the quantitative evidence, we also corroborate our argument with references to specific cases.

Certain audiences to whom we have presented these findings do not find them surprising. Like Captain Renault of *Casablanca*, who feigns being "shocked to find that gambling is going on" in Rick's nightclub, many people simply expect that foreign aid follows political motives. Such a relationship certainly fits the assertion of Hans Morgenthau (1962: 302), scholar and statesman, who claimed that "the transfer of money and services from one government to another performs here the function of a price paid for political services rendered or to be rendered." Yet, some of the policy practitioners actually involved with the activities of the UN, as well as those who work with foreign aid and multilateral organizations, find our results hard to believe. They contend that these trades of money for influence over the UNSC do not happen – or happen rarely. So, it turns out that our robust empirical findings raise a number of challenging questions.

---

[7] Kuziemko and Werker (2006) authored the seminal study in this line of research, examining U.S. bilateral aid. Also see Tamura and Kunieda (2005). Regarding Germany, see Dreher, Nunnenkamp, and Schmaljohann (2013). For the effect of UNSC membership on IMF programs, see Dreher, Sturm, and Vreeland (2009b, 2013). For the World Bank, see Dreher, Sturm, and Vreeland (2009a). For UNICEF, see Kuziemko and Werker (2006). For the AsDB, see Lim and Vreeland (2013). Our work thus contributes to a growing literature examining the informal relationships across international organizations. For work on the interconnectedness of trade organizations, see Ingram et al. (2005) and Alter and Meunier (2009).

Is the political support of the elected members of the UNSC really so important that favors must be rendered in return? Do the ambassadors in New York, who do care about the votes, have the political leverage to mobilize aid bureaucracies? If so, why complicate transactions by tapping into so many aid bureaucracies – the IMF, the World Bank, the Asian Development Bank, the United Nations Children's Fund (UNICEF) – when bilateral aid is available? Can money really buy legitimacy? And finally, what are the consequences for the governments that trade away their political influence in return for money? We consider each of these questions in turn.

1.2 Do UNSC Votes Matter?

The governments of developing countries serving on the UNSC occupy a unique perch. The international press covers their public statements with much greater scrutiny than those of most other developing countries. UNSC members also take turns to occupy the UNSC presidency, which rotates monthly (according to English alphabetic order). The president meets with each of the UNSC members individually to set an agenda for the month. He or she then approves the agenda and presides over UNSC meetings. The president also has the formal authority to call special meetings (or fail to do so, as in a notable case that we address in Chapter 3).[8] Many governments have historically used their turn as president to bring attention to a particular issue important to them. Ultimately, however, UNSC members are important because they vote on matters concerning forceful foreign policies.

UNSC votes go on the public record – members do not enjoy the protection of a secret ballot. Passing a resolution requires nine out of fifteen votes – and no vetoes from the permanent members. Given these voting rules, how powerful is an elected member?

In terms of formal voting power, we have a short answer: not very. The long answer? It's complicated. One way social scientists typically measure formal voting power is to consider how likely a voter is to be pivotal in *making* or *breaking* a resolution.[9] When it comes to *breaking*

---

[8] See Rules 1, 7, 18, 19, and 20 of the *Provisional Rules of Procedure of the Security Council*, available at http://www.un.org/Docs/sc/scrules.htm (accessed June 17, 2011).

[9] O'Neill (1996) relies mainly on the approach of Shapley and Shubik (1954). Another widely used approach is that of Banzhaf (1965). Also see Strand and Rapkin (2011) and Winter (1996). For an application to another international institution, the IMF, see Dreyer and Schotter (1980).

a resolution, the permanent members always have the option of blocking with their individual veto power. So they are always pivotal. Elected members can only "break" a resolution if the coalition supporting the resolution includes exactly nine members. In this situation, if any one of them defects, the resolution fails – so all voters are pivotal. If a coalition supporting a resolution includes more than nine countries, none of the elected members – alone – has the ability to block it. A vote is pivotal in *making* a UNSC resolution if the coalition supporting it includes exactly eight members without it. One additional vote pivots the resolution from failing to passing. For a coalition of any other size, however, no particular voter is pivotal in passing a resolution. That is, if there are more than nine supporters, no single addition or subtraction makes a difference – the resolution will pass. If there are seven or fewer supporters, the resolution fails, regardless of whether an additional member joins or leaves the coalition. To summarize this formal approach to voting power, permanent members can always make a resolution fail, whereas elected members are only pivotal in *breaking* when there are nine supporters and in *making* when there are eight supporters. So, according to this formal idea of pivotal votes, the single vote of an elected UNSC member should rarely matter.

Using this basic concept of voting power, O'Neill (1996) analyzes all possible combinations of hypothetical coalitions and finds that more than 98 percent of voting power belongs to the permanent members.[10] Turning to voting data, we observe 1,517 resolutions that have passed the UNSC from 1966 to 2006. The average size of the winning coalition – 14.3 – far exceeds the minimum winning coalition of nine votes. Only in three cases are there exactly nine supporters.[11] For most

---

[10] Thus there is good reason that many studies of the UNSC focus on the permanent five (P5) as opposed to the elected ten (E10). See, for example, Luck (2006).

[11] These three resolutions were numbered 275 (passed in 1969), 312 (passed in 1972), and 387 (passed in 1976). Resolution 275 deplored Portugal's shelling of villages in Guinea from Portuguese territory in Guinea-Bissau. China, Colombia, France, Spain, the United Kingdom, and the United States all abstained, while voting in favor were Algeria, Senegal, Zambia, Pakistan, Nepal, Paraguay, Finland, Hungary, and – importantly – the Soviet Union. Resolution 312 called on Portugal to end colonization. Argentina, Belgium, France, Italy, the United Kingdom, and the United States abstained, while Guinea, Sudan, Somalia, India, Japan, Panama, and Yugoslavia voted in favor, along with China and the Soviet Union. Resolution 387 condemned South African incursions into Angola. France, Italy, Japan, the United Kingdom, and the United States abstained while China chose not to participate. Voting in favor were Benin, Libya, Tanzania, Pakistan, Panama, Guyana, Sweden, Romania, and the Soviet Union. It seems that the Soviet Union was more likely to put together minimum winning coalitions than the

resolutions that pass, there are more than enough votes. As for failed proposals, data are not readily available, and severe selection bias would plague any analysis: Most votes that would fail are never proposed. For what it is worth, we have collected the data on the failed proposals available at the UN archives in Geneva (from 1966 to 2006, with potentially missing observations prior to 1999). Out of the total 34 failed proposals that we observe, the average supporting coalition is 4.4.

The bottom line is that elected members rarely decide the formal passage of a UNSC resolution. So why would rich and powerful countries want to buy the political support of elected members of the UNSC?

Powerful countries may have an interest in buying insurance votes, especially if they can buy such votes at low cost. General studies of vote-buying suggest that oversized coalitions tend to be established to ensure success (see, for example, Volden and Carrubba 2004). Thus coalitions with exactly nine affirmative votes have rarely appeared in history perhaps because invested governments have pressured extra governments to join coalitions precisely to avoid such close calls. In an exhaustive study of different national legislatures from around the world, however, Saiegh (2011) shows that political actors only purchase pivotal votes. Perhaps, then, one must look beyond the formal voting rules to understand the importance of elected members of the Security Council. Their votes may be pivotal in other ways.

Consider the battle for votes for the Iraq war in 2003. On one side were the United States and the United Kingdom, who sought UNSC approval for the military venture. On the other side were France, Russia, and China, who could veto any such resolution. Yet, the Associated Press reported, "Promises of rich rewards and hints of bruising punishment are flying as diplomats seek the support of Angola, Cameroon, Chile, Guinea, Mexico and Pakistan over a second United Nations resolution that would authorize military action against Saddam Hussein" (Renfrew 2003). The Bush administration lobbied some of the nonpermanent members of the UNSC with aid packages in an attempt to win their votes, while officials from France pushed in the opposite direction (Eldar 2008: 18; Anderson, Bennis, and Cavanagh 2003; Renfrew 2003; Martin 2003).[12] Attempting to establish a favorable majority of UNSC votes in the face of a veto makes no sense in terms of the institution's formal rules. A single veto from one

United States was. Future research could investigate whether the Soviet Union pressured any of the supporting countries, as each of them cast a pivotal vote.
[12] Also see Chapman (2011: 13).

of the permanent members who opposed a military strike against Iraq – France, Russia, or China – would have prevented a UNSC resolution. But even a simple majority of the votes supporting a vetoed proposal may have provided some legitimacy for the war. Affirmative votes from the elected members would have symbolized support from their region and conveyed information as to the appropriateness of a U.S. invasion.

In this case, of course, the United States did not have the support, and a vote was never taken. Instead, the United States built an ad hoc "Coalition of the Willing," which included nearly fifty countries.[13] Interestingly, according to the analysis by Chapman and Reiter (2004), the number of allied countries involved in a military strike does little to sway public opinion, whereas UNSC resolutions have a statistically significant impact.

This story suggests that every UNSC vote may count. The vote of an elected UNSC member matters not only because of the formal rules but also because every member of the UNSC has a global voice intended to represent an entire region. This view is consistent with the observation that there is a premium for getting (nearly) unanimous votes (see, for example, Doyle 2001: 223). The United States and other important countries may seek the support of the UNSC for reasons of legitimacy (Hurd 2007; Voeten 2005; Caron 1993; Claude 1966).[14]

The story of Yemen and the Gulf War perhaps best illustrates the importance of a single vote. When Yemen threatened to vote against the use of armed forces against Iraq in 1990 – for reasons of domestic and regional politics discussed in Chapter 3 – Secretary of State James Baker III declared "this will be the most expensive no vote they have ever cast" (Baker 1995: 325).[15] When Yemen did vote no, the United States cut all of its $70 million in aid. Yet the famous Resolution 678 enjoyed the support of twelve other members of the UNSC and easily

---

[13] See http://georgewbush-whitehouse.archives.gov/infocus/iraq/news/20030327%13;10 .html (accessed June 17, 2011). For a critical analysis of the coalition and how it was formed, see Anderson et al. (2003).

[14] The legitimacy of the UNSC has, of course, long been questioned. For a detailed examination of its place in international law, see Arend and Beck (1993). Lieber (2005: 4) acknowledges that the UNSC can contribute to the "perceived legitimacy of collective action," but argues that the institution pales in importance to the real strength behind most UN action, the sovereign power of the United States. Edelstein (2008: 149) contends that the legitimating approval of the United Nations may fail to placate an occupied population.

[15] As a fledgling Arab country, located on the Arabian peninsula, siding with the West against another Arab country would have raised the dangerous ire of its own citizens, not to mention many Arabs throughout the region as well as, of course, Iraq.

passed without Yemen's support.[16] So the pressure on and punishment of Yemen makes no sense in terms of the rules governing the UNSC. The formal rules require nine affirmative votes for a resolution to pass, so a favorable vote from Yemen should have served as but a mere luxury. Yet the formal rules of the UNSC did not encompass the entirety of U.S. policy objectives. Voeten (2001) cites the memoirs of Secretary Baker (1995: 278), which emphasize U.S. *domestic* support as the main reason that the government sought a multilateral solution to the Gulf War. To the extent that Yemen represented Arab states on the global stage, their vote would have conveyed information about the support for the Gulf War in the Arab world, as well as carried symbolic importance. So, while not pivotal in a formal sense, the United States viewed Yemen's vote as crucial in a political sense. For both informational and symbolic reasons, UNSC votes send a coordinating signal to less-informed governments and citizens around the world to support – or at least not resist – forceful foreign policy actions.

Hence, the legitimacy that the vote of a UNSC member brings may be both symbolic and informational (see Voeten 2005; Thompson 2006; Chapman 2007; Hurd 2007; Fang 2008; Kahler 2011). From a symbolic point of view, the vote of an elected member of the UNSC indicates that a resolution has the support of the duly appointed regional representative.

From an informational point of view, members of the UNSC have access to sensitive documents and private discussions regarding the importance of taking international action. Countries that are not current members of the UNSC, especially if they are small and do not have a strong presence at the UN headquarters in New York, may take cues from their representatives on the UNSC. Indeed, citizens of countries all over the world may take cues from the elected representatives. As Chapman (2011) explains, voters may question if an apparently aggressive foreign policy pursued by their government is overzealously hawkish, but they do not have enough information. A favorable vote from a UNSC member who has access to better information and is known as dovish on matters of international security conveys a credible signal to citizens all over the world that the policy is appropriate.

The legitimacy conferred by UNSC votes can generate greater international support for a forceful foreign policy. Even powerful countries can garner obvious benefits from such support. Economic sanctions, for example, cannot be effective if the targeted country can trade with other

---

[16] Cuba voted against, along with Yemen; China abstained. See Weston (1991: 516, fn2).

countries that refuse to support the embargo. War efforts can be facilitated through several channels, for example, by granting access to air space and shipping lanes, by providing territorial bases of operation, and by providing additional troops and military hardware (see Sandler and Hartley 1999).

Domestic support may be more important. U.S. presidents, for example, hesitate to take foreign policy actions without the support of the American public. Winning the approval of the UNSC can generate increased popular support for a policy, as demonstrated by the research of Chapman and Reiter (2004). They argue that the American public is risk-averse to the use of military force, preferring to use it prudently and only for defensive purposes.[17] U.S. presidents may have expansionist objectives and be willing to use military force more readily than the public would like. This generates a principal-agent problem, where the agent (the U.S. president) has better information than – but divergent preferences from – its principal (the U.S. public). Chapman and Reiter argue that the UNSC has conservative preferences over the use of military force, which are actually closer to those of the U.S. public than they are to those of a given U.S. president. To the extent that the American public perceives the UNSC as an independent third party, a UNSC resolution can act as a credible signal of the appropriateness, prudence, and desirability of the military action that the U.S. president advocates. The argument also holds for the chief executives of other powerful countries.[18]

Consider Figure 1.1, which depicts threat levels on a scale of 1 to 7, along with the preferences of three actors: a chief executive, a typical voter, and a UNSC member. An actor prefers the use of force against threats that meet (or exceed) his threshold – a low threshold represents a war-loving hawk, whereas a high threshold represents an indulgent dove. In the stylized scenario presented in Figure 1.1, the hawkish executive has a low threshold: He prefers the use of military force for any threat above level 2. The more dovish voter prefers the use of force only for threats of level 4 or greater. The cautious UNSC member advocates the use of force against threats of level 6 or higher. The voter knows the preferences of the executive and the UNSC member but never observes the

---

[17] See Jentleson (1992, 2003), Jentleson and Britton (1998), Groeling and Baum (2008: 1069–1070), and Perla (2011).

[18] For a detailed discussion of the argument as it applies to Japan, see Lim and Vreeland (2013). Byman and Waxman (2002: 239) discuss the importance to the United States of securing both domestic and foreign support for coercive strategies they pursue against other states. For seminal work on multilateral coercion, see Martin (1992).

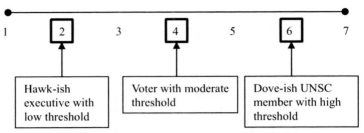

FIGURE 1.1. Hypothetical threat level with "action" thresholds for three actors. *Notes:* The scale from 1 to 7 represents potential threat levels in international relations. The boxes represent the "action" thresholds for three actors: a chief executive of a powerful country (2), a typical voter from that country (4), and an elected member of the UNSC (6). Each actor prefers to take aggressive action against threat levels that meet or exceed his/her threshold. So, the hawkish executive prefers to take action for all threats of level 2 or higher. The more conservative voter only prefers to take action for threats of level 4 or higher. The dovish UNSC member prefers action only for extreme threats of level 6 or higher. The executive and the UNSC member observe threat levels perfectly, whereas the voter can only observe the signals of the executive and the UNSC member. If the UNSC member votes in favor of a resolution calling for action, the voter knows that the threat level is at least 6, and thus supports the executive's preference for action. If the voter can observe payoffs from the executive to the UNSC member that entice the UNSC member to vote in favor of resolutions at lower threat levels, information can still be conveyed, provided that there is a limit to the effectiveness of payoffs. If the UNSC member can be enticed to vote for resolutions only when the threat level is 4 or higher, for example, then the UNSC member's votes will mirror the voter's preferences, and UNSC votes convey appropriate information from this voter's point of view. If the UNSC member can be enticed to vote for resolutions when the threat level is 2 or higher, then UNSC votes convey no more information to voters than the signals from the executive.

true threat levels represented by various international crises – the voter neither has the access to information nor the time to study these situations carefully. The executive and the UNSC member, however, observe the threat level perfectly. Now, suppose they observe a level 6 threat. The executive announces to the voter that they should take military action, but the public does not know if the executive is telling the truth. Maybe the true threat level is only 3. An affirmative vote from the UNSC member would indicate that the threat level is at least 6 – so the voter would know to support the executive's proposed action.

Chapman and Reiter present compelling evidence. Consider Figure 1.2, which shows that American public opinion on a war to liberate Kuwait from Iraq dramatically shifted from 37 percent in favor before the UNSC

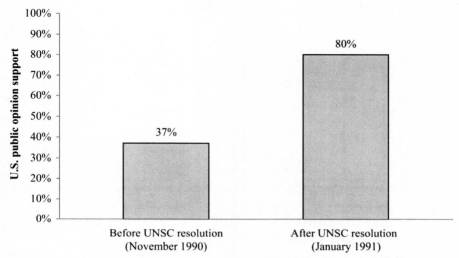

FIGURE 1.2. U.S. public support for a war to liberate Kuwait (UNSC Resolution 678, authorizing the use of force, November 29, 1990). *Notes:* Prior to the UNSC resolution authorizing the use of force against Iraq's invasion of Kuwait, U.S. public support was relatively low, compared to its level after obtaining UNSC support. *Source:* Chapman and Reiter (2004: 892).

resolution to 80 percent in favor after the resolution. Of course, this observation constitutes merely suggestive evidence.[19] Consider, however, the broader data. Figure 1.3 suggests that when a U.S. president leads the country into military action, the average effect on his approval ratings is rather flat. But for the half-dozen actions when he has the backing of the UNSC, the effect is noticeably positive, and the difference is statistically significant.[20] Besides the Gulf War, notable shifts in public opinion are associated with the Korean War, the Yugoslav civil war, and the war in Afghanistan, where public support increased by nine points in each case. Importantly, the pattern holds when controlling for other potential determinants of U.S. public support, such as whether the president enjoys bipartisan support, the number of U.S. allies involved, the support of a

[19] The polls were conducted two months apart (in November 1990 and January 1991); the UNSC resolution was finally passed on January 14, 1991, and many other efforts to generate U.S. support were being conducted domestically. For further examination of the broader question, see Kull and Destler (1999).

[20] When we highlight statistically significant results, we refer to, at least, the 10 percent level of confidence. Many of our results hold at higher thresholds of confidence. See Chapters 4, 5, and 6 for details. (Note that the Chapman and Reiter (2004) datafile is available: http://jcr.sagepub.com/content/48/6/886/suppl/DC1, accessed June 17, 2010).

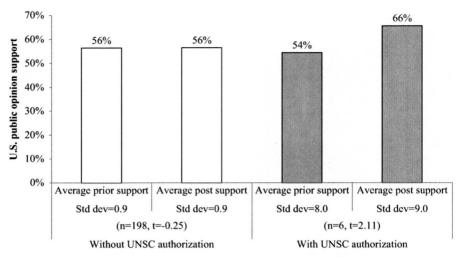

FIGURE 1.3. Public support of the U.S. president before and after military action, without UNSC authorization versus with UNSC authorization. *Notes:* The white columns compare U.S. public support for the U.S. president before and after military action, depicting no discernible effect. The shaded columns make the same comparison when the military action has the authorization of a UNSC resolution – the difference is visible and statistically significant, though based on only six observations. *Source:* Chapman and Reiter (2004).

regional organization, or press coverage (see Chapman and Reiter 2004; Chapman 2011). The effect also holds both during and after the Cold War (although the Cold War effect is driven by the Korean War observation – again, see Chapman and Reiter 2004; Chapman 2011). Chapman and Reiter (2004) and Chapman (2011) show that the relationship also holds up to more rigorous statistical scrutiny. American public support of the president increases by about 9 percent when he enjoys UNSC support. The analysis implies that the UNSC has a unique ability to influence U.S. public opinion.

This argument broadly accords with B. Peter Rosendorff's game-theoretic approach to understanding international relations. He contends that many different types of international institutions serve as independent third parties, sending credible signals to domestic audiences. Along with his coauthors, Rosendorff has shown that (1) entering into trade agreements can signal credible policy on trade, (2) ratifying human rights agreements can signal credible "resolve" to remain in office, and

(3) reporting economic data to international institutions can signal credible transparency.[21]

In our case, we argue that favorable votes on the UNSC may send credible signals to both domestic and international audiences. Chapman and Reiter (2004) focus on the signal to the American audience. Lim and Vreeland (2013) extend this logic to Japanese politics. Most of the examples we discuss throughout the book in fact pertain to domestic audiences. Yet for conflicts where regional tensions could erupt – or where governments seek the goodwill of a regional public – UNSC approval can serve a similar function as it does with domestic audiences. During the Arab Spring, policy-makers in the West wanted to ensure both domestic support and broad appeal throughout the Middle East when intervening in Libya, and UNSC Resolution 1973 helped to facilitate a positive image for their military actions, which ultimately led to the ouster of President Muammar Gaddafi.

Of course, when executives handpick supportive governments, putting together a "coalition of the willing," they send a weaker signal because they can simply select allies with preferences similar to their own. Returning to Figure 1.1, if the endorsement comes from a government with a threshold preference of 2 (exactly the same as the executive), then the voter gains no new information. The independent selection of the UNSC member by the UN General Assembly constitutes the key to the credibility of the signal.

The central premise of this book, however, questions the independence of UNSC votes. Does the buying and selling of UNSC votes damage the credibility of the information conferred by those votes? We suggest that while political deals might weaken signals, they need not destroy their value. We offer two reasons as to why:

First, payoffs have limits. Suppose that a UNSC member will "move" his preference a maximum of two points lower on the threshold scale if he receives a healthy payoff. If the voter knows this and knows that the

---

[21] The work on trade agreements was coauthored by two of the leading scholars of international relations, Edward D. Mansfield of the University of Pennsylvania and Helen V. Milner of Princeton University (Mansfield, Milner, and Rosendorff 2002). The foundation for this work comes from the book by Milner (1997 – also see Milner and Rosendorff 1996 and Milner 1988). This book, in turn, is influenced by Keohane (1984). Also see Milner and Kubota (2005). For Rosendorff's more recent work using these information models to explain human rights treaties, see Hollyer and Rosendorff (2011). For his work on transparency, see Rosendorff and Doces (2006) and Hollyer, Rosendorff, and Vreeland (2011).

UNSC member has a true preference of, say, 6 (as depicted in Figure 1.1), then an affirmative vote indicates a threat of level 4 or higher – which actually matches the preference of the voter. Of course, if the executive can entice the UNSC member to vote for resolutions when the threat level is 2 or higher, then the UNSC vote cannot convey any more credible information than the announcements of the executive. (We address this issue in a different way in Chapter 2 when discussing swing voters.)

Second, the executive and the UNSC member may actually obfuscate their political deals. If the public remains unaware of the deal, they may perceive more credibility in the vote of the UNSC member. Johnson (2011) shows that domestic publics have unfavorable views toward international organizations when these publics are skeptical of that organization's more powerful members. Thus, states may wish to obfuscate their influence over the UNSC by using another organization as a "front." Laundering a "dirty bribe" may represent a key purpose of using multilateral organizations, like the World Bank and the IMF. They can serve to funnel favors to politically important countries (Vaubel 1986, 2006; Yasutomo 1993; Abbott and Snidal 1998). As Ambassador John Bolton explained to us, one should avoid using overt threats because they might easily leak to the press.[22]

Obfuscation may not always be intentional, however. Rather, it can also result from the sheer complexity of the limited toolkit that policy practitioners have at their disposal. As Secretary Madeleine Albright explained to us, the importance of a UNSC member becomes known throughout the various bureaucratic hierarchies, and only the toughest decisions move up the chain to the highest levels.[23] Much of foreign policy work takes place in small ways at low levels through the thousands of daily meetings that occur in Washington and in country capitals throughout the world. As a result, we suspect that even many policy practitioners – and much more so the public – may remain unaware of specific favors provided to important countries.

We return to these issues below. For now, we conclude that policy makers involved in international affairs from all over the world recognize that when a poor, small country is elected to serve on the UNSC, its level

---

[22] Interview with John Bolton, March 31, 2011, American Enterprise Institute, Washington, DC.

[23] Interview with Madeleine Albright, August 29, 2012, Albright Stonebridge Group, Washington, DC. For an analytical framework examining the complex networked systems with and across modern states, see Root (2013).

of importance suddenly rises. Should a significant issue come up during the tenure of such a temporary UNSC member, it behooves powerful countries to have the member government in their good graces – or even in their debt. Providing bilateral foreign aid, as well as loans from the IMF, World Bank, and other international organizations, represents a low-cost means of achieving this goal. The United States and other powerful countries recognize the benefits of putting the elected UNSC members in their debt. Thus, when a country wins election to serve on the UNSC, it moves up on the agendas of policy practitioners. If temporary UNSC members request any of the above forms of foreign aid, powerful governments will pressure the various aid bureaucrats to facilitate the request. Of course, the recipient government runs the risk that the aid might be cut off if the government misbehaves on the UNSC. Our story thus follows the logic of favors, neatly summarized in the opening scene of Francis Ford Coppola's brilliant movie, *The Godfather*[24]:

Someday, and that day may never come, I'll call upon you to do a service for me. But uh, until that day, accept this [foreign aid] as a gift on [your election to the UNSC].

– *Don* Vito Corleone

1.3 Do UN Ambassadors Have Political Leverage over Bilateral and Multilateral Channels of Influence?

Public officials who work in the various bureaucracies around the world face different priorities. The officials who care the most about UNSC votes are the ambassadors serving at the UN in New York City, while officials in other agencies may have quite distinct agendas. Those involved in foreign aid care mainly about achieving development goals in the poor countries where they do their work. So *Don* Corleone's famous line may summarize the end result, but the details work out in a much subtler manner.

Consider, for example, the former Administrator of the United States Agency for International Development (USAID), Andrew S. Natsios. He recalls that in the spring of 1992, he received a phone call from John Bolton about a certain African country – Cape Verde – that was

---

[24] Interestingly, when asked about his favorite movie, then-candidate Barack Obama not only named *The Godfather*, he specifically referenced the scene cited above (CBS, September 23, 2008, see: http://www.youtube.com/watch?v=8Bz9iXernY4 and http://www.cbsnews.com/video/watch/?id=4472911n, accessed 25 June 2013).

serving on the UNSC.[25] At that time, Natsios was serving in USAID as the Assistant Administrator of the Bureau of Humanitarian Assistance, while Bolton was the Assistant Secretary of State for the Bureau of International Organization Affairs (and thus supervised the U.S. relationship with the United Nations). Natsios recalls that Bolton told him that he was trying to get Cape Verde to vote a certain way on the UNSC and thus wanted Natsios to offer food aid to the developing country. For his part, Bolton does not remember the conversation – he says with a smile, "Andrew has an overactive imagination, but it sounds like something I would do."[26] Natsios says that he flat-out refused to put together the food aid package because the country did not qualify as food-insecure. Interestingly, he remembers that Bolton called him a few weeks later to tell him that he could cancel the package because it was no longer needed. Natsios laughs about this because he never initiated the package in the first place.

This story reveals two features of the political economy of the UNSC. First, governments do care about UNSC votes. According to Natsios, Bolton picked up the phone and made the call. Now, to be clear, Ambassador Bolton does not recall this instance or any other where the administration specifically bribed or threatened any government with aid – except in the prominent case of Yemen 1990. But Bolton does report that he regularly pressured ambassadors on how to vote. He might warn about the general "displeasure" that the U.S. government would feel if another government fails to deliver a favorable vote, implying that the country could fall "out of favor" with the United States.[27] He stresses that translating the displeasure into specific favors is simply "not done" on the scene in New York.[28]

Secretary Madeleine Albright also explains that she never told an ambassador, "You do this, and we'll do this."[29] She did develop close working relationships with the other ambassadors with whom she served as U.S. ambassador to the UN from 1993 to 1997. She spent a great deal of time with all of the ambassadors, developing strong friendships with

[25] Interview with Andrew S. Natsios, September 14 , 2011, Georgetown University, Washington, DC.

[26] Interview with John Bolton, March 31, 2011, American Enterprise Institute, Washington, DC.

[27] Ibid.

[28] Ibid.

[29] Interview with Madeleine Albright, August 29, 2012, Albright Stonebridge Group, Washington, DC.

some. For important resolutions, she met individually with every single member of the UNSC to find out how they would vote.[30] She stresses, however, that she and her colleagues were "instructed ambassadors" who represented their countries and acted on policy decided in their country capitals.

Influencing a country on how to vote, therefore, involves a complex web, running from New York, through the various bureaucracies in Washington, and then out to country capitals all over the world. So, ambassadors such as Albright and Bolton would do their part at the UN in New York, and the region-specific bureaus at the State Department would give instructions to their ambassadors in specific countries. At the State Department itself, the assistant secretary for a specific region would meet with the assistant secretary for international organizations, and perhaps the economic assistant secretary, and then USAID might become involved: "There are thousands of these kinds of meetings that take place in government every day."[31]

Now, while Secretary Albright may not agree with all of Ambassador Bolton's policy goals, she stresses that she sees nothing wrong with the use of foreign aid as a tool of foreign policy. As she aptly puts it, "There's not a lot in the toolbox" that practitioners can use to pursue foreign policy goals.[32] She provides a short list: (1) diplomacy (bilateral and multilateral), (2) economic tools – both carrots (such as aid and trade) and sticks (such as embargoes and sanctions), (3) the threat of the use of force, (4) the use of force, and (5) intelligence and law enforcement – "that's it."[33] So, foreign aid simply represents one of the very few tools of foreign policy, and foreign policy, she explains, is simply "trying to get some country to do what you want. That's all it is."[34] She categorically rejects the idea that providing aid – or trading other political or economic favors – represents something negative like bribery. Rather, she views favors such as these as one part of a complicated set of interrelated issues over which governments negotiate. She recalls fondly how much she enjoyed her

---

[30] Ibid.
[31] Ibid.
[32] Ibid.
[33] Ibid. Also see Albright (2009: chapter 1).
[34] Ibid. As she puts it in her 2009 book, "The purpose of foreign policy is to persuade others to do what we want or, better yet, to want what we want" (Albright 2009: 20). In our study, we focus on economic inducements. Kroenig, McAdam, and Weber (2010) provide a careful analysis of nonmilitary and noneconomic inducements – what Nye (2004: 5) calls soft power: "getting others to want the outcomes that you want."

service in the UN and explains that even when representing the most powerful country in the world, her leverage over other ambassadors faced strict limitations. Negotiations therefore require long hours and a great deal of creativity in the application of the tools at hand. Sometimes, she would take the lead in discussion, while other times she would encourage another country to do so. The point about the close working relationships among the ambassadors is that they are operating in the context of many different issues happening at the same time. The United States might not have any direct influence over one specific issue, but it might have influence over another. So while she does not remember wielding the particular tool of foreign aid, she believes that at any given time, depending on the goal, a government may need to use all of the tools, including foreign assistance. She is thus not surprised by our finding of a link between UNSC membership and foreign assistance.

The second feature that the Natsios-Bolton exchange reveals concerns bureaucracies. Their conversations show that governments are not monoliths but rather consist of many different bureaus, which may have competing goals. While one bureau concerns itself with issues of global security, another devotes its work toward promoting economic development – and others work with multilateral financial institutions. Under extraordinary circumstances – such as during the run-up to a war – all of the different components of a government may follow the same strict marching orders. Some of our most obvious and famous examples, such as the Gulf War stories, come from these instances. Under normal circumstances, however, the various bureaucracies may lack a unity of purpose, therefore making it harder to push through favors for the elected members of the UNSC. Secretary Albright explains that when working in foreign policy, one does run into bureaucratic roadblocks – USAID might say, "You can't control my budget. I am into development, and I'm not going to use this for foreign policy."[35] Foreign policy is often decided through the interagency process. The interagency process is meant to bring together different stakeholder agencies to achieve a particular policy goal, and each agency brings forward its perspective – of course, different agencies may disagree as to the means of achieving a goal.

In the chapters that follow, however, we present evidence suggesting that UNSC membership systematically causes increases to many sources of finance: bilateral aid from the United States, Japan, and Germany, and

---

[35] Interview with Madeleine Albright, August 29, 2012, Albright Stonebridge Group, Washington, DC.

multilateral finance from the IMF, the World Bank, the United Nations, the Asian Development Bank, and the African Development Bank. If bureaucratic inertia makes it difficult to push through favors for UNSC members, why do we find effects through so many agencies?

One answer immediately springs to mind: The correlations are spurious. Perhaps strategically important countries are both more likely to win UNSC elections and to receive aid. This is a reasonable guess – but, as we show in Chapters 4 and 5, it is unlikely to account for the whole story. Setting aside the methodologies we use in later chapters to address this potential problem of nonrandom selection, consider, for now, a simple indication that there is something special about UNSC membership: Elected UNSC members receive increased perks while serving on the UNSC, and the perks gradually fade away after exogenous limits end their terms. That is, when exogenously enforced term limits require that elected countries step down after two years on the UNSC, the foreign aid benefits systematically dissipate. This implies a real effect of UNSC membership on foreign aid.

But that still leaves a puzzle: While it may seem plausible that governments trade money for influence over the UNSC, policy practitioners report that it is not so simple. Money must take a long and circuitous path to translate into influence. Consider the recipient country serving on the UNSC: Its ambassadors in New York, who serve on the Security Council, answer to the Ministry of Foreign Affairs, but the bilateral aid agencies and multilateral institutions work mainly with the Ministry of Finance. From the perspective of a donor country, like the United States, the Bureau of International Organization Affairs in the State Department oversees the New York angle, while separate bureaus work on bilateral aid, and yet another set of actors at the U.S. Treasury Department deals with multilateral agencies like the IMF and World Bank. At every node, there are so many complicated bureaucratic channels that it might be surprising that politically motivated money can navigate through any, much less all, of them.

Such bureaucratic challenges, however, can actually help explain why we see effects across so many channels of influence. Consider a U.S. bureaucrat in the State Department looking to generate goodwill with an elected member of the UNSC. He asks a colleague who works at USAID to put together an aid package, but he gets no guarantees. So who does he call next? Multiple channels may be necessary in order for aid to flow.

Some bureaucrats may not even know why a particular country keeps appearing on the agenda. We discussed our research with a former official who had served in the upper echelons of the World Bank hierarchy. He said that while his government certainly pushed him to approve projects for specific countries, it never provided political justifications but rather grounded the reasons for the projects purely in economic terms. In some cases, the World Bank official might guess that the Treasury secretary is taking an interest in a specific country for some political reason, but if so, it was left unsaid. Moreover, he reports that the vast majority of World Bank projects appear to be economically – not politically – motivated.

We also discussed our research with a junior action officer within the State Department's Bureau of Political-Military Affairs back in 2010. During that year, the officer noticed that Brazil and Turkey repeatedly appeared on the agenda of meetings that he attended on a variety of topics – including Middle East security and U.S. policy toward Iran. Office directors and staffers in the room were regularly taking account of how these countries would perceive U.S. actions and statements. While it may have been obvious to the senior officers in the room, the reasons for Brazil's and Turkey's appearance on the agendas were never announced at the meetings, and the junior action officer was curious as to why. When he learned of our research on the UNSC, it suddenly seemed to make sense: Brazil and Turkey were both serving on the Security Council at the time, and the United States was seeking their support for imposing sanctions on Iran. (Interestingly, the support was never forthcoming – a specific issue to which we return in Chapter 7.)

The State Department junior action officer shared with us a further anecdote, which reveals the subtle ways in which a country's profile rises when serving on the UNSC. In the late spring of 2011, President Barack Obama and senior State Department officials met with President Ali Bongo Ondimba of Gabon when he came to Washington, DC. Why would the United States grant such a high-level meeting to the president of a country with a population of just 1.5 million people? The meeting may have come as a reward. Gabon was on the UNSC at a time when the United States depended on the UNSC for key votes on the intervention in Libya. In particular, Gabon supported Resolution 1970 (February 26, 2011), which imposed sanctions on Muammar Gaddafi's regime, and 1973 (March 17, 2011), which established a no-fly zone over Libya and provided the legal basis for the military intervention in the Libyan Civil War. The latter resolution represented a crucial foreign policy goal of the Obama administration, and it passed with only ten votes.[36] Of course, no

---

[36] Besides Gabon, the other supporting votes came from Nigeria, South Africa, Lebanon, Colombia, Bosnia and Herzegovina, Portugal, France, the United Kingdom, and the United States. China, Russia, Brazil, Germany, and India abstained.

one announced President Ondimba's high-level visit as a reward; some observers may regard it as a mere coincidence.

Occasionally, public officials explicitly dispel the notion of coincidence. Having paid an official visit to Togo in 2012, Secretary of State Hillary Clinton explained, "No Secretary of State had ever been to Togo before. Togo happens to be on the UN Security Council. Going there, making the personal investment, has a real strategic purpose.... When you look at... the voting dynamics in key international institutions, you start to understand the value of paying attention to these places."[37]

The junior action officer now assesses the situation as follows: "Senior leaders within the State Department are cognizant of who is or is not on the Security Council. And while there are no 'bald-faced deals,' policy makers appreciate that the opinions and perceptions of UNSC members matter because they can help us achieve (or stand in the way of) some of our most significant foreign policy goals."[38]

While senior officials may implicitly stress the importance of a UNSC member, they do not announce obvious quid pro quos to their staffs. Thus even policy practitioners, who make up the attendance of the thousands of daily meetings, can justifiably express surprise at our results. Some of them can perhaps think of one example where an agenda highlighted the importance of a UNSC member, but, taken individually, each case appears to have followed an idiosyncratic path, one of interpersonal connections and subtle implication, winding itself through various bureaucracies. Our question is whether these diverse channels add up to an overall systematic pattern.

Many other factors certainly help to determine which governments receive foreign aid. According to numerous studies, a country's economic circumstances play the most prominent role, and the country's domestic political situation matters as well. So a policy-maker who spends a career working in a particular African country, for example, may not notice that it was marginally easier to get projects approved during the two years the government served on the UNSC. Most developing countries rarely

---

[37] The quotation comes from Secretary Clinton's remarks at the Foreign Policy Group's Transformational Trends 2013 Forum, held at the Newseum, Washington, DC, November 29, 2012. See http://www.state.gov/secretary/rm/2012/11/201235.htm (accessed January 16, 2013).

[38] Note that this state of affairs recalls the ethnographic work of Anthropologist David Mosse (2005), who argues that aid projects may not always be driven by concerns of best policy but also by other exigencies of the organization, such as maintaining good relations. Also see Marriage (2006) and Ferguson (1994). We are grateful to Tim Allen for suggesting these connections.

serve on the UNSC, and practitioners consistently focus on micro- and macroeconomic factors that more routinely impact their projects. Still, if the pattern of getting more aid – even if just on the margins – holds across the larger sample of countries, then we can report that trading aid for political support is systematic at the UNSC.

Note that the foreign aid provided to UNSC members may also go toward projects that have been underway for many years. The World Bank, for example, has numerous ongoing projects with most developing countries. The World Bank does not suddenly notice a country only when it wins election to the UNSC; to the contrary, some staffers at the World Bank have been paying attention to the country all along. During the time that the country serves on the UNSC, however, when World Bank desk officers in Africa call Washington, they may find more receptive ears. The change is subtle; more projects find their way through bureaucratic channels and get approved by the World Bank Executive Board because the country is now on the radar of many more people in positions of power.

In the meantime, the elected member of the UNSC may also be actively seeking favors through several avenues. As John Bolton notes, after winning election to the UNSC, governments like to "toot their horns."[39] Their position on the UNSC indicates that they have come into international prominence, and they recognize that they have a stronger negotiation posture on the international stage. As such, they seek out more World Bank and IMF loans with softer conditionality and pressure rich countries to provide them with more bilateral aid. Interestingly, Bolton also notes that the same government officials who are thrilled to have a prominent position when they are first elected, are exhausted and "sorry" two years later, after having been pressured so many times on how to vote. They may actually be glad to see their UNSC term come to an end.

Secretary Albright stresses that for many small countries, winning election to the UNSC represents a major achievement, but – all of a sudden – they need a larger delegation.[40] Pressure increases further when – through rotation on the UNSC – they accede to the presidency of the Security Council.[41] Thus, some governments elected to the UNSC may seek out

[margin annotation: It goes both ways!]

---

[39] Interview with John Bolton, March 31, 2011, American Enterprise Institute, Washington, DC.

[40] Interview with Madeleine Albright, August 29, 2012, Albright Stonebridge Group, Washington, DC.

[41] Ibid.

financial favors because they feel emboldened by their newfound status on the international stage, as Ambassador Bolton suggests, while others may seek assistance and guidance from the permanent members because their daunting new position on the international stage is stretching them too thin, as Secretary Albright observes.

Finally, consider again the importance of obfuscating the trades of aid for political influence over the UNSC. As Ambassador Bolton explains, even if a diplomat wanted to make bald-faced trades of aid for political support, doing so would not be effective because they would leak to the press, thereby undermining the appearance of the very political support. If the purpose of providing aid is to win UNSC approval for a foreign policy, and the approval of the UNSC is valuable for the legitimacy it confers, then it would prove counterproductive if the means used to obtain political support appeared somehow illegitimate itself. Eldar (2008) contends that actors almost always trade Security Council votes behind the scenes because governments prefer to escape potential public condemnation. Administrations do not candidly announce to the entire bureaucracy the importance of a country because of its role on the Security Council; instead, the countries simply appear on the agendas of more meetings.

From the viewpoint of recipient countries, more officials must be sent to the United States to deal with UN matters. Global and U.S. media feature them more often in interviews on issues of international security. When meeting with the IMF and World Bank, officials from recipient countries do not explicitly announce that they should receive perks in return for their service on the UNSC; they simply have stronger implied leverage when negotiating.

In the end, a pattern results with larger numbers of programs and more money going to elected UNSC members *on the margins*. If only one channel were used, the transfers would be bigger and the pattern easier to spot. Moreover, most aid bureaucrats would not be willing to make massive transfers on purely political grounds. Small favors, however, can find their way through various bureaucracies, keeping the dirty work of foreign policy from the public eye.

From a game-theoretic perspective, the complete obfuscation of vote-aid trades could, of course, lead to a credibility problem. If a deal were completely secret, it would make it easy to renege on the delivery of foreign aid after voting has taken place on the UNSC. Not surprisingly, more important votes require larger aid packages, and those are exactly the packages that have become the most public. We discuss the fine line between obfuscation and credibility in Chapter 2.

Note that credibility cuts both ways. If an elected UNSC member accepts various favors from a powerful country, there is, of course, a vague implication that it will be cut off if it misbehaves on the UNSC. But neither party really expects this to be an issue. Whether one wants to call these transactions favors, rewards, bribes, or corruption, most of the time, they are not truly consequential in terms of the actions that the UNSC takes. For there to be real consequences, not only does a major issue have to arise for the Security Council to deal with, but it also must be an issue over which the donor and the recipient would actually vote differently in the absence of favors. From the perspective of donor countries, while such a crucial vote may be unlikely, the foreign aid costs them relatively little, so the favors are worthwhile forms of insurance – just in case a major issue arises. From the perspective of recipient countries, the foreign aid is valuable and worth the small risk that they will be asked to vote against their sincere preferences. Note, however, that while this rationalist approach proves helpful in elucidating the logic of our argument – and we use a game-theoretic approach in Chapter 2 for precisely that purpose – it no more reflects the real conduct of foreign policy than does the scene from *The Godfather* described in the previous section. Again, we rely on our interviews. Ambassador Bolton explained that he would have preferred to make bold trades of finance for votes, but he agrees that it is simply not done. Secretary Albright explains that one does not simply say "I need your vote, and I'm going to give you an IMF loan." To the contrary, her approach involved looking for opportunities to work toward common goals, pleasantly suggesting over dinner, "It really would be great to work with you more."[42]

1.4 What Are the Consequences of Politically Motivated Aid?

We find the political economy of the UNSC a fascinating lens through which to understand international relations, and it also provides leverage over further questions central to the study of international political economy.

First, the political economy of the UNSC provides a controlled setting that shines light on the obscured trades of money for political influence on the global stage. Selection bias usually stands as a major obstacle to the study of the causes and consequences of foreign aid. Does Pakistan, for example, receive foreign aid because of its underdevelopment or because

[42] Ibid.

of its strategic geopolitical position? Both reasons probably play a role, but difficulties lie in disentangling the two: Pakistan's poverty levels and strategic importance have both remained relatively constant over time. Ideally, we could gain some analytical leverage by varying one of the factors in an experimental setting, but how can we possibly run experiments over such attributes of a country?

Examining the participation of countries on the UNSC is useful because it partially addresses these problems. While we cannot treat UNSC membership as a true experiment, the idiosyncratic selection process and the exogenously enforced term limits allow us to make controlled comparisons of (1) individual countries on and off the UNSC over time and (2) different countries on and off the UNSC during the same period of time. From a methodological point of view, this helps us to get around the problems of selection bias, which plague so many inquiries in international relations. The political economy of the UNSC thus provides a unique window on how political influence translates into foreign aid.

Second, the study of temporary UNSC members enables us to estimate the economic consequences of politically motivated foreign aid. Again, thanks to the idiosyncratic selection process, we can better distinguish between the circumstances surrounding the provision of foreign aid and its inherent effects. A great deal of research by academics and policymakers alike centers on the effectiveness of politically motivated foreign aid.[43] By focusing on comparisons between countries, on and off the UNSC, we can make a contribution to the understanding of the effects of politically motivated foreign aid.

Finally, the Security Council is the most powerful arm of the UN system. Its resolutions carry the legal authority to take measures to maintain or restore international peace, including the use of economic sanctions, embargoes, and military force. Some situations in which powerful countries have enticed the elected UNSC members to lend them pivotal political support have resulted in consequences of historic proportion.

1.5 Plan of the Book

The book proceeds as follows: Chapter 2 lays out more rigorously the logic of trading money for political influence on the international stage.

---

[43] Consider, for example, Kosack and Tobin (2006); Bobba and Powell (2007); Bearce and Tirone (2010); Headey (2008); Kono and Montinola (2009); Kilby and Dreher (2010); Minoiu and Reddy (2010); Bermeo (2010); and Dreher, Eichenauer, and Gehring (2013).

We then turn to empirically testing our claims. Chapter 3 presents a series of interesting examples of countries receiving perks (or not) while serving on the UNSC. We next turn to analyzing our dataset. We begin in Chapter 4 by examining in detail the question of who wins election to the UNSC. Perhaps the most crucial link in our story, Chapter 5 systematically tests whether membership on the UNSC has a statistically significant effect on foreign aid from various countries (the United States, Japan, Germany, France, and the United Kingdom) and on the loans from various international organizations (the IMF, the World Bank, the United Nations, and regional development banks). After establishing that developing countries receive various financial perks while serving on the UNSC, we explore the consequences of such politically motivated aid in Chapter 6. To conclude, Chapter 7 discusses potential reform of the UNSC.

Regarding our theory (Chapter 2), we lay out a simple but rigorous model that helps to explain why powerful countries are willing to trade aid for votes with smaller countries that serve on the UNSC. The theoretical model implies several testable implications that we explore throughout the rest of the project.

Chapter 3 explores a wide range of historical examples of governments that have made trades of political support for financial favors, and, interestingly, some examples of governments that have chosen not to enter into such deals. The range of examples spans the history of the United Nations, going as far back as the 1950s up to as recently as 2010. The chapter seeks to fulfill the modest goal of suggesting the plausibility of our main hypothesis.

Chapters 2 and 3 suggest something obvious: Powerful countries would rather have friends than enemies elected to the UNSC. Chapter 4 thus addresses the question of endogeneity: What if the countries elected to the UNSC are strategically important to – or are allies of – the United States? Such countries might receive more foreign aid benefits generally, for reasons outside of their UNSC status. This "selection" question looms large, both over the arguments laid out above and over the statistical findings to come. We therefore begin by addressing who gets elected to the UNSC, presenting an historical and statistical analysis of the determinants of election to the UNSC. Chapter 4 first presents the official UN rules for electing temporary members of the Security Council and the descriptive data – the countries that have actually won election. We also delve into the politics of election to the UNSC, tracing some interesting elections. The chapter then presents an innovative statistical model to analyze the

determinants of winning election. The results of Chapter 4 have implications for Chapter 5: They lay the empirical foundation upon which we
base the subsequent analyses. When looking at the effects of UNSC membership, endogeneity looms as a potential problem. That is, as discussed
above, we need to distinguish the effects of UNSC membership from the
circumstances surrounding membership.

Chapter 4 concludes that the selection of countries to serve on the Security Council mainly derives from a compromise between (1) the demands
of powerful countries to win election more frequently and (2) a norm
of giving each country its turn. Importantly, we find no evidence that
countries favored by the United States in terms of foreign aid are more
likely to win UNSC election, although we find some evidence that countries under sanctions are less likely to win under certain circumstances
and tentative evidence that countries receiving U.S. military assistance
may have an advantage in the rare elections contested in the UN General
Assembly. There is also some evidence that populous and rich countries
have greater chances of selection for certain regions during certain time
periods. We thus account for these factors when analyzing the effects
of UNSC membership on receiving foreign aid. Otherwise, we find the
strongest evidence in favor of an exogenous norm of taking turns to fill
UNSC seats, and many idiosyncratic features that determine elections.
So, for the purposes of our study, while selection onto the UNSC does
not represent an experiment, the process comes closer to a random draw
than any existing measure of political importance. By applying country
fixed-effects and controlling for the few factors that do seem to play
a limited role, we can address questions of endogeneity. Furthermore,
the substantial extent to which turn-taking plays a role – particularly in
Africa – makes the election of UNSC members more of an idiosyncratic
process.

Each UNSC election does, of course, have its own story. The stories do
not appear, however, to have systematic commonalities – each case seems
idiosyncratic. Moreover, the patterns that we do observe vary by region.
Latin America and Asia are competitive, with the largest countries – Brazil
and Japan, respectively – winning the most often. Turning to Africa, while
Nigeria has twice jumped the queue, the region has otherwise exhibited
the strongest norm of taking turns or "rotating," as many observers
call the selection process. We take advantage of Africa's commitment
to turn-taking in the chapters that follow. Because of the region's norm
of turn-taking, we can more confidently treat UNSC membership in the
African sample as a quasi-experiment.

Having suggested that selection onto the UNSC is not driven by the same factors that drive foreign aid, we turn to our key question in Chapter 5: Does UNSC membership have a systematic influence over the financial favors that developing countries receive? We begin by testing the effect of UNSC membership on bilateral aid from the most powerful countries in the world during the post–World War II period – the United States, Japan, Germany, France, and the United Kingdom. Interestingly, we find effects for the United States, Japan, and Germany, but not the United Kingdom or France.

We offer the following explanation for this pattern: The United States, the United Kingdom, and France constitute the most important group within the Security Council – commonly called the P3. Almost all major resolutions begin with these three countries. If they are not in agreement on an issue, a proposal will not go forward as they have veto power over one another. Notwithstanding famous disagreements (such as the 2003 invasion of Iraq), these allies tend to vote together. The three then face the collective action problem of convincing the rest of the UNSC to support a resolution. As is standard in many collective action dilemmas, the most powerful actor provides the collective good (Olson 1965). The United States thus systematically takes the lead in lobbying other members of the UNSC with financial perks.

Why then do the other allies of the United States that we consider, Japan and Germany, also provide aid? Japan and Germany constitute part of another group called the G4. The G4 is a group of four countries, also including Brazil and India, that seek permanent status on the UNSC. As losers of World War II, Japan and Germany originally faced exclusion from the entire United Nations system, and the UN Charter carries the infamous "former enemies" clause to this day (UN Charter, article 53). They certainly did not gain access to the UNSC in the early post-war era. With their meteoric rise to global economic prominence, however, the two countries have sought influence over the UNSC. They have campaigned in vain for years to obtain some kind of permanent membership. They have also waged successful campaigns to win temporary membership. They have won election to the UNSC more than any other country in their respective regions. We thus argue that currying favor with the nonpermanent members of the UNSC – by providing them increased bilateral foreign aid – represents a relatively low-cost way to gain political influence over the UNSC.[44] We also find that the regional organization

---

[44] The argument follows Lim and Vreeland (2013).

where Japan holds sway – the Asian Development Bank – also provides more foreign aid to countries when they serve on the UNSC.

Considering international organizations more broadly, Chapter 5 next turns to the IMF, the World Bank, the UN, and various regional organizations. Some scholars have suggested that international organizations can be used to obfuscate political transactions that might damage the reputation of a government. As argued by Vaubel (1986: 48–51, 1996, 2006), delegating "dirty work" to international organizations allows governments to escape public resentment. This desire holds for both donor and recipient countries.[45] As Abbott and Snidal (1998: 18–19) explain, in this way international organizations can serve to "launder" political transactions.

Beyond "political cover," international organizations also provide political leverage and distribute costs across the most relevant countries, as noted above. The IMF and the World Bank do not usually provide an entire loan upfront. In principle, continued disbursements are conditioned on economic policy changes. Their executive boards, however, have the final say on all disbursements, and they have discretion in deeming countries compliant (Stone 2002, 2004; Harrigan, Wang, and El-Said 2006). Many argue that the major shareholders exercise their power to pursue international political goals. While the boards certainly must contend with their internal rules – and all studies of the determinants of IMF and

---

[45] The executive branch of the U.S. government tends to have unfettered control of representation at the IMF, with only occasional direct congressional oversight, such as when seeking to increase the U.S. contribution to the IMF (for example, in 1983 and 1998). Interestingly, Broz and Hawes (2006) and Broz (2008, 2011) show that domestic politics matter here (for similar work on foreign aid in general, see Milner and Tingley 2011). Congressional representatives who receive larger contributions from large private banks and might benefit from increased IMF lending are more likely to approve increases. Representatives of high-skill, pro-globalization districts also favor increases. One interesting possibility is that the executive branch of the U.S. government may rely on the IMF to pressure developing countries more when facing a divided government, that is, when the legislative branch is controlled or partially controlled by a different political party. We explored this possibility by controlling for the years of U.S. divided government (1955–1961, 1969–1977, 1981–1993, and 1995–2003; see Mayhew 2005). We tested an indicator variable for divided government along with the indicator's interaction with UNSC membership. Our initial results are interesting – IMF lending is actually more common under divided government, and lending to UNSC members is also more common under divided government. Yet, when subjected to analysis with control variables under various specifications, we do not find these results to be robust. As an alternative extension, future research might consider partisan effects (see Bermeo, Leblang, and Tingley 2011).

World Bank lending show that economic variables do guide their lending practices – a growing body of literature indicates that international politics matter as well.[46]

As for cost benefits, when they provide foreign aid through the international organizations, the major donors share the burden (Eldar 2008). The IMF and World Bank may be less effective tools when the major shareholders disagree on a specific resolution, but when it comes to temporary UNSC members, their potential importance is readily apparent.[47]

Chapter 6 considers the economic consequences of providing finance to countries serving on the UNSC. We note that many studies have found disappointing effects of foreign aid on economic development, and we argue that the political motivations behind some foreign aid might be responsible for aid's lackluster performance.[48] Political motivations may lower the bar for project quality or monitoring. Thus, the chapter follows the controversial study of Bruce Bueno de Mesquita and Alastair Smith (2010), political scientists at New York University. They study the effect of temporary UNSC membership on economic growth. Their results suggest pernicious consequences – although other scholars have criticized the methodology employed (see Bashir and Lim 2013). We therefore also refer the reader to our results in Dreher, Eichenauer and Gehring (2013), where we specifically consider the effect of foreign aid given to elected UNSC members on economic growth (rather than focusing on membership itself).

Chapter 6 thus goes on to offer a further, more conservative test, focusing on a setting in which "effectiveness" is observed with some precision.[49] Using the ex post performance ratings of World Bank

---

[46] See Sturm, Berger and de Haan (2005), Steinwand and Stone (2008), and Moser and Sturm (2011) for reviews. For in-depth consideration of international political factors, see Thacker (1999), Stone (2002, 2004), Lipscy (2003), Oatley and Yackee (2004), Barro and Lee (2005), Dreher and Jensen (2007), Reynaud and Vauday (2009). For recent studies of the domestic politics of recipient countries, see Mukherjee and Singer (2010); Caraway, Rickard, and Anner (2012); and Cho (2013).

[47] For the importance of agreement across powerful member states, see Copelovitch (2010a, 2010b), Breßlein and Schmaljohann (2013), and Hernandez (2013). For more general work on the logic of delegation and foreign aid, see Nielson and Tierney (2003), Hawkins et al. (2006), Milner (2006), Bradley and Kelley (2008), and, more broadly, Lake (2007).

[48] For example, see Boone (1996), Easterly, Levine, and Roodman (2004), Rajan and Subramanian (2008), and Doucouliagos and Paldam (2009). See Hodler and Dreher (2013) for an explanation of why aid does not robustly correlate with higher economic growth. For a recent exception, showing that aid improves the well-being of women, see the micro-level study of Joshi and Schultz (2013).

[49] This is the approach we take along with our collaborators in Dreher, Klasen, Vreeland, and Werker (2013).

projects, we find that projects granted to governments holding a non-permanent seat on the UNSC are no more likely, on average, to receive a negative quality rating than other projects. When aid is given to Security Council members with elevated short-term debt, however, a negative quality rating is more likely. This set of findings suggests that political influence in aid allocation may impair aid's effectiveness only when the recipient country is in a weak macroeconomic position, as suggested by political scientist Randall Stone (2008) of Rochester University. The research of economist Christopher Kilby (2011a, 2013b) of Villanova University offers a potential mechanism: When facing an economic crisis, politically important countries may use their leverage to rush the preparation stage in order to receive their loans faster – so high-debt UNSC members may have comparatively shorter preparation periods, and, in general, shorter preparation periods result in poor-performing projects.

This finding highlights the importance of the domestic political economy, and thus Chapter 6 concludes by considering the consequences of UNSC membership while accounting for domestic political regime. Revisiting the results of Bueno de Mesquita and Smith (2010), we find that the pernicious effects of UNSC membership on economic development hold only for certain dictatorships in Africa. We do not detect a harmful effect for democratic members of the UNSC. These findings echo what we learned from our conversation with Secretary Albright: While sometimes the United States must work with a strategically important but corrupt dictatorship, usually what the United States is trying to do with a Security Council member fits into the overall strategy for the country.[50]

We conclude the book with some surprises in Chapter 7. Armed with the findings discussed above, we enter into the debate on the various reform proposals for the UNSC. One might expect us to condemn the international system and call for major reforms. Instead, we take a realist approach, suggesting that reforms may be neither useful nor desirable.

If the political manipulation of international institutions were prevented, the great powers would be stripped of an important tool in their limited box to conduct foreign policy. This change would render international institutions less useful to them, and they might cease to participate as members. The lack of support from the world's most powerful countries as members would leave the world with substantially weaker institutionalized, multilateral channels to address a wide range of international issues. Exchanges of money for political support would likely

[50] Interview with Madeleine Albright, August 29, 2012, Albright Stonebridge Group, Washington, DC.

persist in a much more ad-hoc manner and even further weaken institutionalized forms of cooperation. Therefore, the trade-off may not be between manipulable institutions and perfect ones, but rather between corrupted institutions and *no* institutions. For all of their shortcomings, multilateral institutions may be preferable to unilateralism and isolationism. Throughout our analysis, we show that – beyond the international politics – legitimate economic and political concerns drive much of international cooperation and the delivery of foreign aid; it need not have deleterious effects in all cases. So the political manipulation of international organizations may represent a relatively small price to pay for institutionalized global cooperation. After all, if foreign policy is simply the art of getting a government to do something, trades of influence for favors must remain one of the tools.

Still, there are some simple reforms that might make sense and prove politically palatable. Without seeking to completely eliminate side deals, we advocate subtle changes to the election of UNSC members. These reforms would alter the incentives that lead governments to take side deals rather than pursue the interests of the regions that UNSC members are supposed to represent. In contrast with the prominent reform proposals that focus on representational issues – that is, who has a seat at the table – we suggest focusing on accountability. Briefly, our provocative suggestions include (1) abolishing term limits and (2) granting regions, rather than the UN General Assembly, the authority to directly elect their representatives.

Before we can reach any conclusions about how to address the trading of financial favors for political influence, we should first establish the extent of the practice. We begin in Chapter 2 by laying out our theory of money and politics on the international stage.

2

A Theory of Trading Security Council Votes for Aid

2.1 Introducing a Logic of Trading Favors on the International Stage

What is the logic of trading money for political influence on the UN Security Council? This seemingly innocuous question contains a number of analytical puzzles addressed in this chapter. Note that numerous studies have established that governments use foreign aid for certain political purposes. It is not obvious, however, that targeting members of the UNSC represents a good choice. Some governments have strong views on foreign policy and adamantly oppose the United States and its allies. These governments – Cuba under Fidel Castro comes to mind – may prove unwilling to sell their votes. Other governments tend to agree with Western powers and may freely offer their political support with no strings attached. Under what conditions, then, are UNSC votes for sale, and when are they worth buying?

Swing voters may constitute a likely target. Note that when we say "swing," we mean voters who may be willing to change their vote under certain circumstances.[1] Imagine, for example, a country with a weak preference – in the absence of any enticements – of voting against a resolution supported by the United States. If the United States has previously established a strong working relationship with such a country – delivering foreign aid packages, advocating on its behalf at the IMF and the World Bank, and generally supporting that country in subtle ways – the track record of goodwill might influence the country's voting behavior on the Security Council.

---

[1] This concept of "swing voter" is distinct from a pivotal vote, where a change in the vote actually changes the overall outcome on a potential resolution.

Will issues arise during an elected UNSC member's tenure where such swing voting might occur? The relevant actors may not know a priori. Some years, the Security Council holds few important votes. Moreover, even if important issues do come up, the alignment of votes may remain unknown for months in advance. An ostensibly friendly government – consider Yemen before the Gulf War – could find itself at odds with the West if its domestic or regional politics do not line up with Western foreign policy objectives. Because aid packages require some lead time to develop, a donor country might need to put together favorable packages for UNSC members early in their term – just in case an important issue arises down the road. The "gifts" imply, of course, the open possibility of a return favor.[2]

Thus, without knowing what kinds of issues might arise and the local political constraints the various UNSC members will face, donors must decide whether to offer favors, to whom, and of what size. Some countries are too rich or too big to be influenced by foreign aid. As for the smaller, poorer members of the UNSC, if aid costs the donors little and matters a good deal to these UNSC members, the donors may want to target all of them. On the other hand, donor governments may guess which countries will oppose them regardless of receiving aid, which countries will support them regardless of receiving aid, and which countries might cast "swing-able" votes. The powerful donor countries may target only these members of the UNSC.

The elected UNSC members also face a dilemma. They must decide whether to seek out aid and submit to the implicit terms of the arrangement without knowing what issues might arise during their tenure. If they accept gifts, they may find themselves caught between a rock and a hard place – having to choose between international pressure and domestic or regional preferences. This possibility further complicates trading finance for political support.

What is the value of a UNSC vote? We argue in Chapter 1 that UNSC votes provide both symbolic and informational content. Hurd (2007), following on the work of Barnett (1995), Finnemore (1996), Keck and Sikkink (1998), Wendt (1999), and especially Voeten (2005), argues that UNSC resolutions provide a legal framework important for symbolically legitimizing forceful foreign politics. Chapman (2011) argues that UNSC

---

[2] See, for example, Dorussen (2001). Also see Drezner (1999), Bernauer and Ruloff (1999), Cortright (1997), Long (1996), and Wagner (1988). For a more skeptical view, see Moon (1985).

votes are valuable for the information they provide because they represent an independent third party, which can send a credible signal about the appropriateness of a specific foreign policy. Either way, the bald-faced buying of votes may undermine the value of the vote. Vote-buying may appear illegitimate, and it certainly draws into question the credibility of UNSC members as independent third parties. One way to deal with this problem is to obfuscate the trade by going through opaque channels.

Even when a case can be made to trade finance for political support, however, the actors involved may face a time-consistency problem. A powerful donor country may work on putting together a series of favors for a poor country on the UNSC only to have that UNSC member then renege on the implicit deal, voting against an important resolution. Again, the case of Yemen comes to mind. Alternatively, if the UNSC member does deliver the vote, why should the donor actually follow through with the delivery of aid package? Since either party might defect on the deal at distinct points on the timeline, both parties might prefer to avoid the deal in the first place.

On the other hand, they may be able to structure the deal in such a way that addresses these concerns of credibility. In particular, the deal may gain credibility if the donor – who plays the trade game repeatedly over a long time horizon with multiple members of the UNSC – moves last. If this donor government has a valuable reputation as a reliable negotiator, it has an incentive to keep its promises. Here we draw on the logic of Tomz's (2007) work on sovereign debt, which argues that reputation guides inter-temporal trades of international finance. Just as a sovereign borrower would suffer a reputational cost by defaulting for no good reason (a "fair weather" default), so would a powerful country if it "defaulted" on its implicit promise to do favors for friendly UNSC voting behavior.[3] The logic of inter-temporal trades of favors very much resembles Tomz's reputational argument about debt repayment.

The reputation of the donor actually has two opposing effects in our context. If people can observe that the donor government sticks to the deals it makes, it gains credibility for future trades of money for political influence. But recall that these deals undermine legitimacy – the very political commodity that the donor is trying to buy. The donor thus has cross-cutting incentives: a more visible reputation increases the credibility

---

[3] We are grateful to an anonymous reviewer for this suggestion. For experimental work on reputation-building over time, see Tingley and Walter (2011).

of an exceptionally large aid package and simultaneously lowers the very legitimacy being purchased.

These cross-cutting incentives may provide a further explanation of the various channels of aid that the donor-governments and UNSC members choose. During years when they anticipate many important votes, large aid packages may be offered through all channels, including the more visible bilateral channels, to increase their credibility. As a more routine channel, during years where donors do not expect important votes, governments may rely only on multilateral agencies, where aid packages are small enough to remain credible despite a shroud of obscurity that allows for more legitimacy.

In the pages that follow in this chapter, therefore, we have a number of analytical problems to address. They include:

- Does it ever make sense for governments to trade money for political influence on the UNSC?
- Are some UNSC members – perhaps swing voters – better candidates than others for such trades?
- Are trades possible under the uncertainty of whether an important issue will ever arise?
- Are trades credible, given the sequence of moves and the time-consistency problem?
- Do these trades undermine UNSC legitimacy, the specific political commodity being sought?
- Why make the trades through multiple aid agencies?

In the next section, we present a simple game-theoretic model that helps us gain analytical traction over these questions. Following the formal presentation of the game, we address these questions, analyzing archetypical cases in the concluding section.

2.2 The Vote-Aid Trade Game

We present the extended form of the game in Figure 2.1. The appendix to this chapter presents a brief solution to the game with less prose and more mathematics for readers with more advanced experience with game theory. Here in the main text, we discursively present the game and a solution with a broader audience in mind. Nevertheless, we do rely on some technical mathematics.

Because we wish to simplify the political transactions that take place through the thousands of meetings of bureaucrats, our game includes just

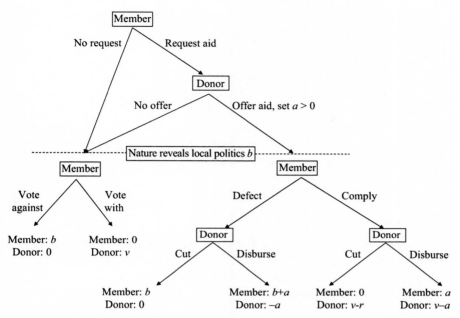

FIGURE 2.1. The vote-aid trade game.

two players: "the Member" (the UNSC member, to whom we refer as "he") and "the Donor" (the potential aid-donor country, to whom we refer as "she"). We assume that the game is played over just one vote on the UNSC, although one could think of this as a portfolio of voting behavior. The Donor supports the resolution and may seek the support of the Member.[4]

The following payoffs are at stake:

- The benefit of local (domestic/regional) politics for the Member: $b \sim F(\bar{b}, \sigma^2)$, where $F(\cdot)$ is an unspecified distribution with mean $\bar{b}$ and variance σ^2. (We specify different distributions in examples below.)
- The value of the vote for the Donor: $v, v > 0$

---

[4] We take this perspective because the main actor we have in mind is the United States. So, in the cases where the Donor might lobby against a resolution she could just exercise her veto power. She would therefore not usually require no-votes from temporary members. That said, the United States might lobby for no-votes on procedural votes, where veto power does not apply, and no-votes might lend legitimacy to a U.S. veto. Donors without veto power, like Japan and Germany, might also play this game. In these cases, one would need to reverse the language (lobbying for opposition, not support), but not the logic of our game.

- The reputational cost to the Donor for reneging on a deal: r, $r > 0$
- The size of the aid package: a, $a > 0$

To be clear from the outset, we treat b as a realization of a random variable (set by Nature); v and r are exogenous variables; and a is the key choice variable, set by the Donor. We explain these variables in more detail in the following sections.

Note that throughout the game, we assume that if the Member is indifferent between voting with or against the Donor, he chooses to vote with her. In Section 2.3, we walk through the details of the game presented in Figure 2.1, explaining each step.

2.3 The Extended Form Game and Payoffs

The game begins when the Member is elected and may choose "Request aid" or "No request." If the Member makes the request, the Donor must then choose between "No offer" and "Offer aid," setting $a = \breve{a} > 0$. For the solution we will eventually present, it is useful to define:

$$\breve{a} = \begin{cases} a^* \text{ if } a^* \le r \\ r \text{ otherwise} \end{cases}$$

and define, implicitly, a^* as the a that solves:

$$a^* = v - \frac{F(a^*)}{F'(a^*)}$$

where, again, F is the cumulative probability distribution of b. Note that if $a^* < 0$, then the "Offer aid" equilibrium does not exist; the Donor cannot offer negative aid. We offer these technical definitions for advanced readers (who may wish to skip ahead to the appendix where we prove the existence of an equilibrium in which the Donor offers a^* and the Member complies with probability $F(a^*)$ – under certain conditions). We will explain how we rely on these definitions as we proceed. For now, the reader should simply keep in mind that if the Donor decides to make an offer of foreign aid (an "Offer aid" equilibrium exists), she sets the offer to $\breve{a}$; otherwise she makes no offer.

As the next step in the game, Nature reveals the value of b, which is drawn from some distribution $F(\cdot)$ with mean $\overline{b}$ and variance σ^2. Neither the Member nor the Donor knows the value of b at the beginning of the game, but the distribution from which b is drawn is common knowledge. For now, assume any generic distribution over any range of numbers covering values where b can be positive or negative. (Below, we alter this assumed distribution, providing different examples in which we assign specific distributions to different types of countries.)

We define b as the "benefit" from local politics (mainly domestic but also regional) to the Member for defying the Donor, and thus voting *against* her. If $b \leq 0$, then the Member and the Donor agree on the issue – or the issue is just not salient to one or both of them. Think of $b > 0$, however, as any situation where a vote arises on the Security Council that matters, jointly, to the Member and to the Donor, and their preferences diverge. Such cases do not always arise for all UNSC members. There are many votes on the UNSC that have no influence over domestic politics for the temporary members of the UNSC and many that the great power donors do not care about. Furthermore, just because both parties care about a vote does not mean that their preferences diverge.

In our model, then, b takes on a non-positive value when (1) the Member does not care about the vote, (2) the Donor does not care, (3) neither cares, or (4) their preferences converge. The value of b is positive if none of those conditions hold, or, in other words, they both care about the vote, and they disagree about it. The probability of such a disagreement depends on the underlying distribution of b, which we will model, below, as a function of the specific UNSC member in question.

2.3.1 No Request or No Offer

Moving down the game tree in Figure 2.1, if there is no request – or no offer – of aid, the Member must decide whether to "Vote with" or "Vote against" the Donor, after having observed b. If he votes with the Donor, he receives a payoff of 0, and the Donor receives v, her valuation of the affirmative vote. If he votes against the Donor, he receives the payoff of b and the Donor receives 0.

2.3.2 The Vote-Aid Trade Subgame

If an aid package is requested and offered, the Member and the Donor enter into the right-hand subgame in Figure 2.1, after having observed b. If the game reaches this juncture, there is now an implicit arrangement in place where foreign aid should be supplied if the Member votes with the Donor. But the Member must still decide whether to "Comply" with the deal – voting with the Donor – or "Defect" – voting against the Donor. Finally, the Donor must decide whether to "Disburse" the aid package or "Cut" it.

2.3.3 The Vote-Aid Trade Payoffs

The right-hand subgame in Figure 2.1 has four potential outcomes: (1) If the Member chooses "Defect," and the Donor chooses "Cut," he receives b, and she receives 0. (2) If the Member chooses "Defect," and the Donor chooses "Disburse," he receives $b + a$, and she receives $-a$. (3) If the Member chooses "Comply" and the Donor chooses "Disburse," he receives a, and the Donor receives $v - a$.[5] (4) If the Member chooses "Comply," and the Donor chooses "Cut," he receives 0, and the Donor receives $v - r$.

Note that if the Member and the Donor make a deal, and the Member complies, but the Donor reneges by cutting the aid, she faces penalty $-r$, $r > 0$. We think of r as the value of having a good reputation as a credible negotiation partner. One can thus think of r as the future stream of the value of being able to play this game repeatedly with many countries in many different situations. Note that some aid packages are too big to be credible. If $a > r$, the Donor will renege because the size of the aid package is so big that it is actually more valuable to the Donor than is her reputation. This feature of the game places a constraint on what the Donor is willing to offer to the Member. As long as her reputation is more valuable to the Donor than is the cost of providing aid (that is, $r > a$), then the Donor's offer of aid is credible. We can assume that r is valuable to some extent (that is, $r > 0$) because the Donor plays similar games over and again with many different countries (those elected to the Security Council and other countries that are important in various political arenas).[6]

2.4 A Solution to the Game

We now offer a solution to the game in Figure 2.1 using the method of backward induction. We begin by analyzing the final decisions made at

---

[5] We could complicate the game, making the utility of a a function of each country's level of economic development. Doing so would reinforce the qualitative conclusions we draw from the game. We address this issue below.

[6] Interestingly, with the way we have structured the payoffs, it is important that the Donor moves last in order for vote-aid trades to be possible. Most developing countries rarely win election to the UNSC, so they do not play this game often – for them, the game represents a one-shot opportunity. If the governments of such countries could cast their UNSC vote after having already secured the aid package, they might have an incentive to renege on this essentially one-shot deal. Allowing the Donor to move last allows for credibility because, while the game may be one-shot for a particular UNSC member, the Donor plays the game again and again with other countries. We are grateful to Kevin Morrison for raising this point. For an innovative approach to international cooperation in a repeated-game setting, see Schneider and Slantchev (2013).

the end of the subgame on the right-hand side of the figure, and then we move backward up the game tree.

2.4.1 To Cut or to Disburse

Down at the bottom of the game, the Donor will surely choose to "Cut" the aid package if the Member chooses "Defect" because $0 > -a$. So, it is easy to see that the payoffs for choosing "Defect" become b for the Member and 0 for the Donor in this situation.

Will the Donor choose "Disburse" or "Cut" on the other side of the subgame, where the Member has chosen "Comply?" The answer to this question depends on the values of r and a. The Donor will disburse the aid package if the reputational costs are high enough: $r \geq a$. If so, the payoffs for complying are a for the Member and $v - a$ for the Donor. If the Member chooses "Comply" and the reputational costs are not high enough – or to put it the other way – the Donor has offered an aid package that is too big to be credible ($a > r$), then the Donor will choose "Cut," thereby reneging on the deal and incurring reputational costs. The payoffs are thus 0 for the Member and $(v - r)$ for the Donor.

It is straightforward to show, however, that the Donor never has an incentive to offer $a > r$ because she can anticipate the incentives this choice will create for both players further down the game tree. The Member must choose between "Comply" and "Defect" after having observed a and b. If the Donor has foolishly set $a > r$ the Member will choose "Comply" only if $b \leq 0$. So, by offering $a \geq r$, the Donor guarantees herself payoffs of 0 if $b > 0$ and $v - r$ if $b \leq 0$. Yet the Donor can do better than this pair of outcomes simply by choosing "No offer," which will guarantee payoffs of 0 if $b > 0$, and v if $b \leq 0$. So, even before observing b, the Donor can anticipate that for any value of b that is revealed, she will be at least as well off – and sometimes better off – by making an offer of $a = \breve{a} \leq r$ (a weakly dominant strategy). In other words, the Donor only makes credible offers of aid.

We have therefore learned that the Donor will always choose "Cut" if the Member chooses "Defect" and will always choose "Disburse" if the Member chooses "Comply." The Member can reliably predict the consequences of his vote. If we now eliminate the weakly dominated moves in Figure 2.1, we can recast the game into the simpler form depicted in Figure 2.2. We can then solve this reduced-form game.

2.4.2 To Comply or to Defect

If the Donor offers an aid package, will the Member comply or defect? The answer to this question depends on domestic politics (the realized

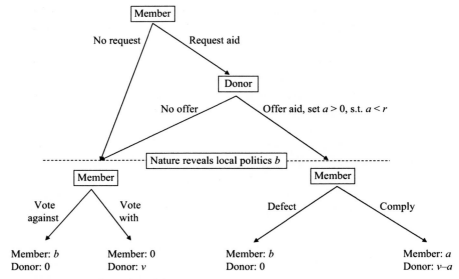

FIGURE 2.2. The reduced-form game.

value of b) and the size of the aid package (the value the Donor has set for $\breve{a}$, which must be positive and is sure to be credible, $0 < \breve{a} \leq r$, as shown above).

Solving this part of the game now becomes straightforward: The payoff for the Member if he defects is b; his payoff for compliance is $\breve{a}$. So, if $b \leq \breve{a}$, the Member chooses "Comply," otherwise, the value of domestic politics is too high, and he chooses "Defect."[7]

2.4.3 To Offer or Not

The crucial question in this game is whether the Donor will offer an aid package and of what size, subject to the constraint $\breve{a} \leq r$. The answer depends on the probability distribution of b. At the beginning of the game, no one knows what issues will arise. Some issues may hold salience for the local political situation of the Member (high b); others may prove completely inconsequential (low b). Without a crystal ball, no one can know for sure what value b will take during the Member's term. The relevant actors may, however, have a sense of the likelihood that b will

---

[7] Also note that we could model the game allowing the Donor to further punish the Member for voting against her – for example, by pushing for harsh terms for an IMF loan. We choose this simpler game, where compliance is less likely, thereby making a harder case for our story.

be high or low. The common-knowledge probability distribution of b captures this sense.[8] Recall that if $b \leq a$, the Member will comply, giving the Donor a payoff of $(v - a)$. If $b > a$, then the Member will defect, giving the Donor a payoff of 0. The probability of the former is denoted by $F(a)$, while the probability of the latter is denoted by the complimentary probability, $[1 - F(a)]$. So, we can calculate the expected value of choosing "Offer aid" as:

$$E^D(a) = F(a)(v - a) + [1 - F(a)]0$$
$$= F(a)(v - a)$$

Let us maximize the above function with respect to the offer, a, so that we can calculate the highest possible offer that the Donor will be willing to make (absent the reputational costs):

$$\frac{\partial E^D(a)}{\partial a} = F'(a)v - F'(a)a - F(a) = 0$$

which in turn yields:

$$v = a^* + \frac{F(a^*)}{F'(a^*)}$$

which represents the offer constraint for the Donor (for proof of the existence of a^* under certain conditions, see the appendix to this chapter). This offer constraint captures the notion that the Donor will offer aid only if there is a reasonable chance that the offer will entice the Member to vote with her. The above equation indicates that the value of the vote must be at least worth the value of the aid (a^*) plus the ratio of the cumulative probability to the marginal probability $[F(a^*)/F'(a^*)]$ that the Member will vote with the Donor if aid is offered. Otherwise, the Donor makes no offer. Now, recall that if $a^* > r$, the Donor is constrained to offer a maximum of r, consistent with the credibility constraint discussed in Subsection 2.4.1. Thus we have arrived at the definition of the offer of foreign aid ($\check{a}$) introduced at the beginning of Section 2.3:

$$\check{a} = \begin{cases} a^* \text{ if } a^* \leq r \\ r \text{ otherwise} \end{cases}$$

---

[8] For example, Middle Eastern countries may have a greater chance of high salience (high b) than do East Asian countries during certain periods of history, as many UNSC resolutions pertain to the Middle East. As an alternative example, a government that faces similar domestic political pressures as the Donor and is a close ally has an expected value of b that is low. See Section 2.6.

Also recall that the "Offer aid" equilibrium exists only if $\check{a} > 0$. Indeed, having calculated $\check{a}$, the Donor must ask herself, "Is it worth it?" What is the value, in terms of foreign aid and other favors, of enticing the political support of the Member, given what will transpire in the absence of such enticement? Recall that if the value of b is negative, the Member will vote with the Donor even in the absence of any aid package. The Donor must, therefore, compare the expected value of offering aid to the expected value of choosing "No offer." We calculate the expected value of "No offer" as:

$$E^D(\emptyset) = F(0)\,v + [1 - F(0)]\,0$$
$$= F(0)\,v$$

where $F(0)$ is the probability that $b \leq 0$, and $1 - F(0)$ is the probability that $b > 0$.

The Donor will choose "Offer aid" if and only if $E^D(\check{a}) \geq E^D(\emptyset)$:

$$F(\check{a})(v - \check{a}) \geq F(0)(v)$$
$$[F(\check{a}) - F(0)]v \geq F(\check{a})\check{a}$$

Note that the probability in the equation above, $[F(\check{a}) - F(0)]$, has substantive implications: $[F(\check{a}) - F(0)]$ is the probability that the realized value of b lies between 0 and $\check{a}$ ($0 < b < \check{a}$), which is the crucial range where offering aid really makes a difference. If $b \leq 0$, the Member will vote with the Donor whether aid is offered or not, and if $b > \check{a}$, the Member will vote against the Donor whether aid is offered or not. However, if the value of domestic politics is somewhere in between (that is, $b \in (0, \check{a}]$), then offering a credible aid package will cause the Member to vote with the Donor, and failing to offer will lead the Member to vote against the Donor. If the probability $[F(\check{a}) - F(0)]$ is sufficiently small, either because the domestic politics of the Member are expected to be very friendly or they are expected to be very unfriendly, the Donor will not bother offering an aid package. Aid is offered to the countries in between: the swing voters.

2.4.4 To Request or Not

Moving a step back on the game tree, the Member must decide whether to request aid before the Donor offers $\check{a}$ and before observing b. It is an easy decision: He should always request. He can anticipate only three possible situations emerging, and, for each of them, he is either indifferent or better off requesting aid:

(1) $b > ă > 0$: Regardless of requesting the aid package, the Member will vote against the Donor, thereby receiving b. He is thus indifferent as to "No request" and "Request."

(2) $b \leq 0$: The member will definitely vote with the Donor. If he does so without requesting aid, he gets 0 for certain. But if he requests aid, he gets 0 if the Donor chooses "No offer" and $a > 0$ if the Donor chooses "Offer aid." So, he might be better off, and cannot be worse off, by requesting aid in this situation.

(3) $ă \geq b > 0$: Without requesting aid, the Member is certain to get b. If he requests aid and the Donor chooses "No offer," he is also sure to get b. If he requests and the Donor chooses "Offer aid," then he will get to make another decision: He will get b or $ă$, choosing the greater of the two. He cannot do worse than b and might do better by choosing "Request aid."

Choosing "Request aid" is, therefore, a weakly dominant strategy for the Member.

2.5 Summarizing Equilibrium Strategies

We can therefore summarize the set of choices each actor should make, that is, their equilibrium strategies:

If $ă$ exists such that $[F(ă) - F(0)]v \geq F(ă)ă$ and $0 < ă \leq r$:

Member: chooses "Request aid"; following "Offer aid," chooses "Comply" if $ă \geq b$, otherwise chooses "Defect."

Donor: chooses "Offer aid," setting:

$$ ǎ = \begin{cases} a^* \; if \; a^* \leq r \\ r \; otherwise \end{cases} $$

where a^* is implicitly defined as: $a^* = v - F(a^*)/F'(a^*)$

Then, if "Defect," chooses "Cut"; if "Comply," chooses "Disburse."

If such $ă$ does not exist:

Member: chooses "Request aid"; following "No offer," chooses "Vote against" if $b > 0$, otherwise chooses "Vote with."

Donor: chooses "No offer."

See this chapter's appendix for further details.

2.6 Archetypes: Too Close, Too Far, and Just Right

Having offered a solution to the game, we now illustrate how it plays out for specific types of cases, each with a different probability distribution of b. We begin by presenting a case where a Member is "too close" to the Donor. It is not worth offering aid in this situation because the Member will vote with the Donor even in the absence of a side payment of size a. Then we turn to a different case, where the Member is "too far." Offering aid does not matter in this situation because the Member will never vote with the Donor even with a side payment. Finally, we present a case that is "just right": the Member might vote with or against the Donor, depending on the aid package – a potential "swing" vote.

To keep the examples easy, we assign values to v and r. For all of these examples, let $v = 1$ and $r = 1$, unless otherwise noted.

2.6.1 Too Close

Consider a case where the Member is sure to vote with the Donor even in the absence of a vote-aid trade. In other words, the preferences of the Member and the Donor closely align. In terms of our game, this scenario implies that the value of voting against the Donor in terms of domestic politics is actually negative. To make the case concrete, assume that the support of b is $(-1, 0)$ and that it is uniformly distributed over the interval. So it is common knowledge that b must take on a negative value.

In this situation, the Donor's optimal offer of aid, if it were made, would not be positive:

$$\left[F(\breve{a}) - F(0) \right] \geq F(\breve{a})\breve{a}$$
$$\Rightarrow [1 - 1] \geq (1)\breve{a}$$

$\Rightarrow \breve{a} \leq 0$, which contradicts the condition that the offer of aid must be positive for the "Offer aid" equilibrium.

So, in this case, the Member may request aid, but the Donor will never offer in equilibrium. Instead, the Donor will choose "No Offer." The expected value of not offering aid is certain because the probability of $\Pr(b < 0) = 1 => E^D(\emptyset) = v$. The payoff to the Member is sure to be 0.

The Donor makes no offer because she knows the Member will vote with her no matter what. The case is really quite simple. If b is negative, the Member will vote with the Donor and take the payoff of 0. Both the Member and the Donor know that the Member will always support the Donor, and no offer of aid is necessary.

2.6.2 Or Too Far

Consider a case where the Member is sure to vote against the Donor even in the presence of a vote-aid trade. In other words, the value of domestic politics is so high it is sure to be greater than the value of the Donor's reputation. Suppose, for example, that the support of b is $(1, 2)$ and that it is uniformly distributed over the interval.

So, we know that $b > 1$. The Member will vote with the Donor only if she can offer him $\breve{a} > 1$. Recall, however, that in this example we have set the reputational costs: $r = 1$. So the maximum (credible) offer that the Donor can make is $\breve{a} = 1$. This offer is insufficient to sway the Member (because he prefers $b > 1$). There is nothing the Donor can do. The Donor's expected value of not offering aid is $E^D(\emptyset) = 0$, and by offering $\breve{a} = 1$, the Donor's expected value is also: $E^D(a) = 0$.

The intuition here is that the benefit for the Member of following domestic or regional politics is too strong, and he cannot be swayed by any (credible) amount of aid from the Donor.

2.6.3 Just Right

Now consider a case where the Member is sure to vote against the Donor in the absence of a vote-aid trade, but could be swayed to vote differently by an enticement. Suppose, for example, that the support of b is $(0, 1)$ and that it is uniformly distributed over the interval. If the Donor makes no offer in this situation, the Member will surely vote against the Donor, receiving payoff $b > 0$, and the Donor will receive a payoff off 0. But the Donor can do better by offering aid. Her expected value of offering aid in this simple setup is $E^D(a) = F(a)(v - a) + [1 - F(a)]0 => a - a^2$. We find the optimal offer, a^*, by taking the derivative, $\frac{\partial E^D(a)}{\partial a} = 1 - 2a$, and setting it equal to zero, which yields $a^* = 0.5 < r.$[9]

In this case, the Member requests aid, and the Donor offers $a^* = 0.5$. The expected value of not offering aid is $E^D(\emptyset) = 0$, and by offering

---

[9] The second order condition for a maximum is also satisfied, as $\frac{\partial^2 E^D(a)}{\partial a^2} = -2$.

$a^* = 0.5$, the Donor's expected value improves: $E^D (a^*) = 0.5 (1 - 0.5) = 0.25$.

So, the Member requests aid, the Donor offers, and the Member complies with probability 0.5. The vote-aid trade swings the vote about half the time.

The examples covered in Subsections 2.6.1 through 2.6.3 thus show that there can be cases where the Donor does not offer aid (when the Member is either too close or too far from her preferences), and an equilibrium where the Donor offers aid. In the equilibrium where the Donor offers aid, the Member may or may not comply with the arrangement, depending on the offer, $\check{a}$, and the realized value of b. We provide further details on the Just Right, Too Far, and Too Close cases in the appendix to this chapter. To foreshadow our empirical work to come in Chapters 3 and 5, we find few cases of "Too far" and "Too Close"; in many empirical cases, there is room for donors to attempt to entice members.

2.7 Changing the Value of the Vote and the Reputation Cost

Suppose there are some years when votes are relatively unimportant to the Donor, and other years when she really cares about UNSC votes. In the model, this possibility can be captured by the value of the vote, v, which we have so far set to 1.

To present an example where the Donor has a relatively unimportant agenda, we can drop the value of v to 0.1 and apply this new value of v to the "just right" case above, where b is uniformly distributed over the $(0, 1)$ interval. To make later examples more interesting, we also drop the value of the Donor's reputation to $r = 0.5$.

The Donor can still improve her expected utility by offering an aid package. Her expected value of offering aid in this setup is $E^D(a) = a (0.1 - a)$. Again, we find the optimal offer, a^*, by taking the derivative, $\frac{\partial E^D(a)}{\partial a} = 0.1 - 2a$, and setting it equal to zero, which yields an offer of $a^* = 0.05 < r$.

The Member still requests aid, but here the Donor only offers $a^* = 0.05$. The expected value of not offering aid is still $E^D (\varnothing) = 0$, and by offering $a^* = 0.05$, the Donor's expected value improves: $E^D(a) = 0.05 (1 - 0.05) = 0.0475$. The Member complies with probability 0.05. In this situation, we still observe offers of finance for political favors, but they more rarely achieve the outcome intended by the Donor because the Donor simply does not care enough to offer large aid packages.

To present a contrasting example, where the Donor has an important Security Council agenda, we can raise the value of the vote to $v = 10$, while keeping the value of the reputation low, $r = 0.5$. Now the Donor cares more about the vote, but faces a credibility constraint because the value of the reputation is relatively low. To give the low reputation value more substance, suppose that the foreign aid package would be obfuscated so that few observers would ever notice if the Donor reneged – perhaps because she used a multilateral agency to deliver the aid package.

In this setup we find $a^* = 5$. Recall that the Donor is constrained, however, to set $\breve{a} \le r = 0.5$. We thus see that a^* is too high to be credible, and the most the Donor can credibly offer is $\breve{a} = 0.5$. Now, the expected value of not offering aid is still $E^D(\varnothing) = 0$, and by offering $\breve{a} = 0.5$, the Donor's expected value improves to: $E^D(a) = 0.5(10 - 0.5) = 4.75$. The Member complies with probability 0.5. In this situation, the low reputation value constrains the Donor, who would like to offer more aid to entice the Member to vote favorably on this important issue, but aid packages beyond 0.5 lack credibility.

What if, however, the Donor can raise the value of r by offering a more public form of aid – say, by offering more public bilateral aid packages instead of more obfuscated multilateral aid packages? If the Donor were to renege on a more public transaction, it would damage her reputation with other governments for future transactions. During a year when the Donor has an important resolution she wishes to pass, the more public offer (with higher r) could thus allow her to offer a larger aid package (that is credible). In the last example where the Donor cares a great deal about the issue ($v = 10$), the Donor could benefit from a higher value of r.

If we alter the last example slightly, raising $r = 0.5$ to $r = 1$, the Donor can credibly offer a bigger aid package, $\breve{a} = 1$. Now the Donor's expected value improves to: $E^D(a) = 1(10 - 1) = 9$. Thus we might expect donors to rely on more public forms of aid during years where they have important resolutions on the agenda.

2.8 Legitimizing Forceful Foreign Policy

Before concluding this chapter, we need to address a logical tension: The purpose of buying UNSC votes, an ostensibly illegitimate activity, is to gain legitimacy for forceful foreign policies. The legitimacy may be symbolic, in that the government demonstrates to the world that it has followed certain global norms in going through the proper channels of the UNSC (Hurd 2007), or it may be informational, in that the UNSC resolution represents the credible endorsement of a foreign policy by an independent third party (Chapman 2011). Buying votes does not seem to fit with either rationale. From a symbolic point of view, buying votes appears to violate the norms of the proper channels of the UNSC. From an informational point of view, buying votes calls into question the independence of the UNSC as a credible third party. How can temporary UNSC members serve as the symbolic representative for their region or convey credible information if their votes can be bought?

We have two answers. The first assumes the open buying of votes, observable by the public, and the second acknowledges that governments actually obfuscate vote-aid trades. The latter possibility – that governments can launder their seemingly dirty politics, for example, through international organizations – raises an interesting paradox with respect to the reputational costs described in the game. If payoffs are visible, they undermine the legitimacy of the UNSC, which is the very political commodity sought.[10] But if payoffs are completely invisible, there can be no reputational costs ($r = 0$), and aid packages are never credible in the game above.[11]

We therefore elaborate on three issues in this section: (1) the value of UNSC votes under open vote-aid trades, (2) obfuscating or laundering dirty politics, and (3) the reputational paradox.

2.8.1 Openly Paying Off UNSC Members

If everyone knows that votes can be bought, does this undermine the legitimacy that the UNSC might provide?

Our theory shows that only under certain circumstances can donors buy votes. *Not all votes can be bought.* In the swing voter example above, there is some probability that local politics will lead a UNSC member to vote against donors, even if this means that the government must renege on a deal. So, even in the presence of vote-aid trades, elected UNSC members still represent their sincere local preferences to a certain extent.

---

[10] One way to incorporate this idea into our model would be to make the value of the vote, v, a function of the public observability of the vote-aid trade (if any).

[11] More precisely in this case, there will be no reputational costs vis-à-vis other countries. The Member will know, of course, but since most developing countries win election to the UNSC rarely, the same government is unlikely to play the game again, and the damage to the Donor's reputation will not matter.

An affirmative vote thus conveys some information – even if the public observes the vote-aid trade.

To put this argument in the formal terms of our model, suppose the public never observes the value of local politics (b), and is thus unsure if the elected UNSC member should support a particular resolution. The public can still imagine three partitions over the distribution of b: (1) values where local politics are so powerfully strong that the UNSC member votes against the resolution even if aid is offered ($b > \breve{a}$), (2) values where local politics would lead the UNSC member to vote against the resolution in the absence of aid, but aid could swing the vote ($0 \leq b \leq \breve{a}$), and (3) values where local politics would lead the UNSC member to vote for the resolution even in the absence of aid ($b < 0$). The public may not be able to distinguish between situations (2) and (3), but it can identify situation (1). Put differently, UNSC votes can convey meaning to the broad public even in the presence of open buying and selling of votes. Specifically, if the UNSC member votes for a resolution, the public knows that the realized value must be below a certain threshold: $b \leq \breve{a}$. A message is thus conveyed, even if the public knows that a donor induced the UNSC member with a side payment of foreign aid. (This answer relates to the simpler discussion of Figure 1.1 in Chapter 1.)

From a symbolic point of view (Hurd 2007), the public knows that if a powerful country gains authorization for a forceful foreign policy through the UNSC, the favorable votes from UNSC members indicate that they were not strongly opposed. If they were, even an offer of foreign aid would not entice them to swing their vote. The process thus still has value because extreme resolutions will not garner the support of some elected UNSC members, despite potential payoffs from donors to elected members of the UNSC.

From an informational point of view (Chapman 2011), the domestic public in a donor country (like the United States) would like to ascertain whether its government is pursuing a recklessly aggressive foreign policy or whether the foreign policy is the right one. Following Chapman's model, the public and the members of the UNSC share conservative preferences on the use of aggressive policies. The U.S. president is more willing to use aggressive foreign policies. When UNSC members vote against a resolution supported by the United States, the American public knows that the situation is extreme: $b > \breve{a}$. An affirmative vote may fail to convey the sincere preference of the UNSC member (that is, whether b is greater or less than 0), but it does convey that the UNSC member, privy to classified and/or detailed information, is not extremely opposed to the policy (that is, the public knows that $b \leq \check{a}$). Once again, even in the presence of side payments, UNSC votes are valuable.[12]

In plainer terms, observers may agree that foreign aid is a tool of foreign policy, as explained by Secretary Albright.[13] The public understands that making arrangements of providing financial assistance in return for political support are part of politics and learns to read the signals with an appropriate filter. Importantly, the public also understands that the power of financial perks faces real constraints, which leaves ample and decipherable room for the sincere domestic preferences of UNSC member countries to play a role. In other words, there are limits on influencing other governments because they have their own national interests.

2.8.2 Obfuscation: Laundering Dirty Politics

Still, the open buying of votes would cheapen their significance. Thus, as Ambassador Bolton explains, explicit public deals are extraordinarily rare, and, in reality, the public tends to be unaware of specific vote-aid trades.[14] Only the instance mentioned in Chapter 1 has received considerable attention by the media: Secretary of State James Baker published in his memoirs that the United States cut all foreign aid to Yemen when the latter's government failed to support the UNSC resolution that authorized the use of force in Iraq in 1990 (Baker 1995: 278). Apart from this case, however, some public policy insiders with whom we have discussed our research have expressed surprise at our claim that UNSC members receive financial perks. Even "insiders" appear unaware of specific arrangements to trade money for political influence.

Some forms of foreign aid are more visible than others, and herein lies the key to the second reason why the public may value UNSC votes in the presence of vote-buying: obfuscation. The public may simply remain unaware of vote-buying. We suspect that favors delivered through multilateral agencies often escape the public eye. Even in the famous case of

---

[12] Following the logic of Crawford and Sobel (1982), the degree of information transmission will be a function of how far the preferences of the public and the UNSC member diverge. For interesting studies of the value of biased information, see Chapman (2011: 38), Johns (2007), Kydd (2003), Lupia and McCubbins (1998), Bawn (1995). Also see Boehmer, Gartzke, and Nordstrom (2004).

[13] Interview with Madeleine Albright, August 29, 2012, Albright Stonebridge Group, Washington, DC.

[14] Interview with John Bolton, March 31, 2011, American Enterprise Institute, Washington, DC.

Yemen, the cutting of U.S. bilateral aid was widely discussed, but what about the country's dealings with multilateral agencies? The fact that the country received no money from the IMF for more than five years after failing to deliver their vote to the United States has gone largely (entirely?) unmentioned in the press. The public pays less attention to the activities of multilateral agencies.

Chapter 1 presents three arguments of why powerful countries may employ international financial institutions, like the IMF and the World Bank, to further foreign policy goals. First, these little-understood international organizations can help to obfuscate political transactions, laundering "dirty" politics (Vaubel 1986, 1996, 2006; Abbott and Snidal 1998).

Second, international organizations also provide political leverage through conditionality. Many scholars argue that the major shareholders exercise their political power over international financial institutions to pursue international political goals.[15]

Third, using multilateral organizations allows for the sharing of costs. When they provide foreign aid through international organizations, the major donors not only share the financial burden, they can also make available tremendous technical expertise to recipient countries. The technical expertise of development banks can prove especially valuable.[16]

Still, governments face a trade-off between employing bilateral aid and using a multilateral channel. Transaction costs increase with a multilateral solution: In addition to negotiating with the (potential) recipients of the funds, the United States, for example, must leverage its influence over the international organization and convince other major shareholders to agree. Thus, the IMF and World Bank may be less effective tools when the major shareholders disagree on a specific resolution (Copelovitch 2010a,b).[17] An important implication of Copelovitch's work is that the

---

[15] Frey and Schneider (1986); Thacker (1999); Stone (2002, 2004); Oatley and Yackee (2004); Barro and Lee (2005); Sturm, Berger, and de Haan (2005); Andersen, Hansen, and Markussen (2006); Fleck and Kilby (2006); Dreher and Jensen (2007); Steinwand and Stone (2008); Kilby (2009a, 2013); Kaja and Werker (2010); Moser and Sturm (2011); Dreher and Sturm (2012); and Morrison (2013).

[16] For these reasons, the value of *a* to the Member may be higher when provided through a multilateral organization, while the cost of *a* to the Donor may be lower.

[17] Also see Hawkins et al. (2006), McLean (2012), Breßlein and Schmaljohann (2013), Hernandez (2013), and Humphrey and Michaelowa (2013). McKeown's (2009) work suggests, however, that U.S. policy-makers can influence international organizations almost as readily as they can use their own resources. On the domestic politics of

relative efficiency of using international organizations as opposed to taking unilateral action depends on a trade-off between the perceived cost of achieving consensus among the major shareholders and the benefit of pooling resources. In our case, however, we believe that the major shareholders typically agree that temporary members of the UNSC are potentially important. The major shareholders can implicitly reach the following consensus: Should a significant issue come up during the tenure of a temporary UNSC member, it behooves the major shareholders to have that country in their debt, and loans from various multilateral financial organizations represent a low-cost means to achieve this goal.

Thus, we suspect that the governments of major shareholder countries subtly highlight the importance of developing countries on the UNSC to their representatives on the executive boards of multilateral financial institutions – even if the precise reason for their importance (their membership on the UNSC) goes unsaid.

2.8.3 Reputational Paradox

With all of the benefits of using international organizations to launder their dirty politics, why would governments ever rely on the more visible bilateral aid channels? We can think of a number of reasons. In Chapter 1, we suggested that governments may rely on multiple channels because of resistance they may encounter in the form of bureaucratic inertia. Governments are not monoliths, and not all bureaucratic agents are willing to sacrifice their stated missions to offer payoffs to UNSC members for political support. Some bureaucratic channels may be closed, whereas others may be open to just a trickle of aid. If swaying a particular member of the UNSC requires a major aid package (large $\check{a}$), multiple channels – both bilateral and multilateral – may be necessary. Moreover, different developing countries may seek out different kinds of financial support during their UNSC terms, depending on their specific needs. Some governments may disdain the IMF and prefer bilateral assistance, and other governments may prefer to work with their regional development bank.

The game presented above offers an additional rationale for employing different channels for favors to UNSC members. As we saw before, when it comes to offering visible or hidden aid, governments face a trade-off.

delegating foreign aid policy to multilateral organizations, see Milner (2006). On the problems associated with delegation, see Nielson and Tierney (2003). On the concepts inherent to international delegation, see Lake (2007).

Hidden aid has the advantage of maintaining the appearance of legitimacy. It also poses, however, a credibility problem. Suppose, in the game above, that there are no reputational costs for the Donor to renege on a deal: $r = 0$. The equilibrium falls apart because the Donor moves last. Once she has secured the vote of the Member (on the right side of the game in Figure 2.1), the Donor can choose "Cut," walking away with the value of the affirmative vote, v, without paying a or r. Anticipating this, the Member should never choose "Comply," and the Donor should therefore never offer aid in the first place. Hence, in order for vote-aid trades to take place, there must be reputational consequences for the donors if they defect. At least some actors, if not the general public, must be able to observe the vote-aid trade in order to generate reputational costs. Larger aid packages require higher reputational costs in order to be credible.

For vote-aid trades that are particularly important to the donor – that is, for high v – donors thus have an incentive to offer more visible forms of aid, such as bilateral aid. More visible aid runs the risk of capturing the attention of the public, but it also has the advantage of lending credibility to larger aid packages. This motivates a hypothesis from above: Donors use more visible forms of foreign aid when they anticipate important votes.

2.9 Testable Hypotheses

The model presented in this chapter illustrates the logic of trading votes for aid and produces a number of testable implications. The most obvious implication is that governments serving on the UNSC should be more likely to receive foreign aid than countries not serving. More specifically, swing voter governments should be targeted. Finally, when donors anticipate important issues arising on the UNSC, they should be more willing to employ more visible forms of aid:

- H1: On average, elected UNSC members receive more foreign aid than nonmembers.
- H2: More specifically, swing voter governments receive more foreign aid than other UNSC members and more than nonmembers.
  - H2a: Non-swing voter countries receive no more foreign aid than nonmember countries.
- H3: Donors use more visible forms of foreign aid when they anticipate important votes.

We explore these hypotheses in qualitative cases (Chapter 3) and test them rigorously with statistical evidence (Chapter 5).

To foreshadow what we find, we present several examples in Chapter 3 that fit into the various categories of "too close," "too far," and "just right." We do note, however, that while these isolated examples exist, demonstrating the overall plausibility of the model, only a few of the examples fit into the extremes of "too close" and "too far"; most of the examples are "just right." We suspect that we find this because the amount of foreign aid matters so little to the donors and so much to the developing country members of the UNSC. Trades are thus highly probable, a priori.

Accordingly, we find a good deal of quantitative evidence in Chapter 5 that supports H1. Countries receive more foreign aid from the United States, Japan, and Germany when serving on the UNSC. They are also more likely to receive loans from several multilateral organizations (such as the IMF and the World Bank). We also find some evidence supporting the swing-voter hypotheses, H2 and H2a. These conditional results are complicated, and we go into the details in Chapter 5. Evidence also supports H3. The United States, at least, appears to employ bilateral aid to influence UNSC members only during years when the Security Council plays a major role in its foreign policy, but the effect of UNSC membership on receiving loans from multilateral organizations does not depend as much on the importance of years.

This chapter has served the purpose of rigorously presenting the logic behind our claims about trading money for political support. Note that the purpose of the game is not to lay out the reality of such deals. As explained in Chapter 1, neither the Donor nor the Member acts as a monolith. Instead, the logic plays out in small ways through the actions of thousands of bureaucrats working in foreign affairs and international finance – in Washington, in New York, and in country capitals all over the world. Still, the basic intuition remains – governments trade finance for political favors.

The task of the chapters that follow is to test the arguments presented here. We begin in the next chapter by presenting a series of cases drawn from history that suggests the plausibility of our arguments. We then turn to testing the generality of the claims by analyzing panel data on UNSC membership and various forms of foreign aid, including bilateral and multilateral.

Appendix 2.1: A More Elegant Solution[18]

1. Definitions

Define, implicitly, a^* as the a that solves:

$$v = a^* + \frac{F(a^*)}{F'(a^*)} \tag{2.1}$$

Define:

$$\check{a} = \begin{cases} a^* \text{ if } a^* \leq r \\ r \text{ otherwise} \end{cases} \tag{2.2}$$

Define Condition I as:

$$(v - \check{a})F(\check{a}) \geq vF(0) \tag{2.3}$$

Define Condition II as:

$$L(a) = \check{a}F(\check{a}) - \int_0^{\check{a}} bF'(b)\, db \geq 0 \tag{2.4}$$

2. Propositions

Lemma 1: *Condition II holds for all offers $a \geq 0$.*

Proof: Note that $L(0) = 0 - 0$, so Condition II holds at $a = 0$. Further note that $L'(a) = F(a) + aF'(a) - aF'(a) = F(a)$ (by Leibniz's integral rule). Now, $L'(a) = F(a) > 0, \forall a \geq 0$. Thus, $L(a) > 0, \forall a \geq 0$.

Lemma 2: *Because Condition II always holds, it is weakly dominant for the Member to always make a request.*

Proof (by backward induction): Member's expected utility of choosing "Request" is:

$$E^M(Request) = \int_{-\infty}^{\check{a}} \check{a}F'(b)\, db + \int_{\check{a}}^{\infty} bF'(b)\, db \tag{2.5}$$

$$= \check{a}F(\check{a}) + \int_{\check{a}}^{\infty} bF'(b)\, db$$

---

[18] We are very grateful to B. Peter Rosendorff for help with this section. Remaining errors are our own.

Member's expected utility of choosing "No request" (∅) is:

$$E^M (\emptyset) = \int_{-\infty}^{0} 0 F'(b)\,db + \int_{0}^{\infty} b F'(b)\,db \qquad (2.6)$$

$$= \int_{0}^{\infty} b F'(b)\,db$$

Member chooses "Request" iff $E^M (Request) \geq E^M (\emptyset)$:

$$\breve{a} F (\breve{a}) + \int_{\breve{a}}^{\infty} b F'(b)\,db \geq \int_{0}^{\infty} b F'(b)\,db \qquad (2.7)$$

$$\breve{a} F (\breve{a}) - \int_{0}^{\breve{a}} b F'(b)\,db \geq 0$$

This reduces to Condition II, above, which always holds in this situation. Choosing "Request" is thus a weakly dominant strategy for Member.

Proposition 1: *If Condition I holds, then the equilibrium strategies are:*

- Member: Chooses "Request aid." Chooses "Comply" if $a \geq b$ and chooses "Defect" otherwise.
- Donor: Offers $\breve{a}$. Chooses "Cut" if Member chooses "Defect" and chooses "Disburse" if Member chooses "Comply."

Proof (by backward induction): After "Comply," Donor chooses "Disburse" because $\breve{a} \leq r$, and Member receives $\breve{a}$. After "Defect," Donor chooses "Cut" because $\breve{a} > 0$ and Member receives b. Hence Member chooses "Comply" if $\breve{a} > b$.

Donor sets a before b is revealed. The ex ante probability that $a \geq b$ is $F(a)$. Hence, Donor's expected utility of offering a is:

$$E^D(a) = F(a)(v - a) + [1 - F(a)]\,0 \qquad (2.8)$$

$$= F(a)(v - a)$$

Taking the derivative of the above with respect to a yields:

$$\frac{\partial E^D(a)}{\partial a} = F'(a)(v - a) - F(a) \qquad (2.9)$$

Setting this equal to zero yields the interior solution a^* which satisfies Equation (2.1) from above: $v = a^* + \frac{F(a^*)}{F'(a^*)}$.

Checking the corners, we have the following two possibilities. If $F'(a)(v - a) - F(a) < 0$ for all $a > 0$, then $a^* = 0$ because $F(a) = 0$ at $a = 0$; if $F'(a)(v - a) - F(a) > 0$ for all $a \geq 0$, then $a^* = \infty$ because

$F(a) = 1$ as $a \to \infty$. Recall, however, the definition of $\check{a}$ (which brings in the credibility constraint):

$$\check{a} = \begin{cases} a^* \text{ if } a^* \leq r \\ r \text{ otherwise} \end{cases}$$

I. Interior Solution: Just Right Case

This is the case where an interior solution exists, with $a^* \in (0, r)$. For instance, if F is a continuous distribution with an increasing hazard rate, then $\frac{F}{F'}$ is monotonically declining. Then the right hand side of Equation 2.1 is an increasing function from 0 at $a = 0$; by the intermediate value theorem it will cross v. If r is large enough, then $a^* \in (0, r)$. Then in equilibrium, the Donor makes an offer, and the Member complies with probability $F(a^*)$.

II. Corner 1: Too Close

This is the case where F has the property that $F'(a)(v - a) - F(a) < 0$ for all $a > 0$. Then from above $a^* = 0$. In equilibrium no positive offer is made (or the offer $\check{a} = 0$ is made). But the Member votes with the Donor anyway.

For instance, if the support of b is $(-1, 0)$, then both the Member and the Donor know that the Member will always support the Donor, and no offer of aid is necessary. In this case, because $a > b$ always holds, $F(a) = 1$. If F is uniform, then $F' = 0$ and hence $F'(a)(v - a) - F(a) = -1 < 0$.

III. Corner 2: Too Far

This is the case where F has the property that $F'(a)(v - a) - F(a) > 0$ for all $a \geq 0$, so $a^* = \infty$. The Donor can make a maximum offer of $\check{a} = r$, which is not enough to generate compliance.

For instance, if the support of b is very large, say (r, ∞), then both the Member and the Donor know that the Donor can never offer enough aid to sway the Member.

3

Examples of Punishments, Threats, and Rewards

3.1 Types of Examples

Exchanging money for political influence seems plausible at every political level – from local politics to international politics. Evidence of these arrangements, however, may elude the public, precisely due to their nature. Mixing finance and politics appears distasteful to many people, and political actors attempt to avoid scrutiny. More importantly, the mechanism may simply defy observation. Political favoritism may come from the highest levels of bureaucratic hierarchies, but the actual agreements may take place at lower levels and specialized bureaus – through thousands of small meetings. The politics of favoritism for UNSC members hardly ever takes place at the United Nations, but rather in the bureaucracies in state capitals all over the world. Rarely do officials actually offer quid pro quo deals; instead, important countries simply find their way to the tops of more agendas in meetings. Can we, therefore, present any evidence that governments trade money for political influence over the UN Security Council?

This chapter presents several examples – examples of governments that have made trades, and, interestingly, some examples of governments that have chosen not to enter into such deals. Recall that the theory presented in Chapter 2 indicates three main types of cases: (1) countries so closely aligned with donors that their political support comes for free, (2) countries too opposed to donors – or too expensive – to buy, and (3) swing voters – arguably the most interesting targets of trades because they offer their political support in certain situations only if enticed. The main donor that we have in mind in this chapter is the United

States – although we find in Chapter 5 that the argument may apply to other donors, notably Japan and Germany, and perhaps key allies of the "West" – the United Kingdom and France. The theory implies that donors and recipients alike should seek to hide these trades. Many cases may thus defy corroboration. Still, we can present a series of archetypical examples that uphold the plausibility of our theory.

By presenting the stories in this chapter, we seek to fulfill a modest objective: to demonstrate the plausibility of our theory's application to the real world. Limitations permeate each example. Alternative hypotheses retain their plausibility: Perhaps the coincidence of aid and voting behavior is just that – a coincidence. Even if we do present convincing evidence of a bribe or reward in return for favorable votes – or a threat and a punishment in return for unfavorable votes – one might reasonably dismiss these examples as exceptions or aberrations.

We therefore pair our examples in this chapter with systematic tests in Chapter 5, where we "control" for alternative explanations in our analysis of an extensive and comprehensive dataset to see if the examples presented here constitute part of a larger pattern. Statistical evidence, of course, also faces limitations: When we cover thousands of observations through data analysis, we cannot delve into the minutia surrounding the events of any of these observations. The real devil remains in the details, and the proper nouns and dates surrounding key examples presented in this chapter constitute the fabric of international politics.

So, the examples in this chapter and the data analyses that follow in subsequent chapters work in tandem to provide a more complete body of evidence of trading money for political influence over the UNSC. We proceed by presenting some remarkable cases from the United States–Iraq conflicts of the early 1990s and the early 2000s. We also discuss cases from throughout the history of the United Nations, as far back as the 1950s and as recent as 2010. We select several cases based on the attention brought to them by the media, and we further supplement our case-selection by applying analytical criteria to our dataset to find examples that fit the systematic patterns that we detect in our quantitative analysis in the next chapter. We then conclude with a discussion of the importance of supporting our qualitative examples with a systematic analysis of quantitative data.

3.2 Zimbabwe 1992

Let us begin with a smoking gun. Following Africa's turn-taking norm, Zimbabwe won an uncontested election to the UNSC in the fall of 1990, shortly before the initiation of the U.S. Operation Desert Storm. During its two-year term on the UNSC, the government also entered into negotiations with the International Monetary Fund for a potential bailout program. Reportedly, the United States threatened Zimbabwe with increased levels of IMF conditionality if it failed to provide political support for key proposals pertaining to Iraq (Pilger 1992, 2002).

For example, on March 2, 1991, Zimbabwe voted in favor of Resolution 686, which imposed conditions on Iraq following the suspension of combat operations in the UNSC-authorized Gulf War. The conditions of Resolution 686 included the obvious rescinding of Iraq's actions to annex Kuwait, but also (1) the acceptance of liability for "any loss, damage or injury arising in regard to Kuwait and third States and their nationals and corporations as a result of the invasion and illegal occupation of Kuwait by Iraq," (2) the release of all Kuwaiti and third-State nationals detained by Iraq, (3) the return of all Kuwaiti property, (4) the cessation of hostile or provocative actions by Iraqi forces against all member states, and (5) the provision of "information identifying Iraqi mines, booby traps as well as any chemical and biological weapons in land or water." The resolution faced controversy: Cuba voted against it, and China, India, and Yemen abstained.

Early on, Zimbabwe's foreign minister described Resolution 686 as "a violation of the sovereignty of Iraq" (Pilger 1992: 182). Nevertheless, he voted in favor of the resolution "after he was reminded that in a few weeks' time he was due to meet potential IMF donors in Paris" (Pilger 1992: 182).

Zimbabwe did not represent an obvious supporter of U.S. foreign policy. Zimbabwe subsequently voted against a U.S.-supported resolution on the repression of Kurds in Iraq (Resolution 688, April 5, 1991). In 1992, Zimbabwe joined China in abstaining on several resolutions pertaining to the evolving situation in Yugoslavia.[1]

---

[1] Specifically, they were Resolutions 757, 770, 776, 777, and 787. Resolution 757 (May 30, 1992) condemned the Federal Republic of Yugoslavia (Serbia and Montenegro) for its continued fighting in Bosnia and Herzegovina, and imposed sanctions. Zimbabwe abstained along with China. Resolution 770 (August 13, 1992) recognized the humanitarian crisis in Bosnia and Herzegovina, and authorized "all measures necessary" to deliver aid (Friedman 1993). Zimbabwe abstained along with China and India. Resolution 776 (September 14, 1992) authorized the enlargement of the mandate and strength of the UNPROFOR in Bosnia and Herzegovina. Zimbabwe abstained along with China and India. Resolution 777 (September 19, 1992) considered that the Socialist Federal Republic of Yugoslavia has ceased to exist and recommended that the Federal Republic of Yugoslavia (Serbia and Montenegro) apply for membership in the United Nations

But during the latter part of 1992, the Zimbabwe government supported the United States on Resolution 773 (August 26, 1992), regarding the demarcation of the Iraq-Kuwait border, and on Resolution 778 (October 2, 1992), regarding the proceeds of sales of Iraqi petroleum and petroleum products. The situation in Iraq represented, of course, the primary focus of U.S. foreign policy at the time.

During this time in 1992, Zimbabwe was concurrently negotiating with the IMF over the conditionality attached to a potential IMF loan. Given the political clout of the United States at the IMF, and the importance to the Bush administration of the UNSC resolutions regarding Iraq, the government of Zimbabwe appears to have read as credible the U.S. threat to impose more stringent conditionality if the government had failed to cooperate at the UNSC. Apparently, the pressure worked, as Zimbabwe voted affirmatively with the United States on both resolutions.

The IMF also approved two simultaneous loan packages for Zimbabwe – with noticeably light conditionality.[2] On the surface, the case of Zimbabwe's 1992–1995 IMF program appears typical. The average number of quarterly conditions attached to the loan roughly equals the mean for the larger sample (8.25 versus 8.26 conditions, on average, per quarterly review). The number of performance criteria for this IMF arrangement also appears typical: an average of 6.25 performance criteria per quarter, as opposed to an average of 5.52 per quarter for the entire sample. So, if anything, the Zimbabwe 1992 arrangement contained an above-average level of performance criteria. The number of "prior actions" required of Zimbabwe stands out, however, as low.

Prior actions constitute the set of policy changes that must go into effect before a government receives any loan installments under an IMF arrangement. Any prior actions negotiated at this point in Zimbabwe's history would have represented the precise policy changes that the government would have had to undertake around the time it cast its vote on

---

as a new member. Zimbabwe abstained along with China and India. Resolution 787 (November 16, 1992) imposed further sanctions on Serbia and Montenegro. Zimbabwe abstained along with China. Also of note, Resolution 748 (March 31, 1992) imposed sanctions on Libya until it complied with investigations of the destruction of Pan Am Flight 103 over Lockerbie and UTA Flight 772 over Chad and Niger. The resolution also invoked Chapter VII of the UN Charter, "stating that Libya's failure to renounce terrorism constituted a threat to international peace and security" (Merrills 2011: 247). Zimbabwe abstained along with Cape Verde, China, India, and Morocco.

[2] Our data on conditions are taken from the IMF's "Monitoring of Fund Arrangements" (MONA) database. For more details on how we derived the number of conditions from there, see Dreher, Sturm, and Vreeland (2013).

Resolutions 773 and 778. On average, there are about eight prior actions for each IMF arrangement in our sample – with a range of 0 to 98 prior actions required under various programs that the IMF has approved. For UNSC members, the average number of prior actions is a little lower – only about 6. Considering that the average number of prior actions for nonmembers is about 8, the difference represents 25 percent. We return to this overall pattern in the next chapter. As for Zimbabwe, how many prior actions were required of the government to receive IMF loan installments on September 11, 1992? There were only two.

The analysis of Zimbabwe's conditionality data – particularly regarding the required prior actions to obtain the loan – suggests the plausibility of the claim that the United States threatened Zimbabwe with increased conditionality if it failed to deliver favorable votes on the Iraq resolutions.

We stress, however, that in our interview with Ambassador John Bolton, he reported that he personally never brought up the IMF with Zimbabwe or any other government. Furthermore, he questioned the source of this case, John Pilger, whom he described, with a smile, as a "left-wing journalist."[3] Pilger is, certainly, a well-known critic of American and British imperialism. We note, however, the wide respect that Pilger has received as a journalist. For example, he has twice won Britain's prestigious Journalist of the Year award (he was the first journalist to win the award for a second time). As for Pilger's allegation that Zimbabwe was threatened with new IMF conditions, he explained to us through personal correspondence that the information came from "a source who could not be named – who was a Zimbabwean with official access in Harare. I'm afraid I've long lost contact with him; I heard he fell out with the regime and had been in some difficulty. He is likely to be abroad now."[4]

Bolton explains that he did not use IMF conditionality as a channel of influence over Zimbabwe or, for that matter, any other government. He certainly agrees that the United States pressures countries on how to vote on UNSC resolutions. Explicit threats, however, would prove counterproductive as they would likely leak to the press. Instead, the strategy involves expressing the "displeasure" that the U.S. government would feel if another government failed to deliver a favorable vote – implying that the country would fall "out of favor" with the

---

[3] Interview with Ambassador John Bolton, March 31, 2011, American Enterprise Institute, Washington, DC.

[4] Personal correspondence with John Pilger, July 6, 2012.

United States.[5] But translating the displeasure into specifics is simply "not done" in New York.[6]

Our conversation with Secretary Albright is instructive on this point. Recall from Chapter 1 that she never made explicit deals such as "You do this and we'll do this" when she served as U.S. ambassador to the UN.[7] Instead, she cultivated close working relationships with many of the ambassadors of temporary UNSC members, while recognizing that, as "instructed ambassadors," they voted according to directives from their home-country capitals. Secretary Albright highlights that there are, therefore, many different – seemingly unconnected – issues at play simultaneously for thousands of people working in government in Washington, New York, and country capitals all over the world. The people at the top may place a country like Zimbabwe high on the agenda, but the political deals may be put together at various different levels of government. Certain key policy goals may result from the interagency process regarding the overall bilateral relationship. And the deals may never be explicitly linked to voting behavior, but rather be the outcome of increased exchanges that result from individuals working in various different bureaucracies doing favors for one another.

3.3 Yemen 1990

Ambassador Bolton notes that Yemen 1990 represents an exception. He clearly remembers offering explicit carrots and making tangible threats in the case of Yemen's vote on Resolution 678 on November 29, 1990. This situation had reached high stakes. Following the Iraqi invasion of Kuwait, the Bush administration was building up support for a war effort to push back the forces of President Saddam Hussein. This objective constituted the first major war effort of the United States since facing high levels of public opposition to the Vietnam War in the 1960s and 1970s. President George Bush wanted UNSC approval specifically to send a signal to the U.S. domestic public that the United States enjoyed the legal support of the international community (Voeten 2001; Chapman 2011). Resolution 678 authorized the use of military force for the so-called

---

[5] Interview with John Bolton, March 31, 2011, American Enterprise Institute, Washington, DC.

[6] Ibid.

[7] Interview with Madeleine Albright, August 29, 2012, Albright Stonebridge Group, Washington, DC.

Gulf War – also known as Operation Desert Storm. As Ambassador Bolton recalls, "Every vote mattered at that point."[8]

The vote on this resolution put Yemen in a terrible position. At the international level, Yemen faced the full force of U.S. diplomatic pressure to support the authorization of military force. At the regional level, Yemen faced Saudi Arabia, a country supportive of Desert Storm, but it also faced neighboring Iraq, which obviously opposed it.

Domestically, Yemen had – as recently as January of that year – undergone reunification of North and South Yemen (Yemen Arab Republic and People's Democratic Republic of Yemen, respectively). Providing explicit, legal, and highly public support for the invasion of a fellow Arab country by a Western power appeared highly disagreeable to many citizens. If the administration of President Ali Abdullah Saleh voted in favor of the Desert Storm operation, it would alienate Arabs both within and also around his fragile country. So the government of this newly reconstituted, poor Arab country found itself in a precarious political position.

Welcoming the newly formed country into the global community, the UN General Assembly elected Yemen to serve on the UNSC starting January 1990. By the end of that year, however, global events had placed the government of Yemen between a rock and a hard place. It could not win. The government had to choose international or domestic punishment.

Local politics triumphed over international pressures. Along with Cuba, Yemen cast a no-vote against UNSC Resolution 678. Secretary of State James Baker III, who attended the Security Council meeting to cast the U.S. vote, then "leaned back to the Americans sitting directly behind him and said, 'That's the most expensive vote they ever cast,'" according to Ambassador Bolton (Bolton 2008: 37).[9]

Bolton further notes, "U.S. foreign assistance was thereupon cut dramatically, something I have wished was more widely known" (Bolton 2008: 37). The United States indeed cut all of its $70 million in aid to Yemen. Despite real needs deriving from an impoverished and stagnant economy – not to mention the management of merging the economies and currencies of the People's Democratic Republic of Yemen and the Yemen Arab Republic, the new Republic of Yemen did not enter into an IMF arrangement for six years. Yemen did obtain funding for new World Bank projects – five in 1990 and four in 1991, so perhaps the vote did not

---

[8] Interview with John Bolton, March 31, 2011, American Enterprise Institute, Washington, DC.

[9] Also see Pilger (1992: 182; 2002), Bandow (1992), Baker (1995), Voeten (2001), and Thompson (2009).

have an impact on its relationship with this institution. However, World Bank projects typically take eighteen months to prepare, and the number of new World Bank projects noticeably dropped to two in 1992, one new project a year from 1993–1995, before returning to five new projects in 1996. The average number of new projects for the Yemen Arab Republic for 1980–1989 was 5.6, with a minimum of three new projects in 1988 and a maximum of eleven new projects in 1982. So, the drop-off in 1992 is noticeable. As Pilger (1992: 182; 2002) reports, "Yemen suddenly had problems with the World Bank and the IMF; and 800,000 Yemeni workers were expelled from Saudi Arabia." Note that Bolton claims no knowledge of the role of the IMF or World Bank. If the vote impacted Yemen's relationship with these organizations, "it would have to come from Washington" not New York (and he is skeptical that there was an impact).[10] The impact on Yemen's foreign aid from the United States did follow directly from the New York meeting, but Ambassador Bolton describes this case as unique.

Still, the story of Yemen serves as a foreboding exemplar of what can happen when a country resists U.S. pressure on an important vote. Below, we argue that this case continues to haunt developing countries. To avoid ending up in the same situation as Yemen, countries have often voted with the United States against their own sincere preferences. Indeed, our story is mainly about countries that do yield to the pressure applied by powerful donor countries, and the Gulf War provides other examples of these types of cases.

3.4 Zaire 1990–1991

The case of Zaire merits attention because its government not only delivered an affirmative vote on Resolution 678 (authorizing the U.S. war effort), but it also used its power as UNSC president to favor the U.S. position.

Members of the UNSC take turns occupying the Council Presidency, which rotates monthly according to the alphabetical order of the (English) names of the member countries. As mentioned in Chapter 1, the president of the UNSC possesses the power to approve the agenda, preside over UNSC meetings, and has the formal authority to call special meetings.[11]

---

[10] Interview with John Bolton, March 31, 2011, American Enterprise Institute, Washington, DC.

[11] See Rules 1, 7, 18, 19, and 20 of the *Provisional Rules of Procedure of the Security Council*, available http://www.un.org/Docs/sc/scrules.htm (accessed June 17, 2011).

Strictly speaking, when another government requests a special meeting, the president faces the obligation to hold one – but it does not always happen.

Consider the example of Zaire, which is now known as the Democratic Republic of Congo. In November 1990, Zaire delivered an affirmative vote on Resolution 678, authorizing Operation Desert Storm. Shortly thereafter, Zaire took its turn as president of the Security Council. During its one-month term, Cuba, Yemen, and India made formal requests to convene an emergency meeting to discuss the events unfolding in Iraq (Pilger 1992: 181–182; 2002). Such a meeting would not suit the United States because it would have opened up a debate about whether the military tactics employed by the United States exceeded the mandate of Resolution 678. So, as John Pilger (2002) explains, "Zaire was offered undisclosed 'debt forgiveness' and military equipment in return for silencing the Security Council when the attack was under way."[12] Zaire faced a compromised position because it had participated in an IMF program from June 1989 to June 1990, drawing down about $100 million in loans, and the World Bank initiated three new projects each year from 1989 to 1991, for a total of nine new projects.

The example of Zaire refusing to convene a meeting of the UNSC illustrates that influence over an elected member of the UNSC can serve useful purposes beyond just votes. In this case, U.S. pressure on Zaire helped to avoid a meeting of the Security Council that could have produced inconvenient debate during the execution of the war.

Note that this example may not represent the first time that Zaire faced U.S. pressure on how to behave on the UNSC. Consider some circumstantial evidence regarding Zaire's UNSC membership and its relationship with the World Bank – an organization where the United States, Japan, Germany, the United Kingdom, and France exercise formal political control through their vote shares on the organization's executive board as well as substantial informal control through their influence over the World Bank staff and management.

From 1960 to 1981, Zaire received between zero and three new World Bank projects each year, with an average of 1.2 per year. In 1981, Zaire won election to serve on the UNSC for 1982 to 1983 – and the number of new projects for those latter two years jumped up to six and four, respectively. Figure 3.1 illustrates the overall pattern from 1970 to 2004. Now, Zaire certainly qualified for World Bank assistance on economic

---

[12] Also see Pilger (1992: 181–182).

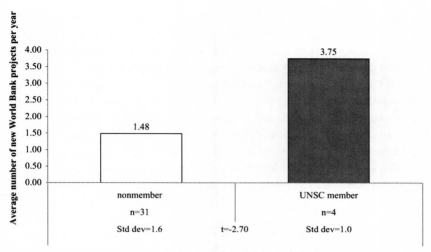

FIGURE 3.1. Average number of new World Bank projects per year for Zaire/ Democratic Republic of Congo (1970–2004).

grounds throughout this period. The deplorable economic conditions of Zaire are well known. Zaire also represented a reliable Cold War ally for the West, and so may have received World Bank assistance in part because of its more general political support. But there was nothing economically remarkable about Zaire during the years 1982–1983 or 1990–1991. Zaire appears to have received more World Bank projects simply when it served on the UNSC.

3.5 So Close: Overdetermined Cases

We can list other examples of governments that supported the United States during the Gulf War. Consider a case like Ecuador, which served on the UNSC in 1991–1992. On the one hand, we can report that Ecuador received healthy portions of U.S. foreign aid as well as loans from the World Bank and the IMF. The government, for example, entered into an IMF arrangement in 1991 and ended up receiving nearly 20 million Special Drawing Rights (SDR) from the IMF.[13] We can also report that Ecuador mostly voted with the United States on the UNSC resolutions

---

[13] The IMF calls its unit of account Special Drawing Rights. The value of an SDR is calculated as a weighted basket of four currencies (the British pound, the euro, the Japanese yen, and the U.S. dollar). Before the formation of the euro, the basket included the French franc and the German mark.

pertaining to Iraq. While abstaining on two resolutions, it voted for twelve other resolutions against Iraq.[14] Most importantly, we highlight that the U.S. ambassador in Quito warned Ecuador of "devastating economic consequences" if it voted against Resolution 686 (Pilger 1992: 182).

This snapshot of evidence supports our hypothesis. Consider, however, a broader view of Ecuador: The country received healthy portions of U.S. aid throughout the 1980s and 1990s, and the World Bank initiated new projects every year (except 1983, 1984, and 1999). Ecuador did enter into a new IMF arrangement in 1991, coincident with its service on the UNSC – and perhaps the United States helped to facilitate the IMF loan in return for influence over its voting behavior at the UNSC – but Ecuador also entered into new IMF programs in 1983, 1985, 1986, 1988, and 1994.

So, Ecuador may appear to fit our story, but – because the country regularly returns as a customer of U.S. foreign aid and of the multilateral institutions where the United States has political leverage – the evidence does not actually appear particularly strong. Consider the counterfactual: Even if Ecuador had not served on the UNSC in 1991–1992, we can easily imagine that the government would have received the aforementioned sources of finance.

Romania represents another overdetermined case. The Romanian government served on the UNSC in 1990 and 1991. The government signed an IMF arrangement in 1991 for 380.5 million SDR, of which 318.1 million was disbursed. Why such generous treatment? Perhaps it has something to do with Romania's voting record on resolutions pertaining to Iraq: The Romanian UN ambassador voted in favor of every U.S.-supported resolution.[15]

Again, however, consider the broader picture. As Romania emerged from the Soviet Bloc, the government forged strong ties to Western Europe and a close friendship with the United States. Romania appears to have received perks while serving on the UNSC, but the reason had more to do with its sincere affinity for the West than a trade of money for political support at the Security Council. Indeed, Romania went on to join NATO in 2004 and the European Union in 2007. Of course, Romania certainly earned goodwill toward these ends by supporting the United States during its term on the UNSC. The case of Romania, like the case of Ecuador

---

[14] The government abstained on 687 and 773 but voted for Resolutions 686, 688, 689, 692, 699, 700, 705–707, 712, 715, and 778.

[15] That is, Security Council Resolutions 660–662, 664–667, 669, 670, 674, 677, 678, 686–689, 692, 699, 700, 705, 706, 707, 712, and 715.

above, does not represent evidence against our hypothesis. The case is simply overdetermined.

3.6 And So Far: The Exception that "Proves the Rule"

If the United States did not need to pressure Romania, it did not bother to pressure Cuba. The Cuban government served on the UNSC from 1990 to 1991, during the important Gulf War period. On the U.S.-supported resolutions pertaining to Iraq, Cuba voted against eight of them and abstained on three others, making Cuba's voting record more opposed to the U.S. record than that of any other country on the UNSC at the time.[16] As for the crucial resolution authorizing the use of military force, Cuba stood as one of only two no-votes.

Of course, Cuba did not receive any U.S. foreign aid. It received just trivial grants from other G7 countries, mostly in the range of hundreds of thousands of dollars. Indeed, with the exceptions of Germany and Italy, all of the other G7 countries gave less than $1 million in aid to Cuba in 1990–1991. Germany did provide about $1 million in 1990 and nearly $2 million in 1991. Italy, interestingly, provided about $3 million in grants and $2 million in loans in 1989, and more than $10 million in loans in 1990 – clearly departing from its previous pattern of providing trivial amounts.[17]

In contrast to Romania, with the collapse of the Eastern Bloc, Cuba remained relatively independent from the West and adamantly opposed to the United States, and its borrowing patterns reflect as much. The country received no money from the World Bank or the IMF. Cuba had ceased its memberships in these organizations back in 1964, and the Castro regime continued to view the IMF and World Bank as tentacles of Western capitalism and tools of U.S. foreign policy. Cuba thus appears to represent the archetypical case of an unwinnable or un-swingable vote, so Western governments do not even try to buy Cuban votes.[18]

---

[16] Regarding Iraq, Cuba voted against Resolutions 666, 670, 678, 686, 687, 688, 706, and 712 and abstained on Resolutions 661, 674, and 692. Cuba also voted against Resolution 683, which ended the U.S. trusteeship of the Marshall Islands and Micronesia.

[17] The spikes in Italian aid are striking – it is possible that Italy attempted some influence over the country as it served on the UNSC – but it is also likely that the spike is related to the collapse of the Soviet empire, on which the economy of Cuba had depended. Grants from Italy to Cuba continue to trend upward following the end of Cuba's service on the UNSC.

[18] In terms of our model in Chapter 2, one could argue that Cuba did not even initiate the "request aid" step – indifference breaks the other way for this extreme government.

Cuba has not always laid claim to such anti-Western politics. During the period before the Cuban Revolution and the Castro regime's subsequent turn toward communism, the United States could entice Cuba to support its policies.

Cuba actually served on the UNSC twice during the period before the Cuban Revolution, in 1949–1950 and 1956–1957. During its first term, Cuba voted along U.S. lines on twenty-one of twenty-three resolutions. On one important vote, Cuba joined the United States in opposing a resolution: Resolution 87 (September 29, 1950) deferred the consideration of the declaration by the People's Republic of China (PRC) "regarding the armed invasion of the island of Taiwan" by the government of the Republic of China (ROC). The resolution furthermore invited a representative of the PRC to attend a future meeting to discuss the declaration. As this resolution involved a procedural matter, the United States could not exercise its veto power.[19] So the resolution passed with seven affirmative votes, three no-votes, and one abstention (at this point in time, the UNSC included only eleven members, so seven votes sufficed to pass a resolution). China, Cuba, and the United States voted against the resolution, and Egypt abstained. At this point in history, the government of the Republic of China (ROC) – located in Taiwan – still held the permanent seat of China on the UNSC. Obviously, this government voted against this resolution, as it opened the door to legitimizing the PRC and delegitimizing the ROC. The United States joined the ROC's opposition, as did Cuba. Cuba continued to support the U.S. position of recognizing the ROC, as opposed to the PRC, by voting against Resolution 88 (November 8, 1950), which called for the presence of a representative of the PRC during a discussion of the situation on the Korean Peninsula. Cuba's no-vote came despite an affirmative vote from the United States, which did not fully support the resolution but decided to vote affirmatively because it would have been impossible to get a majority to amend it (Hamilton 1950). On this vote, therefore, Cuba took a more hardline American stance than the United States itself. The remaining resolution where Cuba departed from the U.S. position was trivial: Cuba abstained on a resolution to reimburse travel expenses to governments assisting in

---

[19] The UN Charter implies in section 2 of article 27 that procedural matters require a supermajority of the votes but does not grant veto power; veto power applies "on all other matters," where "the concurring votes of the permanent members" are required (article 27, section 3). For a thorough treatment of supermajority rules and veto power, see Schwartzberg (2013). Also see Diermeier, Prato, and Vlaicu (2013).

commissions in Indonesia, India, and Pakistan (Resolution 75, September 27, 1949).

Most importantly, Cuba voted with the United States to condemn the invasion of South Korea by North Korea (Resolution 82, June 25, 1950). This resolution called upon UN member states "to render every assistance" in pushing North Korea to withdraw to the 38th parallel. Cuba also supported Resolution 83 (June 27, 1950), which recommended that the UN "furnish such assistance to the Republic of Korea as may be necessary to repel the armed attack and to restore international peace and security in the area." Cuba supplied crucial support for the resolution, which passed with seven out of eleven total votes. Yugoslavia voted no, Egypt and India did not vote, and the Soviet Union was absent (in protest of China's representation by the ousted government in Taiwan, as opposed to the new government of the PRC). Again, as the Security Council included only eleven members, seven votes constituted the precise supermajority required to pass a resolution.[20]

Cuba next served a term from 1956 to 1957. During this term, Cuba voted with the United States 100 percent of the time. All sixteen resolutions supported by the United States also received an affirmative vote from Cuba.[21]

Interestingly, during Cuba's entire history it has entered into only one arrangement with the IMF. The IMF arrangement happened to concur with its service on the UNSC. More precisely, Cuba served on the UNSC from January 1, 1956 through December 31, 1957, and it entered into its only IMF arrangement ever on December 7, 1956 – the IMF arrangement expired on June 6, 1957.

Bilateral aid from the United States to Cuba also spiked during the 1956–1957 UNSC term. From 1946 through 1960, total bilateral aid and military support from the United States to Cuba averaged $240,000 per year. In 1956, however, U.S. aid to Cuba reached $433,000 and then further increased in 1957 to $1.11 million – the highest level ever granted to Cuba during this period of history.[22] These observations, circumstantial to be sure, constitute an interesting piece of an overall pattern. Although the high voting affinity between the United States and Cuba reflects the

---

[20] See UNGA Resolution 1991 (A, 1, c).

[21] Resolutions 111–126.

[22] We use the data of Kuziemko and Werker (2006) for the bilateral aid and military support from the United States to Cuba, 1946–1960. We observe the pattern only for Cuba's second term on the UNSC.

generally warm relationship between the two governments during the 1950s, the timing of the U.S. bilateral aid and the IMF loan may have provided added insurance for the United States to safeguard Cuban support during its 1956–1957 UNSC term.

In sum, while Cuba's recent voting at the UNSC and its disdain for U.S.-tainted money reflects our game-theoretic model's "too far" scenario, the Cuba of the 1950s was much more open to U.S. policies and, perhaps, financial leverage. Cuba readily supplied political support, and the United States supported the Cuban regime financially.

3.7 Great Powers and Emerging Markets

Up to now, we have discussed small, developing countries. Powerful countries also face pressure on how to vote, however, and trades of money for political influence occur with the governments of these types of countries as well. Examples of the United States pressuring these countries – sometimes successfully and other times not – have gained some notoriety.

Consider again the Gulf War period. In 1991, the United States supported a World Bank loan for China and lifted the trade sanction that had been in place since the Tiananmen Square massacre in 1989. In exchange, China supported Security Council Resolution 678, authorizing the use of military force against Iraq (Eldar 2008: 17).

A similar exchange transpired in 1994, when China agreed to abstain on the Resolution 940 to restore democracy in Haiti. The United States again facilitated a World Bank loan for China and also granted the government security guarantees regarding Taiwan (Eldar 2008: 18).

The United States also pressured Russia regarding the resolution to restore democracy in Haiti. In this case, the United States traded its own political support. As Secretary Albright explained to us, the United States had opposed Russian leadership of a UN observer mission in Georgia because of the historic relationship between the two countries and the fact that they shared a border.[23] Secretary Albright's Russian counterpart at the time, Ambassador Yuli Vorontsov, used the same argument to oppose U.S. leadership of a force in Haiti.[24] Now, Secretary Albright pointed out that the U.S. relationship with Haiti was quite different from that of Russia and Georgia, but ultimately the United States and Russia came

---

[23] Interview with Madeleine Albright, August 29, 2012, Albright Stonebridge Group, Washington, DC.
[24] Ibid.

to an agreement.[25] The United States voted in favor of Resolution 937, authorizing peacekeeping forces in Georgia – led by Russia. In return, Russia abstained on Resolution 940, thereby granting legal sanction to U.S. efforts to restore democracy in Haiti (Eldar 2008: 18; Malone 1998: 107).

In the meantime, the United States had also managed to garner Russian support for a series of important resolutions pertaining to the escalating violence and eventual breakup of Yugoslavia. In particular, Russia voted in favor of the initial arms embargo (Resolution 713, September 25, 1991), the establishment of a peacekeeping mission, known as the United Nations Protection Force (UNPROFOR, Resolution 743, February 21, 1992), the authorization to expand UNPROFOR's strength to "enable the Force to control the entry of civilians into the United Nations Protected Areas" (Resolution 769, August 7, 1992), and extensions of UNPROFOR's mandate (Resolution 871, October 4, 1993; and Resolution 908, March 31, 1994).

Of course, during this time, Russia became a member of the IMF for the first time. As the country transitioned into a market economy, inflation spiked, with the ruble depreciating rapidly against the dollar. Russia soon found itself negotiating with the IMF for a bailout. The IMF staff and management insisted on tough austerity measures in return for a loan, but the U.S. government "urged the IMF to soften its usual requirements. . . . The commitments that Russia undertook under the new agreement were predictably watered down" (Stone 2002: 119–120). Furthermore, Russia did not even follow all of the conditions attached to the loan. Thanks to interventions by the U.S. government on Russia's behalf, the bailout money kept flowing, thus keeping Russia in Washington's debt (Stone 2002: 125). Secretary Albright cannot attest to any link between Russia's behavior on the UNSC and U.S. support for Russia at the IMF. As she worked through the State Department, which has no control over the IMF, such support ultimately would have come from the Treasury Department. She does not, however, find it hard to believe that the United States would use every tool available to influence an important country on a salient issue. As she explains, "If we think something is important enough, and there aren't a lot of ways to get a country to do what you want then . . . why not?"[26]

---

[25] Ibid.
[26] Ibid.

As another example, consider the events of 1999. In January, when the United States called for a military response to human rights violations attributed to Serbian forces in Kosovo, Russia's anger "fell on deaf ears" (Stone 2002: 159). Russia had strong ethnic, cultural, and economic ties to Serbia. For many Russians, the support of UNSC resolutions that essentially hurt Serbia's position in the conflict represented a betrayal. Yet, rather than exercising a veto, Russia merely abstained on Resolution 1239 (May 14, 1999), which invited the UN and other humanitarian personnel operating in Kosovo into Serbia and Montenegro. Russia actually voted in favor of Resolution 1244 (June 10, 1999), which authorized "Member States and relevant international organizations to establish the international security presence in Kosovo" and to establish an interim administration (United Nations Interim Administration Mission in Kosovo) to oversee "the development of provisional democratic self-governing institutions" in Kosovo.

During this time, Russia negotiated and entered into yet another IMF arrangement. Now, mid-level officials at the IMF opposed another soft agreement for a government that had repeatedly failed to comply with the conditions of previous arrangements. Russia still had the support, however, of the U.S. government. The United States exercised its political influence over the IMF, and Russia obtained another IMF bailout. Stone (2002: 159) observes, "The timing strongly suggests that an agreement with the IMF was the price of Russia's relatively moderate opposition to the NATO campaign" against Serbia. The IMF arrangement was approved in July.

Of course, many examples of China and Russia vetoing U.S.-sponsored resolutions also exist, which demonstrates that the United States cannot always pressure countries to offer their political support. Beyond China and Russia, other important emerging market countries have also recently asserted themselves at the UNSC, resisting U.S. pressure.

Consider Brazil and Turkey, which both served on the UNSC in 2010.[27] The United States attempted in vain to win the support of these countries for a resolution against Iran. Specifically, the United States sponsored Resolution 1929, which noted that Iran had not complied with previous resolutions regarding the nonproliferation of nuclear weapons and thus imposed sanctions against the country. The resolution represented a fourth round of sanctions, expanding the arms embargo and imposing severe restrictions on Iranian finance (indeed, preventing the provision

---

[27] Brazil's term was 2010–2011, and Turkey's was 2009–2010.

of financial services to Iran).[28] Resolution 1929 passed with twelve affirmative votes, including all five permanent members, with one abstention from Lebanon, and the two negative votes of Brazil and Turkey.

Brazil and Turkey voted against the resolution in part because it went directly against a side deal that they had brokered with Iran, whereby Iran would deposit low-enriched uranium with Turkey in return for reactor fuel, which could be used for nuclear energy, but not as weapons (BBC News 2010). The Obama administration not only pressured Brazil and Turkey to support Resolution 1929, it vigorously opposed their efforts to broker a side deal with Iran. Recall from Chapter 1 that our conversation with an employee of the U.S. State Department revealed that during this time, he noticed Brazil and Turkey at the top of the agenda of nearly every meeting he attended.

Despite U.S. pressure, Brazil and Turkey resisted, asserting themselves as rising powers by brokering their own deal with Iran and opposing the U.S.-sponsored resolution. Given our earlier reference to *The Godfather*, this scenario recalls the scene where an upstart gangster named "The Turk" has just executed an assassination attempt against the once-powerful Godfather and notes that the *Don* was "slipping": "Ten years ago, could I have gotten to him?" In fact, ten years prior to the resolution, Brazil actually had served on the UNSC, in 1998–1999. During this earlier term, Brazil voted along with the United States on 100 percent of 138 resolutions, including controversial resolutions pertaining to Iraq, the former Yugoslavia, and Haiti.[29]

But ten years later, Brazil stood up against nearly all members of the UNSC on a U.S.-sponsored resolution. So what changed?

The U.S.–Brazilian UNSC relationship traces the interesting rise of an emerging market challenger throughout two decades. During the 1990s, Brazil still depended on assistance during periods of financial instability. At the end of 1998, when the Brazilian real required major shoring-up in the wake of financial crises in Thailand, Korea, Indonesia, and Russia, Brazilian president Fernando Henrique Cardoso negotiated an IMF package for $41.5 billion (Vreeland 1999). The Cardoso administration found itself in no position to make waves with the United States

---

[28] The previous resolutions included 1696 (2006), 1737 (2006), 1747 (2007), 1803 (2008), 1835 (2008), and 1887 (2009).

[29] The 138 resolutions were numbered 1147 through 1284. For more lessons about international relations through an excellent and thorough analysis of *The Godfather*, see Hulsman and Mitchell (2009). On the decline of U.S. power, see Nexon and Wright (2007).

during its 1998–1999 term on the UNSC. Moreover, Secretary Albright traces the good working relationship between the two delegations at the UN all the way up to the friendship between the two presidents: "Cardoso and Clinton were good friends."[30] She explains that their friendship helped in getting Brazil's support for many U.S.-supported UNSC resolutions in the late 1990s. "There's no question that Clinton got along very well with Cardoso, and I believe a lot in personal relationships."[31]

Thus, in the years surrounding the IMF loan, including Brazil's term on the Security Council, the countries' roles remained largely in harmony: Brazil received its IMF funds, and the United States enjoyed Brazilian support on many UNSC resolutions it sponsored. But by 2010, with the political power that comes with a strong emerging economy, not to mention a different set of actors in Brasília and Washington, the Brazilian government felt much less compelled to adhere to U.S. political pressure. In the early 1990s, Brazilian leaders were "positioning themselves as kind of leaders of Latin America," inching towards leadership of Latin America.[32] In 2010, instead of offering political support for U.S.-sponsored initiatives – leveraged through IMF loans and personal friendships – Brazil now postured itself as an equal, brokering its own side deal with Iran that competed with the U.S. proposal, and calling itself a major contender for a permanent seat on the UNSC.

3.8 Resolution 1441 and the Three Types: Too Close, Too Far, and Just Right

Following the logic of the game presented in Chapter 2, we have discussed cases where (1) the United States and its allies successfully pressured governments for some votes, (2) did not bother trying to win over other votes, and (3) did not need to do a thing to win still others. Interestingly, we see a perfect application of this same logic in a journalist's discussion of UNSC Resolution 1441.

Resolution 1441 granted broad powers to weapons inspectors in Iraq. Specifically, the resolutions called on Iraq to provide to the weapons inspectors

immediate, unimpeded, unconditional, and unrestricted access to any and all, including underground, areas, facilities, buildings, equipment, records, and means

---

[30] Interview with Madeleine Albright, August 29, 2012, Albright Stonebridge Group, Washington, DC.
[31] Ibid.
[32] Ibid.

of transport which they wish to inspect, as well as immediate, unimpeded, unrestricted, and private access to all officials and other persons.

The United States viewed the resolution as a "last chance" for Iraq to comply with weapons inspections. The far-reaching resolution, which set the ground for the 2003 invasion, passed unanimously on November 8, 2002. As stated to the *Inter Press Service News Agency* by an Asian diplomat, "Only a superpower like the United States could have pulled off a coup like this" (Deen 2002).

The author of the news story, Thalif Deen, reports that France, China, and Russia agreed to the resolution because U.S. officials assured them that they would return to the Security Council before pursuing a military option against Iraq. (Of course, U.S. officials did indeed return to make a presentation to the UNSC on the matter, but, anticipating that a resolution for a military strike against Iraq would fail, they decided to proceed without asking for a vote.)

Most interesting for our research is the way that Deen (2002) discusses the ten nonpermanent members of the Security Council:

Of the 10, the two Western nations, Ireland and Norway, were expected to vote with the United States. Syria, a "radical" Arab nation listed as a "terrorist state" by the U.S. State Department, was expected to either vote against or abstain. So the arm-twisting was confined mostly to the remaining seven countries, who depend on the United States either for economic or military aid – or both.

This account nicely summarizes the logic we offer in Chapter 2. Consider the "too close" cases in more detail. Norway and Ireland both voted along with the United States on Resolution 1441, as well as every other resolution passed in 2002.[33] Of course, neither Norway nor Ireland received any bilateral foreign aid from the G7 countries – or any loans from the IMF or World Bank. Such assistance would have been out of place as these countries also ranked among the highest incomes in the world. Their favorable votes for U.S.-supported resolutions likely derived from sincere common interests.

As for the "too far" case, Syria ended up supporting Resolution 1441. Its support did not appear obvious, however, as the Syrian government opposed the United States on a total of five votes during 2002: On Resolution 1397 (March 12, 2002), which called for an end to Palestinian acts

---

[33] The United States abstained on Resolution 1435, which called on Israel to end its actions in Ramallah, Palestine, destroying Palestinian civilian and security infrastructure.

of terror against Israelis and proposed a two-state solution (the first resolution to do so), Syria abstained because the resolution was "very weak,"
and treated "the killer and the victim on equal footing" (Left 2002).
Then, Syria walked out of negotiations over Resolution 1402 (March
31, 2002), which actually took a harsh stance against Israel, calling for
a ceasefire and the withdrawal of Israeli troops from Ramallah, the West
Bank city where the Palestinian government kept its headquarters. Syria
still contended that "the resolution was not harsh enough to meet Arab
demands" (Crossette 2002).

In September, Syria and the United States again butted heads – this time
over Resolution 1435, which also addressed the Israeli siege of Ramallah.
In this case, both Syria and the United States offered different drafts of the
resolution; the U.S. version was harsher on Palestinian terrorist attacks,
and the Syrian version was harsher on Israel's occupation (Preston and
Bennet 2002). The compromise resolution demanded that Israel cease
its siege of the Palestine capital city of Ramallah, end the destruction of
civilian and security infrastructure, and withdraw occupying forces from
Palestinian cities. The United States allowed the resolution to go forward,
but it chose to abstain (rather than cast an affirmative vote) because the
resolution failed to explicitly condemn terrorist groups striking against
Israel (Preston and Bennet 2002).

Subsequently, after the suicide-bomb attack of a hotel near Mombasa, Kenya, which killed three Israeli tourists and ten Kenyans, the
UNSC passed Resolution 1450 (December 13, 2002), condemning the
attack (Barrow 2002). Syria cast the sole no-vote because the resolution
explicitly expressed sympathy for *Israeli* victims. Resolution 1450 actually became the first resolution to condemn the killing of Israelis in specific, but it did so without the support of Syria (Preston 2002).

Finally, Syria, along with Russia, abstained on Resolution 1454
(December 30, 2002), regarding an expansion of the list of restricted
goods allowed under Iraq's Oil-for-Food program. Claiming that Iraq
had begun to comply with weapons inspections, Syria objected to the
expansion of restricted goods to Iraq, as well as the speed with which the
United States pushed through this resolution (Kerr 2003).

During this time, Syria received no loans under IMF programs, nor
did the country begin any World Bank projects. Indeed, Syria had not
initiated a World Bank project since 1986, although it had previously
participated in a total of twenty World Bank projects during the 1970s
and 1980s. In terms of bilateral aid, the United States did send a truly
trivial amount in the form of grants in 2001 and 2003 – amounting to

$20,000 and $50,000, respectively – but the United States sent no grant money in 2002. That year, the United States provided a paltry $50,000 in aid that was tied to policy changes. The point is that Syria was not dependent on U.S. foreign aid. Syria had been a "pariah" or "bad guy" in the eyes of U.S. policy-makers long before its turn on the UNSC. This history, paired with Syria's claim that Iraq was now complying with weapons inspections, made it unlikely that Syria would support the resolution.

Still, in the end, Syria offered its vote in favor of Resolution 1441, which gave Iraq a "final opportunity" to comply with weapons inspections. Syria argued that "inspections were the best way to avoid a war against Iraq" (Ghattas 2003).

As for the seven potential "swing" voters for Resolution 1441, consider them one by one:

In his article for the *Inter Press Service News Agency*, Deen (2002) concedes that **Singapore**, like Syria, received no economic aid from the United States, yet his report also highlights that "the United States is the biggest single arms supplier to Singapore, selling the Southeast Asian nation weapons worth 656.3 million dollars last year and an estimated 370 million dollars this year." The article goes on to suggest that Singapore could not easily stand up to the United States or refuse to fall in line with its benefactor.

Bulgaria exhibited a more clear-cut financial connection to the United States: The country received $13.5 million in military grants and was scheduled to receive additional aid through a U.S. program called Support for Eastern European Democracy (Deen 2002). In total, the United States supplied $48.5 million in grants to Bulgaria in 2002 (OECD 2006). Further underscoring the precarious position of Bulgaria, the government entered into an IMF Standby Arrangement in February of 2002 for access to more than $300 million dollars of credit. By April of 2003, the government had drawn on about $185 million of the loan (IMF 2003: 104). Furthermore, the government initiated four new World Bank projects in 2002.

With respect to **Colombia**, the *Inter Press Service News Agency* article points out that in 2002 the Colombian government received $380 million in grants from the United States under the International Narcotics Control and Law Enforcement (INCLE) program (Deen 2002). In 2003, Colombia received a total of $680 million in U.S. grant money (OECD 2006). Columbia also received a new World Bank project loan in 2002 and six new World Bank projects in 2003, as well as an IMF

Standby Arrangement with a line of credit worth more than $2 billion dollars (IMF 2004: 106).

In 2002, **Mexico** received about $12 million under INCLE and $28.2 million in U.S. Economic Support Funds (Deen 2002). During that same year, total grant money from the United States reached nearly $85 million – up from $42 million in 2001 (OECD 2006). Mexico also received eight new World Bank projects in 2002 (up from four projects in 2001).

Regarding **Cameroon**, the *Inter Press Service News Agency* article notes that the United States was providing the government with free surplus weapons as well as $2.5 million in annual grants for military education and training (Deen 2002). We note that, according to OECD figures, U.S. grants spiked in 2002 to $13.1 million (up from $4.8 million in 2001).

As for **Guinea**, U.S. grant money to this country reached a high mark in 2002: $41.31 million (OECD 2006). With Guinea's GDP standing at about $3.05 billion in 2002, this figure alone amounts to 1.6 percent of the country's total GDP (World Bank 2012). Additionally, the World Bank initiated three new projects in Guinea that year.

Finally, the *Inter Press Service News Agency* article highlights that the U.S. aid package to **Mauritius** came through the U.S. African Growth and Opportunity Act and explicitly demanded that the government of Mauritius "not engage in activities contrary to US national security or foreign policy interests" (Deen 2002). According to OECD (2006) data, the 2002 U.S. aid package to Mauritius may appear small: just $500,000. Note, however, that this amount more than quadrupled what the country had received in 2001 ($120,000), and it represents a sizeable sum for this small country, which, in 2002, had a population of only about 1.2 million people and an average annual income of less than $4,000 (World Bank 2012). Moreover, U.S. grant money subsequently dropped off when Mauritius left the UNSC – from $340,000 in 2003 to $250,000 in 2004 and zero in 2005 (see Figure 3.2). According to Phyllis Bennis, a fellow at the Institute for Policy Studies, the experience of Yemen from a decade prior (discussed above), influenced the decision-making of Mauritius on this vote: "The Yemen precedent remains a vivid institutional memory at the United Nations" (Deen 2002). The government of Mauritius actually recalled its ambassador, Jagdish Koonjul, "because he continued to convey the mistaken impression that his country had reservations about the U.S. resolution against Iraq" (Deen 2002). Policy-makers in Port Louis

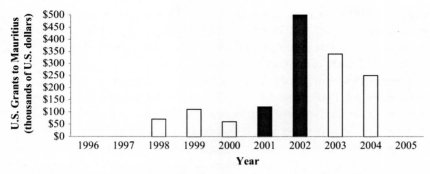

FIGURE 3.2. U.S. grants to Mauritius around the time of Resolution 1441 (November 8, 2002). *Notes:* Shaded columns indicate years when government was serving on the UNSC (2001, 2002). If there is no column, no grant money was received (1996, 1997, 2005). The source of U.S. grant data is OECD (2006).

wanted to send the right signal to their counterparts in Washington and ensure that their support would be registered in New York.

Thus, the United States had some form of financial leverage over nearly all of the developing countries serving on the UNSC. And so, while the controversial Resolution 1441 initially faced opposition, the United States successfully garnered unanimous support for it, winning all fifteen votes.

3.9 Circumstantial Evidence

Beyond the more prominent examples covered by the media, a number of cases have jumped out at us from our analysis of the full set of data on UNSC membership. While, as has been mentioned, all of our examples run the risk of being anecdotal and thus unconvincing, we present these examples more because we find them particularly intriguing. Then, in the chapter that follows, we present our statistical tests of whether a systematic pattern might be driving the interesting examples discussed here.

Take the example of **Kenya**, elected in October of 1996 to serve on the UNSC. During its two-year tenure (1997–1998), it voted along with the United States, the United Kingdom, and France (the P3) on 126 out of 127 resolutions.[34] Regarding the single exception, the P3 itself

---

[34] In 1997, Kenya voted on 53 out of 54 resolutions along with the P3. In 1998, Kenya voted along with the P3 on all 73 resolutions.

actually split, with France abstaining; Kenya similarly abstained (along with China, Egypt, and Russia).[35] Otherwise, Kenya voted in lockstep with the P3 on all resolutions, including several controversial votes where China and Russia abstained.[36]

During this time, from March of 1996 to March of 1999, Kenya was under an IMF program.[37] In terms of the treatment that Kenya received from the IMF, the number of conditions was notably low, with just two prior actions required to obtain the arrangement, a total of thirteen performance criteria and nine structural benchmarks over the life of the three-year program. This amounts to an average of two conditions per quarter, which is among the 20 lowest cases out of the 314 IMF arrangements with 101 countries observed over the 1992 to 2008 period. The 1996 IMF arrangement also stands out when compared to Kenya's other IMF arrangements. The number of conditions averaged 4.75, 3.75, and 5.25 per quarterly review for arrangements negotiated in 1993, 2000, and 2003, respectively – when Kenya did not hold a seat on the UNSC. We present only circumstantial evidence for Kenya here, but we find the case too intriguing to ignore.

Circumstantial evidence also surrounds many World Bank projects.[38] Consider **Argentina's** participation. From 1970 to 1975, Argentina participated in two projects sponsored by the World Bank – both of them started in 1971, while the government was serving on the UNSC. From the 1970s through the 1990s, Argentina became a more regular participant in World Bank projects, averaging about three new projects a year from 1975 to 1995. Still, there are noticeable spikes in 1988, when the World Bank began seven new projects in Argentina, and 1995, when the World Bank initiated thirteen new projects – both years when Argentina was a member of the UNSC. Interestingly, however, the pattern ends with Argentina's fourth term on the UNSC in 1999–2000: new World Bank projects actually dropped down to three and two, respectively, following peaks of fifteen and twelve new projects in 1997 and 1998. So the history

---

[35] Resolution 1134 on Iraq's continued refusal to allow access to sites designated by the UN Special Commission. See http://unbisnet.un.org/ (accessed July 7, 2011).

[36] China abstained on Resolutions 1101 (on Albania, March 28, 1997), 1114 (on Albania, June 16, 1997), 1199 (on Yugoslavia, September 23, 1998), 1207 (on Yugoslavia, November 17, 1998). Russia abstained on Resolution 1129 (on Iraq, September 12, 1997). Both abstained on Resolutions 1203 (on Yugoslavia, October 24, 1998) and 1212 (on Haiti, November 25, 1998).

[37] An Enhanced Structural Adjustment Facility (ESAF) Program.

[38] We originally discussed the examples that follow (Argentina, Ghana, Algeria, Indonesia, and Bangladesh) in Dreher, Sturm, and Vreeland (2009b).

of World Bank projects in Argentina fits our story from 1970 to 1995, but not afterward.

Next, consider **Ghana**. Its first-ever World Bank project was coincident with its first term on the UNSC in 1962–1963. From 1964 to 1985, the country received an average of about 1.5 new World Bank projects per year, with the highest number of new projects being four in some years. Then Ghana once again won election to serve on the UNSC in 1986–1987, and the number of new World Bank projects jumped to its highest level ever: eight in 1987.

Algeria received an average of about one new World Bank project per year from 1962 to 1987, with some years receiving none and other years up to four new projects. In 1988, however, Algeria served on the UNSC, and the number of new projects peaked at five.

Indonesia, as a highly populous country, always has a lot of World Bank projects in place. For example, from 1968 to 1972, Indonesia had between two and eight World Bank–sponsored projects per year with eight new projects in 1970, four in 1971, and seven in 1972. When Indonesia served on the UNSC in 1973, it received a bump in the number of new projects to eleven. Following the UNSC term, the number of new projects remained high, averaging about nine new projects per year from 1975 to 1994. The record number of new projects in Indonesia, however, is seventeen, which was reached while it was serving the second year of a term on the UNSC in 1996.

Bangladesh is a very poor country that typically has multiple World Bank projects in place regardless of international politics. Consider that from independence in 1972 until 1978, the average number of new World Bank projects was almost five per year, ranging from one to seven. Yet, when Bangladesh served on the UNSC in 1979–1980, the number of new World Bank projects jumped up to nine and eleven new projects, respectively. This was unprecedented in Bangladesh and unmatched since – except in 1999 when the country again received eleven new projects. Bangladesh had been elected again to the UNSC that year.

Figures 3.3 through 3.7 depict the patterns of participation in World Bank projects for Argentina, Ghana, Algeria, Indonesia, and Bangladesh, respectively. We stress that this anecdotal evidence from Latin America, Africa and Asia, while intriguing, is purely circumstantial. The World Bank can defend just about any loan to a single developing country as part of its overarching goal to promote development or reduce poverty. We have no doubt that the World Bank staff economists working at the country desks of these countries would be able to justify every project

mentioned above as worthy of World Bank assistance. Not unlikely, they
were each worthy projects, but there were also many other worthwhile
projects that did not receive board approval. Governments of developing countries constantly negotiate and work with the World Bank to
develop new projects. The question for us is, why is it that more projects

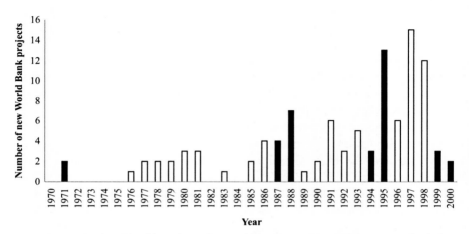

FIGURE 3.3. New World Bank projects in Argentina (1970–2000). *Notes:* Shaded
columns indicate years when government was serving on the UNSC. If there is no
column, there were no new World Bank projects. *Source:* Dreher et al. (2009a).

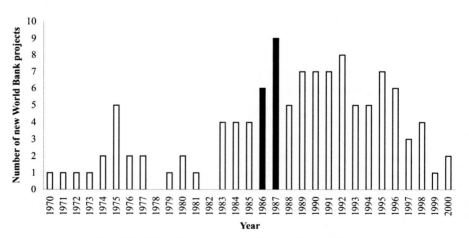

FIGURE 3.4. New World Bank projects in Ghana (1970–2000). *Notes:* Shaded
columns indicate years when government was serving on the UNSC. If there is no
column, there were no new World Bank projects. *Source:* Dreher et al. (2009a).

get approved for some countries in some years? When we consider one country's historical experience and then compare it to the experience of many other countries, we begin to see the pattern that we further explore in Chapter 5. UNSC participation seems to be associated with more World Bank projects.

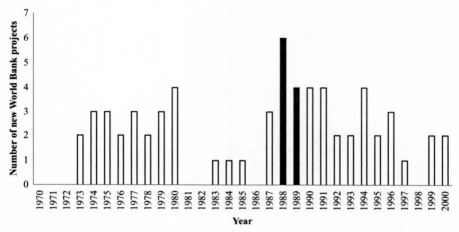

FIGURE 3.5. New World Bank projects in Algeria (1970–2000). *Notes:* Shaded columns indicate years when government was serving on the UNSC. If there is no column, there were no new World Bank projects. *Source:* Dreher et al. (2009a).

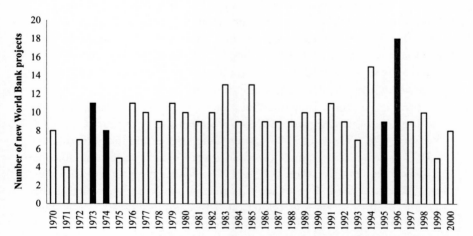

FIGURE 3.6. New World Bank projects in Indonesia (1970–2000). *Notes:* Shaded columns indicate years when government was serving on the UNSC. If there is no column, there were no new World Bank projects. *Source:* Dreher et al. (2009a).

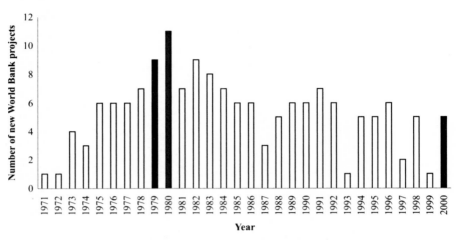

FIGURE 3.7. New World Bank projects in Bangladesh (1971–2000). *Notes:* Shaded columns indicate years when government was serving on the UNSC. If there is no column, there were no new World Bank projects. *Source:* Dreher et al. (2009a).

Finally, consider the circumstantial evidence surrounding **Tanzania** and the IMF. From independence in 1961 until 1974, the country never served on the UNSC, and it never received a loan from the IMF. In 1975, however, Tanzania began its first UNSC term and entered into its first-ever IMF arrangement.

The *Washington Post*, having obtained an early draft of our research, confronted the IMF with the evidence from Tanzania and other similar cases. The IMF claims that international politics had nothing to do with the decision to lend to Tanzania in 1975. Instead, spokesman William Murry explained that "Tanzanian loans were driven in large part by the oil crisis after the Arab oil embargo" (Lynch 2006: A19).

Murry has a point. Tanzanian international reserves dropped in 1974, and the government signed an IMF agreement the next year (Campbell and Stein 1992; Vreeland 2003). After "sluggish" economic performance in 1973 (Johnson 1973), the Tanzanian government accepted only unconditioned financing from the IMF in 1974. First it drew down 10.5 million SDR from the IMF – exactly 25 percent of its quota, which is the maximum allowed without taking on IMF conditions (IMF 1974: 86). Second, it received 6.3 million SDR from the Oil Fund Facility, a special facility designed to meet the impact of increased petroleum prices without imposing conditions (IMF 1974: 86). The government made a second Oil

Facility purchase for 3.15 million SDR in 1975 (IMF 1975: 77). Tanzania escaped conditionality up to this point. Economic problems persisted, however, and Tanzania finally entered into a one-year Standby arrangement for 10.5 million SDR in August 1975. The IMF press release stated that the program was "in support of the government's economic and financial policies of expanding output and tightening fiscal and monetary measures" (IMF 1975: 254).

Yet, Howard Stein, an economist and scholar of African political economy at the University of Michigan, has noted that the policy conditions associated with this arrangement were notably weak (see Stein 1992). The IMF required only that domestic credit usage by the public sector be constrained (Stein 1992: 63). The government did not want any conditions imposed, but it desperately needed foreign exchange. The IMF granted an agreement with very soft conditions, and the government accepted.

Drawing on the research of Kiondo (1992), Stein (1992), and Campbell and Stein (1992), we speculated in a previous publication as to why Tanzania had received such soft treatment from the IMF, suggesting that the prominence of Tanzanian president Julius Nyerere as a leader on the world stage, gave him increased negotiation leverage over the IMF (Vreeland 2003: 26). We now offer a more general explanation here, replacing the proper noun "Nyerere" with the variable "UNSC membership."

3.10 Addressing Skepticism

The theory in Chapter 2 suggests that when it comes to buying the political influence of UNSC members, three archetypes exist:

(1) UNSC members whose preferences closely align with those of the major donor countries, obviating the need to bribe them for their votes;

(2) UNSC members whose preferences line up so far from those of the major donor countries that bribes would typically not suffice to switch their votes; and

(3) UNSC members in the middle, whom the major donors might bribe most fruitfully.

The theory thus predicts that some countries on the UNSC should receive increases in foreign aid while serving on the UNSC, but other countries should not. Specifically, Western powers should not target countries either too close or too far from their policy positions. Instead, swing voters represent the targets of trades of money for political influence.

Of course, much more complexity pervades the real world, and many cases defy simple categorization. One cannot simply know the underlying affinity of governments across a range of issues. Even the countries with preferences furthest away from the major donors might switch their vote if bribed, and even those on the other end of the spectrum might find themselves in a situation where they prefer to vote against the major donors.[39]

We have actually found few cases of governments with preferences that appear too far away from the United States for some attempt to sway their votes. Almost all cases, with the exception of perhaps Cuba during the Gulf War and Syria on issues pertaining to the Middle East, faced some pressure. The famous failure to win the vote of Yemen actually did involve carrots – followed by the stick.

Still, we find it useful to categorize our cases into the three archetypes and present some examples for illustrative purposes. We have thus gone through media reports, scholarly accounts, and our dataset looking for cases that might fit into the different categories.

So, in this chapter, we have briefly discussed some examples where bribes appeared unnecessary – such as Ireland and Norway with respect to weapons inspectors in Iraq (Resolution 1441). We also discussed examples where bribes would do no good in swinging favorable votes on certain resolutions, such as Cuba in 1990 and Syria in 2002. The bulk of the cases we consider, however, reveal that powerful countries – mainly the United States – pressure all sorts of governments on how to vote, using the various means at their disposal.

If we stopped here, we would have no idea if these suspicious cases constitute a systematic pattern in international relations. One could easily dismiss the anecdotes we have presented here. We have seen such skepticism before. Returning to the public reaction of the IMF to our early work, IMF spokesman Murry contended that "the evidence is anecdotal and circumstantial" (Lynch 2006: A19). We consider this to be a reasonable reaction to our cases.

---

[39] The situation becomes more complex if we allow the donors to disagree, as happens in practice. See Copelovitch (2010a, b).

With such skepticism in mind, we turn to more rigorous econometric analysis. In the pages that follow, we present evidence that – in general – governments serving on the UNSC receive more bilateral foreign aid and are more likely to receive loans from the IMF and the World Bank as well as some regional organizations. We begin by addressing the selection question: Who gets elected to the UNSC?

4

Who Wins Election to Represent the World?

4.1 Myths versus Reality

Mistakes about how the world selects temporary members of the UN Security Council permeate casual discussions of the institution. The public, by and large, simply misunderstands the process.

For example, we often hear that UNSC membership "rotates," when, in fact, selection is by election. Some people believe the permanent members of the UNSC (the P5) have veto power over selections, when in fact, they have no such authority. There is also a misconception that regions select their representatives, when, in reality, they merely nominate candidates, and countries can also self-nominate without any regional endorsement. The final decision actually belongs to a two-thirds majority of the UN General Assembly (UNGA).

Grains of truth may drive some of these misunderstandings. There exists no formal rule to rotate membership, for example, but each region has adopted – to varying extents – a norm of taking turns. Officially, the permanent members of the UNSC exert no privileged control over the ultimate selection of temporary members, but they may have enough informal influence to occasionally block truly distasteful candidates from winning. And while the final vote on UNSC members belongs to the UNGA, we observe multiple candidates really contesting elections less than 20 percent of the time. Typically, the regions dominate the process by nominating exactly one candidate per seat, leaving the UNGA to rubber-stamp the selection.

The nuances of the selection process warrant careful study for two reasons: First, they reveal intrinsically interesting features of international relations: our analysis shows that the selection process is driven by a mixture of realist power politics and norms of taking turns.

Second, we need to address the selection question before proceeding to the analysis of the effects of UNSC membership on foreign aid and multilateral lending. The apparent tendency to provide money to UNSC members might result from selecting allies in the first place. Maybe the United States gives foreign aid to countries that it agrees with on foreign policy issues, and the United States also pushes for these countries to win election to the UNSC. If the United States cares about how elected members of the UNSC vote, it may intervene at the election stage to ensure that friends win election more often than do enemies. When we discussed our research with the former head of the United States Agency for International Development (USAID), Andrew S. Natsios, he indeed suggested this alternative explanation.[1] Scholars have also suggested this possibility (see Bashir and Lim 2013). So, beyond any intrinsic interest in the selection process, we also seek to answer the selection question as a means of disentangling the circumstances of election from the inherent effects of membership. As discussed in the previous chapter, we would like to ensure that our empirical investigation of the effects of UNSC membership does not suffer from selection bias. In this chapter, we thus present the formal election rules for the UNSC and then test for empirical patterns that may drive the process.

To motivate this endeavor, consider the following prominent election, which illustrates both the rules of electing UNSC members and the idiosyncratic nature of selection. In 2002, Guatemala announced its candidacy for the October 2006 election of the seat representing the Latin American and Caribbean Group (Torre 2006). In 2004, however, President Hugo Chavez declared Venezuela's candidacy for the same seat (Torre 2006). Now, Chavez did not exactly represent a friendly leader in the eyes of U.S. policy-makers. Indeed, about one month before the election, Chavez delivered a provocative speech to the General Assembly:

It still smells of sulfur.... Yesterday... the President of the United States, whom I call the Devil, came here talking as if he owned the world... As the spokesman of imperialism, he came to share his prescription to try to preserve the current pattern of domination, exploitation, and pillage of the peoples of the world.[2]

---

[1] Interview with Andrew S. Natsios, September 14, 2011, Georgetown University, Washington, DC.

[2] *"Huele a azufre todavía... Ayer... el Señor Presidente de los Estados Unidos, a quien yo llamo el diablo, vino aquí hablando como dueño del mundo.... Como vocero del*

Not surprisingly, the United States opposed Venezuela's election bid and thus put the full weight of its support behind the candidacy of Guatemala. Guatemala enjoyed the regional support of Mexico, Colombia, and fellow Spanish-speaking Central American countries and also received public support from Europe and Canada (MercoPress 2006). Venezuela enjoyed the support of the Caribbean bloc of countries, which opposed Guatemala because of a border dispute with Belize (a member of the Caribbean Community, CARICOM) and because of Guatemala's opposition to preferential treatment of Caribbean banana exports to the European Union (BBC Caribbean 2006). Furthermore, Venezuela received regional support from Argentina, Brazil, Paraguay and Uruguay, and had the support of China, Russia, and the Arab League (Varner 2006). Did U.S. support help Guatemala win? Or did opposition to the United States resonate with other members of the General Assembly, leading to a Venezuelan victory? U.S. opposition to the candidacies of Cuba in 1989 and Syria in 2001 failed to prevent their elections – they each won in a single round of balloting – but U.S. opposition in 2000 contributed to the defeat of Sudan, which lost to Mauritius in four rounds of balloting (Varner 2006, Costa Rica 2005).

In the Guatemala-Venezuela contest, 47 rounds of voting ensued (BBC News 2006). Neither U.S.-backed Guatemala nor wild card Venezuela could garner the required two-thirds majority of UNGA votes. Eventually, both candidates withdrew in favor of a compromise candidate, Panama.

The 2006 electoral contest between Guatemala and Venezuela exemplifies some of the formal rules: Guatemala served as the initial nominee, endorsed by the Latin American and Caribbean region. Then Venezuela decided to nominate itself and enter the race. The supermajority threshold for election by the UNGA loomed large over this election, eventually resulting in both candidates dropping out because neither could win a two-thirds majority of the UNGA votes. The case also reveals the idiosyncratic nature of selection; at the outset, one would not have predicted Panama to win the seat.

This example, however, is atypical. How does the international community usually select its regional representatives? We address this question in the following manner. We begin in Section 4.2 by describing

imperialismo vino a dar sus recetas para tratar de mantener el actual esquema de dominación, de explotación y de saqueo a los pueblos del mundo." Sources: http://www
.youtube.com/watch?v=VPQO7-LE0Gs&feature=related, http://webcast.un.org/ramgen/
ga/61/ga060920am.rm?start=01:02:20&end=01:26:10 (accessed December 15, 2013).

the formal UN rules for the selection process. Then, in Section 4.3, we lay out five theoretical perspectives that might explain the selection process:

(i) Do UN members follow a norm of choosing countries committed to peace, as directed by the *Charter of the United Nations*?
(ii) Does the receipt of foreign aid predict UNSC selection?
(iii) Is selection driven by international power – either by a country's own power or by the power of countries with which it shares strong ties?
(iv) Do shared historical, political, or religious traits play a role?
(v) Do governments practice a norm of taking turns, rotating through the eligible candidates?

Next, in Section 4.4, we present an innovative statistical model developed by Matthew Gould from the University of Westminster and Matthew Rablen of Brunel University.[3] The "multiple discrete-choice" model, specially tailored to the UNSC selection rules, addresses both regional nominations and UNGA elections. Finally, we employ the model in Section 5.5, where we analyze a dataset of 180 elections from 1970 to 2005 to provide empirical answers to the questions above.

To foreshadow our main results, the most robust determinant of UNSC election is turn-taking. This finding holds in some form throughout all regions, although there appears to exist a compromise between the demands of powerful countries to win election more frequently and this norm of giving each country its turn (Dreher, Gould, Rablen, and Vreeland 2014). And in the rare cases where contested elections decide the victor, the UNGA does not respect the turn-taking norm.

Beyond the main compromise between powerful countries and turn-taking, we also find that involvement in inter- and intrastate conflict lowers election probability, while troop contributions to UN peacekeeping missions predict election from the regions. The evidence is patchy, however, and not found for contested elections.

Regarding foreign financial support, evidence is also patchy and somewhat mixed. Development assistance from the United States plays no statistically significant role. Yet, we have some limited evidence from Eastern Europe and the rare instances when the UNGA votes decisively that countries receiving U.S. military assistance are more likely to win

---

[3] See Dreher, Gould, Rablen, and Vreeland (2014).

election.[4] Furthermore, countries facing U.S. or UN sanctions are less likely to win election from Africa and Asia (during the Cold War) and from Latin America (since the Cold War). We return to these factors in Chapter 5 when analyzing the effects of UNSC membership. Beyond these patterns, we find that elections exhibit many idiosyncrasies.

4.2 The UNSC Election Rules

The UNSC election process follows certain written rules – laid out in the UN Charter (article 23) and in UNGA Resolution 1991 (A) – as well as some important unwritten agreements.[5] The written rules define ten seats divided among four regional caucusing groups:

- one country from Eastern Europe (EE);
- two from the Western European and Others Group (WEOG);
- two from the Latin America and Caribbean Group (GRULAC – *el Grupo de Países Latinoamericanos y Caribeños*);
- five from Africa and Asia.[6]

An unwritten but unbroken agreement divides the five seats for Africa and Asia into three seats for Africa and two seats for Asia, and a further unrecorded agreement between Africa and Asia reserves one of their five seats for an Arab state (the "Arab swing seat"), with the regions taking turns every two years to provide a candidate (Security Council Report 2011: 7, Daws 1999: 22–23).

Most of the regional groupings appear intuitive, although the uninitiated usually find the WEOG a strange geographic group – Western Europe plus "Others?" The "others" are the heirs of the old British Commonwealth group – Australia, Canada, and New Zealand – which constituted

---

[4] Note that U.S. military aid does not count as official overseas development assistance, according to the Organization of Economic Co-operation and Development (OECD). In our work in Chapter 5 on the determinants of U.S. development assistance, we do not include U.S. military assistance in our calculation of the dependent variable.

[5] This section follows Dreher, Gould, Rablen, and Vreeland (2014). Much of the background for this section can also be found on the Web site of the Security Council Report, an independent nonprofit organization: http://www.securitycouncilreport.org. We also reference Daws (1999) and draw on Luck (2006).

[6] Before 1966, there were only six elected members of the UNSC. Composition was typically two Latin American countries, one Middle Eastern country, one Eastern European country, and two from the British Commonwealth countries. Sam Daws, a consultant and scholar on UN affairs, provides an excellent account of the development of the UN regional groups (Daws 1999).

a caucus prior to the expansion of the UNSC in the 1960s. The ambiguous name of this caucus has led to interesting developments. Additional countries that have joined the WEOG include Israel (Security Council Report 2011: 6) and Turkey, which won election to represent the WEOG (2009–2010) after having previously won election to represent the Middle East (1951–1952), and Eastern Europe and Asia (1954–1955 and 1961, respectively).

One might think that, because elected members of the UNSC represent specific regions, the regions themselves should elect them, but that is not so. The regional groups caucus informally, usually arriving at a consensus over which candidates to nominate. Countries can self-nominate, however, so a candidate need not have any regional support at all. Indeed, there are cases where a country that would probably not have won election by the region was elected by the required two-thirds majority of the General Assembly (Turkey's election in 2008 comes to mind).

The UNGA conducts staggered elections for five of the ten seats each autumn, with terms beginning in January of the following year.[7] To be eligible for election, a country must belong to one of the five caucusing groups. At present, one UN member (Kiribati) does not participate in any regional grouping, and prior to 2000, when it gained temporary membership in the WEOG, Israel was also without a caucusing group (Security Council Report 2011: 6). Note that while General Assembly Resolution 1991 A (XVIII) lays out the broad guidelines for the groupings, the details about membership are not formally codified in any UN documents that we have found. Membership appears to be a joint decision between the country and the group, and the regional groups appear to operate by consensus. To our knowledge, only Turkey has represented more than one group.

Sometimes governments declare their candidacy years in advance of elections. Other times they do so much later, perhaps in the midst of the elections themselves – ballots even allow for write-in candidates (Security Council Report 2006).[8] Some candidates feel out the waters by hinting

---

[7] During even-numbered years, the two-year terms begin for the Eastern European representative, one of the two GRULAC representatives, one of the two Asian representatives, and two of the three African representatives (the term of the Arab representative also begins as one of the last three seats). During odd-numbered years, the two-year terms begin for both of the WEOG representatives and one of the representatives from each of the GRULAC, Asia, and Africa.

[8] Also see various issues of the *Journal of the United Nations* for details on specific elections (http://www.un.org/en/documents/journal.asp, accessed April 5, 2012).

their interest and gradually make their intentions known, whereas others boldly announce their candidacy. The timing of announcing candidacy appears idiosyncratic, and, as far as we know, no one has recorded a full dataset of such announcements.

The regional caucuses can effectively control the selection of UNSC members by announcing a "clean slate" of candidates: exactly one candidate per eligible seat. This approach usually relegates the UNGA to providing a perfunctory rubber stamp of the regional decision. Contested elections do occur, however, when efforts at agreement at the regional level have failed.

These contested elections, where the UNGA votes actually prove consequential, occur infrequently. Box 4.1 lists all contested elections for the period 1965 to 2005. We arbitrarily define a race "contested" if an additional candidate received at least ten votes.[9] Using this definition, we list a total of 37 contested elections for this time period. For the remaining 168 seats filled (82 percent), the regional candidate won landslide majorities. EE seats appear the most contested (24 percent), while contested elections have decided 22 percent of WEOG seats, 20 percent of GRULAC seats, and 17 percent of Asian seats. For Africa, only 13 percent of elections have seen contestation.[10]

Africa has the most disciplined rules for selecting candidates. Indeed, it is the only region for which we have found references to explicitly codified rules (see the African Union's Rules of Procedure of the Ministerial Committee on Candidatures – Doc. EX.CL/213 (VIII)).[11] This caucusing group operates a system of turn-taking within subregional groups, which should, in theory, ensure that all countries in Africa eventually serve on the Security Council. North Africa and Central Africa rotate one seat every two years; Western Africa has one seat every two years; and Eastern Africa and Southern Africa rotate one seat every two years (Security Council Report 2011: 6).

Even for Africa, however, complexities arise. Malone (2000: 5) reports that Africa, for example, has followed "a strict rotation among its members, although this pattern has been broken occasionally." As Security

---

[9] Little changes if we lower this ten-vote threshold to allow for more elections to count as contested. The qualitative interpretation of the findings we present below hold. These results are available in the book data replication materials.

[10] The Arab swing seat – which alternates between Africa and Asia – has faced the least contestation. Only 11 percent of elections have been contested (2 out of 10 for the African-Arab swing seat and 0 out of 9 for the Asian-Arab swing seat).

[11] African Union (2006: 8). Also see Agam (1999: 41) and O'Brien (1999: 31).

Box 4.1   Contested UNSC elections, 1965–2005

AFRICA (62 seats total)
Africa South of the Sahara (52 seats total):

Multi-round contestation – 5 cases:
- 1977: Nigeria defeated Niger in 5 rounds of balloting, 96 votes to 27. (In the first round, Nigeria received 84 votes, Niger 85.)
- 1984: Madagascar emerged as a compromise candidate in round 11 after Ethiopia and Somalia deadlocked. (In the first round of voting, Ethiopia received 85 votes, and Somalia received 70.)
- 1985: Ghana defeated Liberia in 4 rounds of balloting, 109 votes to 46. (In the first round, Ghana received 45 votes, Liberia 87, and Cameroon 7.)
- 1993: Nigeria defeated Guinea-Bissau in 4 rounds of balloting, 119 votes to 33. (Guinea-Bissau withdrew at that point. In the first round of voting, Rwanda was elected with 153 votes while Nigeria received 99 votes, Guinea-Bissau received 62 votes, and Burundi received 2.)
- 2000: Mauritius defeated Sudan in 4 rounds of voting, 113 votes to 55. (In the first round, Mauritius received 95 votes, Sudan 69.)

One-round contestation – 1 case:
- 1995: Guinea-Bissau defeated Benin in the first round, 128 votes to 60.

African Arab swing seat (10 seats total):

Multi-round contestation – 1 case:
- 1987: Algeria defeated Morocco in 2 rounds of balloting, 113 votes to 42. (In the first round, Algeria received 104 votes, Morocco received 61.)

One-round contestation – 1 case:
- 1983: Egypt defeated Algeria in 1 round, 125 votes to 24.

Total uncontested seats South of the Sahara: 46/52 (88%)
Total uncontested African Arab swing seat: 8/10 (80%)
Total uncontested seats all Africa: 54/62 (87%)

ASIA (41 seats total)
Non-Arab Asia (31 seats total):

Multi-round contestation – 4 cases:
- 1975: Pakistan defeated India in the eighth round of voting when India withdrew (123 votes to 0). (In the first round, India received 60 votes and Pakistan 59.)
- 1978: Bangladesh defeated Japan in 3 rounds of balloting, 125 votes to 2. (In the first round, Bangladesh received 84 votes and Japan 65.)
- 1984: Thailand defeated Mongolia in 4 rounds of balloting, 106 votes to 49. (In the first round, Thailand received 99 votes, Mongolia 59.)
- 1988: Malaysia defeated Bangladesh in 2 rounds of balloting, 143 votes to 5. (In the first round, Malaysia received 104 votes, Bangladesh 55.)

(continued)

Box 4.1 *(continued)*

One-round contestation – 3 cases:
- 1966: India defeated Syria in the first round, 82 votes to 42.
- 1986: Japan defeated India in in the first round, 107 votes to 36.
- 1996: Japan defeated India in the first round, 142 votes to 40.

Asian Arab swing seat (10 seats total) – No cases

Total uncontested seats non-Arab Asia: 24/31 (77%)
Total uncontested Asian Arab swing seat: 10/10 (100%)
Total uncontested seats all Asia: 34/41 (83%)

GRULAC – The Group of Latin American and Caribbean Countries – *Grupo de Países Latinoamericanos y Caribeños* **(41 seats total)**

Multi-round contestation – 5 cases:
- 1979: Mexico famously emerged as a compromise candidate in the 155th round of balloting, when Cuba and Colombia deadlocked. (In the first round, Cuba received 77 votes and Columbia 68.)
- 1980: Panama was eventually elected in the 22nd round. (In the first round, Costa Rica received 89 votes, Guyana 9, Nicaragua 6, Panama 2. Along the 22 rounds of voting, Barbados, Chile, Peru, Dominican Republic, Saint Lucia, Brazil, Grenada, Haiti, Ecuador, Trinidad and Tobago, and Bolivia all received at least one vote.)
- 1982: Nicaragua defeated Dominican Republic in 3 rounds, 104 votes to 50. (In the first round, Nicaragua received 92 votes, Dominican Republic 59.)
- 1996: Costa Rica defeated Bolivia in the second round of voting when Bolivia withdrew (167 votes to 5). (In the first round, Costa Rica received 105 votes and Bolivia 73.)
- 2001: Mexico defeated Dominican Republic in 2 rounds, 138 votes to 40. (In the first round, Mexico received 116 votes, Dominican Republic 60.)

One-round contestation – 3 cases:
- 1977: Bolivia defeated Jamaica in 1 round, 115 votes to 13 (Cuba received 3 votes).
- 1983: Peru defeated Barbados in 1 round, 106 votes to 38.
- 2005: Peru defeated Nicaragua in 1 round, 144 votes to 43.

Total uncontested seats: 33/41 (80%)

WEOG – Western Europe and Others Group (40 seats total)

Multi-round contestation – 6 cases:
- 1978: Portugal defeated Malta in 5 rounds, 99 votes to 45. (In the first round, Portugal received 84 votes, Malta 81.)
- 1982: Malta defeated New Zealand in 3 rounds, 111 votes to 43. (In the first round, Malta received 94 votes, New Zealand 77.)
- 1988: Finland defeated Greece in 3 rounds, 110 votes to 47. (In the first round, Finland received 100 votes, Greece 77.)

(continued)

Box 4.1 *(continued)*

- 1992: New Zealand defeated Sweden in 3 rounds of balloting, 117 votes to 55. (In the first round, New Zealand received 108 votes, Sweden 109.)
- 1996: Portugal defeated Australia in the second round, 124 votes to 57. (In the first round, Portugal received 112 votes, Australia 91.)
- 2000: Norway defeated Italy in 4 rounds of voting, 115 votes to 57. (In the first round, Norway received 114 votes, Italy 94.)

One-round contestation – 3 cases:
- 1980: Spain and Ireland were elected in the first round of balloting with 109 and 107 votes, respectively, while Malta received 74 votes.
- 1986: Italy and Germany were elected in the first round of balloting with 143 and 111 votes, respectively, while Sweden received 16 votes and Ireland 14.
- 1998: Canada and Netherlands were elected in the first round with 131 and 122 votes, respectively, defeating Greece with 87 votes.

Total uncontested seats: 31/40 (78%)

EE – Eastern European Group (21 seats total)

Multi-round contestation – 5 cases:
- 1993: Czech Republic defeated Belarus in 2 rounds of balloting, 127 votes to 47. (In the first round, Czech Republic received 113 votes, Belarus 62.)
- 1999: Ukraine defeated Slovakia in the fourth round of voting when Slovakia withdrew (158 votes to 3). (In the third round, Ukraine received 113 votes, Slovakia 57. In the first round, Ukraine received 92 votes, Slovakia 79.)

One-round contestation – 3 cases:
- 1995: Poland defeated Albania in the first round, 128 votes to 48.
- 1997: Slovenia defeated the former Yugoslav Republic of Macedonia in the first round, 140 votes to 30.
- 2001: Bulgaria defeated Belarus in the first round, 120 votes to 53.

Total uncontested seats: 16/21 (76%).

Total UNGA seats (1965–2005): 205; contested: 37 (18%); uncontested: 168 (82%).
Source: Costa Rica (2005).

Council Report (2011: 6) explains, countries that can claim to straddle more than one geographic region have chosen to shift from one subregion to another, allowing them to run for election more frequently. Even without switching subregions, some members may choose to run more often, whereas others may choose, or are persuaded, to run less frequently or not at all (Security Council Report 2011: 6). The UN official rules offer challengers the right to upset regional norms of rotation. According to the Security Council Report (2009: 6), such queue-jumping occurred three times in our sample period: Ghana queue-jumped Liberia in 1985, and Nigeria queue-jumped Niger in 1977 and Guinea-Bissau in 1993.[12]

So, consequential elections remain rare, but the UNGA does not follow a simple rule of rotation to fill seats. Why, then, do people so often refer to elected UNSC members as "rotating members?" We suggest two reasons.

First of all, the presidency of the UNSC actually does rotate monthly, according to alphabetical order of the English spelling of country names. But this has nothing to do with membership selection.

The second reason for the confusion is more pertinent to this chapter's focus: Regions often – but not always – adhere to a norm of sharing these seats by taking turns, or, in other words, by "rotating" – hence leading to the mistaken idea that selection is by rotation. Africa is particularly known for keeping to the norm.

De jure, the regions may not have much power; they can nominate, but actually any individual country from within the region can self-nominate. De facto, however, regions have dominated the selection process. The vast majority of UNSC elections go uncontested because regions usually nominate a "clean slate" of candidates, with exactly one nomination per regionally designated seat. So the importance of the regional caucuses in the selection of UNSC members should not be underestimated. In most cases, the vote of the General Assembly serves as a rubber stamp on the selections that the regions make, which, in turn, may involve a sort of turn-taking norm.

By contrast, permanent members of the UNSC do not have any de jure privileged role in the selection process. Each permanent member of the UNSC has the same voting power in the General Assembly as every other UN member country. Their veto power, which applies only to substantive matters in UNSC resolutions, does not carry over to UNSC membership selection. Their privileged status in the world may, of course, accord powerful countries more influence in the UNGA, but any such power would be informal. We test for the historic influence of the most prominent members – the United States and the Soviet Union/Russia in Section 4.7.

---

[12] See the *United Nations General Assembly Forty-Eighth Session Official Records* (43rd Plenary Meeting, Friday, October 29, 1993 at 10 a.m. and 3 p.m., respectively), available at http://www.un.org/ga/search/view_doc.asp?symbol=A/48/PV.43 and http://www.un.org/ga/search/view_doc.asp?symbol=A/48/PV.44 (accessed June 24, 2013). We are grateful to Nathaniel Cogley for assistance with this case.

Once a country wins election, it serves a term rigorously limited to two years (see article 23, section 2 of the UN Charter). No elected country has ever served more than two consecutive years.[13] Brazil and Turkey have won the fastest reelections. They both served in 1951–1952 and then were elected anew in October 1953, to serve terms again in 1954–1955.[14] Otherwise, countries always have waited at least two full years before returning.

Bearing in mind the formal rules for UNSC selection, we close this section by presenting our main dependent variable for this chapter in Tables 4.1 through 4.5, which list UNSC participation for each region. Figure 4.1 further presents a map of the world with countries shaded according to the number of years that they served on the UNSC. The map summarizes the pattern that we seek to explain: Why have some countries been elected several times to the UNSC, and others hardly ever or not at all?

A cursory review of the data reveals that Africa appears to have followed a rotational norm – although the queue-jumping by Nigeria and Ghana stands out. Asia and the GRULAC give clear preference to Japan and Brazil, which appear as dominant regional hegemons. The WEOG also seems to have some preference for a hegemon, Germany, but that group also practices a semi-norm of rotation. For example, it usually rotates one seat to a Scandinavian country every four years. The criteria for Eastern Europe do not appear obvious. In the pages that follow in this chapter, we seek to investigate these patterns more rigorously.

4.3 Conjectures

Scant research exists to help guide us in unraveling our puzzle of who wins election to the UNSC.[15] We thus draw on the broader literature in

---

[13] In a handful of cases, countries have served for just one year. Before the expansion of the UNSC in the 1960s, some compromise elections resulted in split terms, where a country from one region served for the first year of the term, and a country from a different region served the second year. In order to set up the staggered elections, some of the original terms – in 1946 and, after expansion, in 1966 – were also cut to one year.

[14] The election of Turkey was controversial as this country contended for the Eastern European seat against Poland, eventually winning after eight rounds of balloting (Costa Rica 2005). Turkey and Poland faced off again in 1959. After 52 rounds of balloting a compromise was finally reached where Poland served in 1960 and Turkey served in 1961, splitting the term.

[15] Like the preceding sections, this section follows Dreher, Gould, Rablen, and Vreeland (2014) and is originally based on Dreher and Vreeland (2009). At this writing, no other published study has addressed the question of UNSC election using quantitative methods. The only published study focuses exclusively on the selection of Western European

TABLE 4.1. *The Africa Group and UNSC Participation (1946–2009)*

	Country	Served on UNSC	Times Elected	UN Membership
Western Africa	Ghana	1962–1963, 1986–1987, 2006–2007	3	1957
	Nigeria	1966–1967, 1978–1979, 1994–1995	3	1960
	Côte d'Ivoire	1964–1965, 1990–1991	2	1960
	Mali	1966–1967, 2000–1001	2	1960
	Senegal	1968–1969, 1988–1989	2	1960
	Guinea	1972–1973, 2002–2003	2	1958
	Benin	1976–1977, 2004–2005	2	1960
	Burkina Faso	1984–1985, 2008–2009	2	1960
	Liberia	1961	1	throughout
	Sierra Leone	1970–1971	1	1961
	Mauritania	1974–1975	1	1961
	Niger	1980–1981	1	1960
	Togo	1982–1983	1	1960
	Cape Verde	1992–1983	1	1975
	Guinea-Bissau	1996–1997	1	1974
	The Gambia	1998–1999	1	1965
Northern/ Central Africa	Egypt	1946, 1949–1950, 1961–1962, 1984–1985, 1996–1997	5	throughout
	Algeria	1968–1969, 1988–1989, 2004–2005	3	1962
	Tunisia	1959–1960, 1980–1981, 2000–2001	3	1956
	Cameroon	1974–1975, 2002–2003	2	1960
	Congo (Rep)	1986–1987, 2006–2007	2	1960
	Gabon	1978–1979, 1998–1999	2	1960
	Libya	1976–1977, 2008–2009	2	1955
	Morocco	1963–1964, 1992–1993	2	1956
	Zaire	1982–1983, 1990–1991	2	1960
	Burundi	1970–1971	1	1962
	Rwanda	1994–1995	1	1962
	Sudan	1972–1973	1	1956
	Never members (membership in the UN in parentheses): Central African Republic (1960), Chad (1960), Equatorial Guinea (1968), Sao Tome and Principe (1975)			
Eastern/ Southern Africa	Zambia	1969–1970, 1979–1980, 1987–1988	3	1964
	Ethiopia	1967–1968, 1989–1990	2	throughout
	Kenya	1973–1974, 1997–1998	2	1963
	Mauritius	1977–1978, 2001–2002	2	1960

Country	Served on UNSC	Times Elected	UN Membership
Tanzania	1975–1976, 2005–2006	2	1961
Uganda	1966, 1981–1982	2	1962
Zimbabwe	1983–1984, 1991–1992	2	1965
Angola	2003–2004	1	1975
Botswana	1995–1996	1	1966
Djibouti	1993–1994	1	1977
Madagascar	1985–1986	1	1960
Namibia	1999–2000	1	1990
Somalia	1971–1972	1	1960
South Africa	2007–2008	1	throughout

Never members (membership in the UN in parentheses): Comoros (1975), Eritrea (1993), Lesotho (1966), Malawi (1964), Mozambique (1975), Seychelles (1976), Swaziland (1968)

international relations and on qualitative accounts of UNSC election to develop several testable hypotheses. We organize these hypotheses into the five questions presented above (Section 4.1).

4.3.1 The UN Charter: International Peace and Security

The UN Charter – chapter V, article 23, section 1 – calls on the members of the UNGA to elect UNSC members on the basis of their contributions to "the maintenance of international peace and security."[16] We thus propose to test the impact of the contributions that countries make to UN peacekeeping missions, measured as the log of the number of troops supplied, on their election to the UNSC (the log of the average annual number of *Peacekeeping troops*). We also include a dichotomous indicator variable to capture whether a country is involved in an international military dispute or a civil war (*War*). We further test for an effect of democracy, which is often associated with openness, justice, and peace (*Democracy*).[17]

countries to various UN committees (Scharioth, 2010). Two working papers on the broader selection of members to the UNSC that have been presented at conferences include Iwanami (2012) and Schmitz and Schwarze (2012). In contrast, several qualitative accounts of the selection of specific UNSC members have been published (see, for example, Malone 1998 and 2000, and Jayakumar 2011).

[16] See: The UN Charter, chapter V, article 23, section 1, available at http://www.un.org/en/documents/charter/chapter5.shtml (accessed December 15, 2013).

[17] On the association of democracy with openness, see Hollyer et al. (2011). On the association with justice see Dowding et al. (2004). On the general proclivity of democracies to peace, see Russett and Oneal (2001). For a contrasting view, see Ferejohn and Rosenbluth (2008).

TABLE 4.2. *The Asia Group and UNSC Participation (1946–2009)*

Country	Served on UNSC	Times Elected	UN Membership
Japan	1958–1959, 1966–1967, 1971–1972, 1975–1976, 1981–1982, 1987–1988, 1992–1993, 1997–1998, 2005–2006	9	1956
India	1950–1951, 1967–1968, 1972–1973, 1977–1978, 1984–1985, 1991–1992	6	throughout
Pakistan	1952–1953, 1968–1969, 1976–1977, 1983–1984, 1993–1994, 2003–2004	6	1947
Philippines	1957, 1963, 1980–1981, 2004–2005	4	throughout
Indonesia	1973–1974, 1995–1996, 2007–2008	3	1950
Malaysia	1965, 1989–1990, 1999–2000	3	1957
Syria*	1947–1978, 1970–1971, 2002–2003	3*	throughout*
Bangladesh	1979–1980, 2000–2001	2	1974
Iraq	1957–1958, 1974–1975	2	throughout
Jordan	1965–1966, 1982–1983	2	1955
Nepal	1969–1970, 1988–1989	2	1955
Turkey*	1951–1952	1	throughout
Bahrain	1998–1999	1	1971
Iran	1955–1956	1	throughout
Kuwait	1978–1979	1	1963
Lebanon	1953–1954	1	throughout
Oman	1994–1995	1	1971
Qatar	2006–2007	1	1971
S. Korea	1996–1997	1	1991
Singapore	2001–2002	1	1965
Sri Lanka	1960–1961	1	1955
Thailand	1985–1986	1	throughout
U.A.E.	1986–1987	1	1971
Yemen*	1990–1991	1	1947
Vietnam	2008–2009	1	1976

Never members (membership in the UN, if after 1946, in parentheses): Afghanistan, Armenia (1992), Azerbaijan (1992), Bhutan (1971), Brunei Darussalam (1984), Cambodia (1955), Cyprus (1960), Democratic People's Republic of Korea (1991), Georgia (1992), Israel (1949), Kazakhstan (1992), Kiribati (1999), Kyrgyzstan (1992), Lao People's Democratic Republic (1955), Maldives (1965)**, Marshall Islands (1991)**, Micronesia (1991)**, Mongolia (1961), Myanmar (1948), Nauru (1999)**, Palau (1994)**, Papua New Guinea (1975)**, Samoa (1976)**, Saudi Arabia, Solomon Islands (1978)**, Tajikistan (1992), Timor-Leste (2002)**, Tonga (1999)**, Turkmenistan (1992), Tuvalu (2000)**, Uzbekistan (1992), Vanuatu (1981)**

* Syria also had representation in 1961 because it had joined with Egypt to form the United Arab Republic in 1958. The United Arab Republic was elected to serve 1961–1962, but Syria left the union in September 1961. Egypt retained the seat (and the name until 1971). Turkey was elected to represent the Middle East. It has also represented EE (twice) and the WEOG (once). People's Democratic Republic of Yemen and Yemen Arab Republic were separate members of the UN until 1990 when the two countries united as the single member Yemen.

** Oceana country.

TABLE 4.3. *The GRULAC and UNSC Participation (1946–2009)*

Country	Served on UNSC	Times Elected	UN Membership
Brazil	1946–1947, 1951–1952, 1954–1955, 1963–1964, 1967–1968, 1988–1989, 1993–1994, 1998–1999, 2004–2005	9	throughout
Argentina	1948–1949, 1959–1960, 1966–1967, 1971–1972, 1987–1988, 1994–1955, 1999–2000, 2005–2006	8	throughout
Colombia	1947–1948, 1953–1954, 1957–1958, 1969–1970, 1989–1990, 2001–2002	6	throughout
Panama	1958–1959, 1972–1973, 1976–1977, 1981–1982, 2007–2008	5	throughout
Chile	1952–1953, 1961–1962, 1996–1997, 2003–2004	4	throughout
Peru	1955–1956, 1973–1974, 1984–1985, 2006–2007	4	throughout
Venezuela	1962–1963, 1977–1978, 1986–1987, 1992–1993	4	throughout
Costa Rica	1974–1975, 1997–1998, 2008–2009	3	throughout
Cuba	1949–1950, 1956–1957, 1990–1991	3	throughout
Ecuador	1950–1951, 1960–1961, 1991–1992	3	throughout
Mexico	1946, 1980–1981, 2002–2002	3	throughout
Bolivia	1964–1965, 1978–1979	2	throughout
Guyana	1975–1976, 1982–1983	2	1966
Jamaica	1979–1980, 2000–2001	2	1962
Nicaragua	1970–1971, 1983–1984	2	throughout
Honduras	1995–1996	1	throughout
Paraguay	1968–1969	1	throughout
Trinidad & Tobago	1985–1986	1	1962
Uruguay	1965–1966	1	throughout

Never members (membership in the UN, if after 1946, in parentheses): Antigua & Barbuda (1981), Bahamas (1973), Barbados (1966), Belize (1981), Dominica (1978), Dominican Republic, El Salvador, Grenada (1974), Guatemala, Haiti, St. Kitts & Nevis (1983), St. Lucia (1979), St. Vincent & Grenadines (1980), Suriname (1975)

Note that the UN Charter also calls for due regard "to equitable geographical distribution."[18] The selection process ensures a specific geographical distribution by assigning seats by region, as outlined above in Section 4.2. The regions themselves may further ensure an equitable distribution within their own geography by practicing a norm of taking turns. We return to this possibility at the end of this section.

[18] UN Charter, chapter V, article 23, section 1. For a discussion, see Thakur (1999).

TABLE 4.4. *The Eastern Europe Group and UNSC Participation (1946–2009)*

Country	Served on UNSC	Times Elected	UN Membership
Poland	1946–1947, 1960, 1970–1971, 1982–1983, 1996–1997	5	throughout
Romania	1962, 1976–1977, 1990–1991, 2004–2005	4	1955
Yugoslavia	1956, 1950–1951, 1972–1973, 1988–1989	4	throughout (ended 1991)
Bulgaria	1966–1967, 1986–1987, 2002–2003	3	1955
Ukraine*	1948–1949, 1984–1985, 2000–2001	3	1991
Czechoslovakia	1964, 1978–1979	2	throughout (ended 1993)
Hungary	1968–1969, 1992–1993	2	1955
Turkey**	1954–1955, 1961	2	throughout
Slovenia	1998–1999	1	1992
Slovakia	2006–2007	1	1993
Belarus*	1974–1975	1	1945
Croatia	2008–2009	1	1992
Czech Republic	1994–1995	1	1993
East Germany	1980–1981	1	1973 (ended 1990)

Never members (membership in the UN in parentheses): Albania (1955), Bosnia and Herzegovina (1992), Estonia (1991), Latvia (1991), Lithuania (1991), Macedonia (1991), Moldova (1992), Montenegro (2006), Serbia (2006, Serbia and Montenegro (1991–2006)
* Not sovereign until 1991.
** Turkey has also represented the Middle East (once) and the WEOG (once).

Nevertheless, while the UN Charter guidelines may hold some influence over how UN member states choose their representatives on the Security Council, the Charter does not constitute a mandate, and the UN delegates in the General Assembly remain free to vote however they wish. We thus turn to variables that may capture their preferences more directly.

4.3.2 Foreign Assistance

Statesmen and scholars alike contend that foreign aid and other financial perks go to strategically important countries.[19] To the extent that foreign

[19] Morgenthau (1962: 302); Maizels and Nissanke (1984); Zimmerman (1993); Boone (1996); Ruttan (1996); Dollar and Pritchett (1998); Schraeder et al. (1998); Lancaster (1999, 2000, 2006); Alesina and Dollar (2000); Kilby (2013b); Berthélemy and Tichit (2004); Kuziemko and Werker (2006); Anwar and Michaelowa (2006); Boschini and Olofsgård (2007); Vreeland (2011); Dreher, Nunnenkamp, and Thiele (2011); Dreher and Fuchs (2011a, 2011b); Mazumder and Vreeland (2013).

TABLE 4.5. *The WEOG and UNSC Participation (1946–2009)*

Country	Served on UNSC	Times Elected	UN Membership
Canada	1948–1949, 1958–1959, 1967–1968, 1977–1978, 1989–1990, 1999–2000	6	throughout
Italy	1959–1960, 1971–1972, 1975–1976, 1987–1988, 1995–1996, 2007–2008	6	throughout
Belgium	1947–1948, 1955–1956, 1971–1972, 1991–1992, 2007–2008	5	throughout
Netherlands	1946, 1951–1952, 1965–1956, 1983–1984, 1999–2000	5	throughout
Australia	1946–1947, 1956–1957, 1973–1974, 1985–1986	4	throughout
Denmark	1953–1954, 1967–1968, 1985–1986, 2005–2006	4	throughout
Germany*	1977–1978, 1987–1988, 1995–1996, 2003–2004	4	1973
Norway	1949–1950, 1963–1964, 1979–1980, 2001–2002	4	throughout
Spain	1969–1970, 1981–1982, 1993–1994, 2003–2004	4	1955
Ireland	1962, 1981–1982, 2001–2002	3	1955
Austria	1973–1974, 1991–1992, 2009–2010	3	1955
New Zealand	1954–1995, 1966, 1993–1994	3	throughout
Sweden	1957–1958, 1975–1976, 1997–1998	3	throughout
Finland	1969–1970, 1989–1990	2	1955
Greece	1952–1953, 2005–2006	2	throughout
Portugal	1979–1980, 1997–1998	2	1955
Malta	1983–1984	1	1964
Turkey**	2009–2010	1	throughout

Never members (membership in the UN, if after 1946, in parentheses): Andorra (1993), Iceland, Israel (1949)***, Liechtenstein (1990), Luxembourg, Monaco (1993), San Marino (1992), Switzerland (2002)

    * East Germany also served once (1980–1981).

  ** Turkey has also represented the Middle East (1951–1952) and EE/Asia (1954–1955, 1961).

*** Israel was without a caucusing group until joining the WEOG in 2000 (Security Council Report 2011: 6).

aid proxies the importance of a country, those that receive these financial benefits may also have a greater chance of winning election to the UNSC. If so, we may confront a problem of endogeneity which would complicate our investigation of the effects of UNSC membership in the analyses to come in Chapter 5.

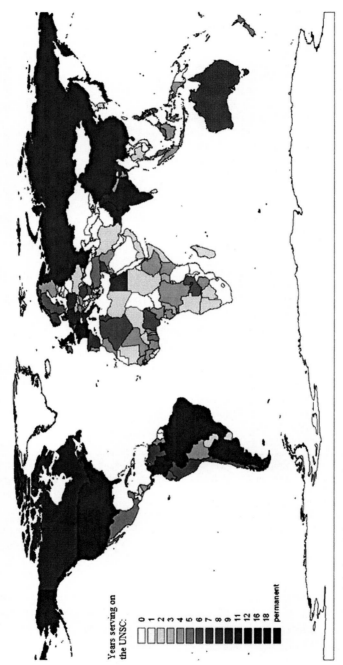

FIGURE 4.1. Global participation on the UN Security Council (1946–2005).

To test for this potential issue, we consider the world's most prominent donor of strategically motivated foreign aid, the United States. We break up U.S. assistance into two components – *U.S. development aid* and *U.S. military assistance* (both measured as the log of constant 2011 dollars). We also consider the two global financial institutions where the United States has the most powerful voice, the World Bank and the IMF. We test whether the number of *New World Bank projects* and *IMF program participation* predict election to the UNSC.[20] We limit our attention to the United States, the World Bank, and the IMF for theoretical and practical reasons. From a theoretical point of view, our focus makes sense because of the prominent place of the United States and the two Bretton Woods Institutions in the world. From a practical point of view, our study requires some degree of parsimony. If we include foreign aid from all potential countries and loans from all multilateral organizations, degrees of freedom become too low for our model to be identified. Our preliminary analyses of foreign aid patterns from other OECD countries and regional organizations do not reveal any statistically significant correlation with UNSC election. We suggest the in-depth exploration of other countries – for example Japan's use of foreign aid to win favor – for future work.

Note that if countries expect financial perks from membership on the UNSC, then perhaps more heavily indebted governments push harder to be elected. Causality may, of course, run the other way – through a type of moral hazard. Perhaps when governments anticipate that they will be elected to the UNSC, they allow their countries to go deeper into debt, anticipating a bailout on the horizon. Either way, levels of indebtedness may predict UNSC membership. We test this hypothesis using *Debt service* as a percentage of gross national income (GNI).

4.3.3 Power: A Realist View

Heavily indebted countries may well desire membership but lack the political and financial capital necessary to win sufficient support. Stiff competition for UNSC seats may lead the most powerful countries to win

---

[20] IMF programs themselves come in cycles (Conway 2007). Omitting participation in IMF programs might thus bias our results in favor of finding a turn-taking norm. Moreover, a substantial literature argues that IMF and World Bank loans might be given for political-economic reasons rather than just need (e.g., Stone 2002; Kilby 2009a, 2013a; Weaver 2008; Reynaud and Vauday 2009).

election most often. Having worked with the Canadian government in their successful 1998 election bid, David M. Malone (2000: 13) notes the importance of campaign funds. Canada, for example, apparently spent US$1.3 million in its efforts to gain a seat at the UNSC table. The former UN representative from Singapore, S. Jayakumar, similarly reports that campaigning takes place over several years and requires considerable political and financial capital (Jayakumar 2011: 65). In his study of the WEOG, Scharioth (2010) finds that "realist" variables, measuring a country's power, predict election to a wide range of UN committees.

To test the impact of a country's global importance, we consider three measures: *Population* (log), per capita income (*GNI per capita*, measured as the log of constant U.S. dollars), and *Territory* size (log).[21]

Political connections may also influence election prospects. Foreign aid, as stated above, may serve as a proxy for the strategic importance of a country. We further measure international connections in four ways. First, we include measures of how frequently countries vote in the General Assembly with the United States and, alternatively, the Soviet Union/Russia (*USA voting in the UNGA* and *Russia voting in the UNGA*). Second, we include a dichotomous indicator *Pariah state* for countries with "pariah" status in the eyes of one or more of the major powers, and hence subject to U.S. and/or UN sanctions, as defined by Morgan, Krustev, and Bapat (2006).[22] Third, we test for the effects

---

[21] Following Dreher, Gould, Rablen, and Vreeland (2014), we use GNI per capita (as opposed to the more common GDP per capita) because it is the income measure used by the UN itself in the computation of member-state contributions to the general and peace-keeping budgets. We also follow the UN's methodology in using U.S. dollar exchange rate estimates of GNI. International, rather than domestic, purchasing power is more relevant in the realist context.

[22] We code a country-year observation as a pariah if it is subject to sanctions imposed by the United States and/or conducted through the UN (through the Security Council or General Assembly). Note that, following Morgan et al. (2006), "The motion need not have been passed [through the United Nations or Security Council], but at least one member of the institution must threaten or propose that the body as a collective adopt sanctions against the target." We do not code country-years as "pariahs" if (1) sanctions target trade practices, (2) data on the type of threat are missing, (3) the anticipated costs are not coded as "major" or "severe" (we consider pariahs only as those under "major" and/or "severe" sanctions), (4) sanctions target a particular industry or industries, or (5) the country acquiesced to demands before sanctions were imposed or capitulated at the threat stage. We use the 2009 updated version of the Morgan, Krustev, Bapat (2006) dataset, called Threat and Imposition of Sanctions (TIES version 3.5). The dataset covers 1971 through 2008. We extend the data by including three major sanctions episodes, which began before 1971: Cuba (1960–present), North Korea (1950–present) and South Africa (1963–1994). Our main findings on the pariah variable hold, however, when

of membership in key UN groupings. For Asia and the GRULAC, we consider membership in the Group of 77 (G77) and the Non-Aligned Movement (NAM) – *G77 and NAM*.[23] For Africa and Asia, we consider membership in the Organisation of Islamic Cooperation (*OIC*). For the WEOG, we consider membership in JUSCANZ (a subset of the WEOG including Australia, Canada, Japan, New Zealand, and the United States) – *JUSCANZ*. Membership in certain non-UN groupings may also matter; we allow for an effect of membership of the European Union (*EU*) and NATO (*NATO*), which may matter for the WEOG and Eastern Europe.

4.3.4 Historical, Political, and Religious Connections

Governments may tend to favor countries with which they share some degree of cultural affinity. Variables we use to test the influence of historical background include indicators of *British* or *French* colonization. We test whether the religious complexion of a country matters by including the percentage of the country that is *Muslim* or, alternatively, *Catholic*.

Beyond historical and religious factors, we test the importance of political affinity within the region, measuring the percentage of the region with which the chief executive shares the same broad political ideology (either left, center, right, or nonideological – *Shared regional ideology*).[24] We further consider another variable that may be related to political culture: the *Control of corruption* within a country. On the one hand, perceived corruption may hurt if regions and the UNGA disdain such countries. On the other, the practice of corruption might also serve as an advantage to governments ready to jump the queue and pay whatever bribes necessary to win support, while showing a complete disregard for any norms of turn-taking.

---

we leave out the sanctions against South Africa, North Korea, and Cuba, and/or we restrict our analysis to the 1971–2008 period. (That is, they hold whether we recode the sanctions for the three countries as zero or whether we drop them from the analysis entirely.) For a discussion of the additional cases see Combs (2012) and Levy (1999).

[23] Again following Dreher, Gould, Rablen, and Vreeland (2014), indicator variables for membership in each cannot be included in the same regression equation because of substantial overlap in membership between G77 and NAM. Instead we create three separate indicator variables: one for countries that are members of both groupings, and one for countries that are members only of G77 (*G77 only, not in NAM*), or, respectively, only of NAM (*NAM only, not in G77*).

[24] We calculate the percentage of the region according to the number of the countries in the region – minus the country in question – sharing the same ideology (left, center, or right). The variable is coded 0 for nonideological governments. See Beck et al. (2001) for the coding of ideology.

4.3.5 Taking Turns

Taking turns has evolved as a widely observed norm among humans and many other species (see, for example, Bendor and Swistak 2001, Colman and Browning 2009, and Franz et al. 2011). In the context of the UNSC election process, the *Turn-taking norm* implies that membership on the UNSC should rotate among the members of each caucusing group. The norm is suggested by the reference in the UN Charter to "an equitable geographical distribution" of the elected members of the UNSC.

Only Africa explicitly claims to operate according to the turn-taking norm, although queue-jumping has occurred a few times even in this region. Still, some evidence of turn-taking exists for each region, as seen in the previous section. But there is also evidence of competition. Even if the region nominates a clean slate and the election is not contested, the selected candidate may have previously served on the UNSC many times (such as Japan, which has won several unopposed elections). We therefore seek to establish whether a turn-taking norm plays a statistically significant role in selecting UNSC members. Is such a pattern systematic or idiosyncratic?

To test the possibility that a region practices the turn-taking norm, we construct a variable, *Turn-taking norm*, which we calculate as the number of years a country has waited to serve on the UNSC divided by the number of countries currently eligible for election. The variable resets to 0 every time the country serves. Under perfect turn-taking with a constant number of countries that have been regularly rotating in the queue, a country's turn should arrive when the value of this variable for that country reaches 1.0. Now, we have seen above that perfect turn-taking does not hold in any region. But if turn-taking holds at all, this variable should be positively correlated with election. It basically represents a measure of how long a country has been "waiting" to serve on the UNSC, conditioned on how many countries potentially are in the queue.

4.3.6 Summary

In sum, we consider five broad perspectives: (1) a commitment to peace, (2) a foreign-aid story, (3) a realist international relations perspective, (4) a story of historical, political, and religious factors, and (5) a turn-taking norm. Table 4.6 summarizes our hypotheses and the variables we use to test them in the pages that follow, along with the sources of our data.

TABLE 4.6. *Hypotheses and Variables Used in Testing the Determinants of UNSC Election*

Do governments follow a norm of choosing countries committed to peace?

War	Indicator coded 1 if a country is engaged in an inter- or intrastate war, 0 otherwise (Themnér and Wallensteen 2012).
Peacekeeping troops (log)	Log of the average monthly military manpower supplied to UN peacekeeping operations per year (plus 1) (Heldt 2008, Heldt and Wallensteen 2006).
Democracy indicator	Indicator coded 1 if contested elections fill the executive and legislative branches of government, 0 otherwise (Cheibub et al. 2010).

Does foreign aid determine election?

U.S. development aid (log)	Log of U.S. development assistance going to the country in constant U.S. dollars (plus 1) (USAID 2011).
U.S. military assistance (log)	Log of U.S. military assistance going to the country in constant U.S. dollars (plus 1) (USAID 2011).
IMF program participation	Indicator coded 1 if a country participated in an IMF program during any part of the year, 0 otherwise (Vreeland 2007).
New World Bank projects	Number of new World Bank projects starting during the year (Dreher et al. 2009a).
Debt service	Debt service as a percentage of gross national income (World Bank 2011).

Is election driven by international power or relationships with powerful countries?

Population (log)	Log of population (UN Statistics Division 2011).
GNI per capita (log)	Log of real GNI per capita in U.S. dollars (UN Statistics Division 2011).
Territory (log)	Log of territorial size in square kilometers (CIA 2012).
USA voting in the UNGA	Voting in line with the United States at the UNGA – % all votes the same; abstain = 0.5 (Voeten and Merdzanovic 2009 and Strezhnev and Voeten 2012; coded as in Dreher and Sturm 2012).
USSR/Russia voting in the UNGA	Voting in line with the Soviet Union/Russia at the UNGA – % all votes the same; abstain = 0.5 (Voeten and Merdzanovic 2009; coded as in Dreher and Sturm 2012).
Pariah state	Indicator coded 1 if a country is subject to UN/U.S. sanctions, 0 otherwise (Morgan et al. 2006).
G77 and NAM	Indicator coded 1 if a country is a member of the G77 and NAM, 0 otherwise.

(continued)

TABLE 4.6 *(continued)*

G77 only, not in NAM	Indicator coded 1 if a country is a member of the G77 and not a member of NAM, 0 otherwise (http://www.g77.org/).
NAM only, not in G77	Indicator coded 1 if a country is a member of NAM and not a member of the G77, 0 otherwise (http://www.nam.gov.za/).
OIC	Indicator coded 1 if a country is a member of OIC, 0 otherwise (http://www.oic-oci.org/).
JUSCANZ	Indicator coded 1 if a country is a member of JUSCANZ, 0 otherwise (http://www.eyeontheun.org/view.asp?p=55&l=11).
EU	Indicator coded 1 if a country is a member of EU, 0 otherwise (http://www.europa.eu/).
NATO	Indicator coded 1 if a country is a member of NATO, 0 otherwise (http://www.nato.int/).

Do shared cultural traits play a role?

Former British colony	Indicator coded 1 if a country is a former British colony, 0 otherwise (Przeworski et al. 2000).
Former French colony	Indicator coded 1 if a country is a former French colony, 0 otherwise (Przeworski et al. 2000).
Shared regional ideology	Proportion of the chief executives in the region sharing the same political ideology – left, center, right (Beck et al. 2001).
% Muslim	Muslims as a proportion of the total population, time invariant (Przeworski et al. 2000).
% Catholic	Catholics as a proportion of the total population, time invariant (Przeworski et al. 2000).
Control of corruption	Score indicating perceptions of the extent to which public power is exercised for private gain (Kaufmann et al. 2011).

Do governments practice a turn-taking norm, rotating membership through eligible candidates?

Turn-taking norm	Number of years since most recently becoming eligible for election to the UNSC divided by number of other countries eligible (author calculations).

Control variable

Arab seat	Indicator for Arab countries eligible for election to the Arab swing seat (coded 1 for Arab countries in Africa every fourth year beginning 1972; 1 for Arab countries in Asia every fourth year beginning 1970; 0 otherwise).

4.4 The Statistical Model

To test the hypotheses discussed in the previous section, we employ a specially tailored statistical model designed to address a number of features specific to the process of selecting temporary UNSC members. The approach, originally developed by Matthew Gould of the University of Westminster and Matthew D. Rablen of Brunel University, builds on existing statistical models that themselves would fail to capture important aspects of UNSC elections. We highlight the two key features of the new model as they differ from standard regression models with which our broad readership may be most familiar:

1. UNSC selection resembles a horse race in that one candidate wins per seat, and all others, by definition, lose that seat. So, observations of countries in a given year cannot be independent of each other. Indeed, the selection of one country to represent a region directly implies the nonselection of the other countries in the region.
2. UNSC selection has a nomination process followed by an election. Regions typically dominate the nomination process and tend to nominate a clean slate of candidates. If, and only if, elections are contested does the UNGA cast a meaningful vote.

The mathematical details of the model are available in Dreher, Gould, Rablen, and Vreeland (2014).[25] Here, we present the intuitions:

To deal with the first issue, we model the probability that a country wins UNSC election *conditioned* on the total number of open seats for the region to which the country belongs – either zero, one, or two seats per year. In other words, rather than assuming that each country's status of winning UNSC election represents a random draw, we explicitly account for the fact that if one country wins a seat, no other country can win it that year.

Consider, for example, the thirty-three countries of the GRULAC. Exactly one of these countries wins election each year to serve a two-year term. In any given year, one country is currently serving on the UNSC, and one country is facing a term limit as it is stepping down from serving on the UNSC and so cannot run for reelection. This leaves thirty-one countries eligible for election, and we know that exactly one of them

---

[25] Also see the appendix to this chapter.

must be selected. In terms of our dependent variable, one country wins (and is coded 1), while the others lose (and are coded 0). There exists a definitional relationship between the coding of winners and losers, so they cannot represent independent, random draws. Scholars of econometric models will recognize that we follow McFadden (1973) and Chamberlain (1980) in addressing this issue.[26] (For readers familiar with this literature, this aspect of the model is similar to a logit conditioned on year by region.)

Turning to the second issue, we note that, depending on the region, the caucusing group decides between 76 percent and 87 percent of the seats, but the UNGA decides the remaining seats, holding contested elections (recall Box 4.1). The model incorporates this two-stage process explicitly with a simple weighting of the preferences of the caucusing group (which shape the nominations) and those of the UNGA (which votes over nominated candidates). We include a parameter that measures the weight attributable to the preferences of the UNGA. Formally, we call the parameter $\alpha_{j,t} \in [0,1]$, where the subscript j denotes the region and t denotes the year so the parameter may vary by region and year. More formally, we define the parameter as

$$\alpha_{j,t} = (\text{Nominations}_{j,t} - \text{Seats}_{j,t}) \,/\, (\text{Eligible Countries}_{j,t} - \text{Seats}_{j,t}).$$

Putting the above equation into words, the parameter $\alpha_{j,t}$ equals the number of nominated candidates – minus the number of seats eligible for a region, divided by the number of eligible countries – again – minus the number of seats eligible for a region. Hence, when the region nominates exactly as many candidates as there are seats, the above equation reduces to zero, $\alpha_{j,t} = 0$, and we place all of the weight on the region's preference. This situation actually holds for about 83 percent of our cases. Now, if a region were to nominate all eligible countries (which has never happened), then the above equation would result in $\alpha_{j,t} = 1$, and we would place all of the weight on the UNGA's preferences. The intuition is clear: Nominating all of the eligible countries in a region would essentially abdicate the decision from the region to the UNGA. While this extreme outcome never happens, the number of nominations exceeds the number of seats in about 17 percent of the cases, and in these cases, our parameter places some weight on the UNGA: $\alpha_{j,t} > 0$. In other words, we model the first

---

[26] Also see Green et al. (2001). We build on these models, following Manski and Sherman (1980) to allow for multiple-discrete choices in our model.

stage as reducing the choice set for the UNGA, leaving the UNGA to remain decisive only to a partial extent.[27]

Putting the two pieces of the model together, Equation 4.1 presents (for advanced readers) the probability that a given country wins UNSC election in a given year from a given region as:

$$\Pr\left(y_{i,j,t} = 1\right) = \alpha_{j,t}\left[\beta'_{GA} x_{i,j,t}\right] + \left(1 - \alpha_{j,t}\right)\left[\beta'_j x_{i,j,t}\right] + \varepsilon_{i,j,t}, \quad (4.1)$$

where $y = 1$ if country i of region j wins election in year t, and 0 otherwise; β_{GA} denotes a vector of parameters that captures the effects of variables x for the UNGA, while β_j denotes a region-specific vector of parameters that captures the effects of variables x for region j. In order to make the model mathematically tractable, we must assume, following Manski and Sherman (1980), that draws of the stochastic component, $\varepsilon_{i,j,t}$, are independent across regions and time (and have identical type-1 extreme value distributions).

The appendix to this chapter presents more technical details. For now, we summarize the model for people who have some familiarity with econometric modeling:

One may think of the model as the sum of two logits, weighted by a parameter $\alpha_{j,t}$ so they sum up to one. The weight, $\alpha_{j,t}$, is a function of the degree of choice granted to the UNGA – how much the UNGA preferences matter compared to the preferences of the region.

4.5 Year, Country, and Cold War Effects

During certain years, the selection of UNSC members has proven more contentious than others. The model we employ addresses such idiosyncrasies by implicitly accounting for fixed-effects of years. (For advanced readers, it does so in a manner much the same as does a conditional logit, conditioned on year. It is indeed important to account for the fact that zero, one, or two countries may be selected from a given region each year, as mentioned above.)

We might further like to address fixed-effects of countries – although it is not obvious that we should do so. We would certainly have a more

---

[27] Some readers may wonder why we do not explicitly model the probability of winning a contested UNGA election conditional on winning regional nomination. We have found that such a mathematically complicated model does not converge for the limited dataset that we have.

accurate assessment of the robustness of the determinants of UNSC selection if we employed a country fixed-effects model. Such a model, being more restrictive, would likely rule out certain findings. In fact, we report below that some of our statistically significant findings are really driven by a single idiosyncratic case. Beyond discovering the determinants of UNSC election, however, another overarching goal of this chapter is to identify variables that might lead to selection bias when we assess the effects of UNSC membership in the next chapter. From this point of view, we may want a less restrictive model that does not include country fixed-effects.[28]

At any rate, the data resolve this debate: We simply do not have enough degrees of freedom to include country indicators – if we do so, the model fails to converge. So, below, we present the model without country fixed-effects. Note, however, that Matthew Gould and Matthew Rablen developed a methodology in our work with them to test for the most important country-outliers and include control variables for them in the model. Thus, in addition to the results that we present here, we also reference our findings in Dreher, Gould, Rablen, and Vreeland (2014), where we include fixed-effects for country-outliers.

Finally, we consider the potential preference change that occurred with the end of the Cold War. Kim and Russett (1996) present evidence that voting patterns in the UNGA shifted from an East-West orientation toward a North-South orientation when the Cold War ended – although Voeten's (2000) analysis suggests much subtler changes between the two periods (also see Stent and Shevtsova 2002).

Ideally, we would report separate sets of results for the Cold War and post–Cold War period. Again, however, data and model limitations trump: When we analyze only one of the time periods, the model fails to converge.[29] Gould and Rablen's approach for selecting the most robust predictors of UNSC selection also addresses this problem. In our research with them, we report separate estimates for these two periods for variables where the effects for each period differ. Our main results presented in Section 4.7 thus focus on the pooled results for the entire time period, and we also discuss differing effects for certain variables during and after the Cold War period that come from our study with Gould and Rablen.

---

[28] We are grateful to Erik Voeten for this suggestion.

[29] We also found this problem even when we examined certain specifications using a simpler conditional logit model in our early work (Dreher and Vreeland 2009).

4.6 Model Estimation

Table 4.7 presents the results from estimating the model described in the previous section for 180 UNSC elections between 1970 and 2005 using a sample of 189 countries for a total of 5,330 country-year observations (the panel is unbalanced because new UN member states enter the sample, and a few exit).

We employ the full set of independent variables discussed in Section 4.3. To match the timing of the election process, we lag the independent variables by one year relative to UNSC membership. We account for the *Arab swing seat* by including an indicator for Arab countries eligible for election to the seat in a given year for Africa, Asia, and the UNGA. As the arrangement to select one Arab country – from, alternatively, Africa or Asia – has been respected throughout, the variable has a strong positive significant effect for both regions. It has no effect at the UNGA level because these selections are almost never contested. Obviously, we do not include the Arab swing seat variable for the other regions. We also drop indicator variables with insufficient variation for certain regions – mostly variables indicating membership in a group but also the Pariah state and War indicators for EE and the WEOG. Model convergence has proven a problem when we include variables with so little (or no) variation.

Regarding missing data, while each individual variable in our dataset is well-populated, when taken together as a group, a significant number of country-years have observations missing for at least one variable (2,396 observations out of a total of 5,342 observations). Dropping incomplete country-years is problematic for both practical and theoretical reasons. From a practical perspective, if we exclude all observations that suffer from some missing data, the sample size becomes too small for the results to remain meaningful for some regions (especially for Eastern Europe, where we have the most missing data). Again, model convergence becomes a problem. From a theoretical perspective, because observations are not independent, excluding one country-year because of missing data can bias the estimates for the remaining countries in that year. We therefore impute missing data and then correct the estimation of our standard errors for the imputed data.[30]

---

[30] The variables with missing data include voting with the United States/Russia in the UNGA (*USA voting in the UNGA, Russia voting in the UNGA*), debt service (% *GNI*), shared regional ideology, and control of corruption. We impute each of these using a

TABLE 4.7. *The Determinants of UNSC Election*

Variable	Africa	Asia	EE	GRULAC	WEOG	UNGA
Turn-taking norm	3.17***	2.38***	0.88***	0.51	3.00***	− 4.62
	(4.65)	(2.84)	(3.03)	(0.92)	(5.46)	(0.70)
War	− 1.25	− 1.84*		0.72		16.65
	(1.58)	(1.82)		(0.86)		(0.59)
Peacekeeping	0.15	0.26*	0.15	0.21*	0.56***	− 2.09
troops (log)	(1.61)	(1.92)	(0.56)	(1.83)	(2.91)	(0.67)
Democracy	− 0.12	0.57	0.67	− 0.19	14.55***	− 13.09
	(0.19)	(0.71)	(0.51)	(0.38)	(4.00)	(0.77)
U.S. development	0.01	0.03	− 0.04	0.02	− 0.18*	2.13
aid (log)	(0.31)	(0.66)	(0.34)	(0.37)	(1.92)	(1.39)
U.S. military	− 0.03	0.05	0.36*	− 0.05	− 0.11	2.45***
assistance (log)	(0.92)	(1.06)	(1.81)	(1.50)	(1.47)	(3.32)
IMF program	0.36	0.10	0.80	0.33	2.03	0.92
participation	(0.80)	(0.16)	(0.76)	(0.60)	(1.37)	(0.06)
New World Bank	0.11	0.07	− 0.03	0.06	0.73	− 6.72**
projects	(1.08)	(0.64)	(0.19)	(0.78)	(1.03)	(2.42)
Debt service (%	0.53*	0.12	0.08	0.95**	− 0.37	3.91
GNI)	(1.73)	(0.23)	(0.12)	(2.04)	(0.65)	(0.39)
Population (log)	0.31	1.59***	− 0.30	0.28	1.55***	15.97**
	(1.59)	(3.26)	(0.26)	(0.80)	(3.03)	(2.15)
GNI per capita	0.39*	0.79**	0.20	1.29***	0.29	− 2.23
(log)	(1.67)	(2.14)	(0.32)	(3.43)	(0.16)	(0.24)
Territory (log)	− 0.03	− 0.43*	1.29	0.18	− 0.07	− 10.62**
	(0.19)	(1.95)	(0.87)	(0.82)	(0.23)	(2.33)
USA voting in the	− 6.78**	7.30	− 0.12	− 2.56	− 14.89	245.96
UNGA	(1.99)	(1.33)	(0.02)	(0.39)	(1.51)	(1.51)
Russia voting in	3.14	2.34	1.38	7.24	− 13.86*	335.76**
the UNGA	(0.91)	(0.41)	(0.16)	(1.18)	(1.69)	(2.26)
Pariah state	− 0.92	1.39		0.62		24.34
	(0.74)	(1.12)		(0.41)		(0.69)
G77 and NAM		− 0.94		4.23***		1.42
		(0.95)		(2.89)		(0.04)
G77 only, not in		− 13.02***		3.86***		− 9.30
NAM		(6.21)		(2.78)		(0.21)
NAM only, not in						18.08
G77						(0.53)
OIC	− 0.23					39.62
	(0.37)					(1.23)
JUSCANZ					− 1.03	64.38**
					(0.64)	(2.08)
EU			32.54***		0.97	− 7.20
			(14.68)		(0.62)	(0.25)
NATO			− 17.50***		0.26	− 20.80
			(9.06)		(0.19)	(0.97)

(*continued*)

TABLE 4.7 *(continued)*

Variable	Africa	Asia	EE	GRULAC	WEOG	UNGA
Former British	0.57	1.61**		1.50	0.81	15.59
colony	(1.15)	(2.15)		(1.53)	(0.35)	(0.97)
Former French	0.56					19.47
colony	(1.24)					(0.65)
Shared regional	− 0.08	− 1.86	3.34*	2.17	1.80	− 4.64
ideology	(0.07)	(0.63)	(1.75)	(1.64)	(0.61)	(0.15)
Muslim (%)	0.09	1.35	− 3.53	12.77	− 23.30	− 29.57
	(0.11)	(0.90)	(1.01)	(1.54)	(0.84)	(0.70)
Catholic (%)	0.05	1.85	0.01	3.28	0.85	− 1.71
	(0.07)	(1.07)	(0.00)	(1.60)	(0.51)	(0.10)
Control of	− 0.69**	− 0.07	− 0.13	− 0.55	0.63	9.93
corruption	(2.22)	(0.12)	(0.14)	(1.49)	(0.66)	(0.84)
Arab swing seat	1.90***	18.53***				− 5.21
	(5.24)	(20.93)				(0.21)

Notes: The dependent variable is an indicator for election to the UNSC. Estimation is with MLE. The sample includes 5,330 country-year observations from 1970 to 2005 covering a total of 189 countries (panel is unbalanced due to states entering and leaving the sample). Numbers in parentheses are the absolute values of t-statistics. As per convention, we mark coefficients with * if $p < 0.10$ (statistical significance at the 10% confidence level); with ** if $p < 0.05$ (statistical significance at the 5% confidence level); and with *** if $p < 0.01$ (statistical significance at the 1% confidence level). Some variables are not included for all regions due to insufficient variation, which prevents model convergence.

We report robust standard errors, adjusted for the imputed data, and clustered on region × year, which allows for within-region and within-year correlation, respectively, and heteroskedasticity.

We stress caution regarding the results for Eastern Europe and the UNGA because of the limited number of observations that these groups include. The EE group contains the fewest countries and the most imputed data. As for the UNGA, only 36 out of the 180 elections in our sample

truncated regression (to reflect, for example, non-negativity constraints) that includes as independent variables all those variables that are fully observed. IMF program participation is the only binary variable to have some missing observations; we similarly impute data for this variable, but with a logistic regression. For most of these variables, we need only impute one observation per country-year, so only a small proportion (around 6 percent) of the data points that enter the regression analysis are imputed. To correct the standard errors, we perform ten imputations. For a methodological discussion of missing data and imputation in political science, see King, Honaker, Joseph, and Scheve (2001). For substantive discussions of the determinants of missing data, see Hollyer, Rosendorff, and Vreeland (2011) and Mitchell (1998).

(1970–2005) are contested, for an average of exactly one of the five elections held each year.

Note that the order of magnitude of the estimated effects for the UNGA is misleading. Recall that the model weighs UNGA preferences by $\alpha_{j,t}$, and group preferences by $(1 - \alpha_{j,t})$ in the composite utility function. For many years, $\alpha_{j,t} = 0$, and even for election years with non-zero values of $\alpha_{j,t}$, its value is typically close to zero: the mean of alpha is 0.008 and the maximum value is 0.111. So the UNGA coefficients that we estimate are offset by the very low weight UNGA preferences receive in the composite preference. That said, the calculation of the marginal effects of this model are highly technical, and we refer interested readers to Dreher, Gould, Rablen, and Vreeland (2014).[31] We restrict our discussion to the direction of correlation (positive or negative) and its statistical significance as our primary purpose is to present an initial analysis of factors that may matter in the selection of UNSC members and to identify potential control variables for Chapter 5.

A minor concern regards the threshold we use to define an election as contested in the UNGA. We arbitrarily set the threshold as whenever at least one additional candidate receives at least ten votes in the UNGA, but we also lowered the threshold down to three votes, effectively allowing for more votes to count as contested. (Three votes seems the lowest reasonable number because it could imply some possible coordination between two countries beyond the candidate country itself, but even in this case the countries might not coordinate.) The results with the lower threshold so much resemble the ten-vote threshold that reporting both would actually be redundant.[32] We thus report only the results using the ten-vote threshold.

4.7 Discussion of the Results

We organize our discussion of the results presented in Table 4.7 according to the five broad perspectives that we presented above in Section 4.3: (1) a commitment to peace, (2) a foreign-aid story, (3) a realist international relations perspective, (4) a cultural approach, and (5) a turn-taking norm.

---

[31] That study calculates elasticity and marginal effect estimates for the final year of the sample. They can be obtained using the "mi predict" command in Stata 12 at the group-specific means.

[32] We do, however include both sets of results in the replication materials for the book. Note that if we raise the threshold, thereby counting fewer elections as contested, eventually, there are too few observations left for the UNGA for the model to converge.

4.7.1 Commitment to Peace

If the selection of UNSC members follows the guidelines in the UN Charter, then a country's contributions to "the maintenance of international peace and security" should matter. We find only limited evidence to support this conjecture.

Table 4.7 shows that countries involved in inter- or intrastate conflict (War) are less likely to win election from Asia. In our work with Gould and Rablen, however, the finding for Asia does not hold; instead, we find countries from Africa and the GRULAC that are engaged in conflict have become less likely to win election since the end of the Cold War. Interestingly, we also find, in that study, a positive effect of conflict during the Cold War for the GRULAC. The finding is driven by the nomination of Peru in 1983, which was then engaged in civil conflict with *Sendero Luminoso* (Shining Path). Note that Barbados contested that election (unsuccessfully) as a second GRULAC candidate.

Peacekeeping troop contributions play a noteworthy role. Table 4.7 reports a positive and marginally statistically significant effect for Asia and the GRULAC, and a stronger effect for the WEOG. In our work with Gould and Rablen, where we address country outliers, we find that only the Asia finding is robust – its statistical significance holds at the 1 percent level. In that model, we also detect a positive effect of peacekeeping troops in Africa.[33]

Finally, we find that democracy matters in the WEOG (statistically significant at the 1 percent level). The only authoritarian regime ever elected to represent the WEOG was Spain in 1968, while the dictatorships in Portugal and Greece never won election. Since democratizing, however, Spain has won election three times, and Portugal and Greece have each been elected twice. Democratizing thus apparently has a positive impact on the chances of winning support from the Western European group.

In the work with Gould and Rablen, we further find positive effects of democracy for EE and the GRULAC for the post-Cold War period. Interestingly, democracy had negative effects in these two regions during the Cold War, although the negative effect in EE is essentially spurious as

---

[33] We are grateful to Birger Heldt of the Folke Bernadotte Academy (Ministry of Foreign Affairs, Sweden) for providing us with the peacekeeping troop data. For studies on the source of UN peacekeeping troops, see Lebovic (2010), and on their effectiveness, see Fortna (2004) and Howard (2007). On the consequences of temporary membership on the UNSC for UN peacekeeping contributions, see Voeten (2011).

only one country-year is coded as a democracy – Poland in 1989 – which happened not to stage a serious campaign that year (it received just one vote).

The UNGA exhibits no preference for countries that are not at war, that contribute peacekeeping troops, or that are democratic. We conclude, not surprisingly, that there is little commitment to the charter guideline of selecting UNSC members contributing to "the maintenance of international peace and security," as measured by our variables. Perhaps, however, our measures misinterpret the concept of contribution. It may be that UN members consider the countries contributing to international peace as the most powerful, in a realist sense. We return to this view below.

4.7.2 Foreign Aid and Multilateral Lending

When it comes to international security, the most strategically relevant developing countries may be those that receive the most foreign aid – especially military aid. We find only weak evidence that foreign aid plays a role, however, and the evidence does not go in a consistent direction.

Governments that receive more U.S. foreign aid are not more likely to win UNSC election. In fact, we detect a negative effect for the WEOG, which is confirmed as robust during the Cold War period by our work with Gould and Rablen.

When it comes to U.S. military assistance, we see a slightly different picture. We estimate a positive and statistically significant effect for EE (at the 10 percent level) and for the UNGA (at the 1 percent level). Both findings are confirmed by our work with Gould and Rablen. Of course, these groups have the fewest observations – the UNGA finding is based on just thirty-six elections. Still, the finding suggests that we should account for U.S. military assistance in our assessment of the effect of UNSC membership on development aid (we do so in Chapter 5).

By contrast, Table 4.7 reports no statistically significant positive effects of IMF program participation or new World Bank projects in any of the regional groups. In our work with Gould and Rablen, we find some evidence of a positive effect of participation in new World Bank projects for Asia and the WEOG and also a similar effect for Africa during the Cold War, although not one that is robust across models. For the UNGA, we actually find a negative effect of participation in new World Bank projects – both here and in our work with Gould and Rablen. The overall picture for the World Bank is thus somewhat unclear, and we stress the importance of focusing on Africa when looking at the effects of UNSC membership on World Bank lending – with important controls for country and year fixed-effects. For our work on the effect of UNSC membership on IMF lending, endogeneity does not appear to be an issue. If anything, the study with Gould and Rablen finds a negative effect for Asia.[34]

Finally, Table 4.7 reports that more heavily indebted countries are more likely to be elected from Africa and the GRULAC. As debt service contains the most imputed values of our variables, it is sensible to be cautious in interpreting these results. Indeed, the result for Africa holds only at the 10 percent confidence level, and the GRULAC result is not robust throughout the study with Gould and Rablen. With respect to Africa, we do not believe that the region has a preference for highly indebted countries. Instead, since we find evidence of a strong turn-taking norm in this region, we suspect that governments may have a good idea of when they will get their chance to serve on the UNSC and thus pursue lax macroeconomic policies in anticipation of the windfall of foreign aid that UNSC membership brings, as we show in Chapter 5.

4.7.3 International Power and Political Connections

Turning to the role of international power, we find that large countries, as measured by population, tend to win election more often than small countries in Asia and the WEOG, according to Table 4.7. According to our work with Gould and Rablen, these findings are robust – and once we account for country outliers, we also find robust positive effects of population for the GRULAC since the Cold War ended and for Africa throughout both time periods. Large countries from their respective regions – Nigeria, Egypt, Japan, India, Bangladesh, Brazil, and Germany – help drive this result. Only in Eastern Europe does the result not hold. Table 4.7 also reports a positive effect of population for the UNGA, although we do not find this to be robust in our work with Gould and Rablen. Still, at least at the regional level, we conclude that large countries, as measured by population, have an advantage in UNSC elections.

Rich countries from the developing world also do well. We estimate a statistically significant positive effect of per capita income for Africa, Asia, and the GRULAC. All three of these findings prove robust in our work with Gould and Rablen.

---

[34] There is also a non-robust, marginally significant positive effect for the WEOG, but this group plays little role in our study of developing countries.

Territorial size has ambiguous effects. In Table 4.7, we report negative effects for Asia and the UNGA, but these findings do not hold in our work with Gould and Rablen. Instead, we actually find positive effects for Asia, EE, and the GRULAC, though none of these is robust to the inclusion of all control variables. We thus make no strong claims about territory.

So populous and rich countries have some advantage in winning elections – what about countries with high levels of political affinity with the most powerful countries? When it comes to voting with the United States in the UNGA, affinity does not appear to help. If anything, African countries voting in alignment with the United States at the UNGA are actually less likely to win nomination, according to Table 4.7 – although this finding does not hold in our work with Gould and Rablen. High affinity with Russia/the Soviet Union has a different story. It has a positive effect in the rare elections contested at the UNGA level, a finding that does hold in our work with Gould and Rablen. Table 4.7 reports a negative effect of voting with Russia/the Soviet Union for WEOG countries, although this finding does not hold in our other study. Instead, our other study suggests a positive effect for voting with Russia/the Soviet Union for Africa and the GRULAC, but this finding is not robust to the inclusion of all control variables. The upshot is that, if anything, the countries aligned with the historic rival of the United States have the advantage in UNSC elections (except from the WEOG). We find no evidence that friends of the United States on the floor of the UNGA have an advantage in Security Council elections.

Pariah states – those under U.S. or UN sanctions – may have a disadvantage in UNSC elections. Table 4.7 does not report any statistically significant effects of this variable because its effects vary according to time period. In our work with Gould and Rablen, pariahs were less likely to win nomination from Africa or Asia during the Cold War. Since the Cold War's end, Nigeria (in 1993) and Sudan (in 2000) have contested as African nominees, and Indonesia (in 1994) and Syria (in 2001) have won the Asian endorsement – despite facing sanctions. Nigeria triumphed in a contested vote and Sudan lost in one. Indonesia and Syria won uncontested clean slate elections.

Nevertheless, states under sanctions have not seen election to the UNSC often. African Cold War cases where governments facing sanctions were not selected to serve on the UNSC include: Libya 1978–2004, South Africa 1963–1994, and Rhodesia 1972–1979 (we list the full range of the sanctions, including the years after the Cold War ended).[35] Interestingly, Libya won election in 1975 and 2007 – right before and right after facing sanctions. Asian cases where governments facing sanctions were not selected to serve on the UNSC during the Cold War include: Iran 1979–present, Laos 1975–1995, and Myanmar 1988–present.[36] The only sanctioned country to win the regional nomination in the GRULAC did so right on the cusp of the two time periods: Cuba 1989. In our work with Gould and Rablen, we find a negative effect for pariahs in GRULAC since the end of the Cold War, but its statistical significance depends on which year we code as the end of the Cold War. Other sanctioned GRULAC countries during the Cold War did not win election: Nicaragua 1977–1979 and Panama 1987–1989. The only other case of sanctions during the post–Cold War period in the GRULAC is Haiti (1991–1994, 2000–2004), which has never won election to the UNSC. Note that in 1989, Cuba won a clean slate election in a single round of balloting despite U.S. opposition (Varner 2006, Costa Rica 2005).

How should we address pariah states in our study? Given the close connection between sanctions and foreign aid – which is practically a definitional one in that cutting foreign aid represents a common sanction against countries – we adopt this variable as an important control in our work on the effects of UNSC membership on foreign aid in the next chapter. While the United States may not have the power to select its favorite countries for the UNSC, it may have stood as a block in certain cases.

Finally, we investigate the role of connections to political groupings within the UN. It turns out, however, that such membership plays little role. We find evidence that such membership matters in some groups, but not in others, and the effects go in different directions. For example, membership in the G77 – but not in the NAM – has a negative effect in Asia but a positive effect in the GRULAC. In the GRULAC, dual membership in NAM and G77 also positively predicts regional nomination. OIC membership has no statistically significant effects.[37] All of these findings are confirmed by our other study with Gould and Rablen. JUSCANZ membership has a statistically significant positive effect for

[35] Note that Rhodesia was never even a member of the UN.
[36] "Present" refers to this writing: 2013.
[37] We do not control for OIC in Asia due to collinearity with the Muslim variable. When we do include them together, neither variable is statistically significant at conventional levels.

UNGA contested elections, but the finding does not hold in our other study. As for groupings external to the UN, EU membership appears to raise a country's probability of receiving a regional nomination in EE but not in the WEOG; NATO membership has a pronounced negative effect on regional nomination probability for members of EE but has no effect in the WEOG. These findings are confirmed by our other study but are not of particular relevance for most of the developing world.

We conclude that while there is evidence that powerful countries win election more often than weaker states, developing countries favored by the United States have no clear advantage. Still, in the next chapter, we take a conservative approach, controlling for pariah status and U.S. military assistance as well as country fixed-effects to address other endowments of countries in our examination of the determinants of foreign aid.

4.7.4 Colonial Heritage, Political Ideology, Religion, and Corruption

Do the historical, religious, and political traits of a country influence its election prospects? Regarding colonial heritage, countries with a history of British colonialism enjoy an advantage in Asia – a finding confirmed by our other study, which also detects a positive effect of British colonialism for the GRULAC and the WEOG.[38] The effect does not hold for Africa or the UNGA. Countries with a history of French colonialism do not appear to have greater probabilities of election from Africa either.

Turning to political cultures, governments sharing a common political ideology with other governments in its region have a greater likelihood of election from EE. Our other study confirms this finding and indicates evidence of a positive effect for the GRULAC as well.[39]

We also consider religion, as measured by the proportion of a country's population that is either Muslim or Catholic. Table 4.7 reports no statistically significant effects for either variable.

As the last variable in this section, the control of corruption has a negative effect for Africa. Ironically, Africa's commitment to fairness in taking turns may be what makes corruption pay in this region. Countries willing to break the rules can have an advantage in the region where the rules are strictly followed. By contrast, our study with Gould and Rablen suggests that the UNGA has tended to shun more corrupt countries since

---

[38]   The former British colonies in the WEOG are Ireland (elected twice) and Malta (elected once).

[39]   Note that Potrafke (2009) finds that government ideology affects UNGA voting behavior.

the end of the Cold War; that study shows the control of corruption to have a positive effect in the UNGA during the post–Cold War era.

We conclude with only weak evidence of the role of historical, political, and religious factors. The factors that do matter can be addressed in the next chapter with attention to country fixed-effects.

4.7.5 Turn-Taking and Rotation

We conclude this discussion with our most important result: We find widespread evidence of the operation of a turn-taking norm – and not only in Africa. Generally speaking, the longer a country has been waiting to appear on the Security Council the higher the probability of receiving the endorsement of the regional caucus. Table 4.7 shows the importance of the effect at the 1 percent significance level or stronger for all regions except the GRULAC.

The GRULAC appears to have adopted a modified turn-taking rule, alternating between a small set of large countries – mainly Brazil, Argentina, and Colombia – that tends to fill one of the two GRULAC seats, and the rest of Latin America and the Caribbean. In our study with Gould and Rablen, where we control for country-outliers, we find a positive effect of the turn-taking norm in the GRULAC – significant at the 5 percent level.

So, turn-taking norms exist in all regions, with simply a more complex norm in the GRULAC. The common misperception that membership on the UNSC rotates therefore finds some support in the electoral patterns at the regional level. Interestingly, however, the UNGA itself does not appear influenced by the turn-taking rights that apply within the regions.

The statistically significant finding of the turn-taking norm for the regions, coupled with the non-finding for contested UNGA elections, suggests that the pattern of taking turns derives from norms of trading important positions on international committees shared by members of the same region. These countries negotiate among each other for positions on many international committees, both within the United Nations and in other international organizations. When a country queue-jumps, however, the UNGA does not base its decision on which country has waited the longest for its turn.

4.8 The Way Forward

The main systematic pattern that appears to drive UNSC selection represents a compromise between selecting rich, populous countries and a commitment to taking turns. Beyond this, we see limited evidence that the UNGA follows the UN Charter in selecting countries committed to peace – countries involved in some form of warfare are less likely to win election to the UNSC, while contribution to peacekeeping troops helps. We also find some evidence that pariah states – those facing U.S. and/or UN sanctions – were less likely to be selected to serve on the UNSC during the Cold War, though this preference has disappeared in the contemporary period.

We find little compelling evidence that U.S. development aid or finance from multilateral organizations influences UNSC selection. Few findings hold across all of the models that we have analyzed in our two studies – and some of them are contradictory. This result follows Bueno de Mesquita and Smith (2010: 72), who conclude that "while election to the UNSC is not random, it appears to be largely unrelated to aid and political and economic development." Still, U.S. military assistance plays some role in EE and in the rare elections contested at the UNGA, and pariah status may act as a confounding factor. We thus account for both of these variables in the next chapter.

Turn-taking still stands as the most robust finding across our research on the determinants of UNSC election. It holds at the 1 percent confidence level across all regions except the GRULAC, where a modified rule holds at the 5 percent level of statistical significance. The finding lends confidence as to the exogeneity of UNSC membership to our variables of interest.

Note that – due to data limitations – we have ignored a further set of factors: the local deals done near 760 United Nations Plaza, New York. Interpersonal arrangements among the ambassadors themselves may drive many of the idiosyncrasies behind UNSC selection. Malone discusses the importance of the "New York angle" in selecting UNSC members. He observes that the actual – secret – ballots are cast in New York and what happens at the interpersonal level is the most consequential: "The New York angle is critical. Seasoned observers at the UN estimate that up to a third of the votes are cast solely by New York-based representatives, who either will not have received instructions from their capitals or will ignore them" (Malone 2000: 13). The personal characteristics and interactions of the individuals on the New York scene may therefore hold sway over many elections. A more fruitful avenue of research to discover patterns of UN selection might be to move from the country level to the personal level in New York. Such research would take us away from the focus of our next chapter, which represents the crux of this study: the effect of UNSC membership on foreign aid and multilateral lending.

At the start of this chapter, we set out to determine what factors play a role in determining temporary UNSC membership. The election process is intrinsically interesting to students of international relations, and our results speak to debtates about UNSC reform. For those who favor turn-taking, more power should be granted to regions in selecting their representatives. Others, who favor the selection of strategically important countries, should advocate a strengthened role for the UNGA, where U.S. military assistance and affinity with Russia/the Soviet Union hold influence. We return to questions of UNSC reform in the concluding chapter.

As we look to the next chapter, an understanding of the UNSC selection process matters for our broader purpose of estimating the impact of UNSC membership on foreign aid flows. Through a systematic evaluation of possible influencing factors, we reach the conclusion that the selection of UNSC members is largely idiosyncratic, although we do observe some patterns. Population size, involvement in warfare, pariah status, and the turn-taking norm all play roles to varying extents. In our analyses in the next chapter, we address these factors – either through the inclusion of fixed-effects for countries or the inclusion of the variables themselves. As for the importance of the turn-taking norm, we consider it an advantage for our research. The exogenous nature of this variable helps to attenuate problems of nonrandom selection – especially in Africa, which adheres to the norm more strictly than any other region. To the extent that countries take turns serving on the UNSC, we can – as analysts – consider their membership to be a chance event.

Appendix 4.1: Election Probabilities[40]

In any given year, depending on the region, there may be up to two seats open for election: Seats$_{j,t}$ $\in$ {0,1,2}. We must therefore define three separate probability functions of selecting country i from region j in year t: $p^0_{i,j,t}$ for region-years where no seats are open, $p^1_{i,j,t}$ for region-years where one seat is open, and $p^2_{i,j,t}$ for region-years where two seats are open. We follow Manski and Sherman (1980), assuming that

---

[40] Derived from Dreher, Gould, Rablen, and Vreeland (2014).

draws of $\varepsilon_{i,j,t}$ in Equation 4.1, above, are independent across regions and time and have identical type-1 extreme value distributions. We can then define:

$$p_{i,j,t}^0 \equiv 0$$

$$p_{i,j,t}^1 \equiv \frac{\exp\left(\alpha_{j,t}\left[\beta_{GA}' x_{i,j,t}\right] + (1 - \alpha_{j,t})\left[\beta_j' x_{i,j,t}\right]\right)}{\sum_{k \in E_{j,t}} \exp\left(\alpha_{j,t}\left[\beta_{GA}' x_{k,j,t}\right] + (1 - \alpha_{j,t})\left[\beta_j' x_{k,j,t}\right]\right)}$$

$$p_{i,j,t}^2 \equiv \frac{2 p_{i,j,t}^1 \left(1 - p_{i,j,t}^1\right)}{1 - \sum_{k \in E_{j,t}} \left(p_{k,j,t}^1\right)^2},$$

where the denominators in $p_{i,j,t}^1$ and $p_{i,j,t}^2$ sum over every country k in the set of eligible countries in region j, year t: $E_{j,t}$. The model sets to zero the probability of selecting a country that is ineligible (those currently serving or facing a term limit).

Note that when only one seat is contested in a region, the distributional assumptions on $\varepsilon_{i,j,t}$ imply that the probability of a single country being elected to the UNSC from $E_{j,t}$, that is, $p_{i,j,t}^1$, follows McFadden's (1973) conditional logit form.[41] We then use $p_{i,j,t}^1$ to define $p_{i,j,t}^2$ as the binomial probability of observing a distinct country pair (the denominator corrects for the impossibility of a single country obtaining dual membership). With these probabilities defined, it is straightforward to write the likelihood function. The details can be found in Dreher, Gould, Rablen, and Vreeland (2014).

---

[41] Although these distributional assumptions are strong, we note their necessity for retaining the conditional logit form. Also, when estimating the final likelihood, we allow for the possibility of within-group clustering. Because we model the probability of choosing country i from region j in year t as conditional on the number of eligible countries in year t, our model, like the original conditional logit, implicitly addresses fixed-effects for year. For an approach that relaxes our distributional assumptions at some conceptual and computational cost see Hendel (1999). Also see Golder et al. (2012).

5

Statistical Evidence of Trading Finance for Favors

5.1 Introduction

Do elected UN Security Council members receive perks during their terms? This empirical question constitutes the central concern of this book. Confronting it with quantitative data embodies the task of this chapter. Having presented many examples in Chapter 3, we now seek to test whether the examples represent exceptional cases or, instead, are part of a systematic pattern – and we must do so while remaining mindful of potential selection bias, as discussed in Chapter 4.

We begin our inquiry into the effects of UNSC membership with an examination of bilateral foreign aid. We then examine whether countries trade money for influence through multilateral organizations. Specifically, we consider the IMF, the World Bank, the United Nations, and regional development banks (RDBs). Finally, we address the more nuanced hypothesis of whether donor countries target swing voters on the UNSC.

5.2 Background on Bilateral Aid: The United States, Japan, Germany, the United Kingdom, and France

Throughout the history of the UNSC, the United States has served as the most prominent agenda-setter. Qualitative examples concerning the United States abound and thus fill the pages of Chapter 3. The focus of our quantitative analysis below begins, therefore, with the United States. We follow Kuziemko and Werker (2006), who show that the United States increases bilateral aid to UNSC members, specifically during important years when the Security Council receives heightened media attention.

Other powerful countries may also attempt to win influence over the UNSC through the elected members. Political scientist Mark Copelovitch suggests, for example, that the United States works most effectively when it agrees with its major allies at the IMF and the World Bank: Japan, Germany, France, and the United Kingdom (Copelovitch 2010a, 2010b). Moreover, these latter countries may have their own agendas that they would like to pursue on the UNSC. Thus, they may have separate incentives to influence elected UNSC members.

The other permanent members might seem the most obvious countries with agendas to pursue on the UNSC. Yet, these countries might not need to routinely trade foreign aid for systematic influence on the Security Council precisely because of their permanent status and veto power. Regarding France and the United Kingdom, when they disagree with the U.S. agenda, they can veto proposed resolutions. And when they do agree with the U.S. agenda, they can free-ride, letting the bigger, more powerful leader do the heavy lifting of convincing elected members of the UNSC to cast favorable votes. As for Russia and China, a comprehensive study of their efforts to pressure elected UNSC members certainly interests us, but the historic lack of reliable data from these countries prevents quantitative analysis. Anecdotal evidence suggests, however, that they tend to rely on their veto power when they disagree with the P3 (the United States, United Kingdom, and France). Regarding foreign aid, their votes (or abstentions) have often been the object of lobbying efforts by the United States, as indicated in Chapter 3. So we might not regularly see proactive lobbying efforts from the other permanent members of the UNSC as they already wield tremendous power.

Japan and Germany, on the other hand, emerged as prominent countries that lacked a voice on the UNSC corresponding to their position in global politics. Arguably, Japan and Germany are currently the world's most powerful countries without permanent seats on the UNSC. Importantly, each of them has revealed a preference for more influence over the body. Along with Brazil and India, they are both members of the G4, the group seeking permanent status on the UNSC. Furthermore, they both have won election to the UNSC more often than any other country in their respective regions. Still, the UNSC often leaves them out of important discussions. They do not serve on the Security Council every year, and when they do serve, they do not have veto power. Their lack of status may therefore make them particularly interested in augmenting their informal power on the UNSC by winning favor with temporary members (Lim and Vreeland 2013).

As the principal losers of World War II, Japan and Germany have a peculiar relationship with the UN, an institution that emerged as a specific legacy of the war. The UN Charter still carries the "former enemies" clause (UN Charter, article 53), which implicitly refers to Germany and Japan. Neither country could become a founding member of the UN, much less a permanent member of the Security Council. Both countries have special provisions in their constitutions restricting the use of military force. In Japan, government officials have argued that the Japanese constitution allows its military to be employed overseas only if authorized by the Security Council (Lim and Vreeland 2013; Green 2003; Yasutomo 1995; Ueki 1993). We have therefore argued, in our research with Daniel Yew Mao Lim of Harvard University, that the Japanese government has incentives to seek additional influence over the UNSC (Lim and Vreeland 2013). The arguments also apply to Germany (Dreher, Nunnenkamp, and Schmaljohann 2013; Grieco 1999).

So, in addition to seeking permanent and elected UNSC membership, do Japan and Germany also seek influence over the Security Council by winning favor with elected members? We suspect that they do. Compared to their campaigns for permanent and elected membership, trading foreign aid for influence over elected members actually represents a lower-cost approach toward augmenting their limited power at the UNSC. Japan, in particular, has spent a great deal of international political capital attempting to gain permanent membership (see Weiss 2008). Furthermore, because Japan and Germany compete to win election more often, they must wage costly campaigns. Malone (2004) estimates that winning a WEOG seat entails campaign costs well into the millions of dollars. Given these other obvious – and costly – means that Japan and Germany have employed to augment their voices on the UNSC, providing foreign aid to elected UNSC members strikes us as another plausible avenue that they might pursue.

5.3 Background on Multilateral Organizations: The IMF, the World Bank, the UN, and Regional Development Banks

Beyond bilateral aid, multilateral organizations represent an alternative source through which to funnel favors for elected members of the UNSC. If bilateral channels exist, however, why should governments also pursue influence through multilateral channels? Obviously, the multilateral path involves the additional cost of getting the most powerful members of various organizations to agree, as well as the costs of pressuring the multilateral bureaucracy, which may be more insulated from political pressure (Kosack and Tobin 2006; Schneider and Tobin 2013).[1]

It turns out that both bilateral and multilateral channels incur costs. The exchange that we discussed in Chapter 1, between John Bolton and Andrew S. Natsios, illustrates that government bureaucracies do not stand as united monoliths. Different bureaus, offices, and ministries have different goals. So, it is not obvious that the bilateral channel will consistently represent the path of least bureaucratic resistance.[2]

Moreover, we identify several reasons – also discussed in Chapter 1 – as to why we expect an effect through the multilateral channel. To review, multilateral organizations offer the advantages of (1) leverage, (2) laundering, and (3) lower costs. *Leverage* exists through explicit conditionality, which is institutionalized in the lending programs of the IMF and the World Bank. *Laundering* helps governments – both the provider and the recipient – hide unpalatable trades of political influence for money: Multilateral organizations can do the dirty work. *Lower costs* result from sharing the financial burden across the membership of multilateral organizations.

We therefore investigate the impact of finance provided through various multilateral organizations. We review the findings of our earlier research, which we pursued along with our coauthor Jan-Egbert Sturm of the Swiss Federal Institute of Technology (ETH), on the effect of UNSC membership on participation in IMF and World Bank programs. We also analyze the distribution of foreign aid from the UN, following Kuziemko and Werker (2006). We then turn to RDBs, following the work of Lim and Vreeland (2013), who look at the Asian Development Bank (AsDB), and the work of Bland and Kilby (2012) and Hernandez (2013), who look at the Inter-American Development Bank (IADB). We then present an original analysis of the African Development Bank (AfDB).

---

[1] Schneider and Tobin (2013) specifically argue that the multilateral nature of the European Union reduces the influence that international politics plays in its foreign aid policy. Consistent with this, we have found no effect of UNSC membership on foreign aid from the European Union. Preliminary evidence does suggest, however, that when they control the Presidency of the Council of the European Union, France, the United Kingdom, and Germany do reward temporary UNSC members (see Mazumder, McNamara, and Vreeland (2014).

[2] See McKeown (2009) for further insights based on recently declassified internal assessments of the U.S. government over its perceived influence on major international organizations.

5.4 Measuring the Effect of UNSC Membership

Throughout the above-discussed analyses, we focus on temporary UNSC membership as our primary explanatory variable of interest. We measure membership as a dichotomous indictor coded 1 for both years of a country's two-year term, and coded 0 otherwise.

We further recognize, however, that the incentives of powerful countries to pursue political support on the UNSC might vary over time. In terms of the formal model in Chapter 2, the "value" of UNSC votes (denoted v in the model) might depend on global events as they unfold over time. Thus, we also consider the importance of the Security Council during any given year. We follow Kuziemko and Werker (2006), who measure the importance of the UNSC during a year as a function of how often the media (specifically, the *New York Times*) publishes articles containing the words "United Nations" and "Security Council." Using this approach, the authors identify three (roughly) equal groups of years: (1) unimportant, (2) somewhat important, and (3) important.[3]

Beyond measuring membership on the UNSC, we further seek to capture the underlying political affinity between UNSC members and powerful donor countries. Recall that the theory we present in Chapter 2 proposes swing voters as the most likely targets of trading finance for favors. Testing this hypothesis proves difficult for a number of reasons.

First of all, powerful countries like the United States may consider almost all developing countries that serve on the UNSC to represent potentially swing-able countries. Recall from Chapter 3's discussion of Resolution 1441 (which granted broad powers to weapons inspectors in Iraq), the only countries considered reliable allies of the United States were Ireland and Norway, fellow developed countries. Such developed countries drop out of our analysis because we investigate only developing countries as they are the only recipients of official development assistance

---

[3] Precisely, they code the following years as "important": 1946–1952, 1954–1956, 1958, 1960–1961, 1964–1965, 1968, 1982, 1990–1994, and 1998. They code these years as "somewhat important": 1953, 1957, 1962, 1963, 1966, 1967, 1969, 1971, 1973, 1975–1976, 1979, 1980, 1985, 1988, 1995–1996, and 1999. The remaining years are coded as "unimportant." Our own classification for the 1960-2008 period – taken from the database collected for Dreher, Nunnenkamp, and Schmaljohann (2013) – codes as "important" years: 1960–1961, 1964–1967, 1973, 1990–1994, 1998, 2002–2003, and 2006. Years coded as "somewhat important" are: 1962–1963, 1968–1971, 1975–1976, 1979–1980, 1982, 1999–2000, 2004–2005, and 2007.

and, historically, the main recipients of loans from multilateral organizations. As for countries with preferences too far away to be considered swing-able – like Cuba or Syria – if there are only a few such countries, a special relationship for them may be wiped out by including country fixed-effects in our econometric models.

Secondly, assuming that a distinct group of swing voters exists, measuring the underlying affinity of preferences across countries is not straightforward. We thus take various different approaches toward distinguishing the potential swing voters from "friends," who should provide their votes in the absence of enticements, and "enemies," who may not provide their votes even if they were enticed.

Our first approach involves coding friends and enemies according to military alliances and sanctions, respectively. Focusing on affinity with the United States, we code as friends countries with U.S. military alliances. We code as enemies countries under U.S. or UN sanctions, using the pariah state variable from Chapter 4.

Our second approach relies on vote patterns in the UN General Assembly. We consider how often countries vote along with the United States in the UNGA. From the entire distribution of voting affinity with the United States, we (arbitrarily) code the top 10 percent as U.S. friends, and the bottom 10 percent as U.S. enemies (altering the precise cut-off points results in qualitatively similar results). The intuition is straightforward: Governments that never or rarely vote along with the United States in the UNGA can be considered to have a low level of affinity with the United States. Governments that almost always vote with the United States in the UNGA can be considered to have a high level of affinity with the United States. We can extend this logic back to the formal model presented in Chapter 2: Governments that usually vote with the United States have low b: They rarely gain local political benefits from opposing the United States. Governments that rarely vote with the United States have high b: They often gain local political benefits from opposing the United States. Most governments are in between.

Using each of these approaches, we expect neither the "friends" nor the "enemies" of the United States to be the targets of increased U.S. bilateral aid. Rather, the potential swing voters should stand as the main targets of U.S. enticements, as predicted by the model presented in Chapter 2.

Finally, we offer another approach from ongoing research conducted with Peter Rosendorff, which accounts for the actual votes taken on the UNSC (see Dreher, Rosendorff, and Vreeland 2013). Here, we measure the underlying affinity of elected UNSC members and the United States at two separate levels: (1) voting in the UNSC and (2) voting in the UNGA. Armed with these two measures, we then consider their interaction. That is, we consider the effect of voting against the United States in the UNSC conditioned on how often they vote with the United States in the UNGA during the previous year (which we use to gauge the proximity of a country's preferences to those of the United States prior to joining the UNSC).

Now, for reasons discussed in Chapter 1, votes on most UNSC resolutions tend toward unanimity. We therefore observe little variation. We have collected (1) all voting data on resolutions that have passed, (2) available data on vetoed resolutions, and (3) available data on resolutions that failed to reach the supermajority threshold of nine votes. Still, countries vote with the United States upward of 90 percent of the time. We argue that this is partly due to U.S. pressure on countries to deliver favorable votes – the very subject of this book – but we acknowledge that it is also due to massive selection bias. Members of the UNSC act strategically when proposing resolutions – they are less likely to make proposals that they expect to fail. Such strategic behavior results in data with little variation, and thus we do not find many interesting results when we examine the impact of UNSC voting on most of our dependent variables. We do, however, discuss a fascinating set of results with respect to the lending behavior of the IMF. To anticipate, we find that larger IMF loans go to UNSC members that vote with the United States on Security Council proposals. More specifically, governments with low affinity for the United States do not receive larger loans, presumably because they are not expected to vote with the United States in the first place, while mid- and high-affinity governments face punishment if they fail to deliver favorable votes. So governments serving on the UNSC do receive larger IMF loans, but only if they actually vote with the United States on UNSC proposals.

5.5 Addressing Potential Problems of UNSC Selection Bias

The possibility of selection bias overshadows our empirical analyses. Selection bias would suggest the following: Countries more likely to receive financial perks, such as U.S. development aid, are also the most likely to win election to the UNSC. Our analysis of selection onto the UNSC (presented in Chapter 4) suggests that this situation is probably not the case. At least we found no robust statistical evidence that U.S. development aid, IMF programs, or World Bank programs positively predict selection onto the UNSC. Still, we did find, for example, that more populous countries are more likely to win election under certain circumstances, and more populous countries may enjoy more importance in global affairs and thus receive more financial perks – regardless of their UNSC status. If true, this situation could lead to an overestimation of the effect of UNSC membership. Inter- and intrastate war also appeared as a determinant of election to the UNSC across most regions, and we found some additional systematic determinants beyond population and war, which differed region by region. While perhaps idiosyncratic across regions, these findings indicate that the selection onto the UNSC is non-random.

The pariah state effect stands as perhaps the most important selection variable discussed in Chapter 4. We discovered that, during the Cold War, states under sanctions by the United States or the UN were less likely to win election to represent the regions of Africa, Asia, and the GRULAC. States under sanctions may also see a drop in their foreign aid – indeed, sanctions often involve the explicit cutting-off of foreign aid (see Morgan, Krustev, and Bapat 2006). If pariah states are both less likely to win UNSC election and less likely to receive foreign aid, failing to account for the connection between sanctions and foreign aid could result in an inflated estimation of the positive effect of UNSC membership on foreign aid. We therefore include the pariah state variable in our regression analyses to address this potential source of bias in our estimation of the effect of UNSC membership on financial flows.

U.S. military assistance turns out to serve as an interesting control variable. We include it because, while it plays a role only in Eastern Europe and not in any other region, it does appear to have a positive and statistically significant impact on the contested elections decided by the UNGA. Now, contested elections amount to just 36 out of 180 elections (by our count), so we stress caution in interpreting the UNGA results, as they rely on so few observations. Moreover, controlling for U.S. military assistance is nonstandard in the vast literature on foreign aid and multilateral lending. Some might object to including U.S. military assistance in analyses of U.S. development aid because the two might be so highly correlated for some cases as to be codetermined. Still, we see no harm in including this control variable for our purposes of ascertaining the impact of UNSC membership and prefer to err on the side of caution. We do have an alternative version of this chapter, available on request, that does not include this control variable. All of the qualitative results presented below hold when we drop U.S. military assistance. The only difference is that in some cases where we report statistical significance at the 10 percent level here, we can report stronger confidence when we do not include U.S. military assistance. So our findings only become stronger without this variable. Interestingly, however, it turns out that U.S. military assistance has a positive and statistically significant impact on many of the financial flows that we examine below – not just on U.S. foreign aid.[4] So the inclusion of U.S. military assistance (measured as the natural logarithm of constant 2011 dollars) turns out to represent an important control variable, and its inclusion reduces our concerns of selection bias.

We can further attenuate potential selection bias by controlling for inter- and intrastate war as we have found that these conflicts make UNSC election less likely under certain circumstances, and the literature on foreign aid has shown that conflict may cause foreign aid to drop significantly.[5]

We also include a pair of standard control variables from the foreign aid literature: political regime and economic development (measured as the natural logarithm of purchasing power parity GDP per capita).[6]

Having noted the above concerns, we should stress that selection bias should stand as a much smaller problem for our study compared to the selection problems that confront most studies of international affairs. Recall another systematic determinant of UNSC membership: the turn-taking norm. To the extent that governments take turns, "rotating" onto the UNSC, we can treat membership as an exogenous treatment. Membership becomes a function of a country's arbitrary place in the queue.

Nevertheless, while the arbitrary nature of the election process reassures us that selection bias should not present a major hindrance to our study, selection should not be ignored. Following one simple but important approach, we include fixed-effects for countries (Simmons and Hopkins 2005). A main attribute that makes countries more likely to win election – its relative population size – remains fairly constant over time, and thus we may think of it as a fixed attribute of a country. Country fixed-effects also address issues pertaining to outlying states. Other

---

[4] For a fascinating analysis of U.S. security interests and international trade – particularly the effect of Central Intelligence Agency presence and a country's proclivity to import goods from the United States – see Berger, Easterly, Nunn, and Satyanath (2013).

[5] Important scholarly contributions that evaluate the connections between conflict and foreign aid include Berthélemy (2006), Balla and Reinhardt (2008), Findley, Powell, Strandow, and Tanner (2011), Flores and Nooruddin (2009), Nielsen, Findley, Davis, Candland, and Nielson (2011), and Girod (2012).

[6] GDP per capita is measured in terms of purchasing power parity (PPP) derived from growth rates of domestic absorption at 2005 constant prices, converted using Laspeyres. See Heston et al. (2012).

states exhibit idiosyncratic preferences, such as Mexico and Saudi Arabia, which have systematically avoided election to the Security Council.[7]

We also include fixed-effects for years to account for global idiosyncrasies over time – for example during years of heightened tension during the Cold War or years during which contested elections took place.

We further allow for different trends by region. More specifically, we adopt the "region quartic" approach of Kuziemko and Werker (2006), whereby we allow for differing trends over time for each region.[8] As our dependent variables in this chapter pertain to foreign aid and loans from multilateral financial institutions, the relevant regions pertain to the developing world, not the regions designated for UNSC selection. So, we account for the following regions: Europe and Central Asia, East Asia and the Pacific, Sub-Saharan Africa, Latin America and the Caribbean, and a residual category for countries that do not fit into the previously listed regions.

Beyond correcting for regional, country, and year effects, scholars have provided many alternative methods of addressing problems of nonrandom selection. A convenient method involves the use of instrumental variables, where the researcher relies on a correlation between the treatment variable of interest and some other "instrumental" variable, which is otherwise uncorrelated to the outcome of interest, controlled for the variables in the model. (Often, the correlation between the instrumental variable and the treatment variable is called "instrument relevance," and the lack of connection between the instrumental variable and the outcome variable is called the "exclusion restriction.") In our case, we would need a variable that could reliably predict selection onto the UNSC, with no connection to foreign aid. Such silver-bullet instrumental variables are hard to find.

Generally speaking, in the absence of random experiments to generate counterfactual observations, the selection problem remains a major obstacle to research in international affairs. In our project, however, we have the good fortune of an alternative approach that approximates an experiment, furnished to us by Africa.

---

[7] For more on the Mexican case, see Serrano and Kenny (2006: 298–314), Green (2007), Montaño (2007), and Muñoz Ledo (2007). We are grateful to Diego Dewar for these suggestions.

[8] By including, for each region, a variable measuring time (in years) along with its squared, cubed, and quartic terms, we allow the time trends to take on any reasonable shape, increasing, decreasing, increasing then decreasing, etc.

5.6 The Africa Solution

Africa's commitment to the norm of taking turns serving on the UNSC provides our project with a unique opportunity in the study of international relations. To the extent that we can treat African membership on the UNSC as idiosyncratic, we attenuate concerns about potential selection bias in our analysis. While all regions exhibit some commitment to the turn-taking norm, the region of Africa has exhibited the strongest commitment. Chapter 4 notes that Africa is the only region for which we have found – in writing – an explicit commitment to the norm. Chapter 4 also corroborates Africa's commitment empirically, showing that the turn-taking norm has the largest effect for the African region, after controlling for other possible determinants of selection to the UNSC.

With Africa's turn-taking norm in mind, we revisit our analysis of the effect of UNSC membership focusing exclusively on Africa. Along with each analysis of global data that we present below, we thus provide accompanying results relying on data from Africa.[9]

Now, even though Africa has abided by a turn-taking norm more than any other region, Chapter 4 does present evidence of exceptions to the rule. So, while the African commitment to rotation provides an opportunity, we recognize that UNSC selection for this region still does not represent a truly random draw. We thus remain concerned to correct for potentially confounding factors. Fortunately, as the region of Africa includes about fifty countries – almost all of which qualify for development assistance – we have ample data to test our main hypothesis. The degrees of freedom provided by the large dataset enables us to account for all of the aforementioned factors. We include fixed-effects for countries, which should help to address outliers, such as Nigeria and Ghana, which have occasionally jumped the queue to win election to the UNSC, as well as any countries that have chosen not to take a turn – or lost election, like Guinea-Bissau. We also include fixed-effects for years to account for year-specific shocks. As with the regressions including all regions in the world, we also allow for a separate time trend for each of the two major regions of Africa: North Africa and Africa South of the Sahara.[10]

Importantly, we also include all of the control variables previously mentioned in this chapter: level of economic development, political regime, an indicator for inter- and/or intrastate warfare, U.S. military

---

[9] We thank Kenneth Scheve for this suggestion.

[10] Again, we include a variable measuring time (in years) along with its squared, cubed, and quartic terms, to allow the time trend to take on any reasonable shape.

assistance, and pariah state. The pariah state variable is particularly important to include because of Rhodesia (Zimbabwe) and apartheid-era South Africa. The race-based policies followed by these countries directly lowered their chances of receiving foreign aid and of winning election to the UNSC. After they changed their policies and governments, they were each welcomed back by the global community and did win election to the UNSC. We would not want to confound the effect of UNSC membership on financial flows with the effect of the sanctions that these countries faced because of their domestic policies.

Thus, noting that Africa has the strongest commitment to the exogenous selection rule of rotating seats, we can also account for few exceptions and control for other factors that may influence foreign aid. As Africa has more developing countries than any other region and has the strongest commitment to the exogenous selection rule of rotating seats, the region provides a more restrictive, crucial test of our main hypothesis that UNSC members receive increases in financial perks during their terms.

5.7 Data, Methods, and Analysis

The dataset for this project includes a maximum of 6,058 country-year observations from 148 countries for the 1960–2009 period.[11] The panel is unbalanced due to different dates of independence for certain countries. What is more, some of our variables suffer from missing data, so we analyze smaller sample sizes for our various models. Our Africa sample includes a maximum of 2,149 observations, covering 49 countries also for 1960–2009. The Appendix to this chapter includes a data table that lists all of the variables we use here along with their means, standard deviations, minimum and maximum values, and their sources. We also have the book dataset available on our websites.[12]

Throughout our analyses, we consider the natural logarithm of each continuous dependent variable.[13] This approach reduces the influence of outlier observations, and the distribution of the dependent variables is closer to the assumed normal distribution. We raise the number e

---

[11] When we include the "important year" classification, the sample ends in 2008.

[12] The websites of the authors are, respectively, http://www.profvreeland.com and http://www.axel-dreher.de.

[13] We add 1 to replace 0 values when taking the natural logarithm (the replacement is necessary because the logarithm of 0 is undefined and the logarithm of 1 is 0).

to the power of our estimated coefficients and subtract one in order to calculate the percentage change in the dependent variable for a one unit change in the independent variable (if the independent variable is also measured as a natural logarithm – as is the case for GDP per capita – then the coefficient indicates the percentage change in the dependent variable given a 1 percent change in the independent variable).[14]

We begin by presenting the results for bilateral aid from the United States, Japan, Germany, the United Kingdom, and France. We then turn to multilateral organizations, presenting the results for the IMF, the World Bank, the UN, and the RDBs. In each case, we discuss first the results for the global sample, followed by a discussion of the results from the Africa sample. Finally, we present the analysis of the swing-voter hypothesis.

5.7.1 Bilateral Aid

First, consider some simple comparisons of bilateral aid, measured in terms of constant 2009 U.S. dollars for the period 1960–2009:

The United States provides an annual average of $65 million to developing countries not serving on the UN Security Council during our sample period (n = 5,719). For temporary UNSC members, the average is $112 million (n = 339). UNSC members receive about 1.7 times more U.S. bilateral aid – or more than $45 million each year – than nonmembers.

Japanese aid follows a similar pattern: $49 million to nonmembers, and $98 million to temporary UNSC members. UNSC members receive about twice as much Japanese bilateral aid – again, more than $45 million each year – than nonmembers.

The pattern for German aid is also similar: $38 million to nonmembers, and $74 million to temporary UNSC members. UNSC members receive about 1.9 times more German bilateral aid – or more than $35 million each year – than nonmembers.

Foreign aid from the United Kingdom also disproportionately goes to UNSC members: $20 million to nonmembers, and $41 million to members. Compared to nonmembers, UNSC members receive about double the bilateral aid from the United Kingdom – or more than $20 million each year.

French foreign aid to nonmembers of the UNSC is $38 million, and to temporary members it is $66 million. UNSC members receive about 1.75 times more French bilateral aid than nonmembers – or more than $25 million each year.

---

[14] See Wooldridge (2009: 231–233).

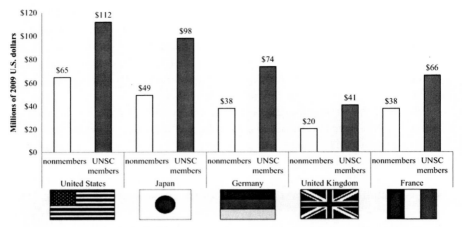

FIGURE 5.1. Bilateral development aid to UNSC members and nonmembers (1960 to 2009). *Notes:* Shaded columns indicate averages for yearly observations of developing countries on the UNSC (n = 339); white columns indicate averages for yearly observations of developing countries not on the UNSC (n = 5,719). *Source of data:* OECD (2012).

Figure 5.1 presents a visual depiction of the patterns of foreign aid to developing countries for the United States, Japan, Germany, the United Kingdom, and France.

The stark pattern of UNSC members receiving more bilateral aid may be due to nonrandom selection. We thus turn to a more rigorous analysis of the data where we control for potentially confounding factors: pariah state, inter-/intrastate war, level of economic development (GDP per capita), political regime, and U.S. military assistance – as well as fixed-effects for countries and years, and regional time trends.

Table 5.1 presents the results analyzing the global dataset on bilateral aid from, respectively, the United States, Japan, Germany, the United Kingdom, and France.

Regarding U.S. foreign aid, we do not find a statistically significant effect of UNSC membership in general (see model 1 of Table 5.1). We do, however, find a statistically significant effect of UNSC membership during years where the UNSC played an important role in global affairs, as indicated by media coverage of the institution (see model 2 of Table 5.1). Specifically, the coefficient of 1.074 suggests that foreign aid increases by nearly 200 percent when countries serve on the UNSC during important years. Our 90 percent confidence interval for the coefficient is wide:

TABLE 5.1. *The Effect of UNSC Membership on Bilateral Aid from the United States, Japan, Germany, the United Kingdom, and France – Global Data Sample*

Variable	Model 1	Model 2	Model 3	Model 4	Model 5	Model 6	Model 7	Model 8	Model 9	Model 10
	USA		Japan		Germany		UK		France	
UNSC member	0.39		0.54**		0.34*		0.07		0.10	
	(1.19)		(2.57)		(1.94)		(0.27)		(0.36)	
UNSC member, unimportant year		−0.37		0.17		0.11		0.32		0.30
		(0.69)		(0.65)		(0.48)		(0.97)		(0.76)
UNSC member, somewhat important year		0.50		0.75**		0.08		−0.83*		−0.10
		(1.08)		(2.12)		(0.36)		(1.70)		(0.21)
UNSC member, important year		1.07*		0.68		0.78**		0.44		−0.10
		(1.90)		(1.53)		(2.13)		(1.09)		(0.22)
Pariah state	−3.89**	−3.69**	−2.20**	−2.20**	−1.68	−1.59	−1.32	−1.04	−1.12	−1.02
	(2.20)	(2.05)	(2.10)	(2.07)	(1.15)	(1.11)	(0.69)	(0.55)	(0.84)	(0.76)
War	−1.18*	−1.17*	−1.86***	−1.88***	−0.77**	−0.77**	−1.09**	−1.12**	−0.22	−0.20
	(1.84)	(1.77)	(3.72)	(3.70)	(2.44)	(2.33)	(2.09)	(2.09)	(0.36)	(0.32)
ln (GDP per capita, PPP)	−0.46	−0.49	0.91*	1.00*	−0.24	−0.28	−1.23**	−1.17**	−0.53	−0.58
	(0.67)	(0.72)	(1.87)	(1.97)	(0.66)	(0.72)	(2.39)	(2.21)	(0.78)	(0.83)
Political regime	0.01	0.02	0.03	0.03	0.06*	0.06*	0.09**	0.10**	0.01	0.01
	(0.37)	(0.41)	(0.79)	(0.72)	(1.97)	(1.94)	(2.34)	(2.38)	(0.39)	(0.36)
U.S. military assistance (const. 2011 dollars)	0.19***	0.19***	0.15***	0.15***	0.11***	0.11***	0.10***	0.10***	0.09***	0.09***
	(6.24)	(6.20)	(5.78)	(5.69)	(5.07)	(5.01)	(3.45)	(3.31)	(3.20)	(3.17)
Number of countries	125	125	125	125	125	125	125	125	125	125
Number of observations	4,974	4,852	4,974	4,852	4,974	4,852	4,974	4,852	4,974	4,852
Period	60–09	60–08	60–09	60–08	60–09	60–08	60–09	60–08	60–09	60–08
R-squared	0.24	0.24	0.60	0.61	0.43	0.45	0.29	0.29	0.61	0.61

Notes: The dependent variables are the natural logarithms of bilateral aid disbursements (plus one) in constant 2009 US dollars by the respective donor (indicated by the column label). Estimation is with OLS. All regressions include country and year fixed-effects and regional quartics. Numbers in parentheses are the absolute values of t-statistics. As per convention, we mark absolute t-statistics with * if p<0.10 (statistical significance at the 10% confidence level); with ** if p<0.05 (statistical significance at the 5% confidence level); and with *** if p<0.01 (statistical significance at the 1% confidence level).

151

0.139 to 2.01.[15] The confidence interval indicates uncertainty about the precise effect, but the interval does not overlap zero, which conveys confidence that the effect of UNSC membership is indeed positive. If we drop the statistically insignificant control variables from the regression, the confidence in the effect of UNSC membership during important years strengthens to the 5 percent level (t = 2.28, not reported in the table but available in the replication materials).

The fact that we find an effect only for important years is basically consistent with the findings of Kuziemko and Werker (2006), who do find a more general effect but report that the effect for important years is more robust. The important-years finding is also consistent with the credibility argument presented in Chapter 2. The United States may use the more obvious channel of bilateral aid to influence UNSC members for important issues.

Turning to Japan, we find a more general effect, regardless of the level of media attention to the UNSC. We estimate that when countries serve on the UNSC, they receive 72 percent more foreign aid from Japan (calculated from model 3 of Table 5.1). The 95 percent confidence interval for the coefficient runs from 0.124 to 0.960, and we thus have confidence that the effect is positive (the p-value of the coefficient is 0.011). Breaking down the effect by the level of media coverage, we find that the effect is driven by the intermediate category: "somewhat" important years (see model 4 of Table 5.1). Recall, however, that we measure media attention by coverage in the American newspaper *New York Times*. So, the importance of the UNSC to Japan may follow another metric. The takeaway from this analysis is a new finding: Membership on the UNSC increases Japanese bilateral aid.

The finding accords with the overall arguments of Lim and Vreeland (2013), where we explain that the UNSC holds an important place in Japanese international affairs because of the legacy of World War II and the "Peace Constitution" that resulted, restricting the use of the Japanese Special Defense Forces.[16]

---

[15] Throughout this section, we refer to confidence intervals for the effects of our key explanatory variables. We do not list these confidence intervals in the tables to save space. They are available in the replication materials.

[16] For an analysis of the political economy of the Japanese and German defense industries, see Clare (2013: chapter 4). For discussions of the importance of the UN for Japan, see Green (2003), Tadokoro (1997), and Ueki (1993). On the ideational motivations behind Japan's global and regional strategy, see Katzenstein and Rouse (1993) and Katzenstein and Okawara (1993). Interestingly, Lim and Vreeland (2013) test for the effect of UNSC

We next analyze bilateral aid from Germany. As with Japanese aid, we find a positive statistically significant effect of UNSC membership (in line with Dreher, Nunnenkamp, and Schmaljohann 2013).[17] We calculate an increase of German foreign aid to UNSC members of about 40 percent during their terms (see model 5 of Table 5.1). The 90 percent confidence interval for this coefficient is 0.049 to 0.627, suggesting confidence in the positive effect. If we drop the statistically insignificant control variables from the specification and reanalyze the data, the statistical significance of the UNSC effect strengthens to the 5 percent level (t = 2.04). When we break up UNSC membership by the importance of the various years, we see that German aid follows a pattern similar to that of U.S. aid: important years drive our result. As reported in model 6 of Table 5.1, we calculate an 117 percent increase in German aid for UNSC members serving during important years (the 95 percent confidence interval of the coefficient is 0.054 to 1.498).

We thus find that both Japan and Germany increase their bilateral aid to countries elected to the UNSC. Recall that Japan and Germany seek permanent status on the UNSC through their membership in the Group of Four (G4). As for election to the UNSC, Germany has won more often than any other country in Western Europe, and Japan has won more often than any other country in Asia. In addition to these avenues for more influence over the UNSC, Japan and Germany appear to seek informal influence over the UNSC by providing increased foreign aid to developing countries when they serve.

Our analysis of bilateral aid from the United Kingdom and France reveals a different pattern. Model 7 of Table 5.1 reports a relatively small, positive coefficient that is not statistically significant for the effect of UNSC membership on aid from the United Kingdom. Model 8 reports

membership on Japanese bilateral aid to Asian countries and find no effect. Instead, they detect an effect through the AsDB, where Japan exercises privileged power in governance (Krasner 1981: 304). They argue that the AsDB allows Japan to obfuscate the politically driven finance. It may be that Japan prefers to use its leverage in the AsDB to win favor with Asian members of the UNSC but relies more on bilateral aid with countries outside of the Asian region as it has comparatively less political leverage over global institutions. Our analysis encompasses all developing countries in the world. For further analyses of Japanese bilateral aid, see Arase (1995), Saito (1996), Katada and McKeown (1998), Kilby (2006, 2011b), Miller and Dolšak (2007), Strand and Tuman (2010), and Gartzke and Naoi (2011).

[17] Dreher, Nunnenkamp, and Schmaljohann (2013) also investigate whether the political ideology of the German government and the relevant ministries influences the effect of temporary UNSC membership on German aid. It does not. Left governments are as likely as conservative ones to give more aid to temporary members of the UNSC.

a statistically significant negative effect of UNSC membership during moderately important years (although we have not found this effect to be robust in other specifications that we have tried). Models 9 and 10 reveal no statistically significant effects of UNSC membership on French foreign aid.

France and the United Kingdom enjoy permanent status along with veto power. Neither country initiates as many resolutions as the United States, and neither has as active an agenda on the UNSC as the superpower. If they agree with the United States, they can often free ride on U.S. efforts to win votes from temporary members of the UNSC. And they can exercise their veto power when they oppose a resolution. Perhaps because they enjoy such power on the UNSC, they need not buy additional influence over temporary members of the UNSC through foreign aid. Japan and Germany do not have the same luxury. The pair that lacks membership on the UNSC – and that has sought both permanent and elected membership – appears more interested in trying to win influence at the UNSC by providing bilateral foreign aid to elected members.

Regarding the possibility that our analysis suffers from problems of endogeneity, we note that the non-findings for the United Kingdom and France reduce our concern that countries that win election to the UNSC are simply important countries in global affairs that generally receive high levels of foreign aid. If countries elected to the UNSC carried broader strategic importance, we would expect effects for the United Kingdom and France. Instead, we find that temporary members of the UNSC are important to the United States only during important years, when the United States government has an agenda to pursue on the UNSC. UNSC members also appear important in general to Japan and Germany, who lack permanent status on the body. We do not find, however, an effect for the United Kingdom or France, as they enjoy permanent veto power on the UNSC and can free ride on U.S. efforts to lobby elected members of the UNSC.

Nevertheless, we seek to further address the possibility of endogeneity. In Table 5.2, we revisit our analysis of bilateral aid, focusing our attention exclusively on Africa. This region's commitment to the turn-taking norm attenuates our concerns about selection bias. We find a remarkably similar set of results.

Regarding U.S. bilateral aid, we find no general effect of UNSC membership for Africa (Table 5.2, model 1), but we do find an effect during somewhat important and important years, as gauged by media coverage. The point estimate and statistical significance for somewhat important

TABLE 5.2. *The Effect of UNSC Membership on Bilateral Aid from the United States, Japan, Germany, the United Kingdom, and France – Africa Data Sample*

Variable	Model 1	Model 2	Model 3	Model 4	Model 5	Model 6	Model 7	Model 8	Model 9	Model 10
	USA		Japan		Germany		UK		France	
UNSC member	0.54		0.74**		0.08		−0.06		−0.15	
	(1.28)		(2.41)		(0.37)		(0.14)		(0.41)	
UNSC member, unimportant year		−0.30		0.41		−0.20		0.16		0.14
		(0.35)		(1.03)		(0.57)		(0.34)		(0.24)
UNSC member, somewhat important year		1.34**		1.12*		0.39		−1.06		−0.03
		(2.29)		(1.86)		(1.41)		(1.12)		(0.04)
UNSC member, important year		0.78*		0.95		0.16		0.65		−0.67
		(1.94)		(1.45)		(0.54)		(1.38)		(1.15)
Pariah state	−7.15**	−7.00**	−5.60***	−5.77***	−5.18	−5.09	−6.15*	−5.94*	−3.78	−3.65
	(2.58)	(2.50)	(4.88)	(5.33)	(1.56)	(1.55)	(1.90)	(1.82)	(1.45)	(1.39)
War	−1.09**	−1.10**	−1.41	−1.44*	−0.57*	−0.57*	−0.57	−0.65	−0.77	−0.75
	(2.09)	(2.06)	(1.64)	(1.68)	(1.77)	(1.76)	(1.00)	(1.20)	(0.80)	(0.76)
ln (GDP per capita, PPP)	−0.10	−0.14	1.90***	2.02***	0.21	0.17	−1.29***	−1.29***	−0.07	−0.15
	(0.14)	(0.18)	(2.88)	(2.90)	(0.37)	(0.27)	(3.23)	(3.09)	(0.09)	(0.18)
Political regime	−0.04	−0.04	−0.03	−0.03	−0.02	−0.02	0.07*	0.07*	−0.09**	−0.10**
	(0.87)	(0.90)	(0.81)	(0.86)	(0.76)	(0.77)	(1.74)	(1.79)	(2.31)	(2.39)
U.S. military assistance (const. 2011 dollars)	0.09***	0.09***	0.09***	0.09***	0.05**	0.05**	0.03	0.02	0.05	0.06
	(2.95)	(3.00)	(2.78)	(2.77)	(2.53)	(2.50)	(1.00)	(0.85)	(1.50)	(1.51)
Number of countries	49	49	49	49	49	49	49	49	49	49
Number of observations	2,149	2,100	2,149	2,100	2,149	2,100	2,149	2,100	2,149	2,100
Period	60–09	60–08	60–09	60–08	60–09	60–08	60–09	60–08	60–09	60–08
R-squared	0.31	0.31	0.68	0.68	0.45	0.45	0.30	0.30	0.62	0.62

Notes: The dependent variables are the natural logarithms of bilateral aid disbursements (plus one) in constant 2009 US dollars by the respective donor (indicated by the column label). Estimation is with OLS. All regressions include country and year fixed-effects and regional quartics. Numbers in parentheses are the absolute values of t-statistics. As per convention, we mark absolute t-statistics with * if $p<0.10$ (statistical significance at the 10% confidence level); with ** if $p<0.05$ (statistical significance at the 5% confidence level); and with *** if $p<0.01$ (statistical significance at the 1% confidence level).

years are actually greater than those for important years. But when we drop the statistically insignificant control variables from the specification, the statistical significance of important years increases, surpassing that of somewhat important years (results available in the replication materials). We conclude that the United States increased bilateral aid to UNSC members from Africa during years when attention to the Security Council reaches moderate to high levels.

For Japanese foreign aid, we find a general effect of UNSC membership in Africa. We estimate an increase in Japanese foreign aid of 110 percent for African countries serving on the UNSC. The 95 percent confidence interval of the coefficient ranges from 0.122 to 1.361. When we break down the effect by the level of media coverage the UNSC received during specific years, we find only a marginally significant effect for somewhat important years, suggesting that either Japan supplies the increase in aid to UNSC members regardless of media attention, or because Japan has different foreign policy objectives than is indicated by the U.S. media.

Turning to Germany, we do not find the same statistically significant effect for aid to Africa as we did in the global sample. We find, for example, a positive coefficient of 0.075, but it is not statistically significant. This result for Germany does not imply that the estimated positive effect of UNSC membership on German foreign aid for the global sample (reported in Table 5.1) is inaccurate. It certainly remains possible that Germany attempts to buy influence with UNSC members outside of Africa, for example, in regions such as Eastern Europe, where Germany has a strong presence, as well as in Asia and in Latin America and the Caribbean. Indeed, the tests using the global data sample presented in Table 5.1 are quite conservative, including a full set of control variables, country and year fixed-effects, and regional time trends. Still, the possibility of selection bias casts a longer shadow for the German result, whereas the results for the United States and Japan stand as more convincing because they are confirmed by examining the data from Africa. So, for more rigorous attention to the UNSC effect on German bilateral aid, we refer readers to Dreher, Nunnenkamp, and Schmaljohann (2013).

Before closing this discussion of bilateral aid, we note the effects of the control variables. The pariah state variable (capturing the influence of U.S. and UN sanctions) has massive negative effects for the United States and Japan, statistically significant at the 5 percent level or stronger. The negative effects of this variable for Germany, the United Kingdom, and France are not statistically significant. We find the same pattern for aid to Africa, except that the negative effect of pariah state is statistically significant at a marginal level for the United Kingdom. These results suggest that the foreign aid policies of the United States and Japan respond in systematic ways to U.S. and UN sanctions.

Turning to war, we find a negative impact on aid from the United States, Japan, Germany, and the United Kingdom. In Africa, the negative effect of war is robust at marginal levels for the United States, Japan, and Germany.

Level of economic development (GDP per capita) has the expected negative effect only for the United Kingdom, where the effect is statistically significant at the 5 percent level; for Japan the effect is strangely positive and statistically significant at the 10 percent level. We find the same pattern for aid to Africa. This set of results is not too surprising given that we control for country fixed-effects and thus use the within-country variation to identify the effects of other variables. Controlled for country fixed-effects, our results imply that changes in per capita GDP from its mean – for the same country – do not robustly predict the amount of aid the country receives.

Political regime appears to matter for Germany (marginally significant) and the United Kingdom – they prefer democracies. For the Africa sample, the statistical significance is at a marginal level only for the United Kingdom, while we find a strange negative effect for France, which appears to prefer African dictatorships – likely due to their colonial ties.

Finally, consider the effect of U.S. military assistance. Not surprisingly, we detect a statistically significant positive correlation between this variable and U.S. foreign aid. Countries that receive more military assistance from the United States also receive more development assistance, both due to their friendship with the superpower. More surprisingly, however, we detect a similar correlation for Japanese, German, UK, and French bilateral aid as well. The effect persists for the United States, Japan, and Germany for aid to Africa. Strategic targets of U.S. military assistance appear to also represent strategic targets of development aid from the most powerful NATO allies and Japan.

5.7.2 IMF and World Bank Programs

The governance structures of the IMF and the World Bank grant privileges to the top five shareholders of the institutions: the United States, Japan, Germany, France, and the United Kingdom. They have more voting power than other countries. In the early years of the IMF, the United States controlled about 34 percent of the votes. Nowadays, the

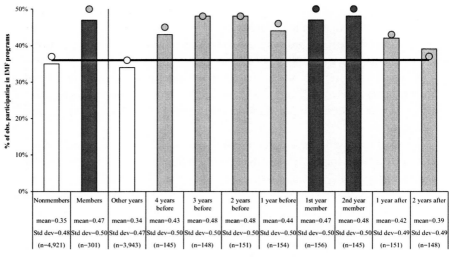

FIGURE 5.2. Participation in IMF programs by UN Security Council member status over time. *Notes:* Horizontal line shows the average rate of participation in IMF programs across the sample. Columns reflect averages for all countries. Circles reflect the averages for only low and lower-middle income countries. *Source:* Dreher et al. (2009b).

United States still controls about 17 percent of the votes, with Japan and Germany controlling 6 percent each, and France and the United Kingdom about 5 percent each.[18] This group has exercised de facto control over the selection and termination of the IMF Managing Director (always a European) and the World Bank President (always an American). Both institutions have their headquarters in Washington, DC, providing convenient access for U.S. policy-makers. It stands to reason that the political control that the United States and its allies enjoy at these Bretton Woods institutions translates into perks for countries considered strategically important to them. Do the major shareholders use their political influence to preference temporary members of the UNSC?

Regarding the IMF, consider first Figure 5.2, which presents the basic pattern of UNSC membership and participation in programs sponsored by the IMF (originally presented in Dreher et al. 2009b).

_____

[18] There currently exists an agreement to increase the vote-shares of emerging market countries, particularly China. As of this writing, however, the reform has yet to be adopted.

The left side of Figure 5.2 shows that the rate of participation in IMF programs is higher for UNSC members than for nonmembers. The columns group all countries in the world, while the dots on the figure focus exclusively on developing countries (low- and lower-middle-income countries). The average annual rate of participation in IMF programs for countries not on the UNSC is 35 percent; for UNSC members, the rate is 47 percent. Focusing on developing countries, the rate is 37 percent for nonmembers and 50 percent for UNSC members.

The right-hand part of Figure 5.2 breaks down participation over time. Focusing on developing countries, we see that four years before membership on the UNSC, the annual rate of participation is 45 percent. During the first and second years serving on the UNSC, the rate of participation increases to 50 percent. Then, exogenous term limits force countries to step down from the UNSC, and participation rates drop to 43 percent. By the second year after ending a term on the UNSC, the rate of participation drops back to 37 percent, which is the average for nonmembers. This circumstantial evidence suggests an association between membership on the UNSC and participation in IMF programs.

More rigorous analyses of these data, which we have conducted with Jan-Egbert Sturm, reveals that the correlation is statistically significant at the 5 percent level and robust across various model specifications (see Dreher, Sturm, and Vreeland 2009b).[19]

Unlike with U.S. bilateral aid, we do not find that the effect of UNSC membership on IMF program participation depends on the level of media attention. The UNSC effect on IMF participation appears to be more general.

Of course, some may wonder if IMF programs really represent a reward for developing countries serving on the UNSC. After all, the IMF is famous – indeed, notorious – for the conditionality attached to its loans. In return for a loan, countries often must undertake painful austerity measures, such as raising interest rates, cutting public expenditures, and raising taxes. Increased access to IMF loans may stand as a benefit for UNSC members, but the policy conditions attached to those loans could be costly.

---

[19] In that study, for example, we address selection bias by exploiting the exogeneity of term limits, employing the first three lags of UNSC participation as instrumental variables, among others. Using the Davidson-MacKinnon (1993) test for consistency of OLS estimates, we cannot reject the null hypothesis at conventional significance levels in any of the models that we analyze, implying that endogeneity does not appear to be a major issue.

We have thus analyzed newly available data on the number of conditions attached to each IMF arrangement in our research with Jan-Egbert Sturm (see Dreher, Sturm, and Vreeland 2013). We find that the number of conditions attached to IMF loans is also associated with UNSC membership: UNSC members receive fewer conditions. We consider the IMF "Monitoring of Fund Arrangements" (MONA) database on the level of conditionality attached to (a maximum of) 314 IMF arrangements with 101 countries over the 1992 to 2008 period. We estimate that Security Council members receive about 30 percent fewer conditions. The overall effect appears to be especially driven by specific policy areas such as debt repayment, trade and the balance of payments, credit to the government, and domestic pricing. The findings suggest that UNSC members have a stronger bargaining position with respect to the IMF, presumably because they enjoy the political support of the major shareholders of the IMF. This conclusion corroborates the examples of Kenya, Tanzania, and Zimbabwe discussed in Chapter 3.[20]

Summarizing what we have found about the IMF, UNSC members enjoy greater access to IMF loans, as indicated by their higher rates of participation, and their loans have fewer policy conditions attached. We also analyze the effect of UNSC membership on the size of loans, but we do not find a substantial effect. So, while UNSC membership influences access to loans and the level of conditionality, the actual size of the IMF loan remains, on average, about the same size as loans to nonmembers of the UNSC. We return to this finding below when we analyze the swing-voter hypothesis. It turns out that loan size is indeed impacted, but to see this, one must account for UNSC voting patterns.

Turning to the World Bank, Figure 5.3 presents the basic pattern of UNSC membership and the annual number of new World Bank projects (originally presented in Dreher et al. 2009a).[21] The left side of the figure

---

[20] The number of IMF conditions has been used as a proxy for stringency of conditionality in several studies (see, for example, Ivanova et al. 2006; Gould 2003; Dreher 2004; Bulíř and Moon 2004; Dreher and Jensen 2007; and Caraway, Rickard, and Anner 2012) – also see Rickard and Caraway (2012). Stone (2008) further suggests the scope of policy conditions. Relatedly, Stone (2002) demonstrates that when governments fail to comply with conditionality, they face lighter punishment if they enjoy strategic importance with the IMF's major shareholders. We discuss the consequences of lighter conditionality in the following chapter.

[21] The IMF typically provides only one loan to a country during a given year, as these loans target macroeconomic objectives. Most World Bank loans go toward a wide range of specific developmental projects, such as building schools or power plants. A government may receive several such loans at a time.

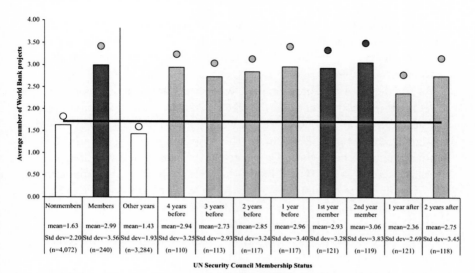

FIGURE 5.3. New World Bank projects by UN Security Council member status over time. *Notes:* Horizontal line shows the average number of World Bank projects across the sample. Columns reflect averages for all countries. Circles reflect the averages for only low and lower-middle income countries. *Source:* Dreher et al. (2009a).

shows that the average number of new World Bank projects is higher for UNSC members than for nonmembers. The columns group all countries in the world, while the dots on the figure focus exclusively on developing countries (low- and lower-middle-income countries – as in Figure 5.2). The average number of new World Bank projects for countries not on the UNSC is 1.6; for UNSC members, it is 2.99. Focusing on developing countries, the average is 1.82 for nonmembers and 3.42 for UNSC members. The right-hand part of the figure breaks down participation over time. The World Bank pattern is not as stark as the IMF pattern. Still, we see a peak average number of new World Bank projects of 3.1 during the second year on the UNSC, followed by a drop off to 2.36 when exogenous term limits force countries to step down from the UNSC. Focusing on developing countries, the peak average number of new World Bank projects is 3.5 during the second year on the UNSC, followed by a drop-off to 2.78 the year that they leave the UNSC.

We have conducted more rigorous analyses of these data with Jan-Egbert Sturm. The analyses reveal that the statistical correlation is significant at the 10 percent level and robust across various model specifications (see Dreher, Sturm, and Vreeland 2009a). We do not find that this effect depends on the level of importance as measured by annual media attention. We conclude that the positive effect of UNSC membership on the number of new World Bank projects that countries receive holds in general.

As for the level of conditionality, when we started with this project, a detailed and comprehensive dataset on World Bank conditions was not publically available. Recently, however, such a database has become available, and Martin Breßlein of the University of Trier and Maya Schmaljohann of Heidelberg University have investigated whether commercial interests of the World Bank's major shareholders drive the number of trade-related conditions attached to World Bank loans (Breßlein and Schmaljohann 2013). They include temporary UNSC membership in the analysis but do not find an effect. Their study does not especially focus on UNSC membership, however, and we leave such analysis to future research.

Turning to the disbursements of World Bank loans, we divide the World Bank data according to the specific agency disbursing the loans. The International Bank for Reconstruction and Development (IBRD) provides loans to middle-income countries, while the International Development Association (IDA) gives credits to poor countries. As with bilateral aid, we observe larger loans for UNSC members than for nonmembers. IBRD loans to nonmembers average $660,000, whereas loans to temporary UNSC members average $1.71 million (measured in constant 2000 U.S. dollars). IDA loans to nonmembers average $320,000 and to temporary UNSC members average $720,000. Addressing these patterns more rigorously, we regress the natural logarithm of annual loan disbursements (plus one) to specific countries on the same set of control variables that we employed for our analyses of bilateral aid above, and we include country and year fixed-effects along with regional time trends. We analyze both the global data sample and the sample of data for just Africa. Table 5.3 presents the results of the analyses.

For the IBRD, we find a positive, statistically significant effect of UNSC membership. For the global sample, we calculate that loan disbursements increase by 87 percent, and the finding is statistically significant at the 5 percent level (see model 1 of Table 5.3). For the Africa sample, we calculate a larger effect of 145 percent (see model 3 of Table 5.3). When we break down the effect by the level of annual media coverage, we find that the effect in the global sample may be driven more by important years, but the level of statistical significance drops to the 10 percent level, so we have more confidence in the overall effect. We see the same pattern

TABLE 5.5. The Effect of UNSC Membership on World Bank Loan Disbursements – Global and Africa Data Samples

Variable	Model 1	Model 2	Model 3	Model 4	Model 5	Model 6	Model 7	Model 8
	IBRD Disbursements		IBRD Disbursements		IDA Disbursements		IDA Disbursements	
	Global Sample		Africa Sample		Global Sample		Africa Sample	
UNSC member	0.63**		0.90**		0.11		0.52*	
	(2.54)		(2.24)		(0.62)		(1.92)	
UNSC member, unimportant year		0.46		0.59		0.53		0.93*
		(1.12)		(0.86)		(1.58)		(1.84)
UNSC member, somewhat important year		0.58		0.24		−0.53		0.18
		(1.55)		(0.43)		(1.39)		(0.38)
UNSC member, important year		0.82*		1.98***		0.28		0.32
		(1.87)		(2.85)		(0.81)		(0.65)
Pariah state	−1.50	−1.54	−3.16	−3.28	−0.70	−0.78	0.11	0.06
	(1.11)	(1.08)	(1.33)	(1.33)	(0.62)	(0.66)	(0.04)	(0.02)
War	−1.45**	−1.46**	−1.20*	−1.29**	−1.28**	−1.30**	−1.79**	−1.75**
	(2.33)	(2.38)	(1.90)	(2.02)	(2.07)	(2.08)	(2.28)	(2.17)
ln (GDP per capita, PPP)	1.86***	1.88***	2.04***	2.11***	−0.69	−0.83	−0.21	−0.32
	(3.08)	(3.07)	(2.81)	(2.84)	(0.77)	(0.89)	(0.19)	(0.28)
Political regime	−0.02	−0.02	−0.07	−0.07	0.06	0.06	0.06	0.05
	(0.41)	(0.54)	(1.17)	(1.12)	(1.55)	(1.49)	(1.10)	(1.00)
U.S. military assistance (const. 2011 dollars)	0.03	0.03	0.04	0.03	0.12***	0.12***	0.14***	0.14***
	(1.25)	(1.14)	(1.00)	(0.93)	(3.77)	(3.74)	(3.77)	(3.78)
Number of countries	125	125	49	49	125	125	49	49
Number of observations	4,974	4,852	2,149	2,100	4,974	4,852	2,149	2,100
Period	60–09	60–08	60–09	60–08	60–09	60–08	60–09	60–08
R-squared	0.46	0.47	0.35	0.36	0.38	0.39	0.52	0.53

Notes: The dependent variables are the natural logarithms of aid disbursements (plus one) in constant 2005 US dollars by the respective donor (indicated by the column label). IBRD refers to the International Bank for Reconstruction and Development. IDA refers to the International Development Association. Together these institutions are commonly called the World Bank. Estimation is with OLS. All regressions include country and year fixed-effects and regional quartics. Numbers in parentheses are the absolute values of t-statistics. As per convention, we mark absolute t-statistics with * if $p<0.10$ (statistical significance at the 10% confidence level); with ** if $p<0.05$ (statistical significance at the 5% confidence level); and with *** if $p<0.01$ (statistical significance at the 1% confidence level).

for the Africa sample, but the size of the coefficient and the level of statistical significance for important years are both substantially higher (see model 4 of Table 5.3).

For the IDA, the results are, by and large, weaker and not as statistically significant. We estimate that the effect of UNSC membership is positive in the global data samples, but the effect is not statistically significant at conventional levels. When we break down UNSC membership by the level of importance received during specific years, we find similar non-results. For the Africa sample, however, we estimate a positive effect significant at the 10 percent level (model 7 of Table 5.3), and a marginally significant positive effect for unimportant years (model 8 of Table 5.3). We conclude that there is an effect of UNSC membership on World Bank loan disbursements, and it appears to operate mainly through the loans to middle-income countries that borrow from the IBRD, although there is also evidence of an effect through IDA lending to poor countries in Africa.

Turning to the control variables, we note that inter- and intrastate war appears to have a robust negative effect on World Bank loan disbursements. Level of economic development – ln(GDP per capita, PPP) – has a positive effect on IBRD disbursements, which makes sense because our sample includes only countries eligible to receive World Bank loans, and the IBRD focuses on the richer countries from within this set (the middle-income countries). The effect of development is not statistically significant for the IDA – this is likely due to the fact that there are "blend" countries that can receive loans from both the IBRD and the IDA (countries like India, for example). We note that neither internationally imposed sanctions (pariah state) nor the domestic level of democracy (political regime) have an effect on World Bank loan disbursements. Interestingly, U.S. military assistance has a highly significant positive effect on IDA lending – both globally and within Africa. Having not originally set out to explore this result, we find it fascinating. The finding resonates with our basic thesis that the political preferences of its major shareholders partly drive World Bank lending.

Summarizing our analyses of the effect of UNSC membership on receiving perks from the IMF and the World Bank, we find that rates of IMF participation and the average number of World Bank loans both increase with UNSC membership, independent of the level of importance in a given year. IMF conditionality, as measured by the number of conditions, is softer for UNSC members. We have thus far not reported an impact of UNSC members on the loan size, but we return to this question below in Section 5.7.6, where we discuss preliminary evidence of an interesting effect when one accounts for voting behavior on the UNSC. To foreshadow, we find smaller IMF loans when governments with high affinity with the United States fail to vote along U.S. lines on the UNSC, presumably as a punishment. As for the World Bank, while we leave detailed analysis for future research, we report initial evidence that World Bank conditionality is not affected by UNSC membership. We do find, however, that disbursements of World Bank loans through the IBRD increase for UNSC members. This finding holds globally as well as for Africa.

5.7.3 The UN

The governance of UN development aid does not follow the model of the Bretton Woods institutions. The underlying logic at the IMF and the World Bank is "one dollar, one vote," and the largest economies in the world have the most say. Now, the vote shares lag behind reality, otherwise China would (already) have more votes than Japan, Germany, France, and the United Kingdom. Still, the basic principle incentivizes powerful countries: The more money they contribute, the more votes they receive. For many UN agencies, however, the basic principle is "one country, one vote." Equitable representation of sovereign nations takes priority over incentivizing donor countries.

The UN also has several aid agencies, including the World Food Program (WFP), the UN Development Program (UNDP), the UN Children's Emergency Fund (UNICEF), the Office of the United Nations High Commissioner for Refugees (UNHCR – also known as the UN Refugee Agency), and the United Nations Regular Program for Technical Assistance (UNTA). Each has a specialized mission, its own bureaucracy, and its own governance – ultimately accountable to the UNGA through various, circuitous channels.

This governance structure may reduce the politicization of UN aid. While Kuziemko and Werker (2006) estimate an effect of UNSC membership on U.S. bilateral aid of more than 50 percent, they estimate a much smaller effect on UN development aid: only about 7 percent. In particular, they find that the effect mainly operates through UNICEF. Interestingly, they note that the United States stands as the largest and most important funder of UNICEF, and they suggest that the United States may, therefore, hold a degree of influence over UNICEF priorities.

If the United States designates a country as politically important, this country may find itself higher up on the agendas of Americans working throughout many bureaucracies, including the UN.

In our analyses of the global dataset, we find little evidence of UN favoritism for UNSC members. Table 5.4 presents the results of our analyses, where we consider (the natural logarithm of) foreign aid from the UN in general (plus one), and then break down the source of aid by specific agency: WFP, UNDP, UNICEF, UNHCR, and UNTA. We find no statistically significant effect of UNSC membership for any of the UN sources of aid, neither in general nor by the importance of year – the only possible exception is the marginally significant positive effect of UNSC membership through the UNHCR, but we have not found the effect to be robust. The non-result for UNSC membership fits with the formal governance of the UN, which does not privilege powerful countries in the same explicit way that the governance of the IMF and the World Bank does.

Turning to the control variables, neither pariah state nor political regime has a statistically significant effect. In line with the organization's charter, war lowers aid from the UN in general, and more specifically through WFP, UNDP, and UNTA. As UN aid targets poor countries, level of economic development has the expected negative effect for the UN in general, specifically through WFP, UNICEF, and UNHCR. Interestingly, U.S. military assistance correlates with UN aid, specifically through UNDP, UNICEF, and UNTA.

In fact, when we turn to the Africa sample (Table 5.5), we do find further evidence that international politics influences the delivery of UN foreign aid. Consider first the effects of the control variables. Pariah state has a large negative effect for UN aid in general (Table 5.5, models 1 and 2), and specifically for UNDP, UNICEF, UNHCR, and UNTA (Table 5.5, models 5–12). So, African countries under U.S. or UN sanctions receive less aid from the UN. Political regime has a negative effect that is marginally significant for UN aid in general and specifically for UNHCR aid (marginally) and UNTA aid (Table 5.5, models 10 through 12). The estimates imply that African democracies receive less aid from the UN than do Africa's nondemocratic governments. African countries engaged in warfare receive less aid from UNDP, UNHCR, and UNTA (Table 5.5, models 5, 6, and 9 through 12). As for U.S. military assistance, we detect no effect in Africa.

Turning to the effect of UNSC membership for African countries, we find a positive effect that is significant at the 10 percent level for UN aid

TABLE 5.4. *The Effect of UNSC Membership on UN Foreign Aid – Global Data Sample*

Variable	Model 1	Model 2	Model 3	Model 4	Model 5	Model 6	Model 7	Model 8	Model 9	Model 10	Model 11	Model 12
	UN	UN	WFP	WFP	UNDP	UNDP	UNICEF	UNICEF	UNHCR	UNHCR	UNTA	UNTA
UNSC member	0.16		-0.29		0.17		0.24		0.47*		0.02	
	(1.35)		(1.02)		(1.16)		(1.36)		(1.73)		(0.18)	
UNSC member, unimportant year		0.22		-0.37		-0.02		0.21		0.55		0.16
		(1.41)		(0.77)		(0.07)		(0.60)		(1.25)		(0.99)
UNSC member, somewhat important year		-0.01		-0.32		0.11		0.21		0.36		-0.09
		(0.09)		(0.67)		(0.60)		(0.83)		(0.74)		(0.44)
UNSC member, important year		0.21		0.12		0.33		0.31		0.43		0.04
		(0.98)		(0.26)		(1.23)		(1.45)		(0.87)		(0.25)
Pariah state	-1.46	-1.42	-0.20	-0.08	-1.69	-1.59	-1.32	-1.26	0.24	0.29	-1.78	-1.76
	(1.32)	(1.30)	(0.19)	(0.07)	(1.28)	(1.20)	(1.07)	(1.01)	(0.16)	(0.20)	(1.60)	(1.58)
War	-0.71*	-0.73*	-1.35*	-1.40*	-0.80**	-0.82**	-0.48	-0.49	-0.67	-0.61	-0.62*	-0.64*
	(1.94)	(1.94)	(1.77)	(1.83)	(2.40)	(2.39)	(1.13)	(1.13)	(1.10)	(1.00)	(1.89)	(1.89)
ln (GDP per capita, PPP)	-0.65*	-0.66*	-2.07***	-2.07***	-0.43	-0.42	-1.06*	-1.09**	-1.43***	-1.47***	-0.05	-0.00
	(1.79)	(1.81)	(3.60)	(3.58)	(1.14)	(1.10)	(1.93)	(2.00)	(2.88)	(2.90)	(0.16)	(0.01)
Political regime	0.04	0.03	0.04	0.03	0.04	0.04	0.01	0.00	-0.02	-0.02	0.01	0.01
	(1.51)	(1.44)	(0.87)	(0.81)	(1.37)	(1.38)	(0.18)	(0.12)	(0.50)	(0.51)	(0.64)	(0.50)
U.S. mil. assistance (const. 2011 dollars)	0.05***	0.05***	0.02	0.02	0.05**	0.05**	0.04*	0.04**	0.00	0.00	0.05***	0.04**
	(2.73)	(2.68)	(0.62)	(0.62)	(2.49)	(2.46)	(1.92)	(1.99)	(0.13)	(0.11)	(2.79)	(2.61)
Number of countries	125	125	125	125	125	125	125	125	125	125	125	125
Number of observations	4,974	4,852	4,922	4,800	4,676	4,554	4,974	4,852	4,974	4,852	4,974	4,852
Period	60–09	60–08	60–09	60–08	60–09	60–08	60–09	60–08	60–09	60–08	60–09	60–08
R-squared	0.87	0.87	0.47	0.47	0.63	0.64	0.75	0.75	0.46	0.47	0.87	0.86

Notes: The dependent variables are the natural logarithms of aid disbursements (plus one) in constant 2009 US dollars by the respective donor (indicated by the column label). Estimation is with OLS. All regressions include country and year fixed-effects and regional quartics. Numbers in parentheses are the absolute values of t-statistics. As per convention, we mark absolute t-statistics with * if $p<0.10$ (statistical significance at the 10% confidence level); with ** if $p<0.05$ (statistical significance at the 5% confidence level); and with *** if $p<0.01$ (statistical significance at the 1% confidence level).

TABLE 5.5. *The Effect of UNSC Membership on UN Foreign Aid – Africa Data Sample*

Variable	Model 1	Model 2	Model 3	Model 4	Model 5	Model 6	Model 7	Model 8	Model 9	Model 10	Model 11	Model 12
	UN		WFP		UNDP		UNICEF		UNHCR		UNTA	
UNSC member	0.20*		0.96***		0.11		0.35**		0.67*		0.03	
	(1.91)		(3.36)		(0.63)		(2.19)		(1.84)		(0.18)	
UNSC member, unimportant year		0.23		0.67		-0.07		0.65**		0.31		0.10
		(1.25)		(1.20)		(0.18)		(2.49)		(0.47)		(0.53)
UNSC member, somewhat important year		0.40*		0.99***		0.48**		0.21		1.38**		-0.02
		(2.15)		(3.77)		(2.40)		(1.18)		(2.55)		(0.06)
UNSC member, important year		-0.01		1.17**		-0.23		0.19		0.72*		0.10
		(0.08)		(2.07)		(1.30)		(0.96)		(1.68)		(0.61)
Pariah state	-4.64**	-4.59**	-3.07	-3.13	-5.25*	-5.02*	-5.11***	-5.09***	-4.37***	-4.30***	-5.33***	-5.33***
	(2.19)	(2.19)	(1.45)	(1.49)	(1.96)	(1.85)	(2.97)	(2.97)	(2.89)	(2.89)	(2.73)	(2.73)
War	-0.77	-0.78	-0.60	-0.68	-0.67**	-0.71**	-0.75	-0.76	-1.89**	-1.97**	-0.80*	-0.82*
	(1.56)	(1.58)	(0.64)	(0.71)	(2.32)	(2.45)	(1.49)	(1.50)	(2.46)	(2.55)	(1.82)	(1.84)
ln (GDP per capita, PPP)	-0.30	-0.31	-2.34**	-2.30***	-0.07	-0.06	-0.46	-0.46	-1.26***	-1.30***	0.28	0.27
	(0.90)	(0.91)	(3.88)	(3.73)	(0.23)	(0.19)	(0.87)	(0.89)	(2.75)	(2.78)	(1.14)	(1.10)
Political regime	-0.03*	-0.04*	0.02	0.01	-0.02	-0.02	-0.03	-0.03	-0.10	-0.11*	-0.04**	-0.05**
	(1.84)	(1.87)	(0.37)	(0.30)	(1.23)	(1.06)	(1.02)	(1.14)	(1.67)	(1.74)	(2.10)	(2.09)
U.S. mil. assistance (const. 2011 dollars)	0.01	0.01	0.00	-0.00	0.00	0.00	-0.01	-0.01	0.02	0.03	-0.00	-0.00
	(0.56)	(0.64)	(0.03)	(0.01)	(0.17)	(0.26)	(0.65)	(0.55)	(0.75)	(0.81)	(0.29)	(0.20)
Number of countries	49	49	49	49	49	49	49	49	49	49	49	49
Number of observations	2,149	2,100	2,128	2,079	2,020	1,971	2,149	2,100	2,149	2,100	2,149	2,100
Period	60-09	60-08	61-09	61-08	65-09	65-08	60-09	60-08	60-09	60-08	60-09	60-08
R-squared	0.92	0.92	0.57	0.57	0.80	0.81	0.87	0.87	0.51	0.52	0.91	0.90

Notes: The dependent variables are the natural logarithms of aid disbursements (plus one) in constant 2009 US dollars by the respective donor (indicated by the column label). Estimation is with OLS. All regressions include country and year fixed-effects and regional quartics. Numbers in parentheses are the absolute values of t-statistics. As per convention, we mark absolute t-statistics with * if $p<0.10$ (statistical significance at the 10% confidence level); with ** if $p<0.05$ (statistical significance at the 5% confidence level); and with *** if $p<0.01$ (statistical significance at the 1% confidence level).

in general. The effect appears to be strongest for UNSC members serving during somewhat important years, as measured by media attention to the UNSC. For the WFP, the positive effect is statistically significant at the 1 percent level and appears to be driven by UNSC members serving during somewhat important and important years. For UNDP and UNHR, we find a positive effect, significant at the 5 percent level, for UNSC members serving during somewhat important years. For UNICEF, we find a positive effect for UNSC membership in general – significant at the 5 percent level – and the effect appears counterintuitively strongest during unimportant years. The magnitudes of the statistically significant coefficients range from 0.196 (for general UN aid – model 1, Table 5.5) to 1.376 (UNHCR during somewhat important years – model 10, Table 5.5). Calculating the percentage change, the range goes from 22 percent to 296 percent.

Having found no effect at the global level, we are surprised to find this set of positive and statistically significant effects for Africa. We cannot, however, easily dismiss them. The effects for UNICEF and for UN aid in general are consistent with the findings of Kuziemko and Werker (2006). Moreover, the focus on Africa represents a more restrictive test on the subset of the data where we can expect the lowest level of selection bias due to Africa's commitment to the turn-taking norm. We conclude that international politics appears to influence the foreign aid practices of the UN with respect to Africa.

5.7.4 Regional Development Banks

RDBs resemble the IMF and World Bank in granting more formal votes to large-economy countries. Their missions follow that of the World Bank; they sponsor development projects in lower- and middle-income countries. The main difference is that the projects of regional development banks focus exclusively on the countries of their respective regions. Importantly, political power also differs: Regional members are privileged in the allocation of votes at each RDB. The size of a country's vote-share – and thus its political influence – reflects the size of its contribution to the organization, which, in turn, reflects (1) the overall size of its economy and (2) whether it is a member of the region in question. So, unlike the World Bank, where the United States, Japan, Germany, the United Kingdom, and France are the major shareholders, regional hegemons – as well as the poorer regional borrower countries – have a stronger voice (Krasner 1981).

In terms of formal political power, consider the RDBs one by one:

The most powerful members of the Asian Development Bank (AsDB) are Japan and the United States, which both control around 12.5 percent of the total votes. The president of the AsDB has always been Japanese, and the AsDB executive board has (de facto) allowed the Japanese finance ministry to choose the president of this regional organization. Both qualitative and quantitative research suggests that Japan has more leverage than the United States at the AsDB (see, for example, Yasutomo 1993 and Kilby 2006). Overall, the cumulative vote-shares of all of the poorer member countries, which actually borrow from the AsDB, is less than the total share of the richer member countries.

The United States stands as the most powerful member of the Inter-American Development Bank (IADB), with a massive 30 percent vote-share, because it has the largest economy in the world and is a member of the Americas. The next largest vote-shares, however, belong to Brazil and Argentina, which control over ten percent each.[22] Note that while the United States has more individual power at the IADB than it does in any other multilateral development bank, the cumulative vote shares of all of the poorer member-countries, which borrow from the IADB, is actually greater than 50 percent. So, unlike at the AsDB, the IADB borrower countries can outvote the richer member countries on the executive board.

The major shareholders at the African Development Bank (AfDB) have varied over time. The African country that has historically controlled the most votes is Nigeria. The United States has been a major nonregional vote-holder, but so have France, Canada, Japan, and Germany. As with the AsDB, the cumulative vote-shares of all of the poorer member countries, which borrow from the AfDB, is less than the total share of the richer member countries. As of this writing, the regional members of the AfDB control 49.7 percent of the votes at the institution.[23] This situation, however, has not always been the case.

Until 1982, AfDB membership remained closed to nonregional countries (African Development Bank 2012). In 1982, the AfDB invited non-regional governments to both contribute financially and, therefore, play a

---

[22] At this writing – the vote-shares evolve over time. Note that each of these directors (except the one representing the United States) represents a group of other countries that have elected them. See http://www.iadb.org/en/about-us/executive-directors-and-alternate-executive-directors,1327.html (accessed November 2, 2012).

[23] Again, at this writing. These vote-shares have also evolved over time. See http://www.afdb.org/fileadmin/uploads/afdb/Documents/Boards-Documents/2011-vp-eng-june.pdf (accessed November 2, 2012).

role in the governance of the institution. So, prior to 1982, African countries controlled the AfDB, and since 1982, Western influence has grown to dominate the executive board (although the president of the AfDB has always been African – see African Development Bank 2012).

We stress that analyzing the effect of UNSC membership on AfDB lending presents a unique opportunity in the study of international relations. Not only do we observe borrower countries both with and without political importance (when they are on/off the UNSC), but we also observe the international institution itself both with and without Western political influence. The fact that this opportunity arises in the region that practices the strongest turn-taking norm provides us additional methodological leverage.

Global politics drove the founding of each of these regional institutions. The IADB, established in 1959, coincided with the Cuban Revolution. The AfDB, established in 1964, coincided with the decolonization of Africa. The AsDB, established in 1966, coincided with the escalating Vietnam War. As Cold War institutions, the political purpose of each was to provide a means for the West to reach out to developing countries in each of the respective regions (for the AfDB, post-1982). That politics should continue to impact RDB lending activities should thus come as no surprise, although we stress that the bulk of each organization's lending activity involves the promotion of development projects.

When countries win election to the UNSC, do they receive favorable treatment from the RDBs? Again, we consider them one by one:

The answer for the AsDB appears to be yes. Lim and Vreeland (2013) investigate whether Japan leverages its privileged position at the AsDB to facilitate project loans for the elected Asian members of the UNSC. As noted above, Japan has a special relationship with the UNSC. As a result of World War II, Japan adopted its "peace constitution," which forbids it from using its armed forces in international conflict, except for self-defense. Legal arguments have been made in Japan, however, that the government can employ the military overseas for missions authorized by the UNSC. The government may thus seek leverage over UNSC members, and providing loans through the AsDB represents one avenue.

Analyzing panel data of AsDB loan disbursements to twenty-four developing member countries from 1968 to 2009, Lim and Vreeland (2013) find that temporary UNSC membership increases AsDB loans, particularly during the post-1985 period when Japan asserted greater political influence in multilateral organizations (see Green 2003; Wade 1996; Ueki 1993; Yasutomo 1993). They estimate an average increase of about 30 percent and argue that because of Japan's checkered history of imperialism, the AsDB provides a convenient mechanism by which to obfuscate favors for politically important countries. The organization can be used as a "nonpolitical cloak" to "legitimize controversial policies, helping Japan to share the risks and the blame" (Yasutomo 1993: 339).

Note that we cannot reanalyze the AsDB results for Africa because the organization lends only to Asian countries. We highlight, however, that Lim and Vreeland (2013) apply rigorous matching methods as a robustness test of their findings to attenuate concerns about selection bias.[24]

Turning from Asia to the Americas, and in contrast to the AsDB, the IADB does not appear to favor UNSC members elected from the GRULAC. A study by Christopher Kilby, an economist at Villanova University, along with researcher Elizabeth Bland (2012), and another study by Diego Hernandez (2013), a researcher at Heidelberg University, have evaluated the political determinants of IADB lending, and while they find some evidence that certain political factors may matter, they do not find an overall effect of UNSC membership. Hernandez does report an effect of UNSC membership on projects that have immediate payoffs (such as projects focused on industry, mining, trade, and financial services). He attributes the overall non-effect of UNSC membership to the IADB's long-term projects (such as those focusing on education, health), which do not appear to be influenced by politics. He argues that aid with a faster impact generates large rents – both political and economic – and may thus represent the main targets of politically motivated lending (also see Clemens et al. 2012).

Still, the more constrained effects of UNSC membership on IADB lending can be connected to its governance structure. Recall that while the United States has a substantial vote-share at the IADB – larger than the share it has at the IMF, World Bank, and the other RDBs – the poorer borrower countries control a majority of the votes on the executive board. Possibly, the vote-power of the recipient countries curtails the use of the IADB for the specific political purpose of influencing UNSC members. The work of Copelovitch (2010a, 2010b) suggests that the political manipulation of an international institution is more likely when the major shareholders agree on the importance of a country. After the executive director representing the United States, the next five directors

---

[24] In their matching methods analysis, Lim and Vreeland rely on Leuven and Sianesi (2003), Imai and van Dyk (2004), Ho et al. (2007), Imai et al. (2008: 495–498), and Iacus et al. (2012).

with the largest vote-shares are (currently) Argentina, Brazil, Mexico, Japan, and Venezuela. It may not be worth the political capital to persuade these other actors to show preference to UNSC members, especially since the United States and Japan have other avenues through their bilateral aid, the IMF, the World Bank, and the AsDB.

Finally, we consider the AfDB. Does the Western influence over this institution lead to political favoritism? To address this question, we analyze the loans from the AfDB's African Development Fund (AfDF), which provides loans at concessional interest rates.[25]

The overall results, presented in models 1 and 2 in Table 5.6, indicate that UNSC membership matters, and we stress that the effects for the AfDB obviously come from the Africa subset of the data. So, we expect that these findings are least tainted by selection bias due to the region's commitment to the turn-taking norm.

For the AfDF (models 1 and 2 of Table 5.6), we find a statistically significant effect for loans to UNSC members. The estimated coefficient of 1.388, statistically significant at the 5 percent level, indicates an increase of lending to UNSC members by about 300 percent. Breaking down the effect by the level of importance of the UNSC during specific years, we find evidence of an increase during both unimportant years and important years, although we do not estimate a positive or statistically significant effect for somewhat important years. Logically, it does not stand to reason that UNSC members would be favored during unimportant and important years, but not during somewhat important years, so the effect is probably driven by general membership on the UNSC. We thus conclude that UNSC membership has a positive effect on AfDF lending.

Interestingly, none of the control variables that we include in the general sample has a statistically significant effect on the lending practices of the AfDF except for war, which lowers aid.

Note that Western countries did not join the AfDB until 1982. We argue that the AfDB provides more loans to UNSC members because the rich Western powers on the institution's executive board use their influence to favor strategically important countries. If our argument is correct, we should therefore find an effect of UNSC membership only from 1982 onward and not prior to 1982. We thus revisit the findings

---

[25] We obtain similar results when analyzing the AfDB's market rate loans, but do not report the results as we have only limited data (available since 2001). Results are available with the replication materials.

TABLE 5.6. *The Effect of UNSC Membership on African Development Bank Lending*

Variable	Model 1	Model 2	Model 3	Model 4	Model 5	Model 6
	All Years		Pre-1982		1982 and Onward	
UNSC Member	1.39**		− 0.16		1.65***	
	(2.62)		(0.09)		(3.37)	
UNSC Member, unimportant year		1.04**		1.72		0.69
		(2.12)		(0.82)		(1.06)
UNSC Member, somewhat important year		0.12		− 2.11		2.28**
		(0.09)		(0.99)		(2.13)
UNSC Member, important year		3.21***				2.42***
		(5.14)				(3.88)
Pariah state	1.85	1.80	6.78***	6.83***	1.52	1.61
	(1.02)	(0.98)	(4.53)	(4.71)	(0.76)	(0.75)
War	− 1.69**	− 1.50**	0.06	− 0.12	− 1.02	− 0.79
	(2.60)	(2.17)	(0.03)	(0.06)	(1.34)	(0.95)
ln (GDP per capita, PPP)	1.04	1.42	7.29**	7.24**	1.32	1.80
	(0.97)	(1.32)	(2.43)	(2.38)	(0.98)	(1.33)
Political regime	0.01	0.00	− 0.04	− 0.05	0.01	0.00
	(0.12)	(0.06)	(0.30)	(0.34)	(0.11)	(0.01)
U.S. military assistance (const. 2011 dollars)	0.05	0.04	− 0.13	− 0.14	0.10	0.09
	(0.87)	(0.70)	(1.51)	(1.66)	(1.62)	(1.48)
Number of countries	49	49	45	45	49	49
Number of observations	1,693	1,644	355	355	1,338	1,289
Period	74-09	74-08	74-81	74-81	82-09	82-08
R-squared	0.35	0.36	0.40	0.40	0.08	0.09

Notes: The dependent variables are the natural logarithms of aid disbursements (plus one) in constant 2009 US dollars by the AfDB's African Development Fund (AfDF). Estimation is with OLS. We split the sample in 1982 because this is the year that Western donors joined the AfDB and thus gained political influence over lending decisions. All regressions include country and year fixed-effects and regional quartics (for North Africa and Africa South of the Sahara). Numbers in parentheses are the absolute values of t-statistics. As per convention, we mark absolute t-statistics with ** if p<0.05 (statistical significance at the 5% confidence level); and with *** if p<0.01 (statistical significance at the 1% confidence level).

for the pre-1982 sample (models 3 and 4 of Table 5.6) and for the 1982 onward sample (models 5 and 6 of Table 5.6).

For the pre-1982 sample, we see no effect of UNSC membership, in line with our expectations. Western powers had no direct political leverage over the organization, and UNSC members did not receive perks. We do have interesting results for the control variables (see models 3 and 4 of Table 5.6). During this period, the AfDF does not lend to pariah states. Of course two pariah states in Africa during this period were Rhodesia and South Africa. The African governments on the executive board did no business with these countries, given their racist policies. In the post-1982 sample, after major changes in Zimbabwe and – eventually – in

South Africa, the pariah state variable does not have a statistically significant effect.

The other interesting control-variable finding is that per capita income has a statistically significant positive effect, indicating that richer countries were more likely than poor ones to receive the AfDF's concessional loans. Note that one main reason that the AfDB opened up its membership to include nonregional members was to increase access to resources and improve its credit rating so that the institution could deliver developmental loans to its poorest members (African Development Bank 2012). In the post-1982 sample, the statistically significant positive effect for ln(GDP per capita, PPP) accordingly disappears; the institution's improved credit rating enabled it to lend to poorer, higher-risk borrower governments.

By opening up the membership to the money of outsiders, however, the AfDB also opened itself up to the political influence of these members. Thus, we see a statistically significant positive effect of UNSC membership in general (model 5 of Table 5.6), which appears to be driven by the somewhat important and the important years (model 6 of Table 5.6). The statistical significance of the effects of UNSC membership on AfDF lending holds at levels stronger than the 5 percent level.

We thus conclude that the AfDB has given preferential treatment to countries when they serve on the UNSC ever since the organization granted formal political influence to Western powers. These results strike us as particularly interesting for the reasons noted earlier in this section: In the region that most closely follows the norm of rotation, we observe borrower countries both with and without political importance (when they are on/off the UNSC), and we also observe the international institution itself both with and without Western political influence. This kind of setup is rare in international relations, and the results confirm our central hypothesis. When Western countries have political power over the international organization, the countries that are strategically important to them receive larger loans.

5.7.5 Targeting Swing Voters

Does the United States target swing voters? As mentioned in the introduction to this chapter, addressing this question demands a lot from the data. First, we require a measure of underlying political affinity between the creditor country and the recipient country. Such measures give a sense of how likely the country is to vote on UNSC resolutions with a powerful donor country – we focus on the United States in this section – in the absence of political carrots or sticks.[26]

We seek to test three propositions derived from the theory presented in Chapter 2: (1) Enemies of the United States do not receive a benefit in terms of foreign aid for serving on the UNSC because no one expects them to vote with the United States. (2) Friends of the United States do not receive a benefit for serving on the UNSC because they are expected to vote with the United States anyway. (3) The in-between governments are thus the targets of foreign aid benefits.

Above, we show that UNSC members serving during important years receive increased foreign aid from the United States. We now revisit that finding, testing whether it applies to the enemies and friends of the United States or only to the countries in between.

We measure the underlying political affinity for the United States in two ways. First, for enemies of the United States, we use the pariah-state indicator variable, and for friends of the United States we employ an indicator variable for a military alliance with the United States (defense pacts, neutrality/nonaggression pacts, and ententes – see Gibler and Sarkees 2004 and Gibler 2009). We interact these variables, respectively, with UNSC membership during important years, thereby allowing UNSC membership to have three separate effects for friends, enemies, and countries in between. We perform this analysis only for the global sample because there is only one observation of a pariah state from Africa serving on the UNSC during an important year (Nigeria 1994), and the United States has no military alliances with African countries.

We consider neither the pariah-state variable nor the ally variable as perfect measures of enemy/friend status. The pariah-state variable may not be sufficient to cover all countries that are systematically opposed to the United States, and the military alliance variable may overstate the similarity of preferences between the U.S. government and the governments of other countries. Still, the approach represents a plausible test of whether the United States targets potential swing voters.

We perform a similar analysis using an alternative approach to categorizing friend/enemies of the United States. As noted above, we employ vote patterns in the UNGA to measure the underlying affinity with the United States. We construct an index of the share of UNGA votes where

---

[26] Using Japan or Germany is less feasible because they are not always members of the UNSC, so we do not have observations of their voting patterns on the UNSC for every year.

a country votes along with the United States during a given year. We follow Kegley and Hook (1991), who discard abstentions or absences and consider only how often countries are in agreement when they vote yes or no.[27] We then code the low-affinity (or "enemy") indicator as 1 for observations in the *lowest tenth percentile* of the entire distribution – and 0 otherwise. We code the high-affinity (or "friend") indicator as 1 for observations in the *highest tenth percentile* of the entire distribution and 0 otherwise. (The tenth percentile cut-off is, of course, arbitrary. We obtain qualitatively similar results when we use a higher or lower cut-off, for example, the twentieth or the fifth percentile, respectively.) As with the pariah and ally variables, we interact the low- and high-affinity indicators with the indicator for UNSC membership during important years.

Again, the approach is not perfect. The General Assembly votes on different types of issues than the Security Council, and UNGA voting profiles may not reflect the true preferences of governments. Moreover, there may be an endogenous relationship between voting at the UNGA and at the UNSC. Still, we consider this approach to represent a further plausible test of whether the United States targets potential swing voters.

For each of the analyses – the pariah/allies approach and the low-/high-affinity approach – we include the same set of control variables as above where we consider U.S. bilateral aid (in models 1 and 2 of Table 5.1). Table 5.7 presents the results.

Consider the results from model 1 of Table 5.7. The interactive effects of UNSC membership during important years with, alternatively, pariah state and U.S. ally are not straightforward to interpret, so we present them on the right-hand part of Table 5.7. For UNSC members during important years that are neither pariah states nor U.S. allies, we estimate a coefficient of 1.236, implying an increase in U.S. bilateral aid of 244 percent. For pariah states (pariah state=1), we estimate a coefficient of −0.136, which is not statistically significant. For U.S. allies (U.S. ally=1), we estimate a coefficient of 0.955, which is similarly not statistically significant. In both of these cases, the 95 percent confidence intervals overlap zero. So, in accordance with the hypothesis of Chapter 2, we estimate no effect for friends or enemies on the UNSC; only the governments in the middle

---

[27] For a new approach, see Bailey, Strezhnev, and Voeten (2013). In their ongoing research, they provide historically comparable dynamic estimates of governments' ideal points on a dimension capturing the Western/U.S.-led liberal order. Other studies using UNGA voting and foreign aid include Ball and Johnson (1996), Boschini and Olofsgård (2007), Alesina and Weder (2002), Fleck and Kilby (2006), Dreher, Nunnenkamp, and Thiele (2008), and Dreher and Sturm (2012). Chung and Woo (2012) offer a contrasting view.

TABLE 5.7. *Swing-Voter Hypothesis*

Variable	Model 1 Pariah & Ally Approach, Global Sample	Model 2 Low- & High- Affinity Approach, Global Sample	Model 3 Low- & High- Affinity Approach, Africa Sample
UNSC member,	1.24**	1.00*	0.85*
important year	(2.21)	(1.68)	(1.91)
Pariah state	−3.66**		
	(2.00)		
Pariah state interaction	−1.37		
with UNSC member,	(0.80)		
important year			
U.S. ally	−0.03		
	(0.03)		
U.S. ally interaction with	−0.28		
UNSC member,	(0.20)		
important year			
Low affinity with the		0.14	−0.15
United States (at the		(0.37)	(0.37)
UNGA)			
Low-affinity interaction		−1.71	−0.88
with UNSC member,		(1.52)	(0.60)
important year			
High affinity with the		0.60	−3.05
United States (at the		(0.71)	(1.40)
UNGA)			
High affinity interaction		1.20	
with UNSC member,		(0.72)	
important year			
War	−1.17*	−0.79	−0.50
	(1.78)	(1.16)	(0.82)
ln (GDP per capita, PPP)	−0.49	−0.24	−0.02
	(0.71)	(0.36)	(0.03)
Political regime	0.02	0.04	0.00
	(0.40)	(1.11)	(0.05)
U.S. military assistance	0.19***	0.20***	0.10***
(const. 2011 dollars)	(6.39)	(6.31)	(3.27)
Number of countries	125	125	49
Number of observations	4,852	4,746	2,042
Period	60–08	60–08	60–08
R-squared	0.24	0.23	0.27

(*continued*)

TABLE 5.7 *(continued)*

Interpreting the Interaction Terms:

Model 1 (Pariah and Ally Approach, Global Sample)

Value of Pariah State	Marginal Effect of UNSC Member, Important Year	Abs. t-Statistic	95% Confidence Interval	
0	1.236**	2.21	0.14	2.33
1	−0.136	0.08	−3.41	3.14

Value of U.S. Ally	Marginal Effect of UNSC Member, Important Year	Abs. t-Statistic	95% Confidence Interval	
0	1.236**	2.21	0.14	2.33
1	0.955	0.72	−1.66	3.57

Model 2 (Low-Affinity and High-Affinity Approach, Global Sample)

Value of Low Affinity	Marginal Effect of UNSC Member, Important Year	Abs. t-Statistic	90% Confidence Interval	
0	1.003*	1.68	0.02	1.98
1	−0.708	0.78	−2.21	0.79

Value of High Affinity	Marginal Effect of UNSC Member, Important Year	Abs. t-Statistic	90% Confidence Interval	
0	1.003*	1.68	0.02	1.98
1	2.202	1.28	−0.64	5.04

Model 3 (Low-Affinity and High-Affinity Approach, Africa Sample)

Value of Low Affinity	Marginal Effect of UNSC Member, Important Year	Abs. t-Statistic	90% Confidence Interval	
0	0.848*	1.91	0.12	1.58
1	−0.035	0.03	−2.15	2.08

Notes: The dependent variable is the natural logarithm of aid disbursements (plus one) in constant 2009 US dollars by the United States. Estimation is with OLS. All regressions include country and year fixed-effects and regional quartics. Numbers in parentheses are the absolute values of t-statistics. As per convention, we mark absolute t-statistics with * if $p<0.10$ (statistical significance at the 10% confidence level); with ** if $p<0.05$ (statistical significance at the 5% confidence level); and with *** if $p<0.01$ (statistical significance at the 1% confidence level).

receive the statistically significant increase in U.S. aid when they serve on the UNSC during important years.

Now, the pariah-state result is driven by the five observations of pariah states serving on the UNSC during important years: Cuba 1990, Cuba

1991, Nigeria 1994, Syria 2002, and Syria 2003. While the cases are few, it is reassuring to see that the effect of UNSC membership on U.S. bilateral aid is not driven by cases that would make no sense according to our theory – indeed, the Cuba and Syria results precisely fit examples discussed in Chapter 3. The U.S. ally finding is driven by more observations (thirty-three in total), mostly from Latin American countries, with whom the United States has defense pacts, and also Turkey 1961, as well as Romania 1990 and 1991. The Romania result is also reassuring as it fits with the discussion of the case in Chapter 3.

We next consider the alternative approach to measuring enemies, friends, and swing voters, using voting affinity in the UNGA. For countries in the middle of the distribution (observations that lie within the middle 80 percent range of the entire UNGA voting distribution), we estimate a coefficient of 1.003, implying an increase in U.S. bilateral aid of 173 percent. The statistical significance of this finding holds only at the 10 percent level, so with 90 percent confidence, we can report that the coefficient is between 0.02 and 1.98. For low-affinity states (low-affinity = 1), we estimate a coefficient of -0.708, which is not statistically significant. For high-affinity states (high-affinity = 1), we estimate a coefficient of 2.202, which is similarly not statistically significant at the 10 percent level. Again, we find that neither friends nor enemies of the United States receive an increase in U.S. bilateral aid when they serve on the UNSC. Instead, the UNSC effect targets governments that lie in the middle range of U.S. affinity. The low-affinity result is driven by eleven observations of states serving on the UNSC during important years: again Cuba (1990 and 1991) and Syria (2002 and 2003), as well as Yemen (1990 and 1991). There are also Pakistan 2003, Guinea 2002 and 2003, Republic of Congo 2006, and Ghana 2006. The high-affinity result relies on ten observations of countries serving on the UNSC during important years – again mainly from Latin America, as well as Turkey 1961. The analysis focusing on the Africa data sample (model 3 of Table 5.7) confirms the low-affinity finding – basically the positive effect of UNSC membership during important years is not driven by the countries that do not often vote with the United States in the UNSC (Guinea 2002 and 2003, Republic of Congo 2006, and Ghana 2006). There are no high-affinity cases in Africa.

The upshot of this analysis is that the effect of UNSC membership on U.S. bilateral aid is driven *not* by the extreme cases of enemies or friends of the United States, but rather by countries in the middle. The United States does not target governments expected to vote against its preferences, nor does it target governments that it can rely on for favorable votes. Rather, the United States targets the swing-voter governments that might vote either way, depending on the enticements.

5.7.6 Voting Behavior on the UNSC

Do the UNSC votes themselves carry financial consequences for the developing countries that cast them? The above analysis suggests that the United States targets countries because of their potential voting behavior on the UNSC. Yet, up to now, we have not considered any systematic evidence of actual voting on the UNSC. The famous story of Yemen voting against Desert Storm in 1990 suggests that voting against the United States can have real repercussions, but does this one case represent an exception, or is it part of a systematic pattern? We close this chapter with an analysis that includes the UNSC voting record to address this question.

Now, before discussing UNSC voting data, we must acknowledge that there is a major problem of selection bias: Most UNSC resolutions pass with overwhelming majorities, often with unanimous support. We have, of course, argued that this is partly due to the pressure on UNSC members to vote with the United States, but the skewed voting record also results from the fact that governments propose resolutions strategically. Governments do not randomly propose resolutions for the UNSC to vote on; they carefully gauge political support. Consequently, we do not observe many instances of countries voting against the most prominent member of the UNSC, the United States. Lim and Vreeland (2013), for example, report that Asian countries serving on the UNSC vote with the United States about 94 percent of the time and vote with Japan about 96 percent of the time.

With so little variation, it is not surprising that in our analyses of the effect of UNSC voting patterns, we obtain mostly inconclusive results. IMF loans stand out as the major exception. Our ongoing research with Peter Rosendorff on the lending patterns of the IMF yields an interesting set of results (see Dreher, Rosendorff, and Vreeland 2013).

Recall from Section 5.7.2 that in our initial analysis of the effect of UNSC membership, we found increased participation rates in IMF programs with fewer conditions attached to the loans, but we did not detect an impact on the actual size of loans (Dreher et al. 2009b). It turns out, however, that UNSC membership does impact IMF loan size.

We propose that the impact of UNSC membership on IMF loans depends on two crucial factors: the underlying political affinity between the UNSC member and the United States, and the UNSC member's voting record at the UNSC. More specifically, we find that UNSC members with high affinity for the United States receive larger loans – provided that they do not vote against the United States at the UNSC. If a high-affinity UNSC member votes against the United States, we detect a substantively and statistically significant negative impact in the size of the loan that the country receives. As for low-affinity countries, they do not receive a significant increase in their IMF loans and thus do not face punishment for voting against the United States. When these countries vote in line with the United States, this is more likely to be the result of coincidence than of successful U.S. pressure. In other words, the United States only targets punishment on countries that it expects, a priori, to vote favorably on the UNSC.

We reach these conclusions through an analysis where we interact the affinity of governments with the United States and their voting records when they serve on the UNSC. We measure the underlying political affinity between the United States and other countries by, once again, relying on the index of voting alignment with the United States at the UNGA. We lag the variable by one year so that it is not measured contemporaneously with UNSC voting. We code UNSC voting according to the percentage of UNSC proposals for which the country votes against the United States. Note that we code observations of countries not serving on the UNSC as 0. So, the lowest possible scores go to countries that either do not serve on the UNSC or vote in perfect alignment with the United States. The highest scores go to countries that vote most against the United States during a given year. We thus also continue to employ the indicator variable coded 1 during years that a country is a temporary member of the UNSC to distinguish UNSC members and nonmembers.

While we present the full analysis of the data in our research with Rosendorff, we provide the data for the project along with the replication materials for this book. The data on UNSC voting patterns come from various sources. Voting data on successful Security Council resolutions are available from the official UN Web site (http://unbisnet.un .org/). We supplement this information with data on proposals that were vetoed, which are available from the official UN veto list (UN document A/58/47), and also with data from archival research in the UN library in Geneva. Data on failed majorities (as opposed to vetoed proposals) have proven the most difficult to obtain. We include voting behavior on these failed majorities obtained from our research in the UN library (these data are, however, incomplete). Overall, we obtained data for 1,489 resolutions, 165 vetoed proposals, and 18 failed majorities over the 1951–2004 period. Our dataset represents the most extensive and comprehensive on UNSC voting of which we are aware at this writing.

As our dependent variables, we consider the dichotomous indicator of participation in IMF programs as well as the (natural logarithm of) IMF loan commitments.[28]

For both dependent variables, we begin with the same model specification used in our study of IMF participation with Jan-Egbert Sturm (Dreher, Sturm, and Vreeland 2009b), which includes as control variables past participation in IMF programs, (log) per capita GDP, investment (in percent of GDP), debt service (in percent of GNI), (log) checks and balances, and the government's budget surplus (in percent of GDP).[29] We also include U.S. military assistance, given its statistical significance in the preceding analyses. The analysis reveals similar results for both dependent variables. We find that for countries with low affinity with the United States, voting against the United States has no effect. Again, they are not expected to vote with the United States in the first place, and if they do vote in line with the United States, this behavior more likely reflects coincidence than evidence of U.S. pressure. Overall, any apparent positive effect of UNSC membership is counterbalanced by a country's low affinity with the United States, so it does not actually receive an increase in IMF participation rates or loan size. The net effect for these countries is statistically indistinguishable from zero.

But for countries with high affinity with the United States – those that can expect a boost in IMF participation for serving on the UNSC – there is a statistically significant negative consequence for voting against the United States on UNSC proposals. The United States expects these countries to vote with them on the UNSC, and these countries can expect more and larger loans from the IMF provided that they supply the favorable

---

[28] Data on IMF participation come from the update to Vreeland (2007) – originally from Przeworski and Vreeland (2000). Note that our indicator variable for concessional programs is coded 1 if a concessional loan program is in effect for at least five months during a particular country-year. These data come from an update to Dreher (2006).

[29] The specification has been derived with a general-to-specific procedure to a specification including the most robust control variables as identified by Sturm, Berger, and de Haan (2005). See Sturm, Berger, and de Haan (2005) and Moser and Sturm (2011) for a detailed description of the associated hypotheses.

votes. If they do not, they face punishment in terms of smaller loans – or no loans at all – from the IMF.

Thus, we can conclude this section with a preliminary finding on the size of IMF loans. It turns out that governments serving on the UNSC may receive larger loan commitments from the IMF, but only if they vote with the dominant shareholder of the institution – they must vote with the United States.

5.8 Conclusion: Summarizing the Main Findings

This chapter presents a series of crucial tests of our main hypotheses. When considered along with the anecdotal evidence presented in Chapter 3, these results corroborate the main idea of this book: Money and politics do mix on the international stage. The specific stories recounted in the previous chapter constitute a part of a larger, systematic pattern whereby the United States, along with Japan and possibly Germany, use their bilateral foreign aid and influence in multilateral organizations, such as the IMF, the World Bank, the AfDB, and the AsDB to favor the elected members of the UNSC in return for their political support on the Security Council.

In the interest of providing a helpful reference summarizing the wealth of data analyses presented in this chapter, we conclude with the following list of twelve empirical takeaway points:

1. Temporary UNSC membership has a positive effect on **US** bilateral aid during important years, as measured by media coverage of the Security Council. The finding holds for the global sample, as well as the Africa sample. The results broadly confirm the findings of Kuziemko and Werker (2006).
2. Temporary UNSC membership has a positive effect on **Japanese** bilateral aid. The finding holds for the global sample as well as the Africa sample.
3. Temporary UNSC membership has a positive effect on **German** bilateral aid, in line with Dreher, Nunnenkamp, and Schmaljohann (2013). The finding holds for the global sample but not for the Africa sample.
4. Temporary UNSC membership does not influence French or British bilateral aid.
5. Our previous research shows that temporary UNSC membership has a positive effect on participation in **IMF** programs and on the

number of **World Bank** projects initiated during a year (Dreher, Sturm, and Vreeland 2009a, 2009b. UNSC members also have lower levels of policy conditionality associated with their IMF loans (Dreher, Sturm, and Vreeland 2009b, 2013).

6. Temporary UNSC membership has a positive effect on **World Bank loans through the IBRD lending window to middle-income countries.** The finding holds for both the global and the Africa samples.

7. Temporary UNSC membership does not appear to influence UN development aid in the global sample; however, we do find positive effects that are marginally significant in the Africa sample for overall **UN development aid**, the **World Food Program, UNICEF**, and the **UNHCR**.

8. Previous research shows that temporary UNSC membership has a positive effect on the size of loans from the **Asian Development Bank** (Lim and Vreeland 2013).

9. Our analysis of data on lending to American countries from the Inter-American Development Bank (not reported) does not reveal a statistically significant effect of UNSC membership, consistent with the studies of Bland and Kilby (2012) and Hernandez (2013). Hernandez (2013) does report a UNSC-membership effect on fast-impact projects in policy areas such as industry, mining, trade, and financial services.

10. Temporary UNSC membership has a positive effect on loans to African countries from the **African Development Bank** during important years, and on loans from the **African Development Fund** in general. The finding holds only for the post-1982 sample, during which Western powers hold political influence over the institution.

11. The effect of temporary membership on U.S. bilateral aid during important years holds only for potential **swing voters.** We do not detect an effect for potential enemies of the United States, such as pariah states (under U.S. or UN sanctions) or low-affinity states that do not vote with the United States in the UNGA, nor do we detect an effect for potential friends of the United States, such as U.S. military allies or countries that tend to vote with the United States in the UNGA.

12. Finally, our ongoing research indicates that the effect of voting with the United States at the UNSC on (a) **participation in IMF programs** and (b) **the size of IMF loan commitments** depends on political affinity with the United States, as measured by voting at the UNGA (Dreher, Rosendorff, and Vreeland 2013).

The original work focusing on the effects of UNSC membership focuses on U.S. foreign aid (Kuziemko and Werker 2006). Our work here shows, clearly, that the effects range far beyond just this variable. Our qualitative research indicates many other dependent variables that we suggest for future research, such as free-trade arrangements and high-level government meetings.[30]

Returning to our own findings in this chapter, an important "so what" question remains: What are the implications of providing finance for political favors on the UNSC? Most countries get a turn to participate on the UNSC, so what is the harm in providing each of them bonus foreign aid during their tenure? The next chapter examines this question.

Appendix 5.1: Describing the Data Used in this Chapter

TABLE 5.a1. *Descriptive Data*

Variable	Mean	Std. Dev.	Min.	Max.	Source
U.S. bilateral aid disb. (Overseas Development Assistance – ODA, mill.)	$67.60	$175	0	$2,150	OECD (2012)
Japanese bilateral aid disb. (ODA, mill.)	$52.10	$160	0	$2,110	OECD (2012)
French bilateral aid disb. (ODA, mill.)	$39.30	$102	0	$2,090	OECD (2012)
German bilateral aid disb. (ODA, mill.)	$40.10	$90.90	0	$1,820	OECD (2012)
UK bilateral aid disb. (ODA, mill.)	$21.40	$72.50	0	$2,100	OECD (2012)
UN aid disb. (ODA, mill.)	$22.00	$38.60	0	$566	OECD (2012)
WFP aid disb. (ODA, mill.)	$6.09	$17.00	0	$307	OECD (2012)
UNDP aid disb. (ODA, mill.)	$5.69	$8.12	0	$132	OECD (2012)
UNICEF aid disb. (ODA, mill.)	$3.40	$8.13	0	$123	OECD (2012)
UNHCR aid disb. (ODA, mill.)	$2.99	$12.50	0	$265	OECD (2012)
UNTA aid disb. (ODA, mill.)	$1.52	$1.70	0	$20.60	OECD (2012)
AfDB aid disb. (ODA, mill.)	$0.24	$4.03	0	$131	OECD (2012)
AfDF aid disb. (ODA, mill.)	$5.69	$37.50	0	$1,270	OECD (2012)
World Bank IBRD disb. (mill.)	$0.72	$2.56	0	$49.70	World Bank (2012)

(continued)

[30] Indeed, researchers have begun to investigate many new areas far afield of what we have covered, including, for example, global culture. Frey, Pamini, and Steiner (2013) have found UNSC members to be more likely to have their sites of cultural value included on the World Heritage List, designed to protect global heritage. Voeten (2011) focuses on the provision of public goods and finds that temporary members of the UNSC provide substantially larger UN peacekeeping troops.

TABLE 5.a1 *(continued)*

Variable	Mean	Std. Dev.	Min.	Max.	Source
World Bank IDA disb. (mill.)	$0.34	$1.26	0	$22.50	World Bank (2012)
IMF loan comm. (mill.)	SDR128	SDR1,011	0	SDR27,375	IMF (2011)
UNSC member	0.056	0.23	0	1	UN (2012)
Pariah state	0.051	0.22	0	1	Morgan, Krustev, and Bapat (2006), Combs (2012), Levy (1999)
War	0.094	0.29	0	1	Themnér and Wallensteen (2012)
GDP per capita, PPP	$4,218	$4,333	$124	$32,382	Heston et al. (2012)
Political regime	−1.021	6.85	−10	10	Marshall et al. (2002)
U.S. mil. assistance (obligations, const. 2011 mill. dollars)	$35.20	$248.00	0	$6,490	USAID (2011)
U.S. ally	0.254	0.44	0	1	Gibler and Sarkees (2004), Gibler (2009)
Affinity with USA (UNGA)	0.392	0.15	0	0.90	Voeten and Merdzanovic (2009), Kilby (2009b)
Voting against USA (UNSC)	0.004	0.03	0	0.42	UN (unbisnet.un.org, UN document A/58/47, UN Geneva library)

6

Consequences of Politically Motivated Aid

6.1 Does Foreign Aid Help or Hurt?

UN Security Council membership has thus far been shown to increase the likelihood of receiving financial perks. With this finding in mind, we turn to a crucial question: What are the consequences? Does the foreign aid funneled to UNSC members have a beneficial, benign, or negative impact in the recipient countries?

Note that the financial favors to UNSC members might result in minimal consequences. If so, then we can report a straightforward conclusion to our analysis: (1) The UNSC is important enough to powerful countries that they are willing to offer bribes and rewards to the countries elected to serve, and (2) a UNSC seat is thus a useful commodity for the government of a developing country even if the financial favors do little for the population as a whole. The donor government gains political support on the UNSC while the recipient government receives a payoff. No harm, no foul, as they say.

Suppose, however, that we actually observe beneficial consequences from the foreign aid in terms of economic development. Recipient governments may use the foreign aid payoffs to promote growth-enhancing projects back home. The foreign aid may benefit the country as a whole over the long run. If so, then we can conclude that vote-aid trades represent a good deal for the developing world: Almost all countries get their turn to participate in the important deliberations of the UNSC, and, when they do, they receive financial perks – so long as they play ball with the truly powerful countries in the world and do not rock the boat. Perhaps these poor countries ultimately play a fairly inconsequential role on the UNSC, but they rise to prominence on the international stage, and, for their service, they duly receive rewards that benefit their country as a whole.

Yet what if foreign aid actually does some harm to recipient countries? Suppose that recipient governments use their foreign aid payoffs as a means to prop up bad policies. The money may enhance a bad government's grip on a struggling country. Leaders may funnel fungible aid directly to supporters and generate graft from specific projects for loyalists who support the regime. Easy loans may line the pockets of a tight-knit group of elites, leaving the rest of society to pay back the debt. Such "aid" does little good – indeed much harm – to the vast majority of the population.[1]

Economists Alberto Alesina of Harvard University and David Dollar of the World Bank and the U.S. Treasury Department indeed suggest that negative consequences may result from the political nature of aid disbursement. The political allocation of aid "provides evidence as to why it is not more effective at promoting growth and poverty reduction" (Alesina and Dollar 2000: 55). Rather than providing aid to governments determined to use it well, donors provide aid to strategically important countries, who count on this aid as a means to maintain their rule. The distortions that result actually do harm to a country's economic prospects.

The evidence on the effectiveness of aid in general does not neatly answer the question of whether the effects of aid to UNSC members are benign, beneficial, or bad. An obstacle typically stands in the way of studying the effects of politically motivated foreign aid: the selection problem. A researcher usually must disentangle the circumstances surrounding the delivery of foreign aid from the inherent effects of that aid. In our project on the UNSC, we can partially overcome this problem: As Chapter 4 suggests, membership on the UNSC is exogenous to the delivery of U.S. development assistance as well as IMF and World Bank

---

[1] Well-known critiques along these lines include Easterly (2001) and Moyo (2009). For nuanced analyses, see Boone (1996); Easterly, Levine, and Roodman (2004); Dunning (2004); Headey (2008); Bermeo (2008); Rajan and Subramanian (2008); Bearce and Tirone (2010); Doucouliagos and Paldam (2009); Kilby and Dreher (2010); Minoiu and Reddy (2010); Clemens et al. (2012); Dreher, Eichenauer, and Gehring (2013); and Schneider and Tobin (2013). Also see Kaplan (2013, especially chapter 5). As for the impact of foreign aid on the role of the state in the economy, see Remmer (2004). Recent research by Bermeo and Leblang (2012) suggests that donors may also use aid to achieve broader immigration goals.

lending. If we can assume that foreign aid is delivered to UNSC members for reasons exogenous to their economic circumstances, then evaluating the effects of that aid becomes more straightforward.

Still, another methodological obstacle remains: the measurement of effectiveness. Scholars typically measure economic development – the ostensible purpose of most foreign aid – in terms of change in per capita income. Yet, this measure of economic growth fluctuates idiosyncratically, and myriad factors influence it. Roodman (2007) further explains the difficulties that lie in measuring economic growth with any degree of precision. Considering that only about 5 percent of the world serves on the UNSC in any given year, we have few observations with which to ascertain the effect of foreign aid on "noisy" economic growth.

With the above opportunities and obstacles in mind, this chapter proceeds as follows. After reviewing the debate on the effect of foreign aid on economic development (Section 6.2), we consider a study by a pair of political scientists at New York University, Alastair Smith and Bruce Bueno de Mesquita (Section 6.3). They study the effect of foreign aid given to UNSC members on economic growth measured over a four-year period, beginning with the election year of the UNSC member (Bueno de Mesquita and Smith 2010). By considering a four-year time horizon, they hope to avoid yearly idiosyncrasies. They find that temporary membership has pernicious consequences for countries that serve on the UNSC, and they attribute the effect to the increased foreign aid that these countries receive. We reevaluate their findings on a region-by-region basis with a special focus on Africa because of the rotation norm that the region follows in selecting UNSC members. Because Africa tends to follow such a rotation norm, endogeneity is less of a concern when studying this region than perhaps other parts of the world (as discussed in Chapter 4). To foreshadow our results, we find a negative effect of UNSC membership on economic growth in Africa.

The Bueno de Mesquita and Smith study has received criticism from Omar S. Bashir and Darren J. Lim, researchers at Princeton University, for equating UNSC membership with receiving foreign aid. Although we find such a correlation between the two factors in Chapter 5, we also find that not all UNSC members receive such financial perks. Thus, we also refer to our ongoing research with Vera Eichenauer of Heidelberg University and Kai Gehring of the Georg-August-Universität Göttingen, where we focus specifically on the effect of *foreign aid* received by UNSC members on economic growth (Dreher, Eichenauer, and Gehring 2013).

This study confirms the basic findings of Bueno de Mesquita and Smith (2010), with some important additions.

Still, we remain cautious about using only economic growth as a dependent variable. Growth is affected by many variables unrelated to aid, and the time lag by which aid affects growth can be substantial (and hard to capture empirically). Thus, section 6.4 supplements our analysis of the effect of foreign aid to UNSC members by considering a different dependent variable. We choose to "narrow the lens," following the approach employed in our study with Stephan Klasen of Georg-August-Universität Göttingen and Eric D. Werker of Harvard University (2013). We consider the multilateral context and use a less noisy outcome variable: World Bank evaluations of the projects that it has sponsored.

The World Bank's Independent Evaluation Group has rated or audited all of the thousands of projects that it has sponsored in developing countries since the 1970s. We analyze the comprehensive dataset of nearly 6,000 World Bank project evaluations in order to understand how the political motivation of aid affects project quality.

To foreshadow the results of this analysis, we find that when the World Bank grants projects to UNSC members facing economic vulnerability – measured by either their burden of short-term debt or of debt service – project quality suffers. These results suggest that when a UNSC member faces a dangerous economic position, the government may expend political capital that comes with its position to obtain foreign aid that goes toward propping up bad policies. Otherwise, however, the well-intentioned aid bureaucracy may successfully manage projects despite the international political motivations behind them. UNSC members with moderate or low levels of debt receive World Bank projects that are just as likely to succeed as projects granted to other countries.

The effect of aid to UNSC members appears to depend on the specific government that manages the economy. Governments serving on the UNSC that mismanage their economies, as indicated by their debt exposure, have fared worse than those granted to other countries. So, beyond international political factors, the domestic politics of recipient countries may also influence the effectiveness of foreign aid. We therefore conclude this chapter by examining the role of political regime (Section 6.5). We present evidence suggesting that democracies and dictatorships employ foreign aid in different ways. It turns out that the pernicious effects of foreign aid detected by Bueno de Mesquita and Smith (2010) are mainly driven by authoritarian governments, particularly those located in Africa. African democracies perform better.

6.2 The Foreign Aid Debate

The debate over foreign aid is politically charged. Some people oppose foreign aid because it distorts what markets would do naturally. Aid in the form of grants represents a tax on the citizens of rich countries and a subsidy for the governments of poor countries. Aid in the form of concessional loans places a further burden on the average citizens of these poor countries to repay the ineffective loans taken out by governments. If the governments of developing countries would just follow good policy, according to this line of thinking, they would not need to rely on foreign aid.

Other people, meanwhile, argue that rich countries have a responsibility to help poor countries – especially if the rich country enjoys the benefits of a legacy of colonialism or imperialism. They point out that government action has an important role to play in the economy in providing public goods, regulating monopolies, addressing externalities, ensuring the provision of various forms of insurance, deterring moral hazard through regulation, and the list goes on. The role of the state in the economy may be particularly important in underdeveloped countries, and foreign aid can augment the role that an underdeveloped state should play.

Still others take a more moderate position. They recognize that aid might help in some situations but remain skeptical when aid goes to corrupt governments that are strategically important to the donor countries.

We have no interest in entering into the ideological battles that drive the debate, and we acknowledge that all points of view are motivated by valid theories and supported by different forms of evidence. A case can be made, for example, that politically motivated aid should be effective. Consider Cold War donors. They wanted to curry favor with their client states, but they also wanted these allies to succeed economically. The East Asian Tigers received tremendous amounts of politically motivated assistance during the Cold War that does not appear to have prevented their economic development.

Moreover, regardless of the politics involved, once an aid project receives funding, the aid bureaucracy must deliver it. The bureaucratic agents, for their part, may desire to implement effective programs irrespective of the political motivations of donors and recipients. When deciding how to allocate economic aid to Pakistan to increase political support for anti-Taliban operations, for example, a U.S. aid official said, "We had to choose a method of funding that was most likely to produce results efficiently and effectively" (Perlez 2009). Thus, the evidence of political bias in aid allocation need not imply ineffectiveness.

Furthermore, at any given time, the number of worthy projects may exceed the resources available to fund them. Aid bureaucrats may thus have a plethora of investment projects with similar potential effectiveness. If all of the options represent worthwhile projects, choosing from among them according to the political criteria of donors should not reduce the average effectiveness of aid programs.

Yet, politically motivated aid might fall short of delivering development benefits for several reasons. First, allocating aid according to political motives may lead to the approval of lower-quality projects for favored countries, compared with competing projects for other developing countries. A problem may thus emerge at the project-approval stage.

Second, as argued by Kilby (2011a, 2013a, 2013b), political pressure from donors may lead the aid bureaucracy to reduce the project preparation periods, leading to worse outcomes. In short, if political pressure rushes a project, it may suffer from poor planning (Hefeker and Michaelowa 2005).

Third, the granting of the aid may forestall important policy reforms that could promote project success. With specific reference to World Bank projects, for example, Kilby (2009a) suggests that favoritism in project allocation undermines the credibility of policy conditionality, rendering it ineffective. Favoritism might also allow projects to go ahead where governments have failed to meet the policy preconditions.

Now, politics may not always interfere with the delivery of aid. Politically important countries may only employ their leverage when they face economic vulnerabilities (Stone 2008). When a politically important country faces mounting debt, for example, it may seek outside financial assistance to promote short-run economic goals and use its political leverage to avoid following policies that might cause short-run hardship. This course of action may damage the viability of the project and its potential impact on the long-run development of the country. Nevertheless, donors concerned with short-run political objectives may not concentrate on monitoring whether the recipient government complies with policy conditions.

In sum, valid – but opposing – theoretical perspectives make different claims on the effectiveness of foreign aid, and a lack of reliable and transparent evidence makes it difficult to settle the debate. The reason for the

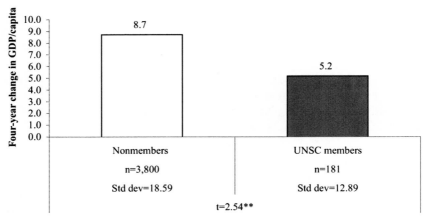

FIGURE 6.1. UNSC membership and economic growth (average four-year change in GDP/capita, 2000 US dollars) – global sample. *Notes:* Average four-year change in GDP/capita by UNSC membership status for the global sample. *Source:* Bueno de Mesquita and Smith (2010).

lack of convincing evidence is due, in part, to the nonrandom allocation of foreign aid. Scholars cannot disentangle, with much certainty, the circumstances surrounding the delivery of foreign aid from the inherent effects of that aid. We thus turn to our own review of the empirical evidence.

6.3 Pernicious Effects

We begin to explore the effectiveness of politically motivated foreign aid by considering the study of Bueno de Mesquita and Smith (2010), who take advantage of the idiosyncratic selection process of UNSC temporary membership. Their study begins with the following observations: (1) selection onto the UNSC is not related to economic development, and (2) UNSC members receive increased foreign aid. They thus treat membership on the UNSC as a "quasi-experiment" through which to test the effects of politically motivated aid on a range of factors, in particular, economic growth.

They find that membership on the UNSC leads to a dramatic reduction in economic growth. They argue that the increased foreign aid that UNSC members receive props up bad policies, bad governments, and distorts market incentives.

We further examine their growth finding, taking it apart region by region. Figure 6.1 presents the average four-year change in GDP per

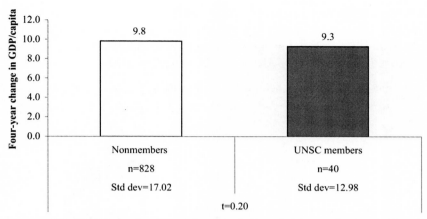

FIGURE 6.2. UNSC membership and economic growth (average four-year change in GDP/capita, 2000 US dollars) – Asia sample. *Notes:* Average four-year change in GDP/capita by UNSC membership status for the Asia sample. *Source:* Bueno de Mesquita and Smith (2010).

capita (measured in 2000 US dollars) for all nonmembers and members of the UNSC. For UNSC members, we treat election year as time-0 and compare the level of GDP per capita in this year to the level reached two years following their two-year term – hence the four-year rate of growth. Figures 6.2 through 6.5 present the same comparisons according to region: Asia (Figure 6.2), Eastern Europe (Figure 6.3), GRULAC (Figure 6.4), and Africa (Figure 6.5).

As for the global sample, including all regions together, the average four-year change in GDP per capita for nonmember countries is 8.7 percent, whereas the rate for UNSC members is just 5.2 percent. The difference of 3.5 percent is statistically significant at the 5 percent level, according to a simple t-test ($t = 2.5$).[2] Turning to the specific regions, however, the effect does not hold at conventional levels of statistical significance for Asia, and Eastern Europe exhibits no difference at all. The descriptive evidence does suggest a statistically significant difference for Latin America (GRULAC), but when subjected to further tests, we do not find the result to be robust.[3] For the African region, we find a different story, which appears to drive the overall results in the global sample. The average four-year change in GDP per capita in the region is 5.5 percent,

---

[2] Bueno de Mesquita and Smith (2010) also consider the effect on the two-year rate of growth and obtain similar, but less robust, results.

[3] Results are available on request.

whereas the average four-year rate of growth for African countries that have served on the UNSC is –1.6 percent. This discrepancy of 7.1 percent is statistically significant at the 5 percent level ($t = 2.2$). The fact that the negative finding holds for Africa should be underscored for two reasons:

1. Of all the regional groupings, Africa adheres most closely to a norm of rotation, so we can most readily treat these data as resulting

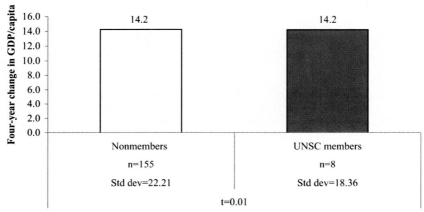

FIGURE 6.3. UNSC membership and economic growth (average four-year change in GDP/capita, 2000 US dollars) – Eastern Europe sample. *Notes:* Average four-year change in GDP/capita by UNSC membership status for the Eastern Europe sample. *Source:* Bueno de Mesquita and Smith (2010).

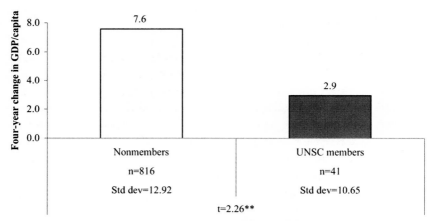

FIGURE 6.4. UNSC membership and economic growth (average four-year change in GDP/capita, 2000 US dollars) – GRULAC sample. *Notes:* Average four-year change in GDP/capita by UNSC membership status for the GRULAC sample. *Source:* Bueno de Mesquita and Smith (2010).

from a quasi-experimental setting. Indeed, the only country that has repeatedly entered into contested elections to represent Africa on the UNSC is Nigeria. When we remove Nigeria from the sample, the results hold (in fact, at higher levels of statistical significance).

2. Africa, more than any other region in the world, has lagged behind when it comes to economic development. It is thus appropriate to focus on this region to understand the impact of foreign aid on development.

It appears that politically motivated aid to Africa has not fared too well. Still, our approach to this region has ignored domestic politics so far. Perhaps some African governments use foreign aid better than others.[4]

Before delving further into the Africa finding, however, we seek to narrow the lens. Measuring change in GDP per capita is notoriously difficult, and we may learn something more nuanced by considering an alternative metric of success. Historically, the agency responsible for providing the most foreign aid to Africa is the World Bank, and this institution carries out self-evaluations of project success. We thus consider the World Bank's own evaluation of projects that it has sponsored as a measure of project success to determine if UNSC membership has an impact in making projects more likely to succeed or to fail.

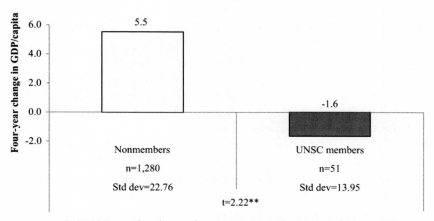

FIGURE 6.5. UNSC membership and economic growth (average four-year change in GDP/capita, 2000 US dollars) – Africa sample. *Notes:* Average four-year change in GDP/capita by UNSC membership status for the Africa sample. *Source:* Bueno de Mesquita and Smith (2010).

---

[4] We focus on regime type below. For a study of the importance of leader-specific characteristics, see Cogley (2013). Also see Chiozza and Goemans (2011).

6.4 A Conservative Analysis[5]

Do foreign aid projects extended to UNSC members result in lower quality outcomes than projects extended to other countries? We address this question by exploiting a recently available dataset from the World Bank, which reports the outcome evaluations for more than 6,000 projects extended to developing countries from 1970 to 2003. Since the 1970s, all World Bank projects have gone through an ex post evaluation by staff involved with the project. The staff conducts the evaluation about six months after a project is completed.[6] Staff judgments may be incorrect or even biased in some cases, but we doubt that a link exists between such potential bias and any political motivations for projects. Frequent staff rotations at the World Bank ensure that the person managing the completion report is rarely the person who supervised the early stages of the project. Furthermore, when it comes to career advancement, the World Bank places more weight on preparing projects and getting them approved than on ex post performance ratings (Mosley et al. 1991). Indeed, the World Bank does not have a formal process to hold individual employees accountable for unsatisfactory projects, and there are no direct consequences in terms of pay or promotion.[7] Even if there were some benefit for the World Bank staff to inflate certain evaluations, it would be risky to do so because all projects stand a chance of undergoing an audit by the Independent Evaluation Group (IEG). The IEG, formerly known as the Operations Evaluation Department (OED), evaluates a sample of World Bank projects every year (World Bank 2003). Having instituted a separate evaluations department in 1971, this department has reported directly to the World Bank executive board, bypassing the Bank's own management layers, since 1975 – the starting point of our analysis.

In terms of our independent variable of interest, donor interests in the recipient country might influence project performance via various paths. Our main hypothesis concerns World Bank decisions about the number, type, and design of projects at the time of project *approval*. We test for

---

[5] This section closely mirrors the study of Dreher, Klasen, Vreeland, and Werker (2013).

[6] The performance rating was binary until 1993 and since then has ranged from highly unsatisfactory to highly satisfactory. For our dependent variable below, we group highly to marginally satisfactory together (coded 1), and highly to marginally unsatisfactory together (coded 0) to generate a binary variable for our full sample. This approach follows the standard practice of the World Bank and Dollar and Svensson (2000). When we recode marginally satisfactory ratings as 0, we obtain similar results in the analysis below. See Dreher, Klasen, Vreeland, and Werker (2013).

[7] The World Bank does hold staff members accountable in rare cases of corruption or criminal behavior associated with granting or supervising loans.

this possibility by including an indicator variable coded 1 if a country is a UNSC member at the time of project approval. This variable directly tests our hypothesis about the effectiveness of politically motivated aid. We also examine whether the performance effect works via a larger number of projects granted to favored countries or through the type and design of projects.

Donor influence might also impact project *implementation* through, for example, the speed of loan disbursement, the degree of supervision, and the enforcement of project conditions (such as counterpart funding requirements) or program conditions (such as macroeconomic or governance) conditionality. We control for this avenue of influence by including a measure of the proportion of the project implementation period during which the country was a temporary member of the UNSC. (To avoid overlap with the approval measure, we code this variable with respect to the second year of project implementation.) While we believe that it is important to test for this mechanism, we consider it less likely than the first, particularly since the shareholders of the World Bank only rarely intervene directly in project supervision issues (Marshall 2008: 76).

Finally, donor influence could bias the *evaluation* of project outcomes. UNSC membership during evaluation cannot change the actual outcome of a project, of course, but it might influence what the World Bank reports. We deem this possibility unlikely because the World Bank kept these reports confidential until recently. Still, we control for this possibility by including UNSC membership at the time of project evaluation.

Equation 6.1 presents the reduced-form empirical specification – which is at the project level (as opposed to the country level):

$$\Pr\left(Performance_{i,j,t} = 1\right)$$
$$= F\left(\begin{array}{c} UNSC_{i,j,t=approval}, \; UNSC_{i,j,t=implementation}, \\ UNSC_{i,j,t=evaluation}, \; x_{i,j,t=approval} \end{array}\right) \quad (6.1)$$

where *Performance* represents the dichotomous indicator of the World Bank's evaluation of project i in country j at year t. UNSC denotes a dichotomous indicator for membership in the UNSC for country j at the time of project approval, implementation, or, alternatively, evaluation. The x denotes a matrix of control variables at the time of project approval (including country or year fixed-effects in some specifications).[8] The function F represents a logit, as the dependent variable is dichotomous,

---

[8] When we include year dummies along with country dummies, many of our regressions fail to converge, so we focus our attention on the specifications with country fixed-effects. While there might be year-specific effects on the likelihood of project success, there is

coded 1 for projects rated as satisfactory and 0 otherwise. We cluster standard errors at the country level and control for country fixed-effects in some models.

To test whether political motivation affects performance in economically mismanaged or vulnerable countries, we interact UNSC membership with two alternative measures of "vulnerability," capturing the recent history of poor decision-making, economic misfortune, or economic desperation: (1) short-term debt as a percentage of total debt, and (2) debt service as a percentage of gross national income (GNI). Sovereigns with poor credit, like other borrowers, find it difficult to borrow from commercial sources over long horizons, and high short-term debt makes countries vulnerable to creditors who may decide not to roll over the debt. Because some of the poorest borrowers may receive loans only from international financial institutions – and such loans are often subsidized and of longer duration – we also look at debt service as a percentage of GNI. This variable captures both the interest rate as well as the overall debt of the country.[9] Equation 6.2 presents the interaction model, where the *Vulnerability* variable represents, alternatively, short-term debt or debt service:

$$\Pr\left(Performance_{i,j,t} = 1\right)$$

$$= F\left(\begin{array}{l} UNSC_{i,j,t=approval}, \; UNSC_{i,j,t=implementation}, \\ UNSC_{i,j,t=evaluation}, \; Vulnerability_{i,j,t=approval}, \\ UNSC_{i,j,t=approval} * Vulnerability_{i,j,t=approval}, \\ x_{i,j,t=approval} \end{array}\right) \quad (6.2)$$

The control variables, x, that we include in our analysis come from Dollar and Svensson's (2000) analysis of the determinants of success of World Bank (structural adjustment) projects: time in office of the borrower government (and its square), ethnic fractionalization and ethnic fractionalization squared, political instability, and democracy. Our measure of time in office comes from Beck et al. (2001). The longest period of time a country's leader has been in office is forty-six years: Jordan in 1999 (King Hussein bin Talal – see Adely 2012: 58; Schwedler 2006: 40). Our measure of ethnic fractionalization comes from Easterly and Sewadeh (2001)

---

no good reason to assume they would be systematically related to temporary UNSC membership.

[9] These two variables have also been used by Stone (2008) as proxies for economic vulnerability. Stone (2008) also suggests trade openness as additional measure of vulnerability.

and ranges from 0 (Republic of Korea) to 93 (Tanzania).[10] Following Dollar and Svensson (2000), we measure instability as the number of government crises. The variable is defined as "the number of any rapidly developing situation that threatens to bring the downfall of the present regime" (Databanks International 2005).[11] The maximum number of crises in a country during one year in our sample is four (in Iran 1978; Liberia 1980, 1981; Argentina 2002). Our measure of political regime, a binary indicator of democracy, comes from Cheibub et al. (2010).[12] We also control for the size and complexity of the project loan, which is included in our database for most but not all of the projects (transformed to real 2000 U.S. dollars using the GDP deflator).[13] We present the descriptive statistics and sources of these variables in the appendix to this chapter.

6.5 Results

We begin our analysis by estimating the model in Equation 6.1. Table 6.1 presents the results. In column 1 we include basic control variables, in the second column we add regional and economic controls, in the third we add year fixed-effects, and in the fourth – our preferred specification – we estimate a country fixed-effects model (conditional logit).

---

[10] Dollar and Svensson (2000: 901) point out that "the political economy literature suggests that ethnic fractionalization and length of tenure affect the probability of successful reform, but does not exactly identify the functional form of this relationship. The quadratic form chosen yields the best results." For a discussion of the problems of measuring this variable, see Posner (2004).

[11] This variable is also used in, for example, Easterly and Levine (1997), Broz (2002), Bueno de Mesquita et al. (2003), and Dreher and Gassebner (2012). It is available to us only through 2003 and thus restricts our sample to projects approved by 2003 (and evaluated by 2006).

[12] The measure of democracy is a binary indicator of whether the chief executive and the legislator are both filled through contested elections, where "contested" is defined by the observation that incumbents face some probability of losing and they actually step down from office when they do. We have also employed the Polity measure to test robustness (Marshall, Gurr, Davenport, and Jaggers 2002).

[13] The World Bank costs include the size of the loan and project-related development. The results are unchanged when only loan size is used. Dollar and Svensson (2000) also include a number of variables related to the World Bank itself, like the time spent by World Bank staff to prepare or supervise a specific project. Their results show that once the endogeneity of World Bank effort is addressed, the World Bank-related variables do not significantly affect project evaluation. The exclusion thus does not likely bias our results (but we do not have access to the effort variable and therefore cannot test for its significance in our specific setting).

TABLE 6.1. *The Effect of UNSC Membership on World Bank Project Evaluation*

	Model 1	Model 2	Model 3	Model 4
UNSC, approval time	− 0.07	− 0.13	− 0.10	− 0.11
	(0.50)	(0.92)	(0.65)	(0.83)
UNSC, project period	− 0.10	− 0.64*	− 0.46	0.07
	(0.25)	(1.67)	(1.21)	(0.17)
UNSC, evaluation time	0.11	0.14	0.14	0.10
	(0.76)	(0.75)	(0.80)	(0.69)
Short-term debt	0.01	0.002	0.003	− 0.004
	(1.13)	(0.37)	(0.51)	(0.73)
Time in office	− 0.02	− 0.01	− 0.01	− 0.02
	(0.81)	(0.53)	(0.48)	(0.83)
Time in office, squared	0.0007	0.0003	0.0003	0.0001
	(0.91)	(0.38)	(0.29)	(0.08)
Ethnic fractionalization	0.01	0.01	0.01	
	(1.50)	(1.32)	(0.97)	
Ethnic fractionalization, squared	− 0.0002*	− 0.0002**	− 0.0002*	
	(1.94)	(2.01)	(1.73)	
Instability	0.0009	− 0.08	− 0.14	0.09
	(0.01)	(0.72)	(1.41)	(0.80)
Democracy	0.26*	0.21	0.04	0.03
	(1.74)	(1.36)	(0.27)	(0.15)
(log) GDP p.c.		− 0.05	− 0.07	
		(0.59)	(0.74)	
(log) Population		0.07	0.05	
		(1.52)	(1.06)	
Lending project cost		− 0.0002	− 0.0003	
		(0.98)	(1.39)	
East Asia		0.69***	0.55**	
		(2.64)	(1.98)	
Latin America		0.09	− 0.09	
		(0.78)	(0.69)	
Middle East		0.34	0.07	
		(0.84)	(0.16)	
South Asia		0.47	0.41	
		(1.45)	(1.22)	
Sub-Saharan Africa		− 0.04	− 0.32	
		(0.15)	(1.01)	
Country fixed-effects	no	no	no	yes
Year fixed-effects	no	no	yes	no
Number of countries	78	76	76	113
Number of observations	5,834	4,499	4,499	6,808
Period (approval year)	75-03	75-03	75-03	75-03
log likelihood	−3,569	−2,660	−2,628	−3,666
Pseudo R2	0.01	0.03	0.04	0.00

Notes: The dependent variable is an indicator for successful project evaluation. Estimation is with a logit model. Unless otherwise noted, all variables are measured at the time of project approval. Numbers in parentheses are the absolute values of z-statistics. Standard errors are clustered at the country level. As per convention, we mark absolute t-statistics with * if $p < 0.10$ (statistical significance at the 10% confidence level); with ** if $p < 0.05$ (statistical significance at the 5% confidence level); and with *** if $p < 0.01$ (statistical significance at the 1% confidence level).
Source: Dreher, Klasen, Vreeland, and Werker (2013).

The coefficient on our key independent variable of interest, UNSC membership at time of approval, is negative but not statistically significant at conventional levels. As for our controls for political importance during other periods over the life cycle of a World Bank project, UNSC membership during the project implementation period is also negative but not statistically significant once we include country fixed-effects. UNSC membership at time of evaluation is positive but not statistically significant, suggesting that UNSC membership does not noticeably bias evaluation reports.

As for the other control variables, only ethnic fractionalization squared (negative) and the indicator variable for East Asia (positive) are statistically significant at the 10 percent level or stronger.[14] According to column 1, the probability of a positive evaluation also increases with democracy (significant at the 10 percent level), but when we introduce additional control variables in column 2, the effect is not statistically significant at conventional levels.[15]

The Dreher, Klasen, Vreeland, and Werker (2013) study divides the sample of World Bank projects between those approved during the Cold War period and those approved during the post–Cold War period. Bermeo (2008, 2011) argues that the political motivations driving foreign aid were stronger and more pernicious during the Cold War. Even the World Bank itself explains: "It is true that during the Cold War years aid was politically motivated. Now however, aid is being delivered to countries most in need and to those who show they are determined to use it well."[16] When it comes to the effect of UNSC membership, we find no effect of UNSC membership for projects approved during either period.

In Table 6.2 we present the results from the model in Equation 6.2, interacting our measures of political importance with vulnerability. The interaction coefficients are negative, and accompanying tests indicate that UNSC members facing high short-term debt or debt service are less likely to have satisfactory projects.[17] Interpreting an interaction effect in a logit

[14] Note however that the significance and sign of the coefficient of an interacted (squared) variable cannot properly be interpreted in the nonlinear logit model without additional calculations (Ai and Norton 2003).

[15] The ethnic fractionalization variables drop out in the country fixed-effects specification, as they do not vary over time.

[16] See the World Bank Web site: http://go.worldbank.org/LXTX3G2B00 (accessed April 12, 2010).

[17] We also interacted short-term debt with UNSC membership during the project period and, respectively, evaluation time. The results show that the effect of UNSC membership does not depend on short-term debt (see Dreher, Klasen, Vreeland, and Werker 2013).

TABLE 6.2. *The Effect of UNSC Membership and Economic Vulnerability on World Bank Project Evaluation*

	Model 1	Model 2
UNSC, approval time	0.121	0.153
	(0.70)	(1.14)
UNSC, project period	0.064	0.010
	(0.16)	(0.03)
UNSC, evaluation time	0.102	0.116
	(0.70)	(0.75)
Short-term debt	− 0.001	
	(0.29)	
UNSC* Short-term debt	− 0.018*	
	(1.76)	
Total debt service		− 0.010
		(1.41)
UNSC* Total debt service		− 0.044**
		(2.10)
Time in office	− 0.020	− 0.014
	(0.86)	(0.61)
Time in office, squared	0.0001	− 0.0001
	(0.11)	(0.05)
Instability	0.095	0.095
	(0.83)	(0.83)
Democracy	0.037	0.037
	(0.18)	(0.17)
Number of countries	113	112
Number of observations	6,808	6,571
Period (approval year)	75-03	75-03
log likelihood	−3,665	−3,508
R2	0.0028	0.0028

Notes: The dependent variable is an indicator for successful project evaluation. Estimation is with a conditional logit model for country fixed-effects. Unless otherwise noted, all variables are measured at the time of project approval. Numbers in parentheses are the absolute values of z-statistics. Standard errors are clustered at the country level. As per convention, we mark absolute t-statistics with * if $p < 0.10$ (statistical significance at the 10% confidence level); and with ** if $p < 0.05$ (statistical significance at the 5% confidence level).
Source: Dreher, Klasen, Vreeland, and Werker (2013).

Marginal Effect of UNSC on Outcome as Short–Term Debt Changes

Dependent Variable: Satisfactory Project Evaluation Dummy

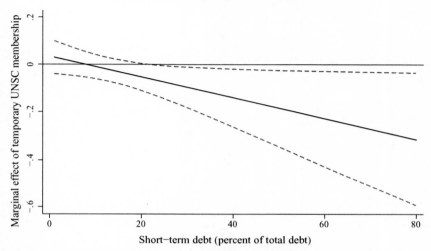

FIGURE 6.6. Marginal effect of UNSC on World Bank project evaluation for different values of short-term debt (from estimates of Table 6.2, column 1). *Notes:* The dashed lines represent the 90% confidence interval. *Source:* Dreher, Klasen, Vreeland, and Werker (2013).

model is, however, not straightforward (Ai and Norton 2003; Greene 2010).[18] So Figure 6.6 illustrates the quantitative effect of UNSC membership at approval time as a function of short-term debt (holding the additional explanatory variables to their means, and setting country fixed-effects to 0). As the figure shows, UNSC membership has a statistically significant negative effect (at the 10 percent level) on project performance when short-term debt as a percentage of total debt is 21 percent or more.[19] Within our sample, this is true for almost 17 percent of the observations. When short-term debt reaches 40 percent of total debt, the probability

---

[18] As Ai and Norton (2003: 123) point out, "the magnitude of the interaction effect in nonlinear models does not equal the marginal effect of the interaction term." It can even be of opposite sign. Moreover, a simple t-test on the coefficient of the interaction term is not appropriate to test for the significance of the interaction. We follow Greene (2010) and conduct a likelihood-ratio test to examine whether the fit of our model improves when including the interaction term. Indeed, the test suggests, at the 10 percent level of significance, that the statistical fit improves.

[19] Note that the mean of short-term debt in the sample is 12.1%; the maximum is 89%.

Marginal Effect of UNSC on Outcome as Debt Service Changes

Dependent Variable: Satisfactory Project Evaluation Dummy

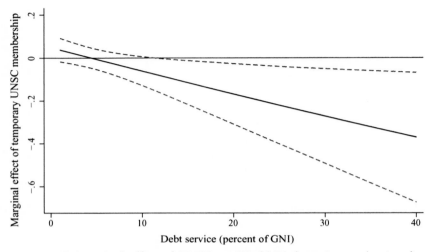

FIGURE 6.7. Marginal effect of UNSC on World Bank project evaluation for different values of debt service as a percentage of GNI (from estimates of Table 6.2, column 2). *Notes:* The dashed lines represent the 90% confidence interval. *Source:* Dreher, Klasen, Vreeland, and Werker (2013).

of a satisfactory evaluation declines by about 15 percentage points with temporary UNSC membership.[20]

Figure 6.7 graphs the effect of UNSC membership at approval time as a function of debt service (again holding the additional explanatory variables to their means, and setting country fixed-effects to 0). Similarly, this figure shows that projects in UNSC member-countries facing debt service greater than 11 percent of GNI (twice the sample mean) are significantly less likely to receive a satisfactory rating. In our sample, this is true for about 7 percent of the observations. At this level of debt service, the estimated negative effect of UNSC membership on project satisfaction is around 8 percentage points.[21] Temporary members of the UNSC with debt service above 11 percent and unsatisfactory project

[20] The cases of UNSC members with short-term debt service above 20% at the time of project approval and unsatisfactory projects include countries from Latin America, Africa, and Asia, such as Argentina (2005), Colombia (1990), Republic of Congo (2007), Ecuador (1991), Nigeria (1995), Thailand (1986), and Zambia (1988), among others.

[21] The likelihood-ratio test again indicates that the interaction increases the fit of the model, significant at the 10 percent level.

ratings include Angola (2003), Côte d'Ivoire (1991), Indonesia (2007), and Nigeria (1995), among others.

In our study with Klasen and Werker, we further explore the negative effect of UNSC membership for countries facing economic vulnerability and discover that the finding proves robust following several alternative approaches. For example, we reevaluate our results focusing only on the projects evaluated by the IEG/OED, which should address any potential bias introduced by the World Bank staff self-evaluation. We obtain similar results as we do in this chapter, indicating a consistency across the self- and the independent evaluations.

In our work with Klasen and Werker, we also introduce control variables for the target sector of the economy for the project: (1) energy and mining, (2) transport, (3) rural and agriculture, or (4) "other" (a World Bank category). Transport and "other" projects are more likely to be successful than projects designed for the rural and agricultural sector (with no significant effect for the energy and mining sector). The coefficients of interest for the vulnerability hypothesis, however, remain nearly unchanged from what we present in this chapter.

The study with Klasen and Werker further adds control variables for development policy loans. Policy loans – including structural and sectoral adjustment loans – differ from typical project loans in several respects: They are disbursed more quickly; they may be granted more often due to financial vulnerability; international political factors may feature more prominently in their approval and supervision; and policy conditionality is a key feature of these loans (see Dollar and Svensson 2000; Mosley et al. 1991). Thus one might expect that our political variables would have a stronger effect for development policy loans, but this does not appear to be the case. The indicator variable for development policy loans actually has a statistically significant positive effect, and the coefficients of interest for the vulnerability-hypothesis are, again, similar to those that we present in this chapter.

We also adjust the timing of the control variables, using average values for the control variables across the period between implementation and evaluation (instead of using project-approval time, as above). Our main vulnerability results hold here as well.

Finally, we address the possibility of nonrandom assignment of projects, using a Heckman two-step approach, where the first step – the selection stage – is the decision to provide World Bank projects to a country in a given year, and the second step – the outcome stage – is the evaluation outcome (see, for example, Heckman 1979). Tests do not indicate that selection bias is a problem, and our main finding holds again.

We thus conclude the following from our analysis of the effect of UNSC membership on the performance of World Bank projects: (1) The average performance does not appear to suffer. (2) Projects awarded to UNSC members facing economic vulnerability perform worse than other projects. So the domestic political economy matters.[22] We measure "vulnerability" using short-term debt and, alternatively, debt service. For a UNSC member where short-term debt as a percentage of total debt is about 40 percent, we estimate that the probability of a satisfactory evaluation is lower by about 15 percentage points. For a UNSC member with debt service greater than 11 percent of GNI, we estimate that the probability of a satisfactory evaluation is lower by about 8 percentage points. Since the average probability of a satisfactory evaluation is about 0.7, this estimate represents a drop of more than 10 percent from the baseline. Substantively, this magnitude approximates the difference between the observed rate of project success in Africa and the rate of success in Western Europe.

So, according to the conservative approach above, which employs World Bank project evaluations to measure performance, foreign aid to UNSC members hurts only highly indebted countries. Yet this conservative analysis faces real limitations. For one, it ignores bilateral aid, focusing only on World Bank projects. We would like to apply our methodology here to bilateral project evaluations, but a comprehensive dataset of such evaluations, such as we have from the World Bank, is unavailable to us.[23] Moreover, the project-evaluation approach ignores the broader question of economic development. For all of the measurement problems noted above, economic growth is simply too important to ignore.

Thus, in further research, with Vera Eichenauer of Heidelberg University and Kai Gehring of the Georg-August-Universität Göttingen, we return to the broader question of whether the donors' political motives matter for the effectiveness of their aid with respect to economic growth (see Dreher, Eichenauer, and Gehring 2013). This new study introduces our measure of temporary UNSC membership to the widely cited growth

---

[22] As one possible transmission channel through which the political economy of a country can make a difference, Kilby (2013a) shows that World Bank project arrangements are rushed for UNSC members when short-term debt is high and that longer preparation improves outcomes.

[23] For the most comprehensive project-specific database, see www.aiddata.org (Tierney et al. 2011).

regressions of Michael Clemens, Steven Radelet, Rikhil Bhavnani, and Samuel Bazzi (2012). Specifically, UNSC membership is interacted with the amount of foreign aid received by a country. The approach thus allows for a separate effect of politically motivated aid on economic growth. This study, therefore, overcomes the Bashir and Lim (2013) critique of the study by Bueno de Mesquita and Smith (2010). Instead of looking just at UNSC membership, it considers the effect of foreign aid to such members. The study finds that this type of aid is indeed less effective, on average. Importantly, these results hold when the sample is restricted to Africa, where the process of UNSC election is, arguably, exogenous. We conclude that when it comes to providing foreign aid, political motives matter.

6.6 Democracy versus Dictatorship

The above analysis shows that UNSC membership can lead to inferior projects when a government faces international economic vulnerability. Under dire circumstances – when governments face high debt – we suspect that UNSC members expend political capital to get a marginally inferior World Bank project approved by the executive board. Under those circumstances, political prominence may lead to project failure. Simply because a country rises to political importance, however, does not imply that it has a bad government. The evidence in the above section suggests that under normal circumstances, UNSC members are just as likely to successfully complete World Bank projects as are other countries. Yet, our ongoing research, which uses the less restrictive approach of looking at general change in the level of economic development, reveals a broader negative effect of foreign aid for UNSC members (Dreher, Eichenauer, and Gehring 2013). Still, this study also finds some (weak) evidence that the negative effect holds in particular for autocratic governments receiving foreign aid while serving on the UNSC. Both approaches thus suggest that specific domestic characteristics of the government in question may play a role. In other words, the domestic political economy matters. With this idea in mind, we return to our analysis of the effect of UNSC membership on economic growth in Africa – now with specific attention to African countries' domestic political circumstances – specifically, regime type.

First, consider the African cases from our dataset that closely fit the finding that highly indebted UNSC members pursue inferior World Bank projects: Zambia (1988), Nigeria (1995), and Republic of Congo (2007). All three of these cases represent governments facing short-term debt

210 The Political Economy of the United Nations Security Council

greater than 20 percent of total debt. All three of these cases represent countries that received World Bank loans for projects that ultimately proved unsatisfactory. We further note that none of these cases represent solidly democratic regimes. Zambia had already lived under the rule of Kenneth Kaunda for over two decades. Nigeria remained under the grip of Sani Abacha's brutal regime. Rule in Congo appeared arguably democratic in 2007, as President Denis Sassou-Nguesso had taken office through competitive elections, but his administration had been in power for well over a decade, and we have yet to see any alternation in power since his original election in 1997. At least the overall economy grew in Congo by about 6 percent over the four-year period after the time of UNSC election (2005).[24] Zambia and Nigeria represent two of the worst performers. Elected in 1986, Zambia's economy contracted by more than 5 percent during the next four years, and Nigeria, elected in 1993, saw a contraction of about 1 percent over the subsequent four-year period.

These cases tentatively suggest that dictatorship may lead to economic vulnerability, which in turn leads governments to exploit political leverage on the UNSC to obtain marginally inferior World Bank projects. Now, when we interact indebtedness, political regime, and UNSC membership in our above analysis of World Bank projects, we do not detect a systematic effect of political regime, but this is asking a lot of the data when we have so few cases. Is there any other evidence that democracies and dictatorships pursue different policies when serving on the UNSC? In this section, we present some tentative economic growth evidence from Africa. Before continuing with Africa, however, consider some global evidence on the interaction of domestic political regime and UNSC membership.

First, some background: According to the seminal study of Adam Przeworski, Jose Cheibub, Fernando Limongi, and Michael Alvarez (2000), democracies and dictatorships grow at about the same average rate: Real GDP per capita increases around 2 percent per year. Yet, the two regimes grow in different ways. While democracies exploit capital more efficiently, dictatorships use labor more "efficiently," by repressing wages.[25] Variance of economic growth is also higher for dictatorships than

---

[24] Republic of Congo economic data come directly from the World Bank. The data for Zambia and Nigeria come from Bueno de Mesquita and Smith (2010), who took their data from the World Bank.

[25] For a study of the connection between wages and debt, see Dymski and Pastor (1990). Also see Pinto and Timmons (2005). On the IMF's role in generating tension in Latin America between the goal of economic growth and the need to attract capital to address the debt crisis, see Shadlen (2007).

democracies (Quinn and Woolley 2001). In other words, democracies tend to grow at a more consistent rate, whereas dictatorships are responsible for both the miracles of economic development and the failures. All of this suggests that the effectiveness of the role of the state in the economy differs by political regime.

In their work with Randolph M. Siverson and James D. Morrow, Bueno de Mesquita and Smith suggest a reason as to why (Bueno de Mesquita et al. 2003). Their "selectorate" theory assumes that governments seek to survive in office, and which policies best help to achieve this goal depends on the political institutions that "select" the government leaders. Under democracy, a large winning coalition of the "selectorate" (in this case, voters) is required to win reelection. Leaders can most effectively deliver benefits to such large swaths of society by providing efficient public goods, which in turn promote economic growth. Governments under democracy thus have incentives to build a productive public infrastructure. Under dictatorship, however, leaders survive in power by catering to a small, loyal elite. Leaders thus bestow benefits in the form of private payoffs and are more likely than democratically elected governments to funnel money to key constituents and engage in graft when promoting public projects.[26] Thus, Bueno de Mesquita et al. (2003) claim that democracies deliver public goods while dictatorships provide private goods to a narrow set of elite supporters of the regime (also see McGillavray and Smith 2008).

With this background in mind, consider our research conducted with political scientist Irfan Nooruddin of Ohio State University on the interaction of UNSC membership and domestic political regime (Nooruddin and Vreeland 2010). This research begins with the observation that the governments of developing countries often face strategic incentives to devote expenditures to public wages and salaries and that such expenditures can play a vital role in fostering economic progress and reducing income inequality. The means available to the government of a developing country to take such action, however, may depend on the role it plays in global governance. Recall from Chapter 5 that when serving as temporary members of the UNSC, governments become more likely to receive loans from the IMF and these loans have fewer conditions attached. IMF

---

[26] For more nuanced typologies of authoritarian regimes, see Gandhi (2008), Geddes (1999), Howard and Roessler (2006), Davenport (2007a, 2007b), Weeks (2008), Falleti (2011), and Levitsky and Way (2010). For an examination of the electoral pressures that democracies face leading them to delay important policy changes, see Walter (2013).

conditionality typically involves austerity measures that can cause the economy to contract. Governments must raise taxes and cut spending, which reduces consumption. If government consumption goes toward productive public goods, as might be true under democracy, the cuts may have negative consequences for long-run economic growth. But if government spending involves the payoff of government cronies, as might be so under dictatorships, then the long-run cuts may have no long-run negative consequences – trimming such government excesses could even stimulate the economy.

Nooruddin and Vreeland (2010) thus consider the effect of IMF reform programs on public wages and salaries, accounting for both UNSC membership and political regime. In general, the dire economic circumstances that governments face when turning to the IMF typically lead them to cut public wages and salaries. This is not surprising. Governments turning to the IMF suffer from problems of excess demand. They may have large government budget deficits, high public debt, low levels of foreign reserves, and an overvalued exchange rate. As a result, their economic circumstances call for them to slash public spending. IMF conditionality can incentivize them to make the hard policy choices because continued disbursements of IMF loans require, in principle, compliance with austere policy conditions (Nooruddin and Simmons 2006). The wages and salaries of civil servants may represent a ripe target for cuts. Yet developing countries often use the civil service to provide both public and private goods to constituencies to maximize their chances of surviving in office (Rudra 2008; Nooruddin and Rudra forthcoming). Cutting expenditures on the wages and salaries of civil servants thus puts governments in jeopardy: Most developing countries face pressure to protect civil servants during economic downturns but typically lack the resources to do so. Economic crises leave them little room but to make the tough choice of cutting public spending.

Elected members of the UNSC hold a trump card. They may have the necessary international political leverage to negotiate favorable treatment from the IMF. So they have the same domestic incentives to protect civil servants as their non-UNSC counterparts *and* the international leverage to obtain the means to do so. IMF participation may enable them to actually increase their budget allocation for public wages and salaries.

The IMF was founded precisely to provide loans of foreign exchange to governments facing a financial crisis.[27] The loans are designed to help

---

[27] Originally, the idea was to make the IMF large enough to be capable of bailing out any country, but the world's largest surplus country at the time – the United States – did not

soften the blow of economic adjustment, but the IMF attaches stringent economic conditions to ensure that the loans do not allow the continuation of the excesses that led to the financial problems in the first place. So even with access to an IMF loan, governments reduce spending, using the loans to pay down national debt, fortify the stock of foreign reserves, or defend the currency. Thus economic austerity and reform are expected to be part of the IMF package. Yet this relies on the IMF actually enforcing the conditions it attaches to loans.[28] In principle, the IMF disburses a loan over time, provided the government complies with specific conditions of economic adjustment, such as cutting government expenditures.

Analyzing the impact of IMF participation on the change in public wages and salaries, Nooruddin and Vreeland (2010) consider a total of 2,354 observations of wages and salaries from 146 countries between 1970 and 1999. We use a two-step instrumental-variable approach to control for nonrandom selection in a regression model with a host of control variables and robust standard errors clustered by country.[29]

For democracies, we obtain the following results: Service on the UNSC does not have a statistically significant effect, nor does IMF participation for democracies *not* serving on the UNSC. But for democracies serving on the UNSC, the effect of IMF participation is to raise public wages and salaries by nearly 1 percent of total expenditures.[30] Once again, we see that countries that are politically important to the major shareholders of the IMF receive benefits. Democratically accountable governments use their political importance to continue to provide public goods – the IMF loan softens the blow of adjustment. There is no similar effect on dictatorships, however, and Nooruddin and Vreeland suspect that these governments use their political leverage to protect smaller constituencies, following Bueno de Mesquita's selectorate theory.

Having seen the role that domestic political incentives may play, we go back to Africa, with a focus on the interaction between UNSC membership and political regime. Again, following Bueno de Mesquita and Smith (2010), we consider the four-year change in per capita income for

trust an international organization with the resources that would have been required. So the IMF was never big enough to manage the ebbs and flows of the trade and financial exchanges in the developed world. The IMF soon found a more suitable clientele – the developing world (see Vreeland 2007).

[28] Dreher (2009) discusses conditionality in the context of IMF programs. See Vreeland (2006) for an analysis of compliance with IMF conditionality.

[29] They estimate, first, a linear probability model of IMF participation and then use the predicted probability of IMF participation in the second stage. The method is explained in technical detail in their appendix (Nooruddin and Vreeland 2010: 105–106).

[30] They estimate a 90 percent confidence interval of 0.11% to 1.74%.

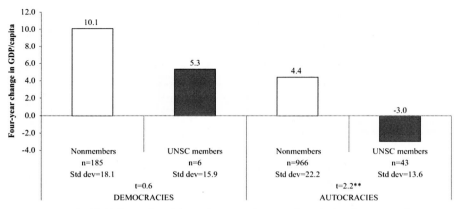

FIGURE 6.8. UNSC membership and economic growth (average four-year change in GDP/capita, 2000 US dollars) by UNSC membership status and by political regime in Africa. *Notes:* Average four-year change in GDP/capita by UNSC membership status and by regime type for the Africa sample. *Source:* Bueno de Mesquita and Smith (2010).

countries elected to the UNSC versus those not elected. This time, we compare this difference across democracies and dictatorships in Africa. We use the measure of political regime employed by Bueno de Mesquita and Smith, a normalized Polity score which runs continuously from 0 to 1 (their cut-off for democracy is a score greater than 0.7 – see Bueno de Mesquita and Smith 2010: 676). Figure 6.8 presents descriptive data.

For African democracies, we observe a difference of 4.8 percentage points: the four-year average rate of growth for the 185 observations of democracies in Africa not on the UNSC is 10.1 percent, and the average rate for the six African democracies elected to the UNSC is 5.3 percent. This difference is not statistically significant, in part due to the size of the difference and in part due to the very few observations of democratic African countries. So, while the average economic performance of African democracies on the UNSC appears poorer, the difference does not constitute a statistically significant pattern.

For dictatorships, we observe a difference of 7.4 percentage points: the four-year average rate of growth for the 966 observations of dictatorships not on the UNSC is 4.4 percent, and the average rate for the 43 observations of dictatorships that served on the UNSC is –3.0 percent. Given the size of the difference, the number of observations, and the variance among the two groups, this difference does represent a statistically significant pattern.

TABLE 6.3. *The Effect of UNSC Membership and Political Regime on Economic Performance in Africa*

Variable	Coefficient	Interactions	Coefficient
Elected to UNSC (T0)	− 6.47*	Effect of UNSC for dictatorships	− 6.47*
	(1.75)	(democracy = 0):	(1.75)
UNSC* Democracy	11.92	Effect of UNSC for democracies	5.45
	(1.20)	(democracy = 1):	(0.71)
Democracy	6.14**	Effect of democracy (UNSC =	6.14**
	(2.17)	0):	(2.17)
Population (logged)	− 8.42***	Effect of democracy on the	18.06**
	(4.64)	UNSC (UNSC = 1):	(2.46)
GDP/capita (logged)	− 23.38***		
	(10.87)		
Constant	274.70***		
	(9.85)		
Number of countries	48		
Number of observations	1,200		
Period	60-01		
R2	0.14		

Notes: The dependent variable is the four-year change in GDP/capita, taken from Bueno de Mesquita and Smith (2010). Estimation is with OLS, including fixed effects for countries. Data cover only Africa. Numbers in parentheses are the absolute values of t-statistics. As per convention, we mark absolute t-statistics with * if $p < 0.10$ (statistical significance at the 10 percent confidence level); with ** if $p < 0.05$ (statistical significance at the 5 percent confidence level); and with *** if $p < 0.01$ (statistical significance at the 1 percent confidence level).

We note two observations: (1) In Africa, dictatorships generally perform worse on average than democracies, and (2) African dictatorships that enjoy the political clout of UNSC membership represent the set of worst performers. African dictatorships that served on the UNSC not only achieved lower rates of economic growth than any other group, but their economies actually contracted, on average, by 3 percent over a four-year period. This statistically significant finding implies that people living under African dictatorships that served on the UNSC consumed less over the four-year period starting with their terms on the UNSC. Of course, elite constituencies that enjoyed close connections to the government likely fared much better.

These descriptive relationships require more rigorous analysis, so we return to the statistical model of Bueno de Mesquita and Smith. Table 6.3 below follows the same statistical model that they use in their analysis except we include only observations from Africa (see Bueno de Mesquita and Smith 2010: 678, table 4). Following their model, we control for GDP

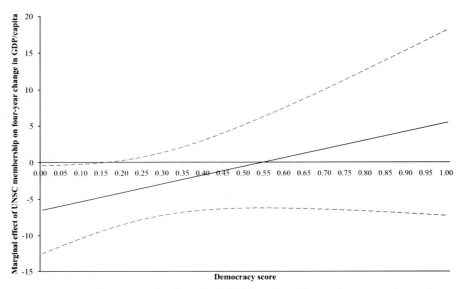

FIGURE 6.9. The marginal effect of UNSC membership on four-year change in GDP/capita for different values of Democracy. *Notes:* The dashed lines represent the 90% confidence interval.

per capita and population (both logged), and we include fixed-effects for countries. Our key variables of interest are election to the UNSC and democracy. We condition the effect of UNSC membership on political regime by including an interaction term (UNSC*Democracy). The first pair of columns presents the main results of the model, and the second pair of columns presents the conditional effects from the interaction term, setting the Democracy variable to 0 and 1, alternatively, for the effect of UNSC membership conditioned on political regime. Figure 6.9 presents the effect of UNSC membership over continuous values of the Democracy variable.

The estimated results presented in Table 6.3 and Figure 6.9 basically confirm the descriptive pattern in Figure 6.8. We find a negative effect of UNSC membership on economic growth for dictatorships. When the democracy variable equals 0, we estimate that UNSC membership leads to a 6.47 percent reduction in growth over the four-year period beginning with election to the UNSC – the finding is statistically significant at the 10 percent level. Now, Figure 6.9 reveals that the negative effect of UNSC membership is statistically significant at the 10 percent level only up to a score of about 0.15 – however, this condition holds for about half of the sample of the 1,200 observations in the analysis.[31] We estimate a positive effect of UNSC membership on economic growth starting at a democracy score of about 0.55. This effect – UNSC membership conditioned on democracy – is not statistically significant.

Looking at the reverse conditional effect – the effect of democracy conditioned on UNSC membership – we estimate that it is positive and statistically significant at the 5 percent level. Democracies perform better than dictatorships in general, and democracies serving on the UNSC perform the best of all. The point estimate is massive – too big to be considered credible: 18.06 percent over the four-year period. The high estimate is due to the small number of observations; recall from Figure 6.8 that we observe only six democracies that serve on the UNSC.[32] The standard error is correspondingly large, but still indicates that the positive effect is statistically significant at the 5 percent level.

The findings for democracies and dictatorships shed some light on the debate that rages between those who favor foreign aid and those who oppose it. Consistent with the assessment of Dollar and Svensson (2000), the effect appears to depend on the political economy of recipient countries. Some governments may do well with foreign aid – at least we detect no negative effect of UNSC membership for democracies in Africa, and we find that UNSC membership may augment the positive effects of democracy. But other governments do poorly – we find a negative effect of

---

[31] More precisely, 632 observations of the 1,200 in this analysis have a democracy score of 0.15 or less. For a thorough examination of the impact of good governance on development assistance, see Neumayer (2003). For an analysis in the context of non-traditional donors, see Dreher, Nunnenkamp and Thiele (2011); on China as a donor, see Dreher and Fuchs (2011b) and Strange et al. (2013). For a study that raises doubts about democracies employing foreign aid for better uses, see Bjørnskov (2010), who shows that foreign aid exacerbates income inequality in democracies but not autocratic countries.

[32] Of the six democracies (according to Bueno de Mesquita and Smith's 2010 measure), four of them fared well: Elected to the UNSC in 1994, Botswana's economy grew by nearly 24% over the next four years. Mali, elected in 1999, grew by about 15% over the next four years. Mauritius, elected in 2000, grew by nearly 13%, while Namibia, elected in 1998, grew by nearly 8%. Two of the democracies did not fare well, however: Guinea-Bissau, elected in 1995, experienced a drastic contraction of the economy by 17% over the next four years. Democratic Nigeria, elected in 1965, saw its economy contract by more than 10% during the next four years. Of course, democracy actually broke down soon after Nigeria's election to the UNSC, so the government was actually a dictatorship during the years it served on the UNSC.

UNSC membership for dictatorships. Note that in the research of Dreher, Eichenauer, and Gehring (2013), we also find that the negative growth effects of foreign aid are mainly driven by autocratic UNSC members.

Thus, international and domestic political factors appear to interact. At the international level, a country's position on the UNSC gives its government political leverage to obtain more foreign aid with fewer policy conditions attached; at the domestic level the regime type shapes the preferences of the government as to how to exploit the foreign aid. Dictatorships may use their international political position to win financial favors from powerful countries that care about their UNSC votes, but this finance does not appear to improve the economic prospects of their countries. While elites connected to the government may benefit from foreign aid, the aid actually harms the economy as a whole, perhaps by propping up bad policies and bad governments.

6.7 Conclusion

The results of this chapter will not settle the foreign aid debate – nor do we intend for them to do so. Indeed, our results call for a nuanced view of foreign aid, one that recognizes that the effects depend partly on a country's international position and partly on its domestic political economy.[33] We have shown that when a country rises in international political prominence by winning election to the UNSC, it becomes more likely to receive various forms of financial perks. The effects of such finance, however, may depend on how well the government has managed the economy and whether the government's survival depends on publicly contested elections or on the support of a narrow elite constituency.

We therefore draw moderate conclusions. Our analysis of World Bank projects suggests that most of the time, UNSC members receive aid that fares no better and no worse than aid extended to other countries. Still, we present some tentative evidence – driven by a few observations in Africa – that UNSC membership may augment the positive effects of democracy on economic performance. Perhaps democratic governments best employ the windfall of foreign aid when serving on the UNSC. We also report some negative results: (1) Economically vulnerable members of the UNSC obtain World Bank projects that result in poor performance, (2) African dictatorships experience economic contractions following their

---

[33] For a more comprehensive approach to the interaction of domestic and international institutions, see Drezner (2002).

participation on the UNSC, and (3) Aid flows are less effective in African dictatorships. We thus suspect that certain governments exploit the temporary political importance they derive from UNSC membership to trade political support for foreign aid that fails their countries in the long run – even if the government enjoys an initial short-run gain from the influx of finance. Perhaps this foreign aid props up bad policies – or even the governments themselves. As these cases are rare, our concluding chapter does not necessarily call for radical changes to the selection of UNSC members or the role that they play. Nevertheless, we do propose some modest changes that might mitigate some of the problems that do exist.

Appendix 6.1: Describing the Data Used in this Chapter

TABLE 6.a1. *Descriptive Data*

Variable	Mean	St. Dev.	Min.	Max.	Source
UNSC, approval time	0.10	0.31	0.00	1.00	Dreher et al. (2009b)
UNSC, project period	0.08	0.13	0.00	0.67	Dreher et al. (2009b)
UNSC, evaluation time	0.09	0.29	0.00	1.00	Dreher et al. (2009b)
Short-term debt (% of total external debt)	12.62	9.39	0.00	88.93	World Bank (2008)
Total debt service (% of GNI)	6.19	5.11	0.00	107.37	World Bank (2008)
Time in office	8.60	8.29	1.00	46.00	Beck et al. (2001)
Time in office, squared	143	254	1.00	2116	
Ethnic fractionalization	52.62	30.08	1.00	93.00	Easterly and Sewadeh (2001)
Ethnic fractionalization, squared	3674	2855	1.00	8649	
Instability	0.17	0.47	0.00	4.00	Databanks International (2005)
Democracy indicator	0.36	0.48	0.00	1.00	Cheibub et al. (2010)
(log) GDP p.c. (constant 2000 US$)	6.59	1.06	4.40	9.01	World Bank (2008)
(log) Population	16.99	1.58	13.29	20.77	World Bank (2008)
Lending project cost, millions of real US$	133	222	0.15	3150	Independent Evaluation Group
IMF program	0.51	0.50	0.00	1.00	Dreher et al. (2009b)
Investment (% of GDP)	12.65	6.87	– 3.46	68.35	Przeworski et al. (2000), extended
Legislative election	0.19	0.39	0.00	1.00	Beck et al. (2001)

Notes: All variables are measured at project approval time, unless noted otherwise.

7

Reforming the UNSC

7.1 And the World Will Live as One?

Imagine a world where governments never manipulate international organizations to further their individual foreign policy objectives – a world where governments cannot trade money for influence over these international organizations – a world where money and politics never mix on the international stage. Is this world a utopia? Or is it, perhaps, a world with no international organizations at all? It just might be a world with lower levels of global cooperation than the world where we actually live. Perhaps governments participate in institutionalized forms of international cooperation only if they can reap some benefits on the side.

Cooperation requires sacrifice. This is true whether we are talking about collaboration between friends or among nations. *Institutionalized* cooperation across independent countries requires the sacrifice of at least some degree of national sovereignty.[1] Generally, people make sacrifices only if they can expect some kind of benefit in return.

This book shows that governments trade financial favors for political influence over the UN Security Council, and some readers may react with calls for reform. But a reactionary rebuke of this mechanism on moral grounds may not be productive. When considering the reform of global

---

[1] See Lake (1996, 1999) and Arend and Beck (1993). Herbst (2007: 137) argues, interestingly, that African leaders have flipped this around, using membership in international organizations to solidify their sovereignty. The effect may depend on the strength of domestic institutions (see Hathaway 2002, Hafner-Burton and Tsutsui 2005). Of course, membership in international organizations has itself been found to impact domestic institutions (Pevehouse 2002, 2005; Mansfield and Pevehouse 2006; Gray 2009).

governance, one should first ask a series of questions. For example, are proposed changes "incentive compatible"? That is, if we adjust the status quo, will governments still have an incentive to participate? Suppose that we could eliminate trades for influence over the UNSC. Perhaps governments would begin to turn their backs on the institution. In other words, governments may only be willing to make the necessary sacrifices to work within the UNSC if trading money for influence remains part of the equation. Side benefits – even unofficial benefits – may be required to entice governments to work with international organizations.[2] We may need to accept trades of political influence for financial favors in order for these international organizations to exist.

Real-world organizations should therefore not be judged by utopian criteria, but should rather be compared to other realistic equilibria, including the option of no international organizations at all. The purpose of writing about the underbelly of the UNSC in this book is not to get people to turn away from the institution in search of the perfect. Instead, we seek to understand the kinds of deals that are necessary for governments to participate. Next, we invite readers to ask whether the world is better off with a perhaps flawed multilateral forum in which to discuss threats to global security – or without any forum at all. Finally, we hope to inspire readers to think about *realistic* changes that might address shortcomings, while still preserving the incentives for countries to participate.

We suggest that even flawed forms of international cooperation may be better than nothing. In this chapter, therefore, we begin by discussing the sacrifices and benefits that governments face when engaging in institutionalized forms of cooperation. We then review the reforms that are currently being debated in the UN and around the world, which mainly concern questions of representation: Who gets to have a permanent seat at the table, and how many seats (permanent and elected) should there be? We see good reasons that the issue of representation has taken center stage. The UNSC derives its authority to legitimize forceful foreign policies through the representational character of the body. Yet, most of the proposals to change representation on the UNSC have little chance of passing. Even if they did pass, they would do little to address the concerns raised by our research. Our research raises the question of accountability – an issue that receives less emphasis in many discussions about

---

[2] See Mitchell and Keilbach (2001) – also see Baccini and Urpelainen (2012).

reforming the UNSC.[3] We thus conclude with a modest proposal to improve accountability, which we can summarize in three words: End term limits.

7.2 Cooperation and Sacrifice

Different types of international organizations require different forms of sacrifice. When it comes to international financial institutions, like the International Monetary Fund and the World Bank, the sacrifice involves money. Governments directly sacrifice some sovereignty over the use of the money that they contribute to the institution. They may retain some voice on the executive board in charge, but the board as a body itself makes the final decisions. Indirectly, the creation of an international institution impacts the relative power of independent states. A new power – the international institution itself – has its own rival presence on the international stage.

When it comes to international security organizations, such as military alliances or the UNSC, the sacrifice involves raw coercive power. Governments directly delegate to the UNSC the power to legitimately authorize forceful foreign policies – like imposing sanctions or even taking military action. UNSC members retain some degree of control over decisions, but the UNSC makes the final decisions as a body. Of course, governments can still take unilateral action and go against the UNSC (see Goldsmith and Levinson 2009: 1793). Nevertheless, the UNSC has become the global focal point for legitimizing forceful foreign policies, either symbolically (Hurd 2007) or by conveying credible information (Chapman 2011).

How much sovereignty in these matters are governments willing to sacrifice? And what do they get in return? The answers to these questions must be commensurate, or cooperation will not be forthcoming. The more benefits that a government receives from an international organization, the more power it may be willing to bestow upon that organization. The benefits that a government can receive from an international organization might involve global public goods as well as benefits tailored to specific governments.

---

[3] Although see Roberts and Zimm (2008: chapter 5) for an exceptional discussion of reform and how it connects to accountability (or fails to). We thank Chester Crocker for this suggestion. For broad approaches to accountability in international organizations, see Zweifel (2005) and Grant and Keohane (2005).

In terms of global public goods, international financial institutions provide a pool of resources to be used for the purposes of stability or development. Since the economic stability and development of one country has spillover effects on others, pooling resources makes sense. Turning to security organizations, these institutions coordinate global efforts to take action against a threat, which, if left unchecked, may have violent spillover effects. Abbott and Snidal (1998) describe the provision of these public goods as a type of repeated prisoner's dilemma with multiple equilibria. In one equilibrium, no one takes the required action to stop a threat, and negative consequences spread. In another equilibrium, individual governments act together, stopping the threat. The international institution serves to coordinate governments on the latter equilibrium, and thus improves global well-being.

Shared benefits, however, may not be enough to entice governments to make the required sacrifices for an international organization to exist. Especially for the most powerful countries – which might be more resilient to negative spillovers and able to prevent them unilaterally – direct individual benefits may also be required.[4]

An international organization can provide one benefit to governments by offering a credible signal of the appropriateness of their preferred policies. To the extent that the public views an international organization as an independent agent, its voice may provide a useful endorsement of governments. In his research with several collaborators, Rosendorff has developed a series of formal models showing that international institutions can send credible signals to domestic audiences about the policies of a government.[5] Chapman (2011) applies this kind of logic directly to the UNSC, showing how Security Council resolutions have helped to provide U.S. presidents with public approval for forceful foreign policies. Trade organizations, as another example, can credibly signal to an uninformed domestic public that its government is pursuing free-trade policies (Mansfield et al. 2002). International financial institutions might signal to voters that a tough austerity package represents the best set of policies to deal with economic problems. Some governments may even use the leverage of an international organization to coerce reticent interest groups so that

---

[4] For a presentation of bribery as an informal institution reinforcing bureaucratic hierarchies, see Darden (2008). He applies his argument to domestic politics, but a related argument can be made for international institutions.

[5] See Mansfield, Milner, and Rosendorff (2002), Rosendorff and Doces (2006), Hollyer and Rosendorff (2011), and Hollyer, Rosendorff, and Vreeland (2011).

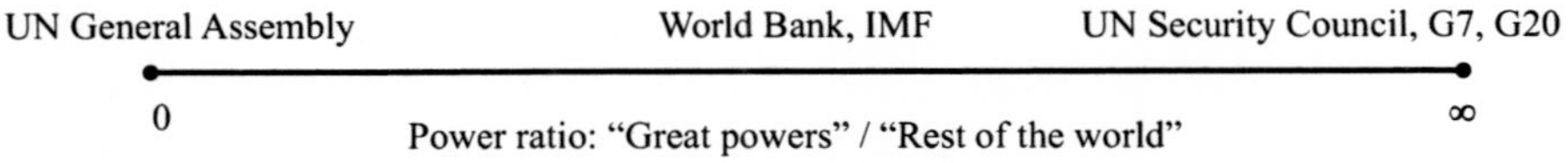

UN General Assembly   World Bank, IMF   UN Security Council, G7, G20

0   Power ratio: "Great powers" / "Rest of the world"   ∞

FIGURE 7.1. Ratio of power in international organizations – "great powers" to the "rest of the world." *Notes:* Different international organizations offer different trade-offs to incentivize the great powers and the rest of the world to participate. At the left extreme are organizations where all countries are treated equally, so no one receives great power status. These organizations favor smaller countries. At the right extreme are clubs where only great powers have membership, leaving out the rest of the world. *Source:* Vreeland (forthcoming). Also see Lake (1996: 7).

they agree to raise taxes or cut expenditures (Vreeland 2003). Depending on the policy and a person's point of view, an organization like the IMF may play the role of scapegoat, bad guy, or dark knight.

This brings us to the "dirty work" that international organizations can do for governments (Vaubel 1986: 48–51). One important benefit that international organizations can provide its members is the ability to obfuscate or launder activities that look bad to the public (Abbott and Snidal 1998: 18–19, Yasutomo 1993: 339). Governments coerce one another, do each other favors, and make trades under the table all of the time – with or without international organizations. International organizations simply provide an additional conduit that might be particularly useful since these institutions are not well understood by outsiders.

In our story, for example, governments use their power in one international organization to gain leverage over another. The top members of the IMF and World Bank can exert their influence on the executive boards of these institutions to provide loans for elected members of the UNSC. At the same time, the elected UNSC members also use their position on the Security Council to gain leverage over international financial institutions. The path runs both ways. The extent to which a government can use its power in an international organization to pursue side objectives depends on how much power the government has in the governance of the international organization. This power, in turn, depends on the country – some get more than others – and with good reason.

One can conceive of international organizations as lying along a continuum of how much power is allocated to the "great" powers and how much voice is left for the "rest of the world" (see Figure 7.1). Our conception takes its inspiration from one of the foremost scholars of international relations, David Lake (1999, 1996: 7), who conceives of cooperation in international security along a continuum from anarchic alliances to hierarchical empires. In our conception, we place the UN General Assembly at the anarchic extreme, where each country gets one vote – there are no "great powers" with special privileges.[6] In between are international financial institutions, where the formula is closer to one dollar, one vote. The more money that a government contributes, the more the international organization allocates power to it (including say over how much power to allocate to emerging countries). Note that while the old powers may resist ceding votes to emerging powers, international financial institutions have institutionalized mechanisms by which they can reallocate votes as the distribution of global GDP evolves. At the hierarchical extreme is the UN Security Council, where about 98 percent of formal voting power is allocated to the great powers, which have permanent status and veto power over resolutions (recall the research of O'Neill 1996 discussed in Chapter 1). The rest of the world vies for the remaining 2 percent of voting power. Moreover, according to the evidence presented in the pages of this book, the little amount of influence that developing countries have over the UNSC is up for sale.

The ways in which power is distributed in each of these institutions may be a function of the purposes each serves.[7] A primary function of the UNGA is to legitimate the existence of sovereign states by granting them membership.[8] All states are treated as equals with respect to their inherent sovereignty, and thus it makes sense to give each one of them the

---

[6] Note that in our conception of international organizations, the World Trade Organization (WTO) is difficult to categorize. Because the organization requires unanimity, it might be considered at the left-most extreme – beyond even the United Nations General Assembly. But, in practice, economically large countries (those with the most at stake on an issue) take the de facto lead in WTO negotiations about specific commodities and issues, and so have powerful agenda-setting power. See McGillivray (2000).

[7] In this discussion, we focus on global institutions. Sacrifices have also been made at the regional level. In Europe, in particular, members of the European Union, and especially the Eurozone, have sacrificed an unprecedented level of sovereignty. As Anderson (1999: 5) notes, "the contingent nature of sovereignty . . . is nowhere more apparent than in contemporary Europe." For further work on regional cooperation in Europe, see Meunier and McNamara (2007); Checkel (2007); Schimmelfennig (2007); and Tucker, Pacek, and Berinsky (2002). For work on regional organizations outside of Europe, see Mansfield and Milner (1997, 1999), Acharya and Johnston (2007), Barnett and Solingen (2007), Dominguez (2007), Khong and Nesadurai (2007), and Desai and Vreeland (2011). For broader approaches to the design of international institutions, see Kahler (2013); Koremenos (2008); Bradley and Kelley (2008); Rosendorff and Milner (2001); Koremenos, Lipson, and Snidal (2001); Downs, Rocke, and Barsoom (1996); and Lake (1996: 15–22, 23–25).

[8] We are grateful to BAN Whi Min for this suggestion. For an extensive study of the historical evolution of the norms of state recognition and sovereignty, see Fazal (2007).

same equal vote. As the forum that legitimizes the constellation of legitimately existing states, the UNGA has the power to select representatives to various other UN committees. Beyond this, the UNGA passes lots of resolutions, but it has little force in and of itself. So, the UNGA has the rather limited authority to certify whether there is broad-based consensus among existing members about the legitimate existence of a state.

International financial institutions provide, of course, finance and are organized much like private banks. Contributions are tied to votes around an executive board. The caveat is that additional shares cannot be purchased without the approval of the existing members, by supermajority. This allows for the power relationships among member states to evolve over time and gives the old powers control over the precise nature of that evolution, including whether changes are allowed at all. Again, the design makes sense, given the purpose.

By granting votes according to the size of contributions, the great powers are incentivized to provide necessary resources for the institution. Voice is afforded to the rest of the world so that they will also participate. They too provide some resources and are also granted a "floor" voice: All members get a minimum number of the votes. As for the great powers, beyond controlling vote shares commensurate with their contributions, the governance of these institutions grants them a great degree of control over the evolution of the vote shares.

By enabling the gradual and controlled evolution of voting power on the executive board, the system of governance helps it to survive the rise and decline of economically powerful countries. If the economy of one power declines, it will no longer be in a financial position to provide the needed resources for the international financial institution, so the membership permits another to take its place. The power of the members of these international organizations must reflect economic realities both to retain their legitimacy and also for their financial viability.

As for the UNSC, its governance grants tremendous power to the major victors of World War II. Not only do they have veto power over resolutions, their special status is, by definition, permanent. The permanence vexes many people who think that the UNSC should reflect evolving power realities – the rise, for example, of Japan and Germany since World War II, and the rise of Brazil and India more recently. It might not be wise, however, to evict an old power from a privileged position. These old powers remain powerful still, and eviction might be, at best, an empty threat and, at worst, interpreted as a provocation.

Taking perhaps a more practical approach, recent debates have focused on the possibility of creating additional permanent seats.[9] But the current permanent UNSC members have veto power over these changes too, and agreement over who to admit into their club is unlikely.

As the UNSC has the authority to legitimize the use of forceful foreign policies – including the use of military force – it makes sense that the great powers required tremendous privilege in return for their support. It touches on one of the defining features of state sovereignty: the monopoly on the legitimate use of violence. Still, some voice for the rest of the world – and the means to allow that voice to evolve over time – has helped the UNSC retain its relevance. If a club is too restrictive and grants no voice to the rest of the world, its legitimacy may not extend beyond its own members – or certainly no further than their members' collective ability and will to impose their views on others. The G7 comes to mind. For nearly thirty-five years, it was sufficient to have seven major economic powers meet to address global financial problems: the United States, Japan, Germany, the United Kingdom, France, Italy, and Canada. They made a minor adjustment at the end of the Cold War, inviting Russia to meetings – not so much for the country's financial power, but rather for its military strength. But with the 2008 Global Financial Crisis, the G7 became irrelevant. The crisis had its origins in the United States, and the major stakeholder in the U.S. economy – China – was not a member of the G7 club. The G7 has no formal mechanism to grant a voice to the rest of the world, no way to incorporate new members as power relationships change, and, in short, no way to evolve. The G7's lack of relevance led to its effective replacement by the G20. The future of this new body, however, is limited as well. Like the G7, the G20 lacks provisions to evolve, nor does it reserve any formal voice for nonmember countries – the rest of the world.[10]

---

[9] For a compelling case and excellent analysis, see McDonald and Patrick (2010). For a critical review, see Hurd (2008). Also see Hosli et al. (2011). For a detailed review of recent reform efforts, see Swart (2013). For discussions of the important legal and normative issues at stake with vote-buying at the international level, see Lockwood (2013) and Freedman (2013).

[10] The membership is already out of date as Argentina dropped from being a top global economy after its crisis in 2001. Iran has since surpassed it in economic weight. Interestingly, the G20 asserts on its Web page, "It is particularly important for the number of countries involved to be *restricted* and *fixed* to ensure the effectiveness and continuity of its activity" (see http://www.g20.org/about_faq.aspx#5_What_are_the_criteria_for_G-20_membership, accessed August 11, 2011; emphasis added). For a discussion of

If the UNSC had been a club of only the United States, the United Kingdom, France, China, and Russia/the Soviet Union, the relevance of this body too may have declined over time. Japan, Germany, Brazil, and India, as well as some other rising military powers, might have asserted independent strength in the world through an alternative, more representative organization. Yet these countries have in fact been afforded a voice on the UNSC. More than any other group of countries in the world, they have sought and won election as temporary members. And thus instead of calling for the dissolution of the UNSC, they have pursued formal channels to amend it.

Amendment is not unprecedented. The UN dramatically changed the voice for the rest of the world in 1965. The number of elected members grew from six to ten, and the UN defined specific regions to represent the many newly independent countries in Africa and Asia. The "Gentlemen's Agreement" of 1945 (Daws 1999: 11) included two elected seats for Latin America, one for the Middle East, one for Eastern Europe, one for Western Europe, and one British Commonwealth country. With the 1965 amendment, the UN formally defined five regions with the following specific seats: one country from Eastern Europe, two countries from the Western European and Others Group (WEOG), two for the Latin America and Caribbean Group (GRULAC), and five from Africa and Asia.

Nevertheless, the UN amendment process makes change unlikely. As laid out in Chapter 18 of the UN Charter, amendments require the support of two-thirds of the UN membership, "including all the permanent members of the Security Council." The founders designed a high threshold for reform precisely to reassure the permanent members of their privileged position; if not, the strong domestic opposition forces within each of the five may have prevented their membership in the first place (Gruber 2000: 88).

Hence, the UNSC includes only limited provisions to evolve over time, and its persistence has come from the privilege it affords the great powers and, importantly, the voice it reserves for the rest of the world. The Security Council provides the opportunity for all countries in the world to be represented – albeit not equally – on the international stage when it comes to matters of global security.

how the 2008 Global Financial Crisis reveals that global governance is out of date, see Mosley and Singer (2009: 423–425).

7.3 Reforming Representation

If representation stands as a key feature of the UNSC, it is perhaps fitting that debates about reforming the institution focus on how to improve this quality. After all, while the UNSC affords some representation to all countries in the world, it appears to provide perhaps too much enfranchisement to the permanent members, leaving the rest of the world to vie for the leftover scraps of voting power.

Proposals approach the question of reform in three main ways: (1) Add new elected/temporary members, (2) Add new permanent members without full privileges (veto power), and (3) Add new permanent members with full privileges (veto power). Note that all of the reforms involve some form of expansion – either in the number of permanent members or in the number of elected members. We address the merits of each proposal in turn.

7.3.1 Adding Elected Members

Inviting more countries to sit around the table gives the impression of more representation. The intuition is correct if the goal is to obtain a literal seat at the table. If we care, however, about the real power held by each seat, then a simple expansion of numbers does not necessarily lead to more representation.

Professor O'Neill of UCLA explains the counterintuitive logic in his 1996 study. He shows that when the UNSC expanded from six to ten elected members, the voice of the rest of the world – in terms of raw voting power – actually declined.

To understand why, one must first recognize that a single vote is most powerful when it makes a difference – that is, when it is pivotal in either making or breaking a resolution. Now, as explained in the introductory chapter to this book, the veto power of the permanent members makes them permanently pivotal when it comes to blocking. Elected members may also be pivotal in breaking a resolution, if the number of votes in favor is exactly equal to the required super majority. Suppose a coalition is just one vote short of the super majority. In this situation, joining the majority causes the resolution to pass, so the vote is pivotal.[11]

Suppose there are eleven UNSC members – five permanent and six who are elected to represent the "rest of the world" – and seven votes

[11] As discussed in Chapter 1, a similar logic applies to breaking a resolution if a voter defects from a bare supermajority. In this case, an additional vote is pivotal in defeating the resolution.

are required for a resolution to pass, as the UNSC existed before the 1965 amendment. Let us consider coalitions of six, with the five permanent members in agreement plus one elected member supporting a resolution. These are the only situations where an additional elected member would be formally pivotal in passing a resolution: one additional vote causes the resolution to pass. (In other situations, there are either too few votes, more than enough, or an opposed permanent member can veto.)[12] The remaining five elected members have an equal opportunity to cast the pivotal vote, thus holding 20 percent of voting power each. Now suppose we are in a similar situation under the post-1965 reforms, with ten elected members and nine votes required to pass a resolution. The critical situation occurs when there are eight supporting votes. Assuming the five permanent members support the resolution along with three elected members, then each of the remaining seven elected members has an equal opportunity to cast the pivotal vote, thus holding 14 percent of voting power each. As there are now more elected members, there is less opportunity for any one of them to cast a pivotal vote.[13] Meantime, the permanent members remain crucial, thanks to their veto power. The upshot is that the power of the rest of the world actually diminishes with the expansion of elected seats, at least in terms of formal leverage around the table. The formal power of the permanent members expands.

Now, setting formal voting power aside, the legitimizing value of each vote may matter – both symbolically (Hurd 2007) and in terms of the information it conveys (Chapman 2011). In this sense, expansion may result in more power for the rest of the world because every single voice on the UNSC can be heard around the world. An argument for expansion can thus be made on these grounds. Even while keeping this logic in mind, the expansion of elected seats may nevertheless diminish the value of the voice. The UNSC perch may not be such a privileged place when too many actors sit upon it. Of course, with more votes for sale, the price of buying a vote may go down (see Saiegh 2011). Still, with an expanded number of seats, each country has a better chance of winning election to the UNSC, which will allow their governments a greater opportunity to vie for the – albeit smaller – set of privileges that UNSC membership affords, including greater access to foreign aid.

---

[12] For simplicity in this mental exercise, we ignore situations where permanent members abstain.

[13] Furthermore, there are fewer situations where one of them will be pivotal, so the cumulative voting power of elected members is also reduced. See O'Neill (1996).

We conclude that expansion does not necessarily lead to more voice. It lowers the value of holding office and does little to address vote-buying – except perhaps by lowering the price. Arguably, expansion strengthens the position of the permanent members, which is, presumably, the very opposite of the intention of the reform.

7.3.2 Adding Permanent Members without Veto Power
In contrast to expanding the number of elected members, expanding the number of permanent members would have a tremendous impact on power relationships at the UNSC. Importantly for our research, the proposed countries – Japan, Germany, Brazil, and India – are far too powerful to be influenced by foreign aid in return for their votes.

Note, however, that if the new permanent members are not granted veto power, the formal voting power of the P5 will not be diminished (assuming the same majority-thresholds). Instead, the dramatic change in power relationships will be between the new class of permanent non-veto members and the rest of the world.

The logic is the same as above. If we keep five permanent members with veto power and expand the number of non-veto members, we diminish the probability that any of the latter group will cast pivotal votes. The formal voting power of the P5 would hence increase. The new non-veto permanent members would have to share a piece of the smaller pie for the rest of the world.

Now, with their new status, the new permanent members would get a permanent slice of a smaller pie, which would represent an improvement for them over the occasional slice of the slightly larger pie that they have been winning. It is therefore understandable that countries like Japan, Germany, Brazil, and India would like to achieve permanent status, even without veto power. Setting aside the question of formal voting power, such status would convey a strong signal of status to their respective domestic audiences as well as to the rest of the world. They would be permanently privy to private UNSC negotiations and have more direct influence over the agenda.

The countries most hurt by the expansion of permanent non-veto members would be the rest of the world. Understandably, regional rivals have therefore objected. Italy opposes Germany's candidacy for permanent status, Argentina and Mexico oppose Brazil's, and Pakistan opposes India's (Ariyoruk 2005). China has played an interesting game with respect to Japan. Its formal power on the UNSC would not be diminished if Japan obtained a permanent seat without veto power, but it would lose relative status as regional power. Right now, China is the sole East Asian country with permanent status on the UNSC, and making Japan a permanent member would change this. Moreover, the Chinese government has cultivated in its domestic politics a continued hatred of Japan for atrocities committed during World War II (Weiss 2008). So when the Bush administration publicly supported Japan's candidacy for permanent status on the UNSC in 2005, the Chinese government released the news domestically and allowed protest to erupt across the nation. In a move that follows the logic of Thomas Schelling (1960), the government then reported to the United States that while it would like to support Japan's candidacy, domestic political constraints would not allow it (Weiss 2008).[14] While the government had initially enabled the protests, it seemed credible that they could not put the genie back in the bottle without resorting to violent repression. Observing the credible constraint that the Chinese government faced domestically, the United States withdrew the proposal (Weiss 2008). The upshot is that regional rivals oppose expansion of the permanent members of the UNSC and can resort to clever tactics to bring down such proposed reforms.

Our purpose is not to dismiss the expansion of permanent members without veto power as a viable reform, although it is not obvious that there is sufficient political will at the global level to see this kind of reform through. We highlight two features: (1) Such expansion introduces a second tier of powerful countries on the UNSC. It does not diminish the formal voting power of the P5, but it does diminish the formal voice of the rest of the world. (2) Expanding permanent members does address vote-buying in that countries of this stature are usually too powerful to be influenced by foreign aid.

7.3.3 Adding Permanent Members with Veto Power

If there is insufficient political will to introduce permanent members without veto power, it is surely lacking to bring them in with veto power. New permanent members with veto power would directly diminish power of the P5. Still, it is worth considering the effects that such changes would bring. Following the work of Tsebelis (1995, 2002), it is straightforward to see that more members with veto power cannot increase the likelihood of resolutions passing – it can only diminish such chances. Resolutions that might pass through the United States, the United Kingdom, France,

---

[14] Also see Putnam (1988).

Russia, and China might not pass through Japan, Germany, Brazil, and India. On many recent issues where Russia and China have abstained, they might have actually exercised their veto if they knew they would be joined by other veto powers.

If it is more difficult to pass resolutions through the UNSC, higher levels of unilateral action might result. In these extreme cases, a country may be willing to take action with or without UNSC authorization – the 2003 invasion of Iraq comes to mind. There may be some policies, however, that a government will pursue only if it has UNSC authorization because such authorization lowers the political and material costs. Chapman and Wolford (2010: 228) contend, "The promise of lowered foreign policy costs... may not only facilitate coercion but also encourage aggressive behavior." They suggest that "if the goal is to reduce the aggregate likelihood of war we should consider crafting institutions that are conservative with their authorization" (2010: 237).

Adding permanent members with veto power may thus be a good thing. These new powers would make the authorization of forceful foreign policies less likely. Successful resolutions would, in turn, provide even more credible signals to the global community. The new permanent members would not be easily swayed by promises of foreign aid. Vote-buying among the elected members would likely continue, but might be less frequent because the UNSC would be necessary only in the rare circumstance when there is both great consensus across a wider range of the world's most powerful countries and a lack of consensus among the smaller countries on the UNSC.

The problem with adding new permanent veto players to the UNSC is that it just does not seem like a realistic option. Any government that would be opposed to new permanent members without veto power would certainly also oppose the more radical proposal of new permanent members *with* veto power. So, observations about opposition to new permanent members discussed above apply here as well. We do see value in considering this option but would also suggest the consideration of more realistic reforms.

7.4 Representation, Accountability, and Term Limits

Most reform proposals for the UNSC address representation and provide no discussion of accountability. Yet, representation without accountability is a farce. Elected members of the UNSC "represent" their regions only in the sense that they happen to come from the region. The election rules provide absolutely no incentive for temporary UNSC members to represent the interests of the other countries in their region. Note that this outcome is by design. Elected UNSC members may be nominated by their respective regions, but governments may also self-nominate, and ultimately the winners are selected not by their designated region but rather the General Assembly. Once elected, temporary members face strict term limits, so immediate reelection is impossible.

Given this setup, it should not be surprising to find that elected members seek to trade their political power on the UNSC for financial favors. Most countries that serve are elected less often than once per decade. A particular government that finds itself on the UNSC may not be in office the next time the country has an opportunity to win election again. Such a government therefore has just one chance to extract as many benefits as it can while serving on the UNSC, and it should disregard the preferences of other governments from the region that it supposedly represents.

To further explore the link between reelection prospects and accountability, consider the work of one of the world's foremost authorities on corruption, Susan Rose-Ackerman of Yale University. She has proposed an inverted U-shaped relationship between the probability of reelection and accountability (called the "paradox of stability" – see Rose-Ackerman 1999: 127). The intuition is simple. People who are guaranteed to keep their jobs have no incentive to work hard. People who are guaranteed to lose their jobs similarly have no incentive to work hard. In both of these extreme situations, people have no incentive to supply effort. To extract effort, contracts should be designed so that there is some chance of keeping and some chance of losing one's job – and the probability should depend on job performance. Accountability is maximized by having some mid-level probability of survival in office. Figure 7.2 illustrates the logic.

With this argument in mind, consider the UNSC, which has two groups: permanent members and term-limited members. The probability of the permanent members keeping their positions is 1; the probability of the term-limited members keeping their positions is 0. The UNSC is, therefore, designed to be unaccountable to the global community. The two groups are positioned at the two extremes along the x-axis in Figure 7.2, where accountability is nil. As for the term-limited members, the one-shot opportunity that they receive to "represent" their region serves as an ideal opportunity to seek "rents" from the global community. They should extract as much as possible during their term.

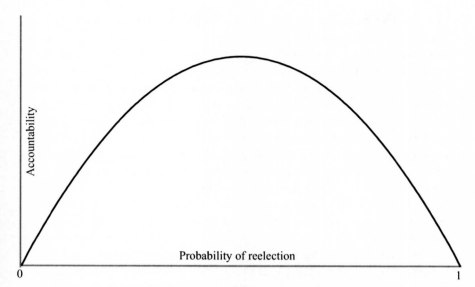

FIGURE 7.2. Accountability and the probability of continuing in power. *Notes:*
Accountability is lowest when governments face either a very low or a very high
chance of winning reelection; accountability is highest in between these extremes.
Unfortunately, the UNSC only has members at the extremes: permanent members
who are guaranteed a continued seat on the body and temporary members who
have zero chance of immediate reelection because of term limits. *Source:* Vreeland
(forthcoming). Inspired by Rose-Ackerman (1999) and Przeworski, Stokes, and
Manin (1999).

Of course, the governments serving on the UNSC all face some degree
of accountability to their home countries. Indeed, the benefits that they
extract during their UNSC term may serve their domestic audiences. Certainly we expect term-limited members to pursue strategies that maximize
their survival chances at home. As argued in Chapter 6, some governments may be able to put the foreign aid that they receive to good use.
Democracies may use the foreign aid they receive particularly well. Still,
governments ridden with debt may attempt to extract foreign aid that
is not well used. The research of Bueno de Mesquita and Smith (2010)
suggests that the effects may even be systematically pernicious. So, there
may be reason to attempt to curtail the practice of trading financial favors
for political influence over the UNSC and to design a more accountable
UNSC.

Note that the quest for foreign aid is not the only reason governments seek elections to the UNSC. Certain governments have domestically driven political incentives that lead them to seek reelection to the UNSC. Japan, Brazil, India, Germany, and other powerful countries have certainly attempted to win election when they can, over and again. They may not be allowed to seek immediate reelection, but they can run for election again after sitting out for a year. These governments seek a powerful voice for their country on the international stage – they are not interested in trading away this political influence for financial favors. To win election, however, these governments must appeal to the countries with the power to elect them – the voters in the UNGA.

Of course, if one wants an institution where regional interests win representation, the nexus of election should not be located in the General Assembly but rather in the regions themselves. Not only does the current institutional design of the selection process fail to incentivize to pursue regional interests, it actually isolates the "representatives" from regional pressures by granting the power to elect them to the General Assembly.

Hence, we suggest two simple reforms that could begin to address the issue of accountability to regions:

1. Abolish term limits.
2. Let regions elect their representatives.

Abolishing term limits stands as the more important of our two suggestions. Allowing for reelection represents the key to accountability. The prospect of reelection provides an incentive for UNSC members to serve on the UNSC in such a way as to win the support of other countries during their next campaign. Under the current system, when deciding how to cast a vote on a UNSC proposal, elected UNSC members must weigh their local political concerns against the prospective bribes of foreign aid. We illustrate this logic in the formal model presented in Chapter 2. If there were no term limits, however, governments would also consider how their voting behavior influences their reelection chances. This new consideration would not eliminate the other two, but it would raise a mitigating factor that would make them tenuously accountable to an electorate.

This reform would also open the door to accommodate rising powers. With the prospect of reelection, countries that are currently elected the most often (for example, Brazil), would likely win reelection the most often, bringing them closer to permanent status. Now, the continued reelection of these regional hegemons might appear to disenfranchise other countries in their respective regions because these other countries would have less chance of winning election. Regional hegemons could win reelection, however, only if other countries felt they were doing a good job. Unlike true permanent members, they would have to win election regularly, and they could do so only by winning favor with voting countries. Part of the strategy for reelection would entail voting in ways that the electorate endorses. Another part of the strategy would involve doing other good deeds for the electorate – perhaps providing them foreign aid. In an interesting turn, elected UNSC members might stop receiving foreign aid and instead start providing it to their electorate. Indeed, this appears to be part of the story already for rich countries that are elected, such as Japan, Germany, and Canada, according to Malone (2004).[15]

Which electorate should choose the representative? This question leads to our second recommendation: Let regions elect their representatives. With term limits abolished, we open the door to accountability but leave open the question of to whom UNSC members should be accountable. As it currently stands, the system guarantees UNSC membership from the African, Asian, Latin American, Eastern European, and the amorphous Western Europe and Others groups. But these groups do not have the final say in selecting their representatives – this power lies in the collective hands of the UNGA.

As shown in Chapter 2, the UNGA has distinct preferences from the regions. While the General Assembly prefers powerful countries, for example, the regions tend to prefer a turn-taking norm. Regions might develop a taste for electing their own most powerful countries if these governments were incentivized to use their power for the benefit of the region. Abolishing term limits and allowing regions to elect their own representatives establishes such incentives. As the most powerful economy of Africa, for example, South Africa could win regular election to the UNSC, but only if the other countries of Africa supported its campaign with their votes. South Africa would thus have a new incentive to pursue good relations with its region. In Latin America, Brazil might face competition from Mexico, Argentina, and Venezuela to stand as the country that does the most for the region, and thus the most deserving of winning

---

[15] Note that O'Brien (1999: 38) proposes that regional groups should be allowed to decide on the length of tenure of its representatives, but he does not specify extending them through reelection. On providing foreign aid to win election to international committees, see Vreeland (2011).

election and reelection to represent Latin America on the international stage of the UNSC. Providing a greater and more formal role to regions in selecting their leadership would serve a secondary purpose of cultivating greater regional ties and a stronger regional identity.[16]

Change remains unlikely, of course. As previously explained, the UN Charter amendment process is difficult by design, and Hosli et al. (2011) argue that evolving voting patterns in the UNSC and UNGA have only made change less likely in recent years. So, we do not believe any of the reform proposals are likely to pass any time soon. Yet change is not unprecedented, and we invite readers to dream of improvements. Even if the reform of global institutions appears unlikely in the short run, aspirations can be realized in the long run – in particular if one plans long in advance. Lord Maynard Keynes, for example, began publishing about an "international loan" in 1919. This idea eventually grew into the Bretton Woods Institutions, founded after World War II. We thus encourage readers to think big about reforms for the future. We recall, however, the importance of making proposals that are incentive-compatible – that provide incentives for both great powers and the rest of the world to participate. As for the current debate, we recognize the importance of representation and understand that this issue should remain part of the reform conversation. We would also suggest including more emphasis on the question of accountability.

As for the incentive compatibility of our own proposal, we note that the biggest winners would include emerging market countries like Brazil and India, whose international political capital is on the rise. The aforementioned G4 – Brazil, Germany, India, and Japan – could become champions for the cause of reelection. They would face opposition, however, from other countries of their respective regions precisely because the reelection of regional hegemons would leave fewer opportunities for other countries of the region to win a seat at the table. Regional rivals have actually organized into a group – known as the "Coffee Club" and also as "Uniting for Consensus" – to oppose the G4 aspirations for permanent seats, arguing instead for additional elected seats (Ariyoruk 2005; von Freiesleben

---

[16] See Desai and Vreeland (2011). Note that this setup would resemble the governance of the Bretton Woods organizations, where there are no term limits for executive board members, which are elected by ad hoc groups of countries. The groups of countries have mostly organized along regional lines. See Kaja and Werker (2010), Vreeland (2011), and Morrison (2013). For a critical assessment of representation at the IMF, see Kapur and Naim (2005).

2013). The Coffee Club includes Italy, Spain, Argentina, Canada, Mexico, South Korea, Pakistan, and others (von Freiesleben 2013: 3; *Oneindia News* 2006). These countries would likely oppose the reelection aspect of our reform proposal.

How can the Security Council accommodate rising powers without alienating their regional rivals? Perhaps a compromise would be to allow for reelection, on the one hand, and greater control at the regional level, on the other. If we allow for regions to fully control the elections (instead of requiring a two-thirds majority of the UNGA), regional rivals and smaller countries would have the means to hold the regional hegemons accountable, or the hegemons would face eviction from office. The hegemons can repeatedly win a high-profile seat on the international stage only if they please their rivals, who might become their power-brokers at the regional level.

The permanent members might, of course, oppose such a reform. As discussed throughout the book, larger emerging market powers can more effectively resist pressure on how to vote than can smaller developing countries. The reform might appeal to the permanent members, however, because it would allow them to accommodate the demands of the powerful countries seeking greater voice on the UNSC without actually extending permanent status or veto power to any additional countries. So, we see possible avenues through which to gain political support for the idea of reelection. Nevertheless, we are not the first to propose this idea, and we recognize that change remains unlikely in the short run.

The path of least resistance remains the expansion of elected seats. Permanent members would gain an expanded set of easier targets to persuade with foreign aid, and the smaller countries would gain increased chances of winning election. But this kind of "reform" would not address the issues raised in this book – it could actually make them worse. So, perhaps another compromise would be to accompany the expansion of seats with the abolition of term limits.[17] The expanded seats would be popular with most developing countries, including the Coffee Club regional rivals, who would realize greater chances of winning election. The end of term limits would serve the interest of the G4, who could achieve a more permanent status on the UNSC by routinely winning reelection. Expansion would benefit the P5, as those countries' real voting power would increase, and, importantly, this kind of reform would help address the looming legitimacy problem for the institution. Increasingly, Brazil,

---

[17] We are grateful to Miles Kahler for this suggestion.

Germany, India, and Japan need to take part in debates over global security, and if the UNSC cannot accommodate them, the institution risks irrelevance, which would not serve the interest of the P5.

Still, we expect that the interests on the various sides of the reform debate will continue to counterbalance each other so that the status quo is likely to prevail. And the status quo does not represent a bad institution for the developing world: Most developing countries win a turn to sit on the UNSC, and they receive certain perks when they do. If they happen to win election during a year when the United States has an active UNSC agenda, they may receive more U.S. foreign aid, particularly if they are identified as a potential swing voter. More generally, they receive increased foreign aid from countries seeking an augmented voice on the UNSC – Japan and Germany. They also may receive more loans from the IMF and the World Bank as well as the Asian Development Bank or the African Development Bank, if they hail from one of these regions. Of course, if an issue arises that arouses local controversy for a UNSC member, domestic political imperatives may force the government to vote against the United States and its allies, leading to punishment. If a government does vote in accordance with the powerful countries and receives financial favors as a result, the money may not always go to good use, depending on the country's political economy. Foreign aid can have pernicious effects in countries already facing high debt or in authoritarian countries. Countries with well managed economies and democratic countries, however, may put their financial perks to good use.

We suggest, nevertheless, that the UNSC might perform better if it engendered greater accountability from elected members. We argue that the best way to incentivize accountability is to allow for the reelection of UNSC members. Furthermore, to strengthen regional relations, the UN could grant the formal power of selecting UNSC members to the regions themselves.

In the meantime, we recommend to readers that while they should always dream of ways to improve international relations, perfect institutions should not become the enemy of good institutions. The existence of an international institution with the legal authority to debate and approve forceful foreign policies provides an important symbol of international law and can, under certain circumstances, convey credible information about the appropriateness of those policies. Even as it currently stands, therefore, the UN Security Council has the potential for good. Do governments trade their political influence on the body in return for financial perks? Absolutely. The cynical implications of such trades are obvious.

Yet they also contain some hope for the future: The fact that such trades take place implies that governments care enough about the Security Council to expend financial and political capital to win its approval. The votes are worth fighting for because the institution matters. Thus, regardless of the reforms we may introduce, trading favors for votes will remain a central aspect of Security Council politics, just as trades of money and influence persist at every level of politics, from local to global.

References

Abbott, Kenneth W., and Duncan Snidal. 1998. Why States Act through Formal International Organizations. *Journal of Conflict Resolution* 42 (1): 3–32.

Acharya, Amitav, and Alastair Iain Johnston. 2007. Comparing Regional Institutions. In Amitav Acharya and Alastair Iain Johnston (eds.), *Crafting Cooperation: Regional International Institutions in Comparative Perspective*. New York: Cambridge University Press: 1–31.

Adely, Fida J. 2012. *Gendered Paradoxes: Educating Jordanian Women in Nation, Faith, and Progress*. Chicago, IL: University Of Chicago Press.

African Development Bank. 2012. Frequently Asked Questions. *Tunis-Belvedère, Tunisia: African Development Bank Group*. Available at: http://www.afdb .org/en/about-us/frequently-asked-questions/#c10288.

African Union. 2006. *Rules of Procedure of the AU Ministerial Committee on Candidatures within the International System*, EX.CL/213 (VIII). Addis Ababa: African Union.

Agam, Hasmy. 1999. Equitable Geographic Representation in the Twenty-First Century. In Ramesh Thakur (ed.), *What Is Equitable Geographic Representation in the 21st Century*. Tokyo: United Nations University: 40–46.

Ai, C. Chunrong, and Edward C. Norton. 2003. Interaction Terms in Logit and Probit Models. *Economics Letters* 80 (1): 123–129.

Albright, Madeleine. 2009. *Read My Pins: Stories from a Diplomat's Jewel Box*. New York: HarperCollins.

Alesina, Alberto, and Beatrice Weder. 2002. Do Corrupt Governments Receive Less Foreign Aid? *American Economic Review* 92 (4): 1126–1137.

Alesina, Alberto, and David Dollar. 2000. Who Gives Foreign Aid to Whom and Why? *Journal of Economic Growth* 5: 33–64.

Alter, Karen J., and Sophie Meunier. 2009. The Politics of International Regime Complexity. *Perspectives on Politics* 7 (1): 13–24.

Andersen, Thomas B., Henrik Hansen and Thomas Markussen. 2006. US politics and World Bank IDA-lending. *Journal of Development Studies* 42 (5): 772–794.

243

Anderson, Jeffrey. 1999. *German Unification and the Union of Europe: The Domestic Politics of Integration Policy*. New York: Cambridge University Press.

Anderson, Sarah, Phyllis Bennis, and John Cavanagh. 2003. *Coalition of the Willing or Coalition of the Coerced?* Washington, DC: Institute for Policy Studies.

Anwar, Mumtaz and Katharina Michaelowa. 2006. The Political Economy of US Aid to Pakistan. *Review of Development Economics* 10 (2): 195–209.

Arase, David. 1995. *Buying Power: The Political Economy of Japanese Foreign Aid*. Boulder, CO: Lynne Rienner.

Arend, Anthony Clark, and Robert J. Beck. 1993. *International Law and the Use of Force: Beyond the UN Charter Paradigm*. New York: Routledge.

Ariyoruk, Ayca. 2005. Players and Proposals in the Security Council Debate. *Global Policy Forum*. Available at: http://www.globalpolicy.org/component/content/article/200/41204.html.

Baccini, Leonardo and Johannes Urpelainen. 2012. Strategic Side Payments: Preferential Trading Agreements, Economic Reform, and Foreign Aid. *Journal of Politics* 74 (4): 932–949.

Bailey, Michael A., Anton Strezhnev, and Erik Voeten. 2013. Estimating Dynamic State Preferences from United Nations Voting Data. Paper presented at the Annual Meeting of Midwest Political Science Association, Chicago, IL.

Bailey, Sydney D., and Sam Daws. 1998. *The Procedure of the United Nations Security Council*. New York: Oxford University Press.

Baker III, James A. 1995. *The Politics of Diplomacy: Revolution, War and Peace: 1989–1992*. New York: G. P. Putnam's Sons.

Ball, Richard, and Christopher Johnson. 1996. Political, Economic, and Humanitarian Motivations for PL 480 Food Aid: Evidence from Africa. *Economic Development and Cultural Change* 44 (3): 515–537.

Balla, Eliana, and Gina Yannitell Reinhardt. 2008. Giving and Receiving Foreign Aid: Does Conflict Count? *World Development* 36 (12): 2566–2585.

Bandow, Doug. 1992. Avoiding War. *Foreign Policy Magazine* 89 (Winter): 156–174.

Banzhaf, John F. 1965. Weighted Voting Doesn't Work: A Mathematical Analysis. *Rutgers Law Review* 19 (2): 317–343.

Barnett, Michael. 1995. Partners in Peace? The United Nations, Regional Organizations, and Peacekeeping. *Review of International Studies* 21 (4): 411–433.

Barnett, Michael, and Etel Solingen. 2007. Designed to Fail or Failure of Design? The Origins and Legacy of the Arab League. In Amitav Acharya and Alastair Iain Johnston (eds.), *Crafting Cooperation: Regional International Institutions in Comparative Perspective*. New York: Cambridge University Press: 180–220.

Barro, Robert J., and Jong-Wha Lee. 2005. IMF-Programs: Who Is Chosen and What Are the Effects? *Journal of Monetary Economics* 52: 1245–1269.

Barrow, Greg. 2002. Syria objects to Israel "as victim." *BBC News*, December 14. Available at: http://news.bbc.co.uk/2/hi/africa/2574907.stm.

Bashir, Omar S., and Darren J. Lim. 2013. Misplaced Blame: Foreign Aid and the Consequences of UN Security Council Membership. *Journal of Conflict Resolution* 57 (3): 509–523.

Bawn, Kathleen. 1995. Political Control versus Expertise: Congressional Choices about Administrative Procedures. *American Political Science Review* 89 (1): 62–73.

BBC Caribbean. 2006. WINFA denounces Guatemala. *BBC Caribbean*, September 27. Available at: http://www.bbc.co.uk/caribbean/news/story/2006/09/060927_bananaguatemala.shtml.

BBC News. 2006. Panama agreement ends UN seat row. *BBC News*, November 2. Available at: http://news.bbc.co.uk/2/hi/americas/6108556.stm.

BBC News. 2010. UN votes for new sanctions on Iran over nuclear issue. *BBC News*, June 9. Available at: http://www.bbc.co.uk/news/10276276.

Bearce, David H., and Daniel C. Tirone. 2010. Foreign Aid Effectiveness and the Strategic Goals of Donor Governments. *Journal of Politics* 72 (3): 837–851.

Beck, Thorsten, George Clarke, Alberto Groff, Philip Keefer, and Patrick Walsh. 2001. New Tools and New Tests in Comparative Political Economy: The Database of Political Institutions. *World Bank Economic Review* 15 (1): 165–176.

Bendor, Jonathan, and Piotr Swistak. 2001. The Evolution of Norms. *American Journal of Sociology* 106 (6): 1493–1545.

Berger, Daniel, William Easterly, Nathan Nunn, and Shanker Satyanath. 2013. Commercial Imperialism? Political Influence and Trade During the Cold War. *American Economic Review* 103 (2): 863–896.

Bermeo, Sarah Blodgett. 2008. Foreign Aid, Foreign Policy, and Strategic Development. Dissertation, Politics Department, Princeton University.

Bermeo, Sarah Blodgett. 2010. Development and Strategy: Aid Allocation in an Interdependent World. SSRN. Available at: http://ssrn.com/abstract=1681104.

Bermeo, Sarah Blodgett. 2011. Foreign Aid and Regime Change: A Role for Donor Intent. *World Development* 39 (11): 2021–2031.

Bermeo, Sarah Blodgett and David Leblang. 2012. Foreign Interests: Immigration and the Political Economy of Foreign Aid. Manuscript, University of Virginia.

Bermeo, Sarah Blodgett, David Leblang, and Dustin Tingley. 2011. Clowns to the Left of Me, Jokers to the Right: How Partisanship Shapes the Allocation of Foreign Aid. Manuscript, Sanford School of Foreign Policy, Duke University.

Bernauer, Thomas, and Dieter Ruloff (eds.). 1999. *The Politics of Positive Incentives in Arms Control*. Columbia, SC: University of South Carolina Press.

Berthélemy, Jean-Claude. 2006. Bilateral Donors' Interest vs. Recipients' Development Motives in Aid Allocation: Do All Donors Behave the Same? *Review of Development Economics* 10 (2): 179–194.

Berthélemy, Jean-Claude, and Ariane Tichit. 2004. Bilateral Donors' Aid Allocation Decisions: A Three-Dimensional Panel Analysis. *International Review of Economics and Finance* 13 (3): 253–274.

Bjørnskov, Christian. 2010. Do elites benefit from democracy and foreign aid in developing countries? *Journal of Development Economics* 92 (2): 115–124.

Bland, Elizabeth, and Christopher Kilby. 2012. Informal Influence in the Inter-American Development Bank. Villanova School of Business Economics Working Paper 22.

Bobba, Matteo, and Andrew Powell. 2007. Aid Effectiveness: Politics Matters. Inter-American Development Bank Research Department Working Paper 601.

Boehmer, Charles, Erik Gartzke, and Timothy Nordstrom. 2004. Do Intergovernmental Organizations Promote Peace? *World Politics* 57 (1): 1–38.

Bolton, John. 2008. *Surrender Is Not an Option: Defending America at the United Nations*. New York: Threshold Editions.

Boone, Peter. 1996. Politics and the Effectiveness of Foreign Aid. *European Economic Review* 40 (2): 289–329.

Boschini, Anne, and Anders Olofsgård. 2007. Foreign Aid: An Instrument for Fighting Poverty or Communism? *Journal of Development Studies* 43 (4): 622–648.

Bradley, Curtis A., and Judith G. Kelley. 2008. The Concept of International Delegation. *Law and Contemporary Problems* 71: 1–36.

Breßlein, Martin, and Maya Schmaljohann. 2013. Surrender Your Market! Do the G5 Countries Use World Bank Trade Conditionality to Promote Trade? Universities of Trier and Heidelberg. Draft.

Broz, J. Lawrence. 2002. Political System Transparency and Monetary Commitment Regimes. *International Organization* 56 (4): 861–887.

Broz, J. Lawrence. 2008. Congressional Voting on Funding the International Financial Institutions. *Review of International Organizations* 3 (4): 351–374.

Broz, J. Lawrence. 2011. The United States Congress and IMF Financing, 1944–2009. *Review of International Organizations* 6 (3–4): 341–368.

Broz, J. Lawrence, and Michael B. Hawes. 2006. US Domestic Politics and International Monetary Fund Policy. In Darren Hawkins, David A. Lake, Daniel Nielson, and Michael J. Tierney (eds.), *Delegation and Agency in International Organizations*. New York: Cambridge University Press: 77–106.

Bueno de Mesquita, Bruce, and Alastair Smith. 2010. The Pernicious Consequences of UN Security Council Membership. *Journal of Conflict Resolution* 54 (5): 667–686.

Bueno de Mesquita, Bruce, Alastair Smith, Randolph M. Siverson, and James D. Morrow. 2003. *The Logic of Political Survival*. Cambridge, MA: MIT Press.

Bulíř, Aleš, and Soojin Moon. 2004. Is Fiscal Adjustment More Durable When the IMF is Involved? *Comparative Economic Studies* 46: 373–399.

Byman, Daniel L., and Matthew Waxman. 2002. *The Dynamics of Coercion: American Foreign Policy and the Limits of Military Might*. New York: Cambridge University Press.

Campbell, Horace, and Howard Stein. 1992. Introduction: The Dynamics of Liberalization in Tanzania. In Horace Campbell and Howard Stein (eds.), *Tanzania and the IMF: The Dynamics of Liberalization*. Boulder, CO: Westview Press: 1–20.

Caraway, Teri, Stephanie Rickard, and Mark Anner. 2012. International Negotiations and Domestic Politics: the Case of IMF Labor Market Conditionality. *International Organization* 66 (1): 27–61.

Caron, David D. 1993. The Legitimacy of the Collective Authority of the Security Council. *American Journal of International Law* 87 (4): 552–588.

Carpenter, Charli. 2012. Norms, Networks and Human Security Agenda-Setting. Manuscript, University of Massachusetts-Amherst.

Chamberlain, Gary. 1980. Analysis of Covariance with Qualitative Data. *Review of Economic Studies* 47 (1): 225–238.

Chapman, Terrence L. 2007. International Security Institutions, Domestic Politics, and Institutional Legitimacy. *Journal of Conflict Resolution* 51 (1): 134–166.

Chapman, Terrence L. 2009. Audience Beliefs and International Organization Legitimacy. *International Organization* 63 (4): 733–764.

Chapman, Terrence L. 2011. *Securing Approval: Domestic Politics and Multilateral Authorization for War*. Chicago, IL: University of Chicago Press.

Chapman, Terrence L. and Dan Reiter. 2004. The United Nations Security Council and the Rally 'Round the Flag Effect. *Journal of Conflict Resolution* 48 (6): 886–909.

Chapman, Terrence and Scott Wolford. 2010. International Organizations, Strategy, and Crisis Bargaining. *Journal of Politics* 72 (1): 227–242.

Checkel, Jeffrey T. 2007. Social Mechanisms and Regional Cooperation: Are Europe and the EU Really All That Different?. In Amitav Acharya and Alastair Iain Johnston (eds.), *Crafting Cooperation: Regional International Institutions in Comparative Perspective*. New York: Cambridge University Press: 221–243.

Cheibub, José Antonio, Jennifer Gandhi, and James Raymond Vreeland. 2010. Democracy and Dictatorship Revisited. *Public Choice* 143 (1–2): 67–101.

Chiozza, Giacomo and H. E. Goemans. 2011. *Leaders and International Conflict*. New York: Cambridge University Press.

Cho, Hye Jee. 2013. Impact of IMF Programs on Perceived Creditworthiness of Emerging Market Countries: Is There a "Nixon-Goes-to-China" Effect? *International Studies Quarterly* doi: 10.1111/isqu.12063.

Chung, Eunbin and Byungwon Woo. 2012. A Theory of Vote Buying at the United Nations General Assembly: Lobbying, Counteractive Lobbying, and Strategic Allocation of American Foreign Aid. Paper presented at the 6th Annual Conference on the Political Economy of International Organizations, Universities of Mannheim and Heidelberg.

CIA. 2012. *CIA World Factbook*. Washington, DC: Central Intelligence Agency.

Clare, Thane. 2013. Perilous Waters: Explaining International Warship Exports. Dissertation, Government Department, Georgetown University.

Claude, Inis L. 1966. Collective Legitimization as a Political Function of the United Nations. *International Organization* 20 (3): 367–379.

Clemens, Michael, Steven Radelet, Rikhil Bhavnani, and Samuel Bazzi. 2012. Counting Chickens When They Hatch: Timing and the Effects of Aid on Growth. *Economic Journal* 122 (561): 590–617.

Cogley, Nathaniel Terence. 2013. The Logic of Political Cessation: Social Esteem and Executive Tenure in Africa. Dissertation, Political Science Department, Yale University.

Colman, Andrew M. and Lindsay Browning. 2009. Evolution of Cooperative Turn-Taking. *Evolutionary Ecology Research* 11 (6): 949–963.

Combs, Jerald A. 2012. Embargoes and Sanctions. *Encyclopedia of the New American Nation*. Available at: http://www.americanforeignrelations.com/ E-N/Embargoes-and-Sanctions.html. More specifically, we reference this page: http://www.americanforeignrelations.com/E-N/Embargoes-and-Sanctions-Cold-war-sanctions.html.

Conway, Patrick. 2007. The Revolving Door: Duration and Recidivism in IMF Programs. *Review of Economics and Statistics* 89 (2): 205–220.

Copelovitch, Mark S. 2010a. *The International Monetary Fund in the Global Economy: Banks, Bonds, and Bailouts*. New York: Cambridge University Press.

Copelovitch, Mark S. 2010b. Master or Servant? Common Agency, Preference Heterogeneity, and the Political Economy of IMF Lending. *International Studies Quarterly* 54 (1): 49–77.

Cortright, David. 1997. *The Price of Peace: Incentives and International Conflict Prevention*. Lanham, MD: Rowman & Littlefield Publishers, Inc.

Costa Rica. 2005. Note Verbale dated July 20, 2005 from the Permanent Mission of Costa Rica to the United Nations addressed to the Secretary-General, A/59/881. New York: United Nations.

Crawford, Vincent P. and Joel Sobel. 1982. *Strategic Information Transmission*. *Econometrica* 50: 1431–1451.

Crossette, Barbara. 2002. US Joins Council Vote Telling Israel To Withdraw. *New York Times*, March 31. Available at: http://www.nytimes.com/2002/03/31/ world/mideast-turmoil-united-nations-us-joins-council-vote-telling-israel-to-withdraw.html.

Darden, Keith. 2008. The Integrity of Corrupt States: Graft as an Informal State Institution. *Politics and Society* 36 (1): 35–59.

Databanks International. 2005. *Cross-National Time-Series Data Archive, 1815–2003*. Binghamton, NY: Binghamton University.

Davenport, Christian. 2007a. *State Repression and the Domestic Democratic Peace*. New York: Cambridge University Press.

Davenport, Christian. 2007b. State Repression and the Tyrannical Peace. *Journal of Peace Research* 44 (4):485–504.

Davidson, Russell and James G. MacKinnon. 1993. *Estimation and Inference in Econometrics*. New York: Oxford University Press.

Daws, Sam. 1997. Seeking Seats, Votes and Vetoes. *The World Today* 53 (October): 256–259.

Daws, Sam. 1999. The Origins and Development of UN Electoral Groups. In Ramesh Thakur (ed.), *What is Equitable Geographic Representation in the 21st Century*. Tokyo: United Nations University: 11–29.

Deen, Thalif. 2002. US Dollars Yielded Unanimous UN Vote against Iraq. *Inter Press Service News Agency*, November 9. Available at: http://www.ipsnews .net/2002/11/politics-us-dollars-yielded-unanimous-un-vote-against-iraq/.

Desai, Raj M. and James Raymond Vreeland. 2011. Global Governance in a Multipolar World: The Case for Regional Monetary Funds. *International Studies Review* 13 (1): 109–121.

Diermeier, Daniel, Carlo Prato, and Razvan Vlaicu. 2013. Procedural Choice in Majoritarian Organizations. SSRN. Available at: http://ssrn.com/abstract= 1371288.

Dollar, David and Lant Pritchett. 1998. *Assessing Aid: What Works, What Doesn't Work and Why?* Washington, DC: The World Bank.

Dollar, David and Jakob Svensson. 2000. What Explains the Success or Failure of Structural Adjustment Programs? *Economic Journal* 110 (466): 894–917.

Dominguez, Jorge I. 2007. International Cooperation in Latin America: the Design of Regional Institutions by Slow Accretion. In Amitav Acharya and Alastair Iain Johnston (eds.), *Crafting Cooperation: Regional International Institutions in Comparative Perspective*. New York: Cambridge University Press: 83–128.

Dorussen, Han. 2001. Mixing Carrots with Sticks: Evaluating the Effectiveness of Positive Incentives. *Journal of Peace Research* 38 (2): 251–262.

Doucouliagos, Hristos, and Martin Paldam. 2009. The Aid Effectiveness Literature: The Sad Results of 40 Years of Research. *Journal of Economic Surveys* 23 (3): 433–461.

Dowding, Keith, Robert E. Goodin, and Carole Pateman. 2004. *Justice and Democracy*. New York: Cambridge University Press.

Downs, George W., David M. Rocke, and Peter N. Barsoom. 1996. Is the Good News about Compliance Good News about Cooperation? *International Organization* 50 (3): 379–406.

Doyle, Michael W. 2001. The New Interventionism. *Metaphilosophy* 32 (1–2): 212–235.

Dreher, Axel. 2004. A Public Choice Perspective of IMF and World Bank Lending and Conditionality. *Public Choice* 119 (3–4): 445–464.

Dreher, Axel. 2006. IMF and Economic Growth: The Effects of Programs, Loans, and Compliance with Conditionality. *World Development* 34 (5): 769–788.

Dreher, Axel. 2009. IMF Conditionality: Theory and Evidence. *Public Choice* 141 (1–2): 233–267.

Dreher, Axel, Vera Eichenauer and Kai Gehring. 2013. Geopolitics, Aid and Growth. CESifo Working Paper Series No. 4299.

Dreher, Axel and Andreas Fuchs. 2011a. Does Terror Increase Aid? *Public Choice* 149: 337–363.

Dreher, Axel and Andreas Fuchs. 2011b. Rogue Aid? The Determinants of China's Aid Allocation. Courant Research Centre: Poverty, Equity and Growth Discussion Paper 93.

Dreher, Axel and Martin Gassebner. 2012. Do IMF and World Bank Programs Induce Government Crises? An Empirical Analysis. *International Organization* 66 (2): 329–358.

Dreher, Axel, Matthew Gould, Matthew D. Rablen, and James Raymond Vreeland. 2014. The Determinants of Election to the United Nations Security Council. *Public Choice* 158 (1–2): 51–83.

Dreher, Axel and Nathan M. Jensen. 2007. Independent Actor or Agent? An Empirical Analysis of the Impact of US Interests on IMF Conditions. *Journal of Law and Economics* 50 (1): 105–124.

Dreher, Axel, Stephan Klasen, James Raymond Vreeland, and Eric Werker. 2013. The Costs of Favoritism: Is Politically-Driven Aid Less Effective? *Economic Development and Cultural Change* 62 (1): 157–191.

Dreher, Axel, Peter Nunnenkamp, and Maya Schmaljohann. 2013. The Allocation of German Aid: Self-Interest and Government Ideology. Kiel Institute for
the World Economy Working Paper 1817.

Dreher, Axel, Peter Nunnenkamp, and Rainer Thiele. 2008. Does US Aid Buy
UN General Assembly Votes? A Disaggregated Analysis. *Public Choice* 136
(1): 139–164.

Dreher, Axel, Peter Nunnenkamp, and Rainer Thiele. 2011. Are 'New' Donors
Different? Comparing the Allocation of Bilateral Aid Between NonDAC and
DAC Donor Countries. *World Development* 39 (11): 1950–1968.

Dreher, Axel, B. Peter Rosendorff, and James Raymond Vreeland. 2013. Buying
Votes and International Organizations. Manuscript, Heidelberg University.

Dreher, Axel and Jan-Egbert Sturm. 2012. Do the IMF and the World Bank
Influence Voting in the UN General Assembly? *Public Choice* 151 (1): 363–
397.

Dreher, Axel, Jan-Egbert Sturm, and James Raymond Vreeland. 2009a. Development Aid and International Politics: Does Membership on the UN Security
Council Influence World Bank Decisions? *Journal of Development Economics*
88 (1): 1–18.

Dreher, Axel, Jan-Egbert Sturm, and James Raymond Vreeland. 2009b. Global
Horse Trading: IMF Loans for Votes in the United Nations Security Council.
European Economic Review 53 (7): 742–757.

Dreher, Axel, Jan-Egbert Sturm, and James Raymond Vreeland. 2013. Politics and IMF Conditionality. *Journal of Conflict Resolution* doi: 10.1177/
0022002713499723.

Dreher, Axel and James Raymond Vreeland. 2009. Who Gets Elected to the
United Nations Security Council? Working Paper, March 2009.

Dreyer, Jacob S. and Andrew Schotter. 1980. Power Relationships in the International Monetary Fund: The Consequences of Quota Changes. *Review of
Economics and Statistics* 62 (1): 97–106.

Drezner, Daniel W. 1999. *The Sanctions Paradox: Economic Statecraft and International Relations.* New York: Cambridge University Press.

Drezner, Daniel W. 2002. *Locating the Proper Authorities: The Interaction
of Domestic and International Institutions.* Ann Arbor, MI: University of
Michigan Press.

Dunning, Thad. 2004. Conditioning the Effects of Aid: Cold War Politics, Donor
Credibility, and Democracy in Africa. *International Organization* 58 (2): 409–
423.

Dymski, Gary A. and Manuel Pastor, Jr. 1990. Bank Lending, Misleading Signals,
and the Latin American Debt Crisis. *The International Trade Journal* 6 (2):
151–192.

Easterly, William. 2001. *The Elusive Quest for Growth.* Cambridge, MA: MIT
Press.

Easterly, William and Ross Levine. 1997. Africa's Growth Tragedy: Policies and
Ethnic Divisions. *Quarterly Journal of Economics* 112 (4): 1203–1250.

Easterly, William, Ross Levine, and David Roodman. 2004. New Data, New
Doubts: A Comment on Burnside and Dollar's "Aid, Policies, and Growth"
(2000). *American Economic Review* 94 (3): 774–780.

Easterly, William and Mirvat Sewadeh. 2001. *Global Development Network Growth Database*. Washington, DC: The World Bank.

Edelstein, David. 2008. *Occupational Hazards: Success and Failure in Military Occupation*. Ithaca, NY: Cornell University Press.

Eldar, Ofer. 2008. Vote-Trading in International Institutions. *European Journal of International Law* 19 (1): 3–41.

Falleti Tulia G. 2011. Varieties of Authoritarianism: The Organization of the Military State and Its Effect on Federalism in Argentina and Brazil. *Studies in Comparative International Development* 46 (2): 137–162.

Fang, Songying. 2008. The Informational Role of International Institutions and Domestic Politics. *American Journal of Political Science* 52 (2): 304–321.

Fazal, Tanisha M. 2007. *State Death: The Politics and Geography of Conquest, Occupation, and Annexation*. Princeton, NJ: Princeton University Press.

Fearon, James D. and David D. Laitin. 2004. Neotrusteeship and the Problem of Weak States. *International Security* 28 (4): 5–43.

Ferejohn, John and Francis McCall Rosenbluth. 2008. *Warlike Democracies*. *Journal of Conflict Resolution* 52 (1): 3–38.

Ferguson, James. 1994. *The Anti-Politics Machine: Development, Depoliticization, and Bureaucratic Power in Lesotho*. Minneapolis, MN: University of Minnesota Press.

Findley, Michael G., Josh Powell, Daniel Strandow, and Jeff Tanner. 2011. The Localized Geography of Foreign Aid: A New Dataset and Application to Violent Armed Conflict. *World Development* 39 (11): 1995–2009.

Finnemore, Martha. 1996. *National Interests in International Society*. Ithaca, NY: Cornell University Press.

Fleck, Robert K. and Christopher Kilby. 2006. World Bank Independence: A Model and Statistical Analysis of US Influence. *Review of Development Economics* 10 (2): 224–240.

Flores, Thomas Edward and Irfan Nooruddin. 2009. Financing the Peace: Evaluating World Bank Post-Conflict Assistance Programs. *Review of International Organizations* 4 (1): 1–27.

Fortna, Virginia Page. 2004. *Peace Time: Cease-Fire Agreements and the Durability of Peace*. Princeton, NJ: Princeton University Press.

Franck, Thomas M. 1990. *The Power of Legitimacy Among Nations*. New York: Oxford University Press.

Franz, Mathias, Daniel van der Post, Oliver Schülke, and Julia Ostner. 2011. The Evolution of Cooperative Turn-Taking in Animal Conflict. *BMC Evolutionary Biology* 11: 323.

Freedman, Isaac. 2013. To Ban International Vote Buying? Rethinking Corruption Norms and their International Applicability. Senior Essay, Department of Government, Georgetown University.

Frey, Bruno S., Paolo Pamini, and Lasse Steiner. 2013. Explaining the World Heritage List: An Empirical Study. *International Review of Economics* 60 (1): 1–19.

Frey, Bruno S. and Friedrich Schneider. 1986. Competing Models of International Lending Activity. *Journal of Development Economics* 20 (2): 225–245.

Friedman, Thomas L. 1993. Clinton Asks UN Chief to Meet on Plan for Airdrop to Bosnians. *New York Times*, February 23. Available at: http://www.nytimes .com/1993/02/23/world/clinton-asks-un-chief-to-meet-on-plan-for-airdrop-to-bosnians.html?pagewanted=all&src=pm.

Gandhi, Jennifer. 2008. *Political Institutions under Dictatorship*. New York: Cambridge University Press.

Garrett, Geoffrey and Barry Weingast. 1993. Ideas, Interests, and Institutions: Constructing the European Community's Internal Market. In Judith Goldstein and Robert Keohane (eds.), *Ideas and Foreign Policy: Beliefs, Institutions, and Political Change*. Ithaca, NY: Cornell University Press: 173–206.

Gartzke, Erik and Megumi Naoi. 2011. Multilateralism and Democracy: A Response to Keohane, Macedo and Moravcsik. *International Organization* 65 (3): 589–598.

Geddes, Barbara. 1999. What Do We Know about Democratization after Twenty Years? *Annual Review of Political Science* 2: 115–144.

Ghattas, Kim. 2003. Syria Calm Despite Neighbouring War. *BBC*, March 21. Available at: http://news.bbc.co.uk/2/hi/middle_east/2873661.stm.

Gibler, Douglas M. 2009. *International Military Alliances from 1648 to 2008*. Washington, DC: Congressional Quarterly Press.

Gibler, Douglas M. and Meredith Sarkees. 2004. Measuring Alliances: The Correlates of War Formal Interstate Alliance Data Set, 1816–2000. *Journal of Peace Research* 41 (2): 211–222.

Girod, Desha M. 2012. Effective Foreign Aid Following Civil War: The Nonstrategic-Desperation Hypothesis. *American Journal of Political Science* 56 (1): 188–201.

Glennon, Michael J. 2001. *Limits of Law, Prerogatives of Power: Interventionism after Kosovo*. New York: Palgrave Macmillan.

Glennon, Michael J. 2003. Why the Security Council Failed. *Foreign Affairs* 82 (3): 16–35.

Golder, Matt, Sona N. Golder, and David A. Siegel. 2012. Modeling the Institutional Foundations of Parliamentary Government Formation. *Journal of Politics* 74 (2): 427–445.

Goldsmith, Jack and Daryl Levinson. 2009. Law for States: International Law, Constitutional Law, Public Law. *Harvard Law Review* 122 (7): 1791–1868.

Goldstein, Judith and Robert Keohane. 1993. Ideas, Interests, and Institutions: An Analytical Framework. In Judith Goldstein and Robert Keohane (eds.), *Ideas and Foreign Policy: Beliefs, Institutions, and Political Change*. Ithaca, NY: Cornell University Press: 3–30.

Gould, Erica. 2003. Money Talks: Supplemental Financiers and International Monetary Fund Conditionality. *International Organization* 57 (3): 551–586.

Grant, Ruth W. and Robert O. Keohane. 2005. Accountability and Abuses of Power in World Politics. *American Political Science Review* 99 (1): 29–43.

Gray, Julia. 2009. International Organization as a Seal of Approval: European Union Accession and Investor Risk. *American Journal of Political Science* 53 (4): 931–949.

Green, Donald P., Soo Yeon Kim, and David H. Yoon. 2001. Dirty Pool. *International Organization* 55 (2): 441–468.

Green, Michael Jonathan. 2003. *Japan's Reluctant Realism: Foreign Policy Challenged in an Era of Uncertain Power*. New York: Palgrave.

Green, Rosario. 2007. Consejo de Seguridad. *El Universal*, July 3. Available at: http://www.eluniversal.com.mx/editoriales/37991.html.

Greene, William. 2010. Testing Hypotheses about Interaction Terms in Nonlinear Models. *Economics Letters* 107: 291–296.

Grieco, Joseph M. 1999. Realism and Regionalism: American Power and German and Japanese Institutional Strategies During and After the Cold War. In Ethan Kapstein and Michael Mastanduno (eds.), *Unipolar Politics: Realism and State Strategies After the Cold War*. New York: Columbia University Press: 319–353.

Groeling, Tim and Matthew A. Baum. 2008. Crossing the Water's Edge: Elite Rhetoric, Media Coverage, and the Rally-Round-the-Flag Phenomenon. *Journal of Politics* 70 (4): 1065–1085.

Gruber, Lloyd. 2000. *Ruling the World*. Princeton, NJ: Princeton University Press.

Hafner-Burton, Emilie Marie, and Kiyoteru Tsutsui. 2005. Human Rights in a Globalizing World: The Paradox of Empty Promises. *American Journal of Sociology* 110 (5): 1373–1411.

Hamilton, Thomas J. 1950. UN Body Invites Red China to Discuss Troops in Korea. *New York Times*, November 9 (late city edition): 1, 3.

Harrigan, Jane, Chengang Wang, and Hamed El-Said. 2006. The Economic and Political Determinants of IMF and World Bank Lending in the Middle East and North Africa. *World Development* 34 (2): 247–270.

Hathaway, Oona A. 2002. Do Human Rights Treaties Make a Difference? *The Yale Law Journal* 111 (8): 1935–2042.

Hawkins, Darren G., David A. Lake, Daniel L. Nielson, and Michael J. Tierney. 2006. Delegation Under Anarchy: States, International Organizations and Principal-Agent Theory. In Darren Hawkins, David A. Lake, Daniel Nielson, and Michael J. Tierney (eds.), *Delegation and Agency in International Organizations*. New York: Cambridge University Press: 3–38.

Headey, Derek. 2008. Geopolitics and the Effect of Foreign Aid on Economic Growth: 1970–2001. *Journal of International Development* 20 (2): 161–180.

Heckman, James J. 1979. Sample Selection Bias as a Specification Error. *Econometrica* 47 (1): 153–161.

Hefeker, Carsten and Katharina Michaelowa. 2005. Can Process Conditionality Enhance Aid Effectiveness? The Role of Bureaucratic Interest and Public Pressure. *Public Choice* 122 (1–2): 159–175.

Heldt, Birger. 2008. *Personnel Contributions to UN Peacekeeping Operations, 1970–2005*. Stockholm: Folke Bernadotte Academy.

Heldt, Birger and Peter Wallensteen. 2006. *Peacekeeping Operations: Global Patterns of Intervention and Success, 1948–2004*, 2nd ed. Sandöverken, Sweden: Folke Bernadotte Academy Publications.

Hendel, Igal. 1999. Estimating Multiple-Discrete Choice Models: An Application to Computerization Returns. *Review of Economic Studies* 66 (2): 423–446.

Herbst, Jeffrey. 2007. Crafting Regional Cooperation in Africa. In Amitav Acharya and Alastair Iain Johnston (eds.), *Crafting Cooperation: Regional International Institutions in Comparative Perspective*. New York: Cambridge University Press: 129–144.

Hernandez, Diego. 2013. Does Inclusion Guarantee Institutional Autonomy? The Case of the Inter-American Development Bank. University of Heidelberg, Department of Economics Working Paper 541.

Heston, Alan, Robert Summers, and Bettina Aten. 2012. *Penn World Table Version 7.1.* Philadelphia: Center for International Comparisons of Production, Income and Prices at the University of Pennsylvania.

Ho, Daniel E., Imai Kosuke, Gary King, and Elizabeth A. Stuart. 2007. Matching as Nonparametric Preprocessing for Reducing Model Dependence in Parametric Causal Inference. *Political Analysis* 15 (3): 199–236.

Hodler, Roland and Axel Dreher. 2013. Development (Paradigm) Failures. *Journal of Development Economics* 101: 63–74.

Hollyer, James R. and B. Peter Rosendorff. 2011. Why Do Authoritarian Regimes Sign the Convention Against Torture? Signaling, Domestic Politics, and Non-Compliance. *Quarterly Journal of Political Science* 6 (3–4): 275–327.

Hollyer, James R., B. Peter Rosendorff, and James Raymond Vreeland. 2011. Democracy and Transparency. *Journal of Politics* 73 (4): 1191–1205.

Hosli, Madeleine, Rebecca Moody, Bryan O'Donovan, Serguei Kaniovski, and Anna Little. 2011. Squaring the Circle? Collective and Distributive Effects of United Nations Security Council Reform. *Review of International Organizations* 6 (2): 163–187.

Hovet, Thomas Jr. 1960. *Bloc Politics in the United Nations.* Cambridge, MA: Harvard University Press.

Howard, Lise Morjé. 2007. *UN Peacekeeping in Civil Wars.* New York: Cambridge University Press.

Howard, Marc Morjé, and Philip G. Roessler. 2006. Liberalizing Electoral Outcomes in Competitive Authoritarian Regimes. *American Journal of Political Science* 50 (2): 365–381.

Hudson, Natalie Florea. 2009. Securitizing Women's Human Rights and Gender Equality. *Journal of Human Rights* 8 (1): 53–70.

Hulsman, John C. and A. Wess Mitchell. 2009. *The Godfather Doctrine: A Foreign Policy Parable.* Princeton, NJ: Princeton University Press.

Humphrey, Chris and Katharina Michaelowa. 2013. Shopping for Development: Multilateral Lending, Shareholder Composition and Borrower Preferences. *World Development* 44 (4): 142–155.

Hurd, Ian. 2007. *After Anarchy: Legitimacy and Power in the UN Security Council.* Princeton, NJ: Princeton University Press.

Hurd, Ian. 2008. Myths of Membership: The Politics of Legitimation in UN Security Council Reform. *Global Governance* 14 (2): 199–217.

Hurd, Ian and Bruce Cronin (eds.). 2008. *The UN Security Council and the Legitimacy of International Authority.* Princeton, NJ: Princeton University Press.

Iacus, Stefano M., Gary King, and Giuseppe Porro. 2012. Causal Inference Without Balance Checking: Coarsened Exact Matching. *Political Analysis* 20 (1): 1–24.

Imai, Kosuke, Gary King, and Elizabeth A. Stuart. 2008. Misunderstandings among Experimentalists and Observationalists about Causal Inference. *Journal of the Royal Statistical Society, Series A (Statistics in Society)* 171 (2): 481–502.

Imai, Kosuke and David A. van Dyk. 2004. Causal Inference with General Treatment Regimes: Generalizing the Propensity Score. *Journal of the American Statistical Association* 99 (467): 854–866.

Ingram, Paul, Jeffrey Robinson, and Marc L. Busch. 2005. The Intergovernmental Network of World Trade: IGO Connectedness, Governance, and Embeddedness. *American Journal of Sociology* 111 (3): 824–858.

International Monetary Fund. 1974. Tanzania's Next Five-Year Plan. *IMF Survey* 3 (6): 86.

International Monetary Fund. 1975. Press Releases: Oil Facility Purchases. *IMF Survey* 3 (3): 77.

International Monetary Fund. 2003. *IMF Annual Report*. Washington, DC.

International Monetary Fund. 2004. *IMF Annual Report*. Washington, DC.

International Monetary Fund. 2011. *International Financial Statistics* (November). Washington, DC.

Ivanova, Anna, Wolfgang Mayer, Alex Mourmouras, and George Anayiotos. 2006. What Determines the Implementation of IMF-Supported Programs? In Ashoka Mody and Alessandro Rebucci (eds.), *IMF-Supported Programs – Recent Staff Research*. Washington, DC: International Monetary Fund: 160–188.

Iwanami, Yukari. 2012. Delegating the Power to Govern Security Affairs: The Composition of the UN Security Council. Paper presented at the 5th Annual Conference on the Political Economy of International Organizations, Villanova University.

Jayakumar, S. 2011. *Diplomacy: A Singapore Experience*. Singapore: Straits Times Press.

Jentleson, Bruce W. 1992. The Pretty Prudent Public: Post Post-Vietnam American Opinion and the Use of Military Force. *International Studies Quarterly* 36: 49–74.

Jentleson, Bruce W. 2003. Tough Love Multilateralism. *The Washington Quarterly* 27 (Winter 2003–2004): 7–24.

Jentleson, Bruce W. and Rebecca L. Britton. 1998. Still Pretty Prudent: Post–Cold War American Public Opinion and the Use of Military Force. *Journal of Conflict Resolution* 42: 395–417.

Johns, Leslie. 2007. A Servant of Two Masters: Communication and the Selection of International Bureaucrats. *International Organization* 61 (2): 245–275.

Johnson, Tana. 2011. Guilt by Association: The Link between States' Influence and the Legitimacy of Intergovernmental Organizations. *Review of International Organizations* 6 (1): 57–84.

Johnson, Thomas. 1973. "Abode of Peace" Has Sluggish Economy. *New York Times*, February 4: 4.

Johnston, Alastair Iain. 2001. Treating International Institutions as Social Environments. *International Studies Quarterly* 45 (4): 487–515.

Joshi, Shareen and T. Paul Schultz. 2013. Family Planning and Women's and Children's Health: Long-Term Consequences of an Outreach Program in Matlab, Bangladesh. *Demography* 50 (1): 149–180.

Kahler, Miles. 2011. Legitimacy, humanitarian intervention, and international institutions. *Politics, Philosophy, & Economics* 10 (1): 20–45.

Kahler, Miles. 2013. Rising Powers and Global Governance: Negotiating Change in a Resilient Status Quo. *International Affairs* 89 (3): 711–729.

Kaja, Ashwin and Eric Werker. 2010. Corporate Governance at the World Bank and the Dilemma of Global Governance. *World Bank Economic Review* 24 (2): 171–198.

Kaplan, Stephen B. 2013. *Globalization and Austerity Politics in Latin America.* New York: Cambridge University Press.

Kapur, Devesh and Moises Naim. 2005. The IMF and Democratic Governance. *Journal of Democracy* 16 (1): 89–102.

Katada, Saori N. and Timothy J. McKeown. 1998. Aid Politics and Electoral Politics: Japan, 1970–1992. *International Studies Quarterly* 42 (3): 591–600.

Katzenstein, Peter J. and Nobuo Okawara. 1993. Japan's National Security: Structures, Norms, and Policies. *International Security* 17 (4): 84–118.

Katzenstein, Peter J. and Martin Rouse. 1993. Japan as a Regional Power in Asia. In Jeffrey A. Frankel and Miles Kahler (eds.), *Regionalism and Rivalry: Japan and the United States in Pacific Asia.* Chicago, IL: University of Chicago Press: 217–244.

Kaufmann, Daniel, Aart Kraay, and Massimo Mastruzzi. 2011. The Worldwide Governance Indicators: Methodology and Analytical Issues. *Hague Journal on the Rule of Law* 3 (2): 220–246.

Keck, Margaret E. and Kathryn Sikkink. 1998. *Activists beyond Borders: Advocacy Networks in International Politics.* Ithaca, NY: Cornell University Press.

Kegley, Charles W. Jr. and Steven W. Hook. 1991. US Foreign Aid and UN Voting: Did Reagan's Linkage Strategy Buy Defence or Defiance? *International Studies Quarterly* 35 (3): 295–312.

Keohane, Robert O. 1984. *After Hegemony: Cooperation and Discord in the World Political Economy.* Princeton, NJ: Princeton University Press.

Kerr, Paul. 2003. Oil-for-Food Extended, Goods Review List Revised. *Arms Control Today* January/February. Available at: http://www.armscontrol.org/act/2003_01-02/oilforfood_janfeb03.

Khong, Yuen Foong and Helen E. S. Nesadurai. 2007. Hanging Together, Institutional Design and Cooperation in Southeast Asia: AFTA and the ARF. In Amitav Acharya and Alastair Iain Johnston (eds.), *Crafting Cooperation: Regional International Institutions in Comparative Perspective.* New York: Cambridge University Press: 32–82.

Kilby, Christopher. 2006. Donor Influence in Multilateral Development Banks: The Case of the Asian Development Bank. *Review of International Organizations* 1 (2): 173–195.

Kilby, Christopher. 2009a. The Political Economy of Conditionality: An Empirical Analysis of World Bank Loan Disbursements. *Journal of Development Economics* 89 (1): 51–61.

Kilby, Christopher. 2009b. Donor Influence in International Financial Institutions: Deciphering What Alignment Measures Measure. Villanova School of Business Economics Working Paper 8.

Kilby, Christopher. 2011a. Assessing the Contribution of Donor Agencies to Aid Effectiveness: The Impact of World Bank Preparation on Project Outcomes. Villanova School of Business Economics Working Paper 20.

Kilby, Christopher. 2011b. Informal Influence in the Asian Development Bank. *Review of International Organizations* 6 (3–4): 223–257.

Kilby, Christopher. 2013a. An Empirical Assessment of Informal Influence in the World Bank. *Economic Development and Cultural Change* 61 (2):431–464.

Kilby, Christopher. 2013b. The Political Economy of Project Preparation: An Empirical Analysis of World Bank Projects. *Journal of Development Economics* 105: 211–225.

Kilby, Christopher and Axel Dreher. 2010. The Impact of Aid on Growth Revisited: Do Donor and Recipient Characteristics Make a Difference? *Economics Letters* 107 (3): 338–340.

Kim, Soo Yeon and Bruce Russett. 1996. The New Politics of Voting Aignment in the United Nations General Assembly. *International Organization* 50 (4): 629–652.

King, Gary, James Honaker, Anne Joseph, and Kenneth Scheve. 2001. Analyzing Incomplete Political Science Data: An Alternative Algorithm for Multiple Imputation. *American Political Science Review* 95: 49–69.

Kiondo, Andrew. 1992. The Nature of Economic Reforms in Tanzania. In Horace Campbell and Howard Stein (eds.), *Tanzania and the IMF: The Dynamics of Liberalization*. Boulder, CO: Westview Press: 21–42.

Kono, Daniel Yuichi and Gabriella R. Montinola. 2009. Does Foreign Aid Support Autocrats, Democrats, or Both? *Journal of Politics* 71 (2): 704–718.

Koremenos, Barbara. 2008. When, What, and Why do States Choose to Delegate? *Law and Contemporary Problems* 71: 151–192.

Koremenos, Barbara, Charles Lipson and Duncan Snidal. 2001. The Rational Design of International Institutions. *International Organization* 55 (4): 761–799.

Kosack, Stephen and Jennifer Tobin. 2006. Funding Self-Sustaining Development: The Role of Aid, FDI and Government in Economic Success. *International Organization* 60 (1): 205–243.

Krasner, Stephen D. 1981. Power Structures and Regional Development Banks. *International Organization* 35 (2): 303–328.

Kroenig, Matthew, Melissa McAdam, and Steven Weber. 2010. Taking Soft Power Seriously. *Comparative Strategy* 29 (5): 412–431.

Kull, Steven and I. M. Destler. 1999. *Misreading the Public: The Myth of New Isolationalism*. Washington, DC: Brookings Institution.

Kuziemko, Ilyana and Eric Werker. 2006. How Much Is a Seat on the Security Council Worth? Foreign Aid and Bribery at the United Nations. *Journal of Political Economy* 114 (5): 905–930.

Kydd, Andrew. 2003. Which Side Are You On? Bias, Credibility and Mediation. *American Journal of Political Science* 47 (4): 597–611.

Lake, David A. 1996. Anarchy, Hierarchy, and the Variety of International Relations. *International Organization* 50 (1): 1–33.

Lake, David A. 1999. *Entangling Relations: American Foreign Policy in Its Century*. Princeton, NJ: Princeton University Press.

Lake, David A. 2007. Delegating Divisible Sovereignty: Sweeping a Conceptual Minefield. *Review of International Organizations* 2 (3): 219–237.

Lancaster, Carol. 1999. *Aid to Africa: So Much to Do, So Little Done*. Chicago, IL: University of Chicago Press.

Lancaster, Carol. 2000. *Transforming Foreign Aid: United States Assistance in the 21st Century*. Washington, DC: Institute for International Economics.

Lancaster, Carol. 2006. *Foreign Aid: Diplomacy, Development, Domestic Politics*. Chicago, IL: University of Chicago Press.

Lebovic, James H. 2010. Passing the Burden: Contributions to UN Peace Operations in the Post–Cold War Era. Paper presented at the Annual Meeting of the International Studies Association, New Orleans, LA.

Left, Sarah. 2002. UN Security Council Backs Palestinian State. *The Guardian*, March 13. Available at: http://www.guardian.co.uk/world/2002/mar/13/israelandthepalestinians.unitednations.

Leuven, Edwin and Barbara Sianesi. 2003. PSMATCH2: Stata Module to Perform Full Mahalanobis and Propensity Score Matching, Common Support Graphing, and Covariate Imbalance Testing. Department of Economics, Boston College.

Levitsky, Steven and Lucan A. Way. 2010. *Competitive Authoritarianism: Hybrid Regimes after the Cold War*. New York: Cambridge University Press.

Levy, Philip I. 1999. Sanctions on South Africa: What Did They Do? Center Discussion Paper No. 796. Economic Growth Center, Yale University.

Lieber, Robert J. 2005. *The American Era: Power and Strategy for the 21st Century*. New York: Cambridge University Press.

Lim, Daniel Yew Mao and James Raymond Vreeland. 2013. Regional Organizations and International Politics: Japanese Influence over the Asian Development Bank and the UN Security Council. *World Politics* 65 (1): 34–72.

Lipscy, Phillip. 2003. Japan's Asian Monetary Fund Proposal. *Stanford Journal of East Asian Affairs* 3 (1): 93–104.

Lockwood, Natalie J. 2013. International Vote Buying. *Harvard International Law Journal* 54 (1): 97–156.

Long, William J. 1996. *Economic Incentives and Bilateral Cooperation*. Ann Arbor, MI: Michigan University Press.

Luck, Edward C. 2006. *The UN Security Council: Practice and Promise*. New York: Routledge.

Lupia, Arthur and Matthew D. McCubbins. 1998. *The Democratic Dilemma: Can Citizens Learn What They Need to Know?* New York: Cambridge University Press.

Lynch, Colum. 2006. Security Council Seat Tied to Aid. *Washington Post*, November 1. Available at: http://www.washingtonpost.com/wp-dyn/content/article/2006/10/31/AR2006103101217.html.

Maizels, Alfred and Machiko K. Nissanke. 1984. Motivations for Aid to Developing Countries. *World Development* 12 (9): 879–900.

Malone, David M. 1998. *Decision-Making in the UN Security Council: The Case of Haiti, 1990–1997*. New York: Oxford University Press.

Malone, David M. 2000. Eyes on the Prize: The Quest for Nonpermanent Seats on the UN Security Council. *Global Governance* 6 (1): 3–21.

Malone, David M. 2004. *The UN Security Council: From the Cold War to the 21st Century*. Oxford: Oxford University Press.

Mansfield, Edward D. and Helen V. Milner (eds.). 1997. *The Political Economy of Regionalism*. New York: Columbia University Press.

Mansfield, Edward D. and Helen V. Milner. 1999. The New Wave of Regionalism. *International Organization* 53 (3): 589–627.

Mansfield, Edward D., Helen V. Milner, and B. Peter Rosendorff. 2002. Why Democracies Cooperate More: Electoral Control and International Trade Agreements. *International Organization* 56 (3): 477–514.

Mansfield, Edward D. and Jon C. Pevehouse. 2006. Democratization and International Organizations. *International Organization* 60 (1): 137–167.

Manski, Charles and Leonard Sherman. 1980. An Empirical Analysis of Household Choice among Motor Vehicles. *Transportation Research Part A: General*, 14 (5–6): 349–366.

Marriage, Zöe. 2006. *Not Breaking the Rules, Not Playing the Game: International Assistance to Countries at War*. London: C Hurst & Co Publishers Ltd.

Marshall, Katherine. 2008. *The World Bank: From Reconstruction to Development to Equity*. New York: Routledge.

Marshall, Monty G., Ted Robert Gurr, Christian Davenport, and Keith Jaggers. 2002. Polity IV: 1800–1999. *Comparative Political Studies* 35 (1): 40–45.

Martin, Lisa. 1992. *Coercive Cooperation: Explaining Multilateral Economic Sanctions*. Princeton, NJ: Princeton University Press.

Martin, Patrick. 2003. Bugging, Bribes and Bullying: US Thuggery in Advance of UN Vote. *World Socialist Web site*, March 6. Available at: http://www.wsws.org/articles/2003/mar2003/un-m06.shtml.

Mayhew, David R. 2005. *Divided We Govern: Party Control, Lawmaking, and Investigations, 1946–2002*, 2nd ed. New Haven, CT: Yale University Press.

Mazumder, Soumyajit and James Raymond Vreeland. 2013. O Canada, We Stand on Guard for Thee: Foreign Aid Benefits for Members of the Bretton Woods Canadian-Bloc. Mortara Center Working Paper.

Mazumder, Soumyajit, Kathleen R. McNamara, and James Raymond Vreeland. 2014. The Buck Stops Here: What Global Horse Trading Tells Us about the European Project. Paper presented at the 7th Annual Conference on Political Economy of International Organizations, Princeton University.

McDonald, Kara C. and Stewart M. Patrick. 2010. *UN Security Council Enlargement and US Interests. Council on Foreign Relations*. Council Special Report No. 59. New York: Council on Foreign Relations.

McFadden, Daniel. 1973. Conditional Logit Analysis of Qualitative Choice Behavior. In Paul Zarambeka (ed.), *Frontiers in Econometrics*. New York: Academic Press: 105–142.

McGillivray, Fiona. 2000. Democratizing the World Trade Organization. Hoover Institution Policy Paper No 105.

McGillivray, Fiona and Alastair Smith. 2008. *Punishing the Prince: A Theory of Interstate Relations, Political Institutions, and Leader Change*. Princeton, NJ: Princeton University Press.

McKeown, Timothy J. 2009. How US Decision-Makers Assessed Their Control of Multilateral Organizations, 1957–1982. *Review of International Organizations* 4 (3): 269–291.

McLean, Elena V. 2012. Donors' Preferences and Agent Choice: Delegation of European Development Aid. *International Studies Quarterly* 56 (2): 381–395.

McNamara, Kathleen R. 1998. *The Currency of Ideas: Monetary Politics in European Union*. Ithaca, NY: Cornell University Press.

McNamara, Kathleen R. 1999. Consensus and Constraint: Ideas and Capital Mobility in European Monetary Integration. *Journal of Common Market Studies* 37 (3): 455–476.

MercoPress. 2006. New Names for the UN Security Council Deadlock. *Merco Press South Atlantic News Agency* (Montevideo) October 17. Available at: http://en.mercopress.com/2006/10/17/new-names-for-the-un-security-council-deadlock.

Merrills, J. G. 2011. *International Dispute Settlement, 5th ed*. New York: Cambridge University Press.

Meunier, Sophie and Kathleen R. McNamara (eds.). 2007. *Making History: European Integration and Institutional Change at Fifty*. New York: Oxford University Press.

Miller, Andrew R. and Nives Dolšak. 2007. Issue Linkages in Environmental Policy: The International Whaling Commission and Japanese Development Aid. *University of Illinois Law Review* 7 (1): 69–96.

Milner, Helen V. 1988. *Resisting Protectionism: Global Industries and the Politics of International Trade*. Princeton, NJ: Princeton University Press.

Milner, Helen V. 1997. *Interests, Institutions and Information: Domestic Politics and International Relations*. Princeton, NJ: Princeton University Press.

Milner, Helen V. 2006. Why Multilateralism? Foreign Aid and Domestic Principal-Agent Problems. In Darren Hawkins, David A. Lake, Daniel Nielson, and Michael J. Tierney (eds.), *Delegation and Agency in International Organizations*. New York: Cambridge University Press: 107–139.

Milner, Helen V. and Keiko Kubota. 2005. Why the Move to Free Trade? Democracy and Trade Policy in the Developing Countries. *International Organization* 59 (1): 107–143.

Milner, Helen V. and B. Peter Rosendorff. 1996. Trade Negotiations, Information and Domestic Politics: The Role of Domestic Groups. *Economics & Politics* 8 (2): 145–189.

Milner, Helen V. and Dustin H. Tingley. 2011. Who Supports Global Economic Engagement? The Sources of Preferences in American Foreign Economic Policy. *International Organization* 65 (1): 37–68.

Minoiu, Camelia and Sanjay G. Reddy. 2010. Development Aid and Economic Growth. *Quarterly Review of Economics and Finance* 50 (1): 27–39.

Mitchell, Ronald B. 1998. Sources of Transparency: Information Systems in International Regimes. *International Studies Quarterly* 42 (1): 109–130.

Mitchell, Ronald B. and Patricia M. Keilbach. 2001. Situation Structure and Institutional Design: Reciprocity, Coercion, and Exchange. *International Organization* 55 (4): 891–917.

Montaño, Jorge. 2007. En el Consejo de Seguridad. *El Universal*. May 18. Available at: http://www.eluniversal.com.mx/editoriales/37620.html.

Moon, Bruce E. 1985. Consensus or Compliance? Foreign-Policy Change and External Dependence. *International Organization* 39 (2): 297–329.

Morgan, T. Clifton, Valentin Krustev, and Navin A. Bapat. 2006. Threat and Imposition of Sanctions (TIES) Data User's Manual: Case Level Data. Available at: http://www.unc.edu/~bapat/TIES.htm.

Morgenthau, Hans. 1962. A Political Theory of Foreign Aid. *American Political Science Review* 56 (2): 301–309.

Morrison, Kevin M. 2013. Membership No Longer Has Its Privileges: The Declining Informal Influence of Board Members on IDA Lending. *Review of International Organizations* 8 (2): 291–312.

Moser, Christoph and Jan-Egbert Sturm. 2011. Explaining IMF Lending Decisions after the Cold War. *Review of International Organizations* 6 (3–4): 307–340.

Mosley, Layna and David Andrew Singer. 2009. The Global Financial Crisis: Lessons and Opportunities for International Political Economy. *International Interactions* 35 (4): 420–429.

Mosley, Paul, Jane Harrigan, and John Toye. 1991. *Aid and Power: The World Bank and Policy-Based Lending Volume 2, Case Studies*. New York: Routledge.

Mosse, David. 2005. *Cultivating Development: An Ethnography of Aid Policy and Practice*. London: Pluto Press.

Moyo, Dambisa. 2009. *Dead Aid*. New York: Farrar, Straus and Giroux.

Mukherjee, Bumba and David Andrew Singer. 2010. International Institutions and Domestic Compensation: The IMF and the Politics of Capital Account Liberalization. *American Journal of Political Science* 54 (1): 45–60.

Muñoz Ledo, Porfirio. 2007. La ONU: La Capilla Sixtina. *El Universal* 10. Available at: http://www.offnews.info/verArticulo.php?contenidoID=8466.

Neumayer, Eric. 2003. *The Pattern of Aid Giving: The Impact of Good Governance on Development Assistance*. New York: Routledge.

Nexon, Daniel H. and Thomas Wright. 2007. What's at Stake in the American Empire Debate. *American Political Science Review* 101 (2): 253–271.

Nielsen, Richard A., Michael G. Findley, Zachary S. Davis, Tara Candland, and Daniel L. Nielson. 2011. Foreign Aid Shocks as a Cause of Violent Armed Conflict. *American Journal of Political Science* 55 (2): 219–232.

Nielson, Daniel L. and Michael J. Tierney. 2003. Delegation to International Organizations: Agency Theory and World Bank Environmental Reform. *International Organization* 57 (2): 241–276.

Nooruddin, Irfan and Nita Rudra. Forthcoming. Are Developing Countries Really Defying the Embedded Liberalism Compact? *World Politics*.

Nooruddin, Irfan and Joel W. Simmons. 2006. The Politics of Hard Choices: IMF Programs and Government Spending. *International Organization* 60 (4): 1001–1033.

Nooruddin, Irfan and James Raymond Vreeland. 2010. The Effect of IMF Programs on Public Wages and Salaries. In Jennifer Clapp and Rorden Wilkinson (eds.), *Global Governance, Poverty and Inequality*. London: Routledge: 90–111.

Nye, Joseph S. Jr. 2004. *Soft Power: The Means to Success in World Politics*. New York: Public Affairs.

Oatley, Thomas and Jason Yackee. 2004. American Interests and IMF Lending. *International Politics* 41 (3): 415–429.

O'Brien, Terence. 1999. Electoral Groups Reconfiguration and Present Day Realities. In Ramesh Thakur (ed.), *What is Equitable Geographic Representation in the 21st Century*. Tokyo: United Nations University: 30–39.

OECD. 2006. *Journal on Development, Development Co-operation Report 2005*. Paris: OECD.

OECD. 2012. *Development Assistance Committee (DAC) Data*. Paris: OECD.

Olson, Mancur. 1965. *The Logic of Collective Action: Public Goods and the Theory of Groups*. Cambridge, MA: Harvard University Press.

O'Neill, Barry. 1996. Power and Satisfaction in the United Nations Security Council. *Journal of Conflict Resolution* 40 (2): 219–237.

Oneindia News. 2006. Italy, Pak-Led Coffee Club Opposes New Permanent Members. *Oneindia News*, September 21. Available at: http://news.oneindia .in/2006/09/21/italy-pak-led-coffee-club-opposes-new-permanent-members-on-unsc-1158845848.html.

Perla, Héctor Jr. 2011. Explaining Public Support for the Use of Military Force: The Impact of Reference Point Framing and Prospective Decision Making. *International Organization* 65 (1): 139–167.

Perlez, Jane. 2009. US Fears Pakistan Aid Will Fuel Graft. *New York Times*, September 20: A4. Available at: http://www.nytimes.com/2009/09/21/world/ asia/21aid.html.

Pevehouse, Jon C. 2002. With a Little Help from My Friends? Regional Organizations and the Consolidation of Democracy. *American Journal of Political Science* 46 (3): 611–626.

Pevehouse, Jon C. 2005. *Democracy from Above: Regional Organizations and Democratization*. New York: Cambridge University Press.

Pilger, John. 1992. *Distant Voices*. London: Vintage Books.

Pilger, John. 2002. How the Bushes Bribe the World. *New Statesman*, September 23. Available at: http://www.newstatesman.com/200209230006.

Pinto, Pablo M. and Jeffrey F. Timmons. 2005. The Political Determinants of Economic Performance: Political Competition and the Sources of Growth. *Comparative Political Studies* 38 (1): 26–50.

Posner, Daniel N. 2004. Measuring Ethnic Fractionalization in Africa. *American Journal of Political Science* 48 (4): 849–863.

Potrafke, Niklas. 2009. Does Government Ideology Influence Political Alignment with the US? An Empirical Analysis of Voting in the UN General Assembly. *Review of International Organizations* 4 (3): 245–268.

Preston, Julia. 2002. In a First, UN Notes Israeli Dead in Terror Attack in Mombasa. *New York Times*, December 14. Available at: http://www.nytimes .com/2002/12/14/world/in-a-first-un-notes-israeli-dead-in-terror-attack-in-mombasa.html.

Preston, Julia and James Bennet. 2002. UN Security Council Calls for End to Siege of Arafat. *New York Times*, September 24. Available at: http://www .nytimes.com/2002/09/24/international/middleeast/24CND-MIDE.html? pagewanted=all.

Przeworski, Adam, Michael Alvarez, José Antonio Cheibub, and Fernando Limongi. 2000. *Democracy and Development: Political Regimes and Economic Well-being in the World, 1950–1990*. New York: Cambridge University Press.

Przeworski, Adam and James Raymond Vreeland. 2000. The Effect of IMF Programs on Economic Growth. *Journal of Development Economics* 62 (2): 385–421.

Przeworski, Adam, Susan C. Stokes, and Bernard Manin. 1999. *Democracy, Accountability, and Representation*. New York: Cambridge University Press.

Putnam, Robert D. 1988. Diplomacy and Domestic Politics: The Logic of Two-Level Games. *International Organization* 42: 427–460.

Quinn, Dennis P. and John T. Woolley. 2001. Democracy and National Economic Performance: The Preference for Stability. *American Journal of Political Science* 45 (3): 634–657.

Rajan, Raghuram G. and Arvind Subramanian. 2008. Aid and Growth. *Review of Economics and Statistics* 90 (4): 643–665.

Remmer, Karen L. 2004. Does Foreign Aid Promote the Expansion of Government? *American Journal of Political Science* 48 (1): 77–92.

Renfrew, Barry. 2003. France Battles US to Line Up UN Votes. *Pittsburgh Post Gazette* (*Associated Press*), March 1. Available at: http://old.post-gazette.com/world/20030301franceworld2p2.asp.

Reynaud, Julien and Julien Vauday. 2009. Geopolitics in the International Monetary Fund. *Journal of Development Economics* 89 (1): 139–162.

Rickard, Stephanie J. and Teri Caraway. 2012. The Devil's in the Details: Assessing the Effects of IMF Loan Programs. Prepared for presentation at the Annual Meeting of the American Political Science Association, New Orleans, LA.

Risse-Kappen, Thomas. 1994. Ideas Do Not Float Freely: Transnational Coalitions, Domestic Structures, and the End of the Cold War. *International Organization* 48 (2): 185–214.

Roberts, Adam and Dominik Zimm. 2008. *Selective Security: War and the United Nations Security Council since 1945*. New York: Routledge.

Roodman, David. 2007. Macro Aid Effectiveness Research: A Guide for the Perplexed. Working Paper No. 135, Center for Global Development, Washington, DC.

Root, Hilton L. 2013. *Dynamics among Nations: The Evolution of Legitimacy and Development in Modern States*. Cambridge, MA: MIT Press.

Rose-Ackerman, Susan. 1999. *Corruption and Government: Causes, Consequences, and Reform*. New York: Cambridge.

Rosendorff, B. Peter and John Doces. 2006. Transparency and Unfair Eviction in Democracies and Autocracies. *Swiss Political Science Review* 12 (3): 99–112.

Rosendorff, B. Peter and Helen V. Milner. 2001. The Optimal Design of International Trade Institutions: Uncertainty and Escape. *International Organization* 55 (4): 829–857.

Rudra, Nita. 2008. *Globalization and the Race to the Bottom in Developing Countries: Who Really Gets Hurt?* New York: Cambridge University Press.

Ruggie, John Gerard. 1992. Multilateralism: The Anatomy of an Institution. *International Organization* 46 (3): 561–598.

Russett, Bruce (ed.). 1997. *The Once and Future Security Council*. New York: St. Martin's Press.

Russett, Bruce and John Oneal. 2001. *Triangulating Peace: Democracy, Interdependence, and International Organizations*. New York: W. W. Norton.

Russett, Bruce, Barry O'Neill, and James S. Sutterlin. 1997. Breaking the Restructuring Logjam. In Bruce Russet (ed.), *The Once and Future Security Council.* New York: St. Martin's Press: 153–172.

Ruttan, Vernon W. 1996. *United States Development Assistance Policy: The Domestic Politics of Foreign Economic Aid.* Baltimore, MD: The Johns Hopkins University Press.

Saiegh, Sebastian M. 2011. *Ruling by Statute: How Uncertainty and Vote Buying Shape Lawmaking.* New York: Cambridge.

Saito, Jun. 1996. "Shoeki to Enjo: Nippon no ODA Kunibetsu Haibun Seisaku no Keiryo Bunseki" [Bureaucratic Motives of Foreign Aid Allocation: A Quantitative Analysis of the Country Allocation of Japan's Official Development Assistance]. *Leviathan* (October): 126–145.

Sandler, Todd and Keith Hartley. 1999. *The Political Economy of NATO: Past, Present and into the 21st Century.* New York: Cambridge University Press.

Scharioth, Nicolas. 2010. *Western Democracies in the UN: Who Gets Elected and Why – A Quantitative Examination of Elections to United Nations Councils and Committees.* Berlin: Nomos.

Schelling, Thomas C. 1960. *The Strategy of Conflict.* Cambridge, MA: Harvard University Press.

Schimmelfennig, Frank. 2007. Functional form, identity-driven cooperation: institutional designs and effects in post-Cold War NATO. In Amitav Acharya and Alastair Iain Johnston (eds.), *Crafting Cooperation: Regional International Institutions in Comparative Perspective.* New York: Cambridge University Press: 145–179.

Schmitz, Jan and Johannes Schwarze. 2012. Determinants of the Election of Non-Permanent Members to the United Nations Security Council – An Empirical Analysis. Paper presented at the 5th Annual Conference on the Political Economy of International Organizations, Villanova University.

Schneider, Christina J. and Branislav L. Slantchev. 2013. Abiding by the Vote: Between-Groups Conflict in International Collective Action. *International Organization* 67 (4): 759–796.

Schneider, Christina J. and Jennifer L. Tobin. 2013. Interest Coalitions and Multilateral Aid Allocation in the European Union. *International Studies Quarterly* 57 (1): 103–114.

Schraeder, Peter J., Steven W. Hook, and Bruce Taylor. 1998. Clarifying the Foreign Aid Puzzle: A Comparison of American, Japanese, French, and Swedish Aid Flows. *World Politics* 50 (2): 294–323.

Schwartzberg, Melissa. 2013. *Counting the Many: The Origins and Limits of Supermajority Rule.* New York: Cambridge University Press.

Schwedler, Jillian. 2006. *Faith in Moderation: Islamist Parties in Jordan and Yemen.* New York: Cambridge University Press.

Security Council Report. 2006. *Special Research Report No. 4: UN Security Council Elections 2006.* New York: Security Council Report. Available at: http://www.securitycouncilreport.org/atf/cf/%7B65BFCF9B-6D27-4E9C-8CD3-CF6E4FF96FF9%7D/SpecialReport_SCElections_14%20August%2006.doc.

Security Council Report. 2009. *Special Research Report No. 1: UN Security Council Elections 2009*. New York: Security Council Report. Available at: http://www.securitycouncilreport.org/special-research-report/lookup-c-glKWLeMTIsG-b-5488243.php.

Security Council Report. 2011. *Special Research Report No. 4: Security Council Elections 2011*. New York: Security Council Report. Available at: http://www.securitycouncilreport.org/special-research-report/lookup-c-glKWLeMTIsG-b-7741609.php.

Serrano, Monica and Paul Kenny. 2006. Iraq and World Order: A Latin American Perspective. In Ramesh Thakur and Waheguru Pal Singh Sidhu (eds.), *The Iraq War Crisis and World Order*. Tokyo: UN University Press: 298–314.

Shadlen, Kenneth C. 2007. Debt, Finance and the IMF: Three Decades of Debt Crises in Latin America. In Europa Publications (corp. ed.), *South America, Central America and the Caribbean*. London: Routledge: 8–12.

Shapley, L. S., and Martin Shubik. 1954. A Method for Evaluating the Distribution of Power in a Committee System. *American Political Science Review* 48: 787–792.

Simmons, Beth A. and Daniel J. Hopkins. 2005. The Constraining Power of International Treaties. *American Political Science Review* 99 (4): 623–631.

Slaughter, Anne-Marie. 2003. Misreading the Record. *Foreign Affairs* 82 (4): 202–204.

Stein, Howard. 1992. Economic Policy and the IMF in Tanzania: Conditionality, Conflict, and Convergence. In Horace Campbell and Howard Stein (eds.), *Tanzania and the IMF: The Dynamics of Liberalization*. Boulder, CO: Westview Press: 59–83.

Steinwand, Martin C. and Randall W. Stone. 2008. The International Monetary Fund: A Review of the Recent Evidence. *Review of International Organizations* 3 (2): 123–149.

Stent, Angela and Lilia Shevtsova. 2002. America, Russia and Europe: A Realignment? *Survival: Global Politics and Strategy* 44 (4): 121–134.

Stone, Randall W. 2002. *Lending Credibility: The International Monetary Fund and the Post-Communist Transition*. Princeton, NJ: Princeton University Press.

Stone, Randall W. 2004. The Political Economy of IMF Lending in Africa. *American Political Science Review* 98 (4): 577–592.

Stone, Randall W. 2008. The Scope of IMF Conditionality. *International Organization* 62 (4): 589–620.

Stone, Randall W. 2011. *Controlling Institutions: International Organizations and the Global Economy*. New York: Cambridge University Press.

Strand, Jonathan R. and David P. Rapkin. 2011. Weighted Voting in the United Nations Security Council: A Simulation. *Simulation & Gaming* 42 (6): 772–802.

Strand, Jonathan R. and John P. Tuman. 2010. Foreign Aid Disbursement and Recipient Voting Behavior in an International Organization: The Case of Japan and the International Whaling Commission. Manuscript, University of Nevada, Las Vegas.

Strange, Austin, Bradley C. Parks, Michael J. Tierney, Andreas Fuchs, Axel Dreher, and Vijaya Ramachandran. 2013. China's Development Finance to Africa: A Media-Based Approach to Data Collection. Center for Global Development Working Paper 323, Washington, DC.

Strezhnev, Anton and Erik Voeten. 2012. United Nations General Assembly Voting Data. Georgetown University. Available at: http://dvn.iq.harvard.edu/dvn/dv/Voeten.

Sturm, Jan-Egbert, Helge Berger, and Jakob de Haan. 2005. Which Variables Explain Decisions on IMF Credit? An Extreme Bounds Analysis. *Economics & Politics* 17 (2): 177–213.

Swart, Lydia. 2013. Reform of the Security Council: 2007–2013. In Lydia Swart and Estelle Perry (eds.), *Governing & Managing Change at the United Nations: Security Council Reform from 1945 to September 2013*. New York: Center for UN Reform Education: 23–59.

Tadokoro, Masayuki. 1997. A Japanese View of Restructuring the Security Council. In Bruce Russet (ed.), *The Once and Future Security Council*. New York: St. Martin's Press: 119–134.

Tamura, Fumika and Takuma Kunieda. 2005. Vote-Buying Behavior in the Security Council: Theory and Evidence from U.S. Foreign Aid. Manuscript, Department of Economics, Brown University.

Tannenwald, Nina. 2005. Ideas and Explanation: Advancing the Theoretical Agenda. *Journal of Cold War Studies* 7 (2): 13–42.

Thacker, Strom C. 1999. The High Politics of IMF Lending. *World Politics* 52 (1): 38–75.

Thakur, Ramesh (ed.). 1999. *What Is Equitable Geographic Representation in the 21st Century*. Tokyo: United Nations University.

Tharoor, Sashi. 2003. Why America Still Needs the United Nations. *Foreign Affairs* 82 (5): 67–80.

Themnér, Lotta and Peter Wallensteen. 2012. Armed Conflicts, 1946–2011. *Journal of Peace Research* 49 (4): 565–575.

Thompson, Alexander. 2006. Coercion through IOs: The Security Council and the Logic of Information Transmission. *International Organization* 60 (1): 1–34.

Thompson, Alexander. 2009. *Channeling Power: The UN Security Council and US Statecraft in Iraq*. Ithaca, NY: Cornell University Press.

Tierney, Michael J., Daniel L. Nielson, Darren G. Hawkins, J. Timmons Roberts, Michael G. Findley, Ryan M. Powers, Bradley Parks, Sven E. Wilson, and Robert L. Hicks. 2011. More Dollars than Sense: Refining Our Knowledge of Development Finance Using AidData. *World Development* 39 (11): 1891–1906.

Tingley, Dustin H., and Barbara F. Walter. 2011. The Effect of Repeated Play on Reputation Building: An Experimental Approach. *International Organization* 65 (2): 343–365.

Tomz, Michael. 2007. *Reputation and International Cooperation: Sovereign Debt across Three Centuries*. Princeton, NJ: Princeton University Press.

Torre, Wilbert. 2006. México frena a Venezuela en ONU. *El Universal*, October 19. Available at: http://www.eluniversal.com.mx/notas/382237.html.

True-Frost, C. Cora. 2007. The Security Council and Norm Consumption. *International Law and Politics* 40: 115–217.

Tsebelis, George. 1995. Decision Making in Political Systems. *British Journal of Political Science* 25: 289–326.

Tsebelis, George. 2002. *Veto Players: How Political Institutions Work*. Princeton, NJ: Princeton University Press.

Tucker, Joshua A., Alexander C. Pacek, and Adam J. Berinsky. 2002. Transitional Winners and Losers: Attitudes toward EU Membership in Post-Communist Countries. *American Journal of Political Science* 46 (3): 557–571.

Ueki, Yasuhiro. 1993. Japan's UN Diplomacy: Sources of Passivism and Activism. In Gerald L. Curtis (ed.), *Japan's Foreign Policy after the Cold War*. New York: M. E. Sharpe: 347–370.

United Nations. 2013. *United Nations Security Council: Membership Since 1946. New York: United Nations*. Available at: http://www.un.org/en/sc/members/search.shtml.

United Nations Statistics Division. 2011. *UNData*. New York: United Nations. Available at: http://data.un.org.

USAID. 2011. *U.S. Overseas Loans and Grants: Obligations and Loan Authorizations*. Washington, DC: USAID. Available at: http://gbk.eads.usaidall.net.gov/about/.

Varner, Bill. 2006. Chavez's Push for UN Council Seat Sets Up a Showdown With US. *Bloomberg*, October 11. Available at: http://www.bloomberg.com/apps/news?pid=newsarchive&sid=aHbR19zyxptU&refer=news.

Vaubel, Roland. 1986. A Public Choice Approach to International Organization. *Public Choice* 51: 39–57.

Vaubel, Roland. 1996. Bureaucracy at the IMF and the World Bank: A Comparison of the Evidence. *The World Economy* 19 (2): 185–210.

Vaubel, Roland. 2006. Principal-Agent Problems in International Organizations. *Review of International Organizations*. 1 (2): 125–138.

Voeten, Erik. 2000. Clashes in the Assembly. *International Organization* 54 (2): 185–215.

Voeten, Erik. 2001. Outside Options and the Logic of Security Council Action. *American Political Science Review* 95 (4): 845–858.

Voeten, Erik. 2005. The Political Origins of the UN Security Council's Ability to Legitimize the Use of Force. *International Organization* 59 (3): 527–557.

Voeten, Erik. 2008. A Strategic Approach to Understanding Security Council Authority. In Ian Hurd and Bruce Cronin (eds.), *The UN Security Council and the Legitimacy of International Authority*. New York: Routledge: 43–56.

Voeten, Erik. 2011. Does Participation in International Organizations Increase Cooperation? Evidence from the ICC, UNHRC, and UNSC. SSRN. Available at: http://ssrn.com/abstract=1865201.

Voeten, Erik and Adis Merdzanovic. 2009. United Nations General Assembly Voting Data. Washington, DC: Georgetown University. Available at: http://www9.georgetown.edu/faculty/ev42/UNVoting.htm.

Volden, Craig and Clifford J. Carrubba. 2004. The Formation of Oversized Coalitions in Parliamentary Democracies. *American Journal of Political Science* 48 (3): 521–537.

Von Freiesleben, Jonas. 2013. Reform of the Security Council: 1945–2008. In Lydia Swart and Estelle Perry (eds.), *Governing & Managing Change at the United Nations: Security Council Reform from 1945 to September 2013*. New York: Center for UN Reform Education: 1–23.

Vreeland, James Raymond. 1999. The IMF: Lender of Last Resort or Scapegoat? Paper presented at the Annual Meeting of the Midwest Political Science Association, Chicago, IL.

Vreeland, James Raymond. 2003. *The IMF and Economic Development*. New York: Cambridge University Press.

Vreeland, James Raymond. 2006. IMF Program Compliance: Aggregate Index versus Policy Specific Research Strategies. *Review of International Organizations* 1 (4): 359–378.

Vreeland, James Raymond. 2007. *The International Monetary Fund: Politics of Conditional Lending*. New York: Routledge.

Vreeland, James Raymond. 2011. Foreign Aid and Global Governance: Buying Bretton Woods – The Swiss-Bloc Case. *Review of International Organizations* 6 (3–4): 369–391.

Vreeland, James Raymond. Forthcoming. Domestic Politics and International Institutions: Cooperation, Sacrifice, and Change. In Jennifer Gandhi and Rubén Ruiz-Rufino (eds.), *Handbook of Comparative Political Institutions*. New York: Routledge: pages forthcoming.

Wade, Robert. 1996. Japan, the World Bank, and The Art of Paradigm Maintenance: The East Asian Miracle in Political Perspective. *New Left Review* 217 (1): 3–36.

Wagner, R. Harrison. 1988. Economic Interdependence, Bargaining Power, and Political Influence. *International Organization* 42 (3): 461–483.

Walter, Stefanie. 2013. *Financial Crises and the Politics of Macroeconomic Adjustments*. New York: Cambridge University Press.

Weaver, Catherine. 2008. *Hypocrisy Trap: The World Bank and the Poverty of Reform*. Princeton, NJ: Princeton University Press.

Weeks, Jessica L. 2008. Autocratic Audience Costs: Regime Type and Signaling Resolve. *International Organization* 62 (1): 35–64.

Weiss, Jessica. 2008. The 2005 Anti-Japanese Protests in China and UNSC Reform. Manuscript, Woodrow Wilson School, Princeton University.

Wendt, Alexander. 1992. Anarchy Is What States Make of It: The Social Construction of Power Politics. *International Organization* 46 (2): 391–425.

Wendt, Alexander. 1999. *Social Theory of International Politics*. New York: Cambridge University Press.

Weston, Burns H. 1991. Security Council Resolution 678 and Persian Gulf Decisions Making: Precarious Legitimacy. *American Journal of Law* 85 (3): 516–535.

Winter, Eyal. 1996. Voting and Vetoing. *American Political Science Review* 90 (4): 813–823.

Wooldridge, Jeffrey M. 2009. *Introductory Econometrics: A Modern Approach*, 4th ed. Cincinnati, OH: South-Western College Publisher.

World Bank. 2003. *World Bank Operations Evaluation Department: The First 30 Years*. Washington, DC: The World Bank.

World Bank. 2008. *World Development Indicators, CD-ROM*. Washington, DC: The World Bank.

World Bank. 2011. *World Development Indicators*. Washington, DC: World Bank.

World Bank. 2012. *World Development Indicators*. Washington, DC: World Bank.

Yasutomo, Dennis T. 1993. The Politicization of Japan's 'Post–Cold War' Multilateral Diplomacy. In Gerald L. Curtis (ed.), *Japan's Foreign Policy after the Cold War*. New York: M. E. Sharpe: 323–346.

Yasutomo, Dennis T. 1995. *The New Multilateralism in Japan's Foreign Policy*. New York: St. Martin's Press.

Zimmerman, Robert F. 1993. *Dollars, Diplomacy and Dependency: Dilemmas of US Economic Aid*. Boulder, CO: Lynne Rienner.

Zweifel, Thomas D. 2005. *International Organizations and Democracy: Accountability, Politics, and Power*. Boulder, CO: Lynne Rienner.

Author Index

Subject Index

Note: The letter *b* indicates box, *f* indicates figure, *n* indicates footnote, and *t* indicates table. UNSC and UNGA resolutions numbers are in boldface print.

Lightning Source UK Ltd.
Milton Keynes UK
UKOW05f0717030814

236254UK00001B/56/P